AUTOMATIC TRANSMISSIONS AND TRANSAXLES

SIXTH EDITION

James D. Halderman
Tom Birch

PEARSON

Boston   Columbus   Indianapolis   New York   San Francisco   Hoboken
Amsterdam   Cape Town   Dubai   London   Madrid   Milan   Munich   Paris   Montréal   Toronto
Delhi   Mexico City   São Paulo   Sydney   Hong Kong   Seoul   Singapore   Taipei   Tokyo

Senior Product Manager: Lindsey Prudhomme Gill
Editorial Assistant: Nancy Kesterson
Director of Marketing: David Gesell
Senior Marketing Coordinator: Alicia Wozniak
Program Manager: Holly Shufeldt

Senior Art Director: Jayne Conte
Cover Designer: Bruce Kenselaar
Lead Media Project Manager: April Cleland
Full-Service Project Management and Composition: Integra Software Services, Ltd.
Printer/Binder: RR Donnelley
Cover Printer: RR Donnelley

Library of Congress Cataloging-in-Publication Data

Halderman, James D.
   Automatic transmissions and transaxles/James Halderman, Tom Birch.—Sixth edition.
      pages cm
   Revised editon of: Automatic transmissions and transaxles/Tom Birch. 2012.
   Includes index.
   ISBN-13: 978-0-13-351656-2 (alk. paper)
   ISBN-10: 0-13-351656-3 (alk. paper)
   1. Automobiles—Transmission devices, Automatic.   2. Automobiles—Transmission devices, Automatic—Maintenance and repair.   I. Halderman, James D.   II. Title.
   TL263.B57 2015
   629.2'446—dc23
                                                           2014001274

10 9 8 7 6 5 4 3 2

ISBN 10:   0-13-351656-3
ISBN 13: 978-0-13-351656-2

PREFACE

PROFESSIONAL TECHNICIAN SERIES Part of the Pearson Automotive Professional Technician Series, the sixth edition of *Automatic Transmissions and Transaxles* represents the future of automotive textbooks. The series is a full-color, media-integrated solution for today's students and instructors. The series includes textbooks that cover all eight areas of ASE certification, plus additional titles covering common courses. The series is peer reviewed for technical accuracy.

UPDATES TO THE SIXTH EDITION

- All content is correlated to the latest NATEF and ASE tasks for Automatic Transmissions/transaxles(A2).
- New colored photos and line drawings have been added to this edition.
- A dramatic, new full-color design enhances the subject material.
- Hundreds of new full-color line drawings and photos help bring the subject alive.
- New review and chapter quiz questions are included in this new edition.
- New step-by-step photo sequences show in detail the steps involved in performing specific tasks or service procedures.
- A new chapter covering all aspects of torque converters now discussed in one chapter (Chapter 5).
- A new chapter on hybrid electric vehicle transmissions included in this edition (Chapter 10).
- A new chapter on continuously variable transmissions (CVTs) included in this edition (Chapter 11).
- A new chapter on dual clutch automatic transmissions included in this edition (Chapter 12).
- Content has been streamlined for easier reading and comprehension.

- Two new appendixes included. Sample ASE certification test with answers (Appendix 1) and NATEF correlation chart (Appendix 2).
- Unlike other textbooks, this book is written so that the theory, construction, diagnosis, and service of a particular component or system is presented in one location. There is no need to search through the entire book for other references to the same topic.

ASE AND NATEF CORRELATED NATEF-certified programs need to demonstrate that they use course material that covers NATEF and ASE tasks. All Professional Technician textbooks have been correlated to the appropriate ASE and NATEF task lists. These correlations can be found in the appendix.

A COMPLETE INSTRUCTOR AND STUDENT SUPPLEMENTS PACKAGE All Professional Technician textbooks are accompanied by a full set of instructor and student supplements. Please see page vi for a detailed list of supplements.

A FOCUS ON DIAGNOSIS AND PROBLEM SOLVING The Professional Technician Series has been developed to satisfy the need for a greater emphasis on problem diagnosis. Automotive instructors and service managers agree that students and beginning technicians need more training in diagnostic procedures and skill development. To meet this need and demonstrate how real-world problems are solved, "Real World Fix" features are included throughout and highlight how real-life problems are diagnosed and repaired.

The following pages highlight the unique core features that set the Professional Technician Series book apart from other automotive textbooks.

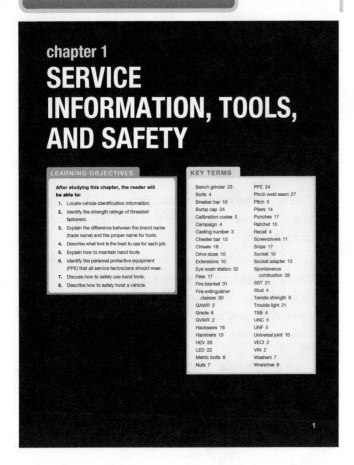

chapter 1

SERVICE INFORMATION, TOOLS, AND SAFETY

LEARNING OBJECTIVES

After studying this chapter, the reader will be able to:

1. Locate vehicle identification information.
2. Identify the strength ratings of threaded fasteners.
3. Explain the difference between the brand name (trade name) and the proper name for tools.
4. Describe what tool is the best to use for each job.
5. Explain how to maintain hand tools.
6. Identify the personal protective equipment (PPE) that all service technicians should wear.
7. Discuss how to safely use hand tools.
8. Describe how to safely hoist a vehicle.

KEY TERMS

Bench grinder 23	PPE 24
Bolts 4	Pinch weld seam 27
Breaker bar 10	Pitch 5
Bump cap 24	Pliers 14
Calibration codes 3	Punches 17
Campaign 4	Ratchet 10
Casting number 3	Recall 4
Cheater bar 13	Screwdrivers 11
Chisels 18	Snips 17
Drive sizes 10	Socket 10
Extensions 10	Socket adapter 13
Eye wash station 32	Spontaneous combustion 26
Files 17	SST 21
Fire blanket 31	Stud 4
Fire extinguisher classes 30	Tensile strength 6
GAWR 2	Trouble light 21
Grade 6	TSB 4
GVWR 2	UNC 5
Hacksaws 18	UNF 5
Hammers 13	Universal joint 10
HEV 33	VECI 2
LED 22	VIN 2
Metric bolts 6	Washers 7
Nuts 7	Wrenches 8

LEARNING OBJECTIVES AND KEY TERMS appear at the beginning of each chapter to help students and instructors focus on the most important material in each chapter. The chapter objectives are based on specific ASE and NATEF tasks.

 **TECH TIP**

It Just Takes a Second

Whenever removing any automotive component, it is wise to screw the bolts back into the holes a couple of threads by hand. This ensures that the right bolt will be used in its original location when the component or part is put back on the vehicle.

TECH TIPS feature real-world advice and "tricks of the trade" from ASE-certified master technicians.

 SAFETY TIP

Shop Cloth Disposal

Always dispose of oily shop cloths in an enclosed container to prevent a fire. ● **SEE FIGURE 1–69.** Whenever oily cloths are thrown together on the floor or workbench, a chemical reaction can occur, which can ignite the cloth even without an open flame. This process of ignition without an open flame is called **spontaneous combustion**.

SAFETY TIPS alert students to possible hazards on the job and how to avoid them.

 REAL WORLD FIX

The Case of the Stretched Shift Cable

The clutch on a Dodge Ram pickup (260,000 km) did not release completely. Adjusting the cable helped, but the end of the adjustment was reached. The transmission and clutch were removed. The clutch was carefully inspected, and it showed little wear and no damage.

After reading some similar cases on www.iatn.net a new cable was purchased, and it was determined that the old cable had stretched. Installation of the new cable repaired this problem.

REAL WORLD FIXES present students with actual automotive scenarios and show how these common (and sometimes uncommon) problems were diagnosed and repaired.

 FREQUENTLY ASKED QUESTION

How Many Types of Screw Heads Are Used in Automotive Applications?

There are many, including Torx, hex (also called Allen), plus many others used in custom vans and motor homes. ● **SEE FIGURE 1–9.**

FREQUENTLY ASKED QUESTIONS are based on the author's own experience and provide answers to many of the most common questions asked by students and beginning service technicians.

NOTE: Most of these "locking nuts" are grouped together and are commonly referred to as *prevailing torque nuts*. This means that the nut will hold its tightness or torque and not loosen with movement or vibration.

NOTES provide students with additional technical information to give them a greater understanding of a specific task or procedure.

CAUTION: *Never* use hardware store (nongraded) bolts, studs, or nuts on any vehicle steering, suspension, or brake component. Always use the exact size and grade of hardware that is specified and used by the vehicle manufacturer.

CAUTIONS alert students about potential damage to the vehicle that can occur during a specific task or service procedure.

☠ **WARNING**

Do not use incandescent trouble lights around gasoline or other flammable liquids. The liquids can cause the bulb to break and the hot filament can ignite the flammable liquid, which can cause personal injury or even death.

WARNINGS alert students to potential dangers to themselves during a specific task or service procedure.

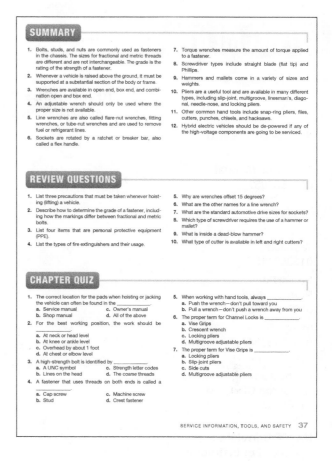

SUMMARY

1. Bolts, studs, and nuts are commonly used as fasteners in the chassis. The sizes for fractional and metric threads are different and are not interchangeable. The grade is the rating of the strength of a fastener.
2. Whenever a vehicle is raised above the ground, it must be supported at a substantial section of the body or frame.
3. Wrenches are available in open end, box end, and combination open and box end.
4. An adjustable wrench should only be used where the proper size is not available.
5. Line wrenches are also called flare-nut wrenches, fitting wrenches, or tube-nut wrenches and are used to remove fuel or refrigerant lines.
6. Sockets are rotated by a ratchet or breaker bar, also called a flex handle.
7. Torque wrenches measure the amount of torque applied to a fastener.
8. Screwdriver types include straight blade (flat tip) and Phillips.
9. Hammers and mallets come in a variety of sizes and weights.
10. Pliers are a useful tool and are available in many different types, including slip-joint, multigroove, linesman's, diagonal, needle-nose, and locking pliers.
11. Other common hand tools include snap-ring pliers, files, cutters, punches, chisels, and hacksaws.
12. Hybrid electric vehicles should be de-powered if any of the high-voltage components are going to be serviced.

REVIEW QUESTIONS

1. List three precautions that must be taken whenever hoisting (lifting) a vehicle.
2. Describe how to determine the grade of a fastener, including how the markings differ between fractional and metric bolts.
3. List four items that are personal protective equipment (PPE).
4. List the types of fire extinguishers and their usage.
5. Why are wrenches offset 15 degrees?
6. What are the other names for a line wrench?
7. What are the standard automotive drive sizes for sockets?
8. Which type of screwdriver requires the use of a hammer or mallet?
9. What is inside a dead-blow hammer?
10. What type of cutter is available in left and right cutters?

CHAPTER QUIZ

1. The correct location for the pads when hoisting or jacking the vehicle can often be found in the _____.
   a. Service manual
   b. Shop manual
   c. Owner's manual
   d. All of the above
2. For the best working position, the work should be _____.
   a. At neck or head level
   b. At knee or ankle level
   c. Overhead by about 1 foot
   d. At chest or elbow level
3. A high-strength bolt is identified by _____.
   a. A UNC symbol
   b. Lines on the head
   c. Strength letter codes
   d. The coarse threads
4. A fastener that uses threads on both ends is called a _____.
   a. Cap screw
   b. Stud
   c. Machine screw
   d. Crest fastener
5. When working with hand tools, always _____.
   a. Push the wrench—don't pull toward you
   b. Pull a wrench—don't push a wrench away from you
6. The proper term for Channel Locks is _____.
   a. Vise Grips
   b. Crescent wrench
   c. Locking pliers
   d. Multigroove adjustable pliers
7. The proper term for Vise Grips is _____.
   a. Locking pliers
   b. Slip-joint pliers
   c. Side cuts
   d. Multigroove adjustable pliers

THE SUMMARY, REVIEW QUESTIONS, AND CHAPTER QUIZ at the end of each chapter help students review the material presented in the chapter and test themselves to see how much they've learned.

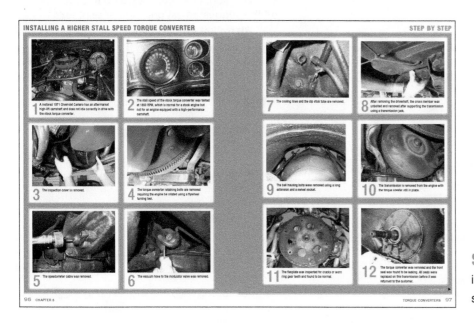

INSTALLING A HIGHER STALL SPEED TORQUE CONVERTER — STEP BY STEP

1. A restored 1971 Chevrolet Camaro has an aftermarket high-lift camshaft and does not idle correctly in drive with the stock torque converter.
2. The stall speed of the stock torque converter was tested at 1800 RPM, which is normal for a stock engine but not for an engine equipped with a high-performance camshaft.
3. The inspection cover is removed.
4. The torque converter retaining bolts are removed requiring the engine be rotated using a flywheel turning tool.
5. The speedometer cable was removed.
6. The vacuum hose to the modulator valve was removed.
7. The cooling lines and the dip stick tube are removed.
8. After removing the driveshaft, the cross member was unbolted and removed after supporting the transmission using a transmission jack.
9. The bell housing bolts were removed using a long extension and a swivel socket.
10. The transmission is removed from the engine with the torque converter still in place.
11. The flexplate was inspected for cracks or worn ring gear teeth and found to be normal.
12. The torque converter was removed and the front seal was found to be leaking. All seals were replaced on this transmission before it was returned to the customer.

96 CHAPTER 6   TORQUE CONVERTERS 97

STEP-BY-STEP photo sequences show in detail the steps involved in performing a specific task or service procedure.

RESOURCES IN PRINT AND ONLINE
Automatic Transmissions and Transaxles

NAME OF SUPPLEMENT	PRINT	ONLINE	AUDIENCE	DESCRIPTION
Instructor Resource Manual 0133564657		✔	Instructors	NEW! The ultimate teaching aid: Chapter summaries, key terms, chapter learning objectives, lecture resources, discuss/ demonstrate classroom activities, MyAutomotiveLab correlation, and answers to the in-text review and quiz questions.
TestGen 013356410X		✔	Instructors	Test generation software and test bank for the text.
PowerPoint Presentation 0133564665		✔	Instructors	Slides include chapter learning objectives, lecture outline of the test, and graphics from the book.
Image Bank 0133748294		✔	Instructors	All of the images and graphs from the textbook to create customized lecture slides.
Instructors Resource CD-ROM 0133564673	✔		Instructors	Take your instructor resources with you! This convenient CD houses the text PowerPoint presentation, Image Bank, instructors manual, and TestGen.
NATEF Correlated Task Sheets – For Instructors 0133564762		✔	Instructors	Downloadable NATEF task sheets for easy customization and development of unique task sheets.
NATEF Task Sheets – For Students 0133564649	✔		Students	Study activity manual that correlates NATEF Automobile Standards to chapters and page numbers in the text. Available to students at a discounted price when packaged with the text.
CourseSmart eText 0133564096		✔	Students	An alternative to purchasing the print textbook, students can subscribe to the same content online and save up to 50% off the suggested list price of the print text. Visit **www.coursesmart.com**

All online resources can be downloaded from the Instructor's Resource Center: **www.pearsonighered.com/irc**

ACKNOWLEDGMENTS

A large number of people and organizations have cooperated in providing the reference material and technical information used in this text. We express sincere thanks to the following organizations for their special contributions to the book:

A-1 Automatic Transmissions
Aceomatic Recon
AFM, Raytech Automotive Components Comp.
Alto Products Corp.
American Honda Motor Company
ATEC Trans-Tool and Cleaning Systems
Autotrans
AxiLine, Hicklin Engineering
BorgWarner, Morse TEC
Tom Broxholm, Skyline College
Chassis Ear, Steelman
Chrysler Corporation
Ethyl Corporation
Mark Ferner, Pennzoil-Quaker State
Fluid Rx
Fluke Corporation
Ford Motor Company
General Motors Corporation
Goodall Manufacturing Co.
Roger Griffen, Nissan North America, Inc.
G-Tec
HECAT Inc.
International Lubricants, Inc.
Tony Jewel, Reedley College
J.S. Products/Steelman
KD Tools
Kent-Moore, SPX Corporation
Life Automotive Products
Dennis Madden, ATRA
The Mighty Mover
Federal-Mogul Corp.
NEAPCO Inc.
Nissan North America, Inc.
OTC, SPX Corporation
Pennzoil-Quaker State Company.
Raybestos Aftermarket Products Co.
Ken Redick
Rostra Precision Controls
Slauson Transmission Parts, Christopher Wilson
Snap-on Tools
Sonnax Industries
SPX Filtran
Superior Transmission Parts
T.C.R.S. Inc., Hicklin Engineering

Toyota Motor Sales, U.S.A., Inc.
Tribco, Inc.
Waekon Corporation
Williams Technology Inc., Division of Delco Remy Int.
Yank Converters
ZF Group North American Operations

TECHNICAL AND CONTENT REVIEWERS The following people reviewed the manuscript before production and checked it for technical accuracy and clarity of presentation. Their suggestions and recommendations were included in the final draft of the manuscript. Their input helped make this textbook clear and technically accurate while maintaining the easy-to-read style that has made other books from the same authors so popular.

Tom Broxholm
Skyline College

Ron Chappell
Santa Fe Community College

Curtis Cline
Wharton County Junior College

Matt Dixon
Southern Illinois University

Kenneth P. Dytrt
Pennsylvania College of Technology

Dr. David Gilbert
Southern Illinois University

Richard Krieger
Michigan Institute of Technology

Russell A. Leonard
Ferris State University

William Milam
Eastfield College

Justin Morgan
Sinclair Community College

Joe Palazzolo
GKN Driveline

Greg Pfahl
Miami-Jacobs Career College

Jeff Rehkopf
Florida State College

Scott Russell
Blue Ridge Community College

Chuck Rockwood
Ventura College

Eugene Talley
Southern Illinois University

Chuck Taylor
Sinclair Community College

Omar Trinidad
Southern Illinois University

Ken Welch
Saddleback College

Special thanks to instructional designer **Alexis I. Skriloff James.**

PHOTO SEQUENCES   We would also like to thank Chuck Taylor of Sinclair Community College in Dayton, Ohio, plus Greg Pfahl and James (Mike) Watson who helped with many of the photos. A special thanks to Dick Krieger, Richard Krieger, Jeff Rehkopf, and Randal Sedwick for their detailed and thorough review of the manuscript before publication and to Richard Reaves for all of his help. Most of all, we wish to thank Michelle Halderman for her assistance in all phases of manuscript preparation.

James D. Halderman

Tom Birch

JAMES D. HALDERMAN Jim Halderman brings a world of experience, knowledge, and talent to his work. His automotive service experience includes working as a flat-rate technician, a business owner, and a professor of automotive technology at a leading U.S. community college for more than 20 years.

He has a Bachelor of Science degree from Ohio Northern University and a Master's degree in Education from Miami University in Oxford, Ohio. Jim also holds a U.S. patent for an electronic transmission control device. He is an ASE-certified Master Automotive Technician and is also Advanced Engine Performance (L1) ASE certified. Jim is the author of many automotive textbooks all published by Pearson. He has presented numerous technical seminars to national audiences, including the California Automotive Teachers (CAT) and the Illinois College Automotive Instructor Association (ICAIA). He is also a member and presenter at the North American Council of Automotive Teachers (NACAT). Jim was also named Regional Teacher of the Year by General Motors Corporation and an outstanding alumnus of Ohio Northern University. Jim and his wife, Michelle, live in Dayton, Ohio. They have two children. You can reach Jim at:

jim@jameshalderman.com.

TOM BIRCH Tom Birch started his automotive service career working as a technician at a Ford dealership. Then, while in the army, he was a wheel vehicle mechanic and worked as a technician on army vehicles when stationed in Europe. He then earned both Bachelor's and Master's degrees from Chico State College, now California State University, Chico and taught in the California school system before going to Yuba College in Northern California. Tom is past president and board member of the California Automotive Teachers (CAT), plus a member and winner of the MVP award of the North American Council of Automotive Teachers (NACAT). He is also a member of the Mobile Air Conditioning Society (MACS) and Automotive Service Council- California (ASC-CA) plus the Society of Automotive Engineers (SAE). Tom is the author of many automotive textbooks, all published by Pearson.

BRIEF CONTENTS

CONTENTS

chapter 1
SERVICE INFORMATION, TOOLS, AND SAFETY

LEARNING OBJECTIVES

After studying this chapter, the reader will be able to:

1. Locate vehicle identification information.
2. Identify the strength ratings of threaded fasteners.
3. Explain the difference between the brand name (trade name) and the proper name for tools.
4. Describe what tool is the best to use for each job.
5. Explain how to maintain hand tools.
6. Identify the personal protective equipment (PPE) that all service technicians should wear.
7. Discuss how to safely use hand tools.
8. Describe how to safely hoist a vehicle.

KEY TERMS

Bench grinder 23
Bolts 4
Breaker bar 10
Bump cap 24
Calibration codes 3
Campaign 4
Casting number 3
Cheater bar 13
Chisels 18
Drive sizes 10
Extensions 10
Eye wash station 32
Files 17
Fire blanket 31
Fire extinguisher classes 30
GAWR 2
Grade 6
GVWR 2
Hacksaws 18
Hammers 13
HEV 33
LED 22
Metric bolts 6
Nuts 7
PPE 24
Pinch weld seam 27
Pitch 5
Pliers 14
Punches 17
Ratchet 10
Recall 4
Screwdrivers 11
Snips 17
Socket 10
Socket adapter 13
Spontaneous combustion 26
SST 21
Stud 4
Tensile strength 6
Trouble light 21
TSB 4
UNC 5
UNF 5
Universal joint 10
VECI 2
VIN 2
Washers 7
Wrenches 8

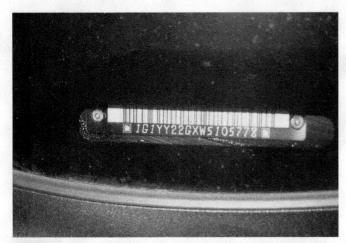

FIGURE 1–1 Typical vehicle identification number (VIN) as viewed through the windshield.

1 = United States	J = Japan	U = Romania
2 = Canada	K = Korea	V = France
3 = Mexico	L = China	W = Germany
4 = United States	M = India	X = Russia
5 = United States	P = Philippines	Y = Sweden
6 = Australia	R = Taiwan	Z = Italy
8 = Argentina	S = England	
9 = Brazil	T = Czechoslovakia	

CHART 1–1

The first number or letter in the VIN identifies the country where the vehicle was made.

A = 1980/2010	L = 1990/2020	Y = 2000/2030
B = 1981/2011	M = 1991/2021	1 = 2001/2031
C = 1982/2012	N = 1992/2022	2 = 2002/2032
D = 1983/2013	P = 1993/2023	3 = 2003/2033
E = 1984/2014	R = 1994/2024	4 = 2004/2034
F = 1985/2015	S = 1995/2025	5 = 2005/2035
G = 1986/2016	T = 1996/2026	6 = 2006/2036
H = 1987/2017	V = 1997/2027	7 = 2007/2037
J = 1988/2018	W = 1998/2028	8 = 2008/2038
K = 1989/2019	X = 1999/2029	9 = 2009/2039

CHART 1–2

The pattern repeats every 30 years for the year of manufacture.

VEHICLE IDENTIFICATION

MAKE, MODEL, AND YEAR All service work requires that the vehicle and its components be properly identified. The most common identification is the make, model, and year of the vehicle.

> **Make:** e.g., Chevrolet
>
> **Model:** e.g., Impala
>
> **Year:** e.g., 2008

VEHICLE IDENTIFICATION NUMBER The year of the vehicle is often difficult to determine exactly. A model may be introduced as the next year's model as soon as January of the previous year. Typically, a new model year starts in September or October of the year prior to the actual new year, but not always. This is why the **vehicle identification number**, usually abbreviated **VIN**, is so important. ● **SEE FIGURE 1–1**.

Since 1981, all vehicle manufacturers have used a VIN that is 17 characters long. Although every vehicle manufacturer assigns various letters or numbers within these 17 characters, there are some constants, including:

- The first number or letter designates the country of origin. ● **SEE CHART 1–1**.

- The fourth or fifth character is the car line/series.

- The sixth character is the body style.

- The seventh character is the restraint system.

- The eighth character is often the engine code. (Some engines cannot be determined by the VIN number.)

- The tenth character represents the year on all vehicles. ● **SEE CHART 1–2**.

VEHICLE SAFETY CERTIFICATION LABEL A vehicle safety certification label is attached to the left side pillar post on the rearward-facing section of the left front door. This label indicates the month and year of manufacture as well as the **gross vehicle weight rating** (**GVWR**), the **gross axle weight rating** (**GAWR**), and the vehicle identification number.

VECI LABEL The **vehicle emissions control information** (**VECI**) label under the hood of the vehicle shows informative settings and emission hose routing information. ● **SEE FIGURE 1–2**.

The VECI label (sticker) can be located on the bottom side of the hood, the radiator fan shroud, the radiator core support, or on the strut towers. The VECI label usually includes the following information:

- Engine identification

- Emissions standard that the vehicle meets

- Vacuum hose routing diagram

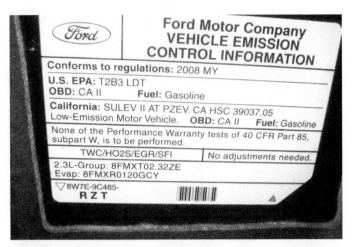

FIGURE 1–2 The vehicle emissions control information (VECI) sticker is placed under the hood.

- Base ignition timing (if adjustable)
- Spark plug type and gap
- Valve lash
- Emission calibration code

CALIBRATION CODES **Calibration codes** are usually located on Powertrain Control Modules (PCMs) or other controllers. Whenever diagnosing an engine operating fault, it is often necessary to use the calibration code to be sure that the vehicle is the subject of a technical service bulletin or other service procedure. ● **SEE FIGURE 1–3**.

CASTING NUMBERS When an engine part such as a block is cast, a number is put into the mold to identify the casting. ● **SEE FIGURE 1–4**. These **casting numbers** can be used to identify the part and check dimensions such as the cubic inch displacement and other information, such as the year of manufacture. Sometimes changes are made to the mold, yet the casting number is not changed. Most often the casting number is the best piece of identifying information that the service technician can use for identifying an engine.

SERVICE INFORMATION

SERVICE MANUALS Service information is used by the service technician to determine specifications and service procedures, and any needed special tools.

Factory and aftermarket service manuals contain specifications and service procedures. While factory service manuals cover just one year and one or more models of the same vehicle, most aftermarket service manufacturers cover

FIGURE 1–3 A typical calibration code sticker on the case of a controller. The information on the sticker is often needed when ordering parts or a replacement controller.

FIGURE 1–4 Casting numbers on major components can be either cast or stamped.

multiple years and/or models in one manual. Included in most service manuals are the following:

- Capacities and recommended specifications for all fluids
- Specifications including engine and routine maintenance items
- Testing procedures
- Service procedures including the use of special tools when needed

ELECTRONIC SERVICE INFORMATION Electronic service information is available mostly by subscription and provides access to an Internet site where service manual–type information is available. ● **SEE FIGURE 1–5**. Most vehicle manufacturers also offer electronic service information to their dealers and to most schools and colleges that offer corporate training programs.

FIGURE 1–5 Electronic service information is available from aftermarket sources such as ALLDATA and Mitchell On Demand, as well as on websites hosted by vehicle manufacturers.

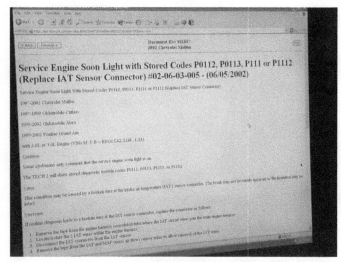

FIGURE 1–6 Technical service bulletins (TSBs) are issued by vehicle manufacturers when a fault occurs that affects many vehicles with the same problem. The TSB then provides the fix for the problem including any parts needed and detailed instructions.

TECHNICAL SERVICE BULLETINS **Technical service bulletins**, often abbreviated **TSBs**, sometimes called *technical service information bulletins (TSIB)*, are issued by the vehicle manufacturer to notify service technicians of a problem and include the necessary corrective action. Technical service bulletins are designed for dealership technicians but are republished by aftermarket companies and made available along with other service information to shops and vehicle repair facilities. **SEE FIGURE 1–6.**

INTERNET The Internet has opened the field for information exchange and access to technical advice. One of the most useful websites is the International Automotive Technician's Network at **www.iatn.net**. This is a free site but service technicians must register to join. If a small monthly sponsor fee is paid, the shop or service technician can gain access to the archives, which include thousands of successful repairs in the searchable database.

RECALLS AND CAMPAIGNS A **recall** or **campaign** is issued by a vehicle manufacturer and a notice is sent to all owners in the event of a safety-related fault or concern. While these faults may be repaired by shops, it is generally handled by a local dealer. Items that have created recalls in the past have included potential fuel system leakage problems, exhaust leakage, or electrical malfunctions that could cause a possible fire or the engine to stall. Unlike technical service bulletins whose cost is only covered when the vehicle is within the warranty period, a recall or campaign is always done at no cost to the vehicle owner.

? FREQUENTLY ASKED QUESTION

What Should Be Included on a Work Order?

A work order is a legal document that should include the following information:

1. Customer information
2. Identification of the vehicle including the VIN
3. Related service history information
4. The "three Cs":
   - Customer concern (complaint)
   - Cause of the concern
   - Correction or repairs that were required to return the vehicle to proper operation.

THREADED FASTENERS

BOLTS AND THREADS Most of the threaded fasteners used on vehicles are **bolts**. Bolts are called *cap screws* when they are threaded into a casting. Automotive service technicians usually refer to these fasteners as *bolts*, regardless of how they are used. In this chapter, they are called bolts. Sometimes, studs are used for threaded fasteners. A **stud** is a short rod with threads on both ends. Often, a stud will have coarse threads on one end and fine threads on the other end. The end of the stud with coarse threads is screwed into the casting. A nut is used on the opposite end to hold the parts together.

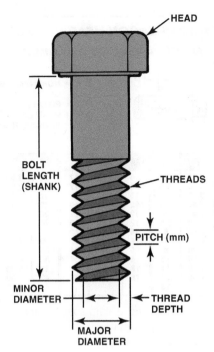

FIGURE 1–7 The dimensions of a typical bolt showing where sizes are measured.

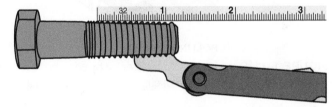

FIGURE 1–8 Thread pitch gauge used to measure the pitch of the thread. This bolt has 13 threads to the inch.

The fastener threads *must* match the threads in the casting or nut. The threads may be measured either in fractions of an inch (called fractional) or in metric units. The size is measured across the outside of the threads, called the *crest* of the thread. ● SEE FIGURE 1–7.

FRACTIONAL BOLTS Fractional threads are either coarse or fine. The coarse threads are called **unified national coarse (UNC)**, and the fine threads are called **unified national fine (UNF)**. Standard combinations of sizes and number of threads per inch (called **pitch**) are used. Pitch can be measured with a thread pitch gauge as shown in ● SEE FIGURE 1–8. Bolts are identified by their diameter and length as measured from below the head, and not by the size of the head or the size of the wrench used to remove or install the bolt.

SIZE	THREADS PER INCH		OUTSIDE DIAMETER INCHES
	NC UNC	NF UNF	
0	..	80	0.0600
1	64	..	0.0730
1	..	72	0.0730
2	56	..	0.0860
2	..	64	0.0860
3	48	..	0.0990
3	..	56	0.0990
4	40	..	0.1120
4	..	48	0.1120
5	40	..	0.1250
5	..	44	0.1250
6	32	..	0.1380
6	..	40	0.1380
8	32	..	0.1640
8	..	36	0.1640
10	24	..	0.1900
10	..	32	0.1900
12	24	..	0.2160
12	..	28	0.2160
1/4	20	..	0.2500
1/4	..	28	0.2500
5/16	18	..	0.3125
5/16	..	24	0.3125
3/8	16	..	0.3750
3/8	..	24	0.3750
7/16	14	..	0.4375
7/16	..	20	0.4375
1/2	13	..	0.5000
1/2	..	20	0.5000
9/16	12	..	0.5625
9/16	..	18	0.5625
5/8	11	..	0.6250
5/8	..	18	0.6250
3/4	10	..	0.7500
3/4	..	16	0.7500
7/8	9	..	0.8750
7/8	..	14	0.8750

CHART 1–3

American standard is one method of sizing fasteners.

Fractional thread sizes are specified by the diameter in fractions of an inch and the number of threads per inch. Typical UNC thread sizes would be 5/16–18 and 1/2–13. Similar UNF thread sizes would be 5/16–24 and 1/2–20. ● SEE CHART 1–3.

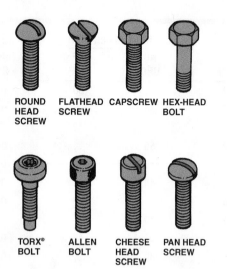

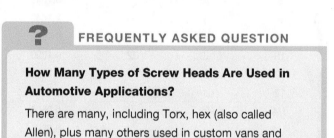

ROUND HEAD SCREW · FLATHEAD SCREW · CAPSCREW · HEX-HEAD BOLT

TORX® BOLT · ALLEN BOLT · CHEESE HEAD SCREW · PAN HEAD SCREW

FIGURE 1–9 Bolts and screws have many different heads which determine what tool is needed.

METRIC BOLTS   The size of a **metric bolt** is specified by the letter *M* followed by the diameter in millimeters (mm) across the outside (crest) of the threads. Typical metric sizes would be M8 and M12. Metric threads are specified by the thread diameter followed by X and the distance between the threads measured in millimeters (M8 X 1.5). ● **SEE FIGURE 1–10.**

GRADES OF BOLTS   Bolts are made from many different types of steel, and for this reason some are stronger than others. The strength or classification of a bolt is called the **grade**. The bolt heads are marked to indicate their grade strength.

The actual grade of bolts is two more than the number of lines on the bolt head. Metric bolts have a decimal number to indicate the grade. More lines or a higher grade number indicate a stronger bolt. In some cases, nuts and machine screws have similar grade markings. Higher grade bolts usually have threads that are rolled rather than cut, which also makes them stronger. ● **SEE FIGURE 1–11.**

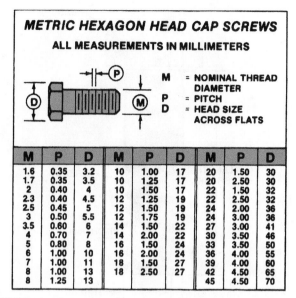

METRIC HEXAGON HEAD CAP SCREWS

ALL MEASUREMENTS IN MILLIMETERS

M = NOMINAL THREAD DIAMETER
P = PITCH
D = HEAD SIZE ACROSS FLATS

M	P	D	M	P	D	M	P	D
1.6	0.35	3.2	10	1.00	17	20	1.50	30
1.7	0.35	3.5	10	1.25	17	20	2.50	30
2	0.40	4	12	1.25	19	22	1.50	32
2.3	0.40	4.5	12	1.50	19	22	2.50	32
2.5	0.45	5	12	1.75	19	24	2.00	36
3	0.50	5.5	14	1.50	22	24	3.00	36
3.5	0.60	6	14	2.00	22	27	3.00	41
4	0.70	7	16	1.50	24	30	3.50	46
5	0.80	8	16	2.00	24	33	3.50	50
6	1.00	10	18	1.50	27	36	4.00	55
7	1.00	11	18	2.50	27	39	4.00	60
8	1.00	13				42	4.50	65
8	1.25	13				45	4.50	70

FIGURE 1–10 The metric system specifies fasteners by diameter, length, and pitch.

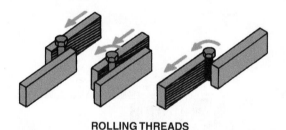

ROLLING THREADS

FIGURE 1–11 Stronger threads are created by cold-rolling a heat-treated bolt blank instead of cutting the threads, using a die.

CAUTION: *Never* use hardware store (nongraded) bolts, studs, or nuts on any vehicle steering, suspension, or brake component. Always use the exact size and grade of hardware that is specified and used by the vehicle manufacturer.

TENSILE STRENGTH OF FASTENERS   Graded fasteners have a higher tensile strength than nongraded fasteners. **Tensile strength** is the maximum stress used under tension (lengthwise force) without causing failure of the fastener. Tensile strength is specified in pounds per square inch (psi).

The strength and type of steel used in a bolt is supposed to be indicated by a raised mark on the head of the bolt. The type of mark depends on the standard to which the bolt was manufactured. Most often, bolts used in machinery are made to SAE Standard J429. ● **SEE CHART 1–4** that shows the grade and specified tensile strength.

SAE BOLT DESIGNATIONS

SAE GRADE NO.	SIZE RANGE	TENSILE STRENGTH, PSI	MATERIAL	HEAD MARKING
1	1/4 through 1 1/2	60,000	Low or medium carbon steel	
2	1/4 through 3/4	74,000		
	7/8 through 1 1/2	60,000		
5	1/4 through 1	120,000	Medium carbon steel, quenched and tempered	
	1 1/8 through 1 1/2	105,000		
5.2	1/4 through 1	120,000	Low carbon martensite steel,* quenched and tempered	
7	1/4 through 1 1/2	133,000	Medium carbon alloy steel, quenched and tempered	
8	1/4 through 1 1/2	150,000	Medium carbon alloy steel, quenched and tempered	
8.2	1/4 through 1	150,000	Low carbon martensite steel,* quenched and tempered	

CHART 1–4

*Martensite steel is a specific type of steel that can be cooled rapidly, thereby increasing its hardness. It is named after a German metallurgist, Adolf Martens.
The tensile strength rating system as specified by the Society of Automotive Engineers (SAE).

Metric bolt tensile strength property class is shown on the head of the bolt as a number, such as 4.6, 8.8, 9.8, and 10.9; the higher the number, the stronger the bolt. ● **SEE FIGURE 1–12.**

NUTS Nuts are the female part of a threaded fastener. Most nuts used on cap screws have the same hex size as the cap screw head. Some inexpensive nuts use a hex size larger than the cap screw head. Metric nuts are often marked with dimples to show their strength. More dimples indicate stronger nuts. Some nuts and cap screws use interference fit threads to keep them from accidentally loosening. This means that the shape of the nut is slightly distorted or that a section of the threads is deformed. Nuts can also be kept from loosening with a nylon washer fastened in the nut or with a nylon patch or strip on the threads. ● **SEE FIGURE 1–13.**

NOTE: Most of these "locking nuts" are grouped together and are commonly referred to as *prevailing torque nuts.* This means that the nut will hold its tightness or torque and not loosen with movement or vibration. Most prevailing torque nuts should be replaced whenever removed to ensure that the nut will not loosen during service. Always follow the manufacturer's recommendations. Anaerobic sealers, such as Loctite, are used on the threads where the nut or cap screw must be both locked and sealed.

WASHERS Washers are often used under cap screw heads and under nuts. ● **SEE FIGURE 1–14.** Plain flat washers are used to provide an even clamping load around the fastener. Lock washers are added to prevent accidental loosening. In some accessories, the washers are locked onto the nut to provide easy assembly.

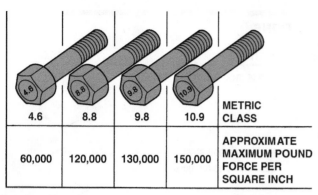

METRIC CLASS	4.6	8.8	9.8	10.9
APPROXIMATE MAXIMUM POUND FORCE PER SQUARE INCH	60,000	120,000	130,000	150,000

FIGURE 1–12 Metric bolt (cap screw) grade markings and approximate tensile strength.

HEX NUT JAM NUT NYLON LOCK NUT CASTLE NUT ACORN NUT

FIGURE 1–13 Nuts come in a variety of styles, including locking (prevailing torque) types, such as the distorted thread and nylon insert type.

FLAT WASHER LOCK WASHER STAR WASHER STAR WASHER

FIGURE 1–14 Washers come in a variety of styles, including flat and serrated used to help prevent a fastener from loosening.

TECH TIP

A 1/2 Inch Wrench Does Not Fit a 1/2 Inch Bolt

A common mistake made by persons new to the automotive field is to think that the size of a bolt or nut is the size of the head. The size of the bolt or nut (outside diameter of the threads) is usually smaller than the size of the wrench or socket that fits the head of the bolt or nut. Examples are given in the following table:

Wrench Size	Thread Size
7/16 inch	1/4 inch
1/2 inch	5/16 inch
9/16 inch	3/8 inch
5/8 inch	7/16 inch
3/4 inch	1/2 inch
10 mm	6 mm
12 or 13 mm*	8 mm
14 or 17 mm*	10 mm

* European (Système International d'Unités-SI) metric.

TECH TIP

It Just Takes a Second

Whenever removing any automotive component, it is wise to screw the bolts back into the holes a couple of threads by hand. This ensures that the right bolt will be used in its original location when the component or part is put back on the vehicle. Often, the same diameter of fastener is used on a component, but the length of the bolt may vary. Spending just a couple of seconds to put the bolts and nuts back where they belong when the part is removed can save a lot of time when the part is being reinstalled. Besides making certain that the right fastener is being installed in the right place, this method helps prevent bolts and nuts from getting lost or kicked away. How much time have you wasted looking for that lost bolt or nut?

HAND TOOLS

WRENCHES Wrenches are the most used hand tool by service technicians. **Wrenches** are used to grasp and rotate threaded fasteners. Most wrenches are constructed of forged alloy steel, usually chrome-vanadium steel. ● **SEE FIGURE 1–15.**

After the wrench is formed, it is hardened, and then tempered to reduce brittleness, and then chrome plated. There are several types of wrenches.

OPEN-END WRENCH. An open-end wrench is usually used to loosen or tighten bolts or nuts that do not require a lot of torque. Because of the *open* end, this type of wrench can be easily placed on a bolt or nut with an angle of 15 degrees, which allows the wrench to be flipped over and used again to continue to rotate the fastener. The major disadvantage of an open-end wrench is the lack of torque that can be applied due to the fact that the open jaws of the wrench only contact two flat surfaces of the fastener. An open-end wrench has two different sizes, one at each end. ● **SEE FIGURE 1–16.**

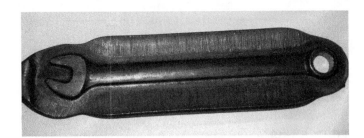

FIGURE 1–15 A wrench after it has been forged but before the flashing, extra material around the wrench, has been removed.

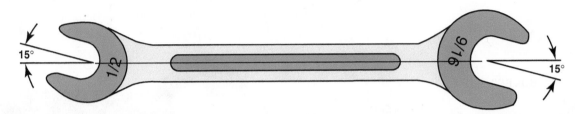

FIGURE 1–16 A typical open-end wrench. The size is different on each end and notice that the head is angled 15 degrees at the end.

BOX-END WRENCH. A *box-end wrench*, also called a *closed-end wrench*, is placed over the top of the fastener and grips the points of the fastener. A box-end wrench is angled 15 degrees to allow it to clear nearby objects.

Therefore, a box-end wrench should be used to loosen or to tighten fasteners because it grasps around the entire head of the fastener. A box-end wrench has two different sizes, one at each end. ● **SEE FIGURE 1–17**.

Most service technicians purchase *combination wrenches*, which have the open end at one end and the same size box end on the other end. ● **SEE FIGURE 1–18**.

A combination wrench allows the technician to loosen or tighten a fastener using the box end of the wrench, turn it around, and use the open end to increase the speed of rotating the fastener.

ADJUSTABLE WRENCH. An *adjustable wrench* is often used where the exact size wrench is not available or when a large nut, such as a wheel spindle nut, needs to be rotated but not tightened. An adjustable wrench should not be used to loosen or tighten fasteners because the torque applied to the wrench can cause the movable jaws to loosen their grip on the fastener, causing it to become rounded. ● **SEE FIGURE 1–19**.

LINE WRENCHES. Line wrenches are also called *flare-nut wrenches*, *fitting wrenches*, or *tube-nut wrenches* and are designed to grip almost all the way around a nut used to retain a fuel or refrigerant line, and yet, be able to be installed over the line. ● **SEE FIGURE 1–20**.

 **TECH TIP**

Hide Those from the Boss

An apprentice technician started working for a shop and put his top tool box on a workbench. Another technician observed that, along with a complete set of good-quality tools, the box contained several adjustable wrenches. The more experienced technician said, "Hide those from the boss." The boss does not want any service technician to use adjustable wrenches. If any adjustable wrench is used on a bolt or nut, the movable jaw often moves or loosens and starts to round the head of the fastener. If the head of the bolt or nut becomes rounded, it becomes that much more difficult to remove.

SAFE USE OF WRENCHES Wrenches should be inspected before use to be sure they are not cracked, bent, or damaged. All wrenches should be cleaned after use before being returned to the tool box. Always use the correct size of wrench for the fastener being loosened or tightened to help prevent the rounding of the flats of the fastener. When attempting to loosen a fastener, pull a wrench—do not push a wrench. If a wrench is pushed, your knuckles can be hurt when forced into another object if the fastener breaks loose or

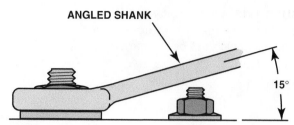

FIGURE 1–17 The end of a box-end wrench is angled 15 degrees to allow clearance for nearby objects or other fasteners.

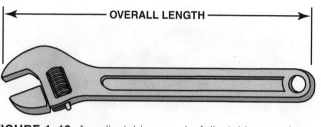

FIGURE 1–19 An adjustable wrench. Adjustable wrenches are sized by the overall length of the wrench and not by how far the jaws open. Common sizes of adjustable wrenches include 8, 10, and 12 inch.

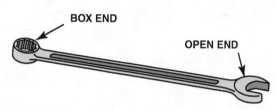

FIGURE 1–18 A combination wrench has an open end at one end and a box end at the other end.

FIGURE 1–20 The end of a typical line wrench, which shows that it is capable of grasping most of the head of the fitting.

if the wrench slips. Always keep wrenches and all hand tools clean to help prevent rust and to allow for a better, firmer grip. Never expose any tool to excessive heat. High temperatures can reduce the strength ("draw the temper") of metal tools.

Never use a hammer on any wrench unless you are using a special "staking face" wrench designed to be used with a hammer. Replace any tools that are damaged or worn.

RATCHETS, SOCKETS, AND EXTENSIONS
A **socket** fits over the fastener and grips the points and/or flats of the bolt or nut. The socket is rotated (driven) using either a long bar called a **breaker bar** (flex handle) or a ratchet. ● SEE FIGURES 1–21 AND 1–22.

A **ratchet** is a tool that turns the socket in only one direction and allows the rotating of the ratchet handle back and forth in a narrow space. Socket **extensions** and **universal joints** are also used with sockets to allow access to fasteners in restricted locations.

DRIVE SIZE. Sockets are available in various **drive sizes**, including 1/4, 3/8, and 1/2 inch sizes for most automotive use. ●SEE FIGURES 1–23 AND 1–24.

Many heavy-duty truck and/or industrial applications use 3/4 and 1 inch sizes. The drive size is the distance of each side

TECH TIP

Right to Tighten

It is sometimes confusing which way to rotate a wrench or screwdriver, especially when the head of the fastener is pointing away from you. To help visualize while looking at the fastener, say "righty tighty, lefty loosey."

of the square drive. Sockets and ratchets of the same size are designed to work together.

REGULAR AND DEEP WELL. Sockets are available in regular length for use in most applications or in a deep well design that allows for access to a fastener that uses a long stud or other similar conditions. ● SEE FIGURE 1–25.

TORQUE WRENCHES
Torque wrenches are socket turning handles that are designed to apply a known amount of force to the fastener. There are two basic types of torque wrenches:

1. **Clicker type.** This type of torque wrench is first set to the specified torque and then it "clicks" when the set torque value has been reached. When force is removed from the

RATCHET REVERSING LEVER

1/2–3/4 INCH SQUARE DRIVE LUG

FIGURE 1–21 A typical ratchet used to rotate a socket. A ratchet makes a ratcheting noise when it is being rotated in the opposite direction from loosening or tightening. A knob or lever on the ratchet allows the user to switch directions.

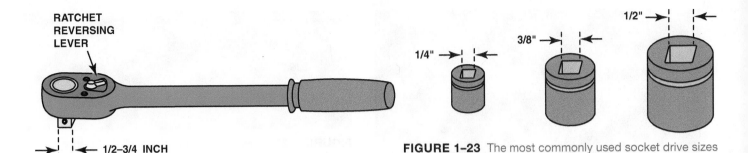

1/4" **3/8"** **1/2"**

FIGURE 1–23 The most commonly used socket drive sizes include 1/4, 3/8, and 1/2 inch drive.

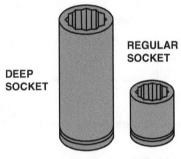

FIGURE 1–22 A typical flex handle used to rotate a socket, also called a breaker bar because it usually has a longer handle than a ratchet and, therefore, can be used to apply more torque to a fastener than a ratchet.

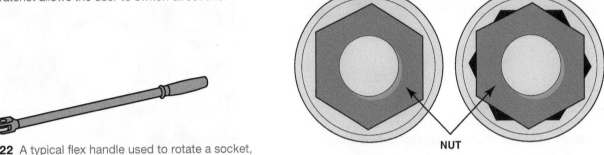

6-POINT SOCKET **12-POINT SOCKET**

NUT

FIGURE 1–24 A 6-point socket fits the head of a bolt or nut on all sides. A 12-point socket can round off the head of a bolt or nut if a lot of force is applied.

torque wrench handle, another click is heard. The setting on a clicker-type torque wrench should be set back to zero after use and checked for proper calibration regularly. ● **SEE FIGURE 1–26**.

2. **Beam-type.** This type of torque wrench is used to measure torque, but instead of presenting the value, the actual torque is displayed on the dial of the wrench as the fastener is being tightened. Beam-type torque wrenches are available in 1/4, 3/8, and 1/2 inch drives and both English and metric units. ● **SEE FIGURE 1–27**.

DEEP SOCKET **REGULAR SOCKET**

FIGURE 1–25 Allows access to the nut that has a stud plus other locations needing great depth, such as spark plugs.

SAFE USE OF SOCKETS AND RATCHETS Always use the proper size socket that correctly fits the bolt or nut. All sockets and ratchets should be cleaned after use before being placed back into the tool box. Sockets are available in short and deep well designs. Never expose any tool to excessive heat. High temperatures can reduce the strength ("draw the temper") of metal tools.

Never use a hammer on a socket handle unless you are using a special "staking face" wrench designed to be used with a hammer. Replace any tools that are damaged or worn.

Also select the appropriate drive size. For example, for small work, such as on the dash, select a 1/4 inch drive. For most general service work, use a 3/8 inch drive and for suspension and steering and other large fasteners, select a 1/2 inch drive. When loosening a fastener, always pull the ratchet toward you rather than push it outward.

SCREWDRIVERS

STRAIGHT-BLADE SCREWDRIVER. Many smaller fasteners are removed and installed by using a **screwdriver**. Screwdrivers are available in many sizes and tip shapes. The most commonly used screwdriver is called a *straight blade* or *flat tip*.

FIGURE 1–26 Using a clicker-type torque wrench to tighten connecting rod nuts on an engine.

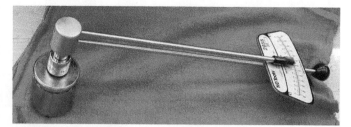

FIGURE 1–27 A beam-type torque wrench that displays the torque reading on the face of the dial. The beam display is read as the beam deflects, which is in proportion to the amount of torque applied to the fastener.

 TECH TIP

Check Torque Wrench Calibration Regularly

Torque wrenches should be checked regularly. For example, Honda has a torque wrench calibration setup at each of its training centers. It is expected that a torque wrench be checked for accuracy before every use. Most experts recommend that torque wrenches be checked and adjusted as needed at least every year and more often if possible. ● SEE FIGURE 1–28.

FIGURE 1–28 Torque wrench calibration checker.

Flat-tip screwdrivers are sized by the width of the blade and this width should match the width of the slot in the screw. ● SEE FIGURE 1–29.

CAUTION: Do not use a screwdriver as a pry tool or as a chisel. Screwdrivers are hardened steel only at the tip and are not designed to be pounded on or used for prying because they could bend easily. Always use the proper tool for each application.

PHILLIPS SCREWDRIVER. Another type of commonly used screwdriver is called a Phillips screwdriver, named for Henry F. Phillips, who invented the crosshead screw in 1934. Due to the shape of the crosshead screw and screwdriver, a Phillips screw can be driven with more torque than can be achieved with a slotted screw.

A Phillips head screwdriver is specified by the length of the handle and the size of the point at the tip. A #1 tip has a sharp point, a #2 tip is the most commonly used, and a #3 tip is blunt and is only used for larger sizes of Phillips head fasteners. For example, a #2 × 3 inch Phillips screwdriver would typically measure 6 inch from the tip of the blade to the end of the handle (3 inch long handle and 3 inch long blade) with a #2 tip.

Both straight-blade and Phillips screwdrivers are available with a short blade and handle for access to fasteners with limited room. ● SEE FIGURE 1–30.

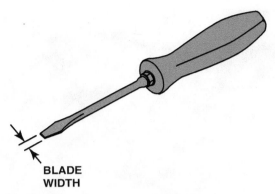

BLADE WIDTH

FIGURE 1–29 A flat-tip (straight-blade) screwdriver. The width of the blade should match the width of the slot in the fastener being loosened or tightened.

FIGURE 1–30 Two stubby screwdrivers that are used to access screws that have limited space above. A straight blade is on top and a #2 Phillips screwdriver is on the bottom.

TECH TIP

Use Socket Adapters with Caution

A **socket adapter** allows the use of one size of socket and another drive size ratchet or breaker bar. Socket adapters are available and can be used for different drive size sockets on a ratchet. Combinations include:

- 1/4 inch drive—3/8 inch sockets
- 3/8 inch drive—1/4 inch sockets
- 3/8 inch drive—1/2 inch sockets
- 1/2 inch drive—3/8 inch sockets

Using a larger drive ratchet or breaker bar on a smaller size socket can cause the application of too much force to the socket, which could crack or shatter. Using a smaller size drive tool on a larger socket will usually not cause any harm, but would greatly reduce the amount of torque that can be applied to the bolt or nut.

TECH TIP

Avoid Using "Cheater Bars"

Whenever a fastener is difficult to remove, some technicians will insert the handle of a ratchet or a breaker bar into a length of steel pipe sometimes called a **cheater bar**. The extra length of the pipe allows the technician to exert more torque than can be applied using the drive handle alone. However, the extra torque can easily overload the socket and ratchet, causing them to break or shatter, which could cause personal injury.

OFFSET SCREWDRIVERS. Offset screwdrivers are used in places where a conventional screwdriver cannot fit. An offset screwdriver is bent at the ends and is used similar to a wrench. Most offset screwdrivers have a straight blade at one end and a Phillips end at the opposite end. ● **SEE FIGURE 1–31.**

IMPACT SCREWDRIVER. An *impact screwdriver* is used to break loose or tighten a screw. A hammer is used to strike the end after the screwdriver holder is placed in the head of the screw and rotated in the desired direction. The force from the hammer blow does two things: It applies a force downward holding the tip of the screwdriver in the slot and then applies a twisting force to loosen (or tighten) the screw. ● **SEE FIGURE 1–32.**

SAFE USE OF SCREWDRIVERS Always use the proper type and size screwdriver that matches the fastener. Try to avoid pressing down on a screwdriver because if it slips, the screwdriver tip could go into your hand, causing serious personal injury. All screwdrivers should be cleaned after use. Do not use a screwdriver as a prybar; always use the correct tool for the job.

HAMMERS AND MALLETS **Hammers** and mallets are used to force objects together or apart. The shape of the back part of the hammer head (called the *peen*) usually determines the name. For example, a ball-peen hammer has a rounded end like a ball and it is used to straighten oil pans and valve covers, using the hammer head, and for shaping metal, using the ball peen. ● **SEE FIGURE 1–33.**

NOTE: A claw hammer has a claw used to remove nails and is not used for automotive service.

A hammer is usually sized by the weight of the head of the hammer and the length of the handle. For example,

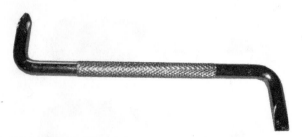

FIGURE 1–31 An offset screwdriver is used to install or remove fasteners that do not have enough space above to use a conventional screwdriver.

 FREQUENTLY ASKED QUESTION

What Is a Torx?

A Torx is a six-pointed star-shaped tip that was developed by Camcar (formerly Textron) to offer higher loosening and tightening torque than is possible with a straight blade (flat tip) or Phillips. Torx is very commonly used in the automotive field for many components. Commonly used Torx sizes from small to large include T15, T20, T25 and T30.

Some Torx fasteners include a round projection in the center requiring that a special version of a Torx bit be used. These are called security Torx bits, which have a hole in the center to be used on these fasteners. External Torx fasteners are also used as engine fasteners and are labeled E instead of T, plus the size, such as E45.

FIGURE 1–32 An impact screwdriver used to remove slotted or Phillips head fasteners that cannot be broken loose using a standard screwdriver.

FIGURE 1–33 A typical ball-peen hammer.

a commonly used ball-peen hammer has an 8 ounce head with an 11 inch handle.

MALLETS. *Mallets* are a type of hammer with a large striking surface, which allows the technician to exert force over a larger area than a hammer, so as not to harm the part or component. Mallets are made from a variety of materials including rubber, plastic, or wood. ●**SEE FIGURE 1–34**.

DEAD-BLOW HAMMER. A shot-filled plastic hammer is called a *dead-blow hammer*. The small lead balls (shot) inside a plastic head prevent the hammer from bouncing off of the object when struck. ●**SEE FIGURE 1–35**.

SAFE USE OF HAMMERS AND MALLETS All mallets and hammers should be cleaned after use and not exposed to extreme temperatures. Never use a hammer or mallet that is

damaged in any way and always use caution to avoid doing damage to the components and the surrounding area. Always follow the hammer manufacturer's recommended procedures and practices.

PLIERS

SLIP-JOINT PLIERS. **Pliers** are capable of holding, twisting, bending, and cutting objects and is an extremely useful classification of tools. The common household type of pliers are called *slip-joint pliers*. There are two different positions where the junction of the handles meets to achieve a wide range of sizes of objects that can be gripped. ●**SEE FIGURE 1–36**.

MULTIGROOVE ADJUSTABLE PLIERS. For gripping larger objects, a set of *multigroove adjustable pliers* is a commonly used tool of choice by many service technicians. Originally designed to remove the various size nuts holding rope seals used in water pumps, the name *water pump pliers* is also used.

FIGURE 1–34 A rubber mallet used to deliver a force to an object without harming the surface.

FIGURE 1–35 A dead-blow hammer that was left outside in freezing weather. The plastic covering was damaged, which destroyed this hammer. The lead shot is encased in the metal housing and then covered.

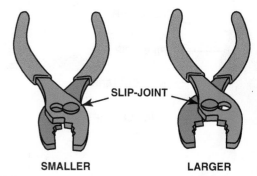

FIGURE 1–36 Typical slip-joint pliers is a common household pliers. The slip joint allows the jaws to be opened to two different settings.

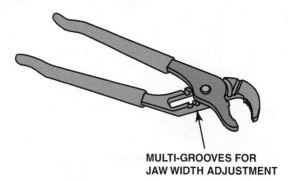

FIGURE 1–37 Multigroove adjustable pliers is known by many names, including the trade name "Channel Locks®."

These types of pliers are commonly called by their trade name *Channel Locks®*. ● **SEE FIGURE 1–37**.

LINESMAN'S PLIERS. *Linesman's pliers* is a hand tool specifically designed for cutting, bending, and twisting wire. While commonly used by construction workers and electricians, linesman's pliers is a very useful tool for the service technician who deals with wiring. The center parts of the jaws are designed to grasp round objects such as pipe or tubing without slipping. ● **SEE FIGURE 1–38**.

DIAGONAL PLIERS. *Diagonal pliers* is designed to cut only. The cutting jaws are set at an angle to make it easier to cut wires. Diagonal pliers are also called *side cuts* or *dikes*. These pliers are constructed of hardened steel and they are used mostly for cutting wire. ● **SEE FIGURE 1–39**.

NEEDLE-NOSE PLIERS. *Needle-nose pliers* are designed to grip small objects or objects in tight locations. Needle-nose pliers

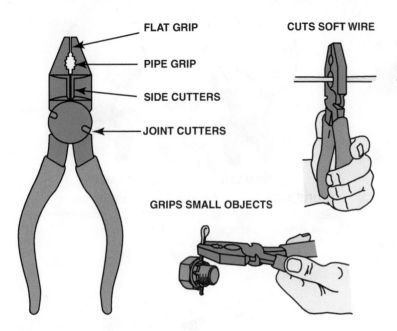

FLAT GRIP

PIPE GRIP

SIDE CUTTERS

JOINT CUTTERS

CUTS SOFT WIRE

GRIPS SMALL OBJECTS

FIGURE 1–38 Linesman's pliers are very useful because it can help perform many automotive service jobs.

CUTTING WIRES CLOSE TO TERMINALS

PULLING OUT AND SPREADING COTTER PIN

FIGURE 1–39 Diagonal-cut pliers is another common tool that has many names.

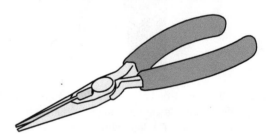

FIGURE 1–40 Needle-nose pliers are used where there is limited access to a wire or pin that needs to be installed or removed.

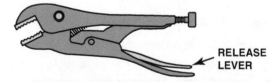

RELEASE LEVER

FIGURE 1–41 Locking pliers are best known by their trade name Vise Grips®.

have long, pointed jaws, which allow the tips to reach into narrow openings or groups of small objects. ● SEE FIGURE 1–40.

Most needle-nose pliers have a wire cutter located at the base of the jaws near the pivot. There are several variations of needle nose pliers, including right angle jaws or slightly angled to allow access to certain cramped areas.

LOCKING PLIERS. *Locking pliers* are adjustable pliers that can be locked to hold objects from moving. Most locking pliers also have wire cutters built into the jaws near the pivot point. Locking pliers come in a variety of styles and sizes and are commonly referred to by the trade name *Vise Grips*®. The size is the length of the pliers, not how far the jaws open. ● SEE FIGURE 1–41.

SNAP-RING PLIERS. *Snap-ring pliers* is used to remove and install snap-rings. Many snap-ring pliers are designed to be able to remove and install both inward, as well as outward, expanding snap rings. Some snap-ring pliers can be equipped with serrated-tipped jaws for grasping the opening in the snap ring, while others are equipped with points, which are inserted into the holes in the snap ring. ● SEE FIGURE 1–42.

SAFE USE OF PLIERS Pliers should not be used to remove any bolt or other fastener. Pliers should only be used when specified for use by the vehicle manufacturer.

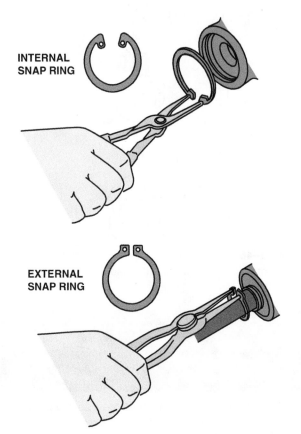

INTERNAL
SNAP RING

EXTERNAL
SNAP RING

FIGURE 1–42 Snap-ring pliers are also called lock ring pliers and most are designed to remove internal and external snap rings (lock rings).

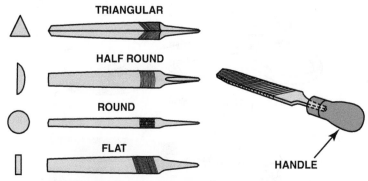

TRIANGULAR

HALF ROUND

ROUND

FLAT

HANDLE

FIGURE 1–43 Files come in many different shapes and sizes. Never use a file without a handle.

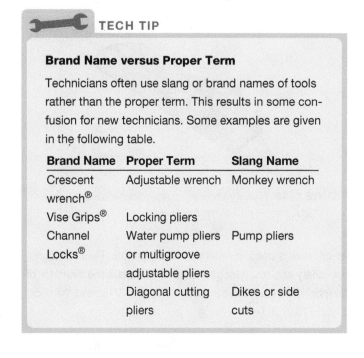

TECH TIP

Brand Name versus Proper Term

Technicians often use slang or brand names of tools rather than the proper term. This results in some confusion for new technicians. Some examples are given in the following table.

Brand Name	Proper Term	Slang Name
Crescent wrench®	Adjustable wrench	Monkey wrench
Vise Grips®	Locking pliers	
Channel Locks®	Water pump pliers or multigroove adjustable pliers	Pump pliers
	Diagonal cutting pliers	Dikes or side cuts

FILES **Files** are used to smooth metal and are constructed of hardened steel with diagonal rows of teeth. Files are available with a single row of teeth called a *single cut file*, as well as two rows of teeth cut at an opposite angle called a *double cut file*. Files are available in a variety of shapes and sizes from small flat files, half-round files, and triangular files. ● **SEE FIGURE 1–43**.

SAFE USE OF FILES Always use a file with a handle. Because files only cut when moved forward, a handle must be attached to prevent possible personal injury. After making a forward strike, lift the file and return the file to the starting position; avoid dragging the file backward.

SNIPS Service technicians are often asked to fabricate sheet metal brackets or heat shields and need to use one or more types of cutters available called **snips**. *Tin snips* are the simplest and are designed to make straight cuts in a variety of materials, such as sheet steel, aluminum, or even fabric. A variation of the tin snips is called *aviation tin snips*. There are three designs of aviation snips including one designed to cut straight (called a *straight cut aviation snip*), one

designed to cut left (called an *offset left aviation snip*), and one designed to cut right (called an *offset right aviation snip*). ● **SEE FIGURE 1–44**.

UTILITY KNIFE A *utility knife* uses a replaceable blade and is used to cut a variety of materials such as carpet, plastic, wood, and paper products, such as cardboard. ● **SEE FIGURE 1–45**.

SAFE USE OF CUTTERS Whenever using cutters, always wear eye protection or a face shield to guard against the possibility of metal pieces being ejected during the cut. Always follow recommended procedures.

PUNCHES A **punch** is a small diameter steel rod that has a smaller diameter ground at one end. A punch is used to drive a

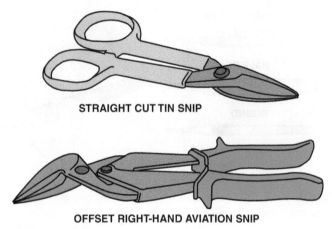

STRAIGHT CUT TIN SNIP

OFFSET RIGHT-HAND AVIATION SNIP

FIGURE 1–44 Tin snips are used to cut thin sheets of metal or carpet.

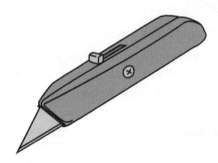

FIGURE 1–45 A utility knife uses replaceable blades and is used to cut carpet and other materials.

pin out that is used to retain two components. Punches come in a variety of sizes, which are measured across the diameter of the machined end. Sizes include 1/16, 1/8, 3/16, and 1/4 inch. ● **SEE FIGURE 1–46.**

CHISELS A **chisel** has a straight, sharp cutting end that is used for cutting off rivets or to separate two pieces of an assembly. The most common design of chisel used for automotive service work is called a *cold chisel*.

SAFE USE OF PUNCHES AND CHISELS Always wear eye protection when using a punch or a chisel because the hardened steel is brittle and parts of the punch could fly off and cause serious personal injury. See the warning stamped on the side of this automotive punch in ● **FIGURE 1–47.**

The tops of punches and chisels can become rounded off from use, which is called "mushroomed." This material must be ground off to help avoid the possibility of the overhanging material being loosened and becoming airborne during use. ● **SEE FIGURE 1–48.**

HACKSAWS A **hacksaw** is used to cut metals, such as steel, aluminum, brass, or copper. The cutting blade of a hacksaw

PIN

FIGURE 1–46 A punch used to drive pins from assembled components. This type of punch is also called a pin punch.

WEAR SAFETY GOGGLES

FIGURE 1–47 Warning stamped on the side of a punch warning that goggles should be worn when using this tool. Always follow safety warnings.

is replaceable and the sharpness and number of teeth can be varied to meet the needs of the job. Use 14 or 18 teeth per inch (TPI) for cutting plaster or soft metals, such as aluminum and copper. Use 24 or 32 teeth per inch for steel or pipe. Hacksaw blades should be installed with the teeth pointing away from the handle. This means that a hacksaw only cuts while the blade is pushed in the forward direction. ● **SEE FIGURE 1–49.**

SAFE USE OF HACKSAWS Check that the hacksaw is equipped with the correct blade for the job and that the teeth are pointed away from the handle. When using a hacksaw, move the hacksaw slowly away from you, then lift slightly and return for another cut.

BASIC HAND TOOL LIST

The following is a typical list of hand tools every automotive technician should possess. Specialty tools are not included.

Safety glasses

Tool chest

1/4 inch drive socket set (1/4 to 9/16 inch standard and deep sockets; 6 to 15 mm standard and deep sockets)

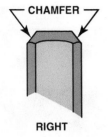

FIGURE 1–48 Use a grinder or a file to remove the mushroom material on the end of a punch or chisel.

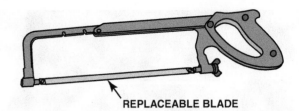

FIGURE 1–49 A typical hacksaw that is used to cut metal. If cutting sheet metal or thin objects, a blade with more teeth should be used.

1/4 inch drive ratchet

1/4 inch drive 2 inch extension

1/4 inch drive 6 inch extension

1/4 inch drive handle

3/8 inch drive socket set (3/8 to 7/8 inch standard and deep sockets; 10 to 19 mm standard and deep sockets)

3/8 inch drive Torx set (T40, T45, T50, and T55)

3/8 inch drive 13/16 inch plug socket

3/8 inch drive 5/8 inch plug socket

3/8 inch drive ratchet

3/8 inch drive 1 1/2 inch extension

3/8 inch drive 3 inch extension

3/8 inch drive 6 inch extension

3/8 inch drive 18 inch extension

3/8 inch drive universal

1/2 inch drive socket set (1/2 to 1 inch standard and deep sockets)

1/2 inch drive ratchet

1/2 inch drive breaker bar

1/2 inch drive 5 inch extension

1/2 inch drive 10 inch extension

3/8 to 1/4 inch adapter

1/2 to 3/8 inch adapter

3/8 to 1/2 inch adapter

Crowfoot set (fractional inch)

Crowfoot set (metric)

3/8 through 1 inch combination wrench set

10 through 19 mm combination wrench set

1/16 through 1/4 inch hex wrench set

2 through 12 mm hex wrench set

3/8 inch hex socket

13 to 14 mm flare-nut wrench

15 to 17 mm flare-nut wrench

5/16 to 3/8 inch flare-nut wrench

7/16 to 1/2 inch flare-nut wrench

1/2 to 9/16 inch flare-nut wrench

Diagonal pliers

Needle pliers

Adjustable-jaw pliers

Locking pliers

Snap-ring pliers

Stripping or crimping pliers

Ball-peen hammer

Rubber hammer

Dead-blow hammer

Five-piece standard screwdriver set

Four-piece Phillips screwdriver set

#15 Torx screwdriver

#20 Torx screwdriver

Center punch

Pin punches (assorted sizes)

Chisel

Utility knife

Valve core tool

Filter wrench (large filters)

Filter wrench (smaller filters)

Test light

Feeler gauge

Scraper

Pinch bar

Magnet

FIGURE 1–50 A typical beginning technician tool set that includes the basic tools to get started.

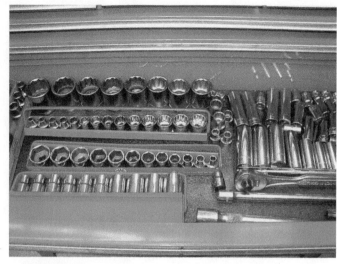

FIGURE 1–51 A typical large tool box, showing just one of many drawers.

FIGURE 1–52 A typical 12 volt test light.

TOOL SETS AND ACCESSORIES

A beginning service technician may wish to start with a small set of tools before purchasing an expensive tool set. ● **SEE FIGURES 1–50 AND 1–51.**

ELECTRICAL HAND TOOLS

TEST LIGHT A test light is used to test for electricity. A typical automotive test light consists of a clear plastic screwdriver-like handle that contains a lightbulb. A wire is attached to one terminal of the bulb, which the technician connects to a clean metal part of the vehicle. The other end of the bulb is attached to a point that can be used to test for electricity at a connector or wire. When there is power at the point and a good connection at the other end, the lightbulb lights. ● **SEE FIGURE 1–52.**

SOLDERING GUNS

ELECTRIC SOLDERING GUN. This type of soldering gun is usually powered by 110 volt AC and often has two power settings expressed in watts. A typical electric soldering gun will produce from 85 to 300 watts of heat at the tip, which is more than adequate for soldering.

ELECTRIC SOLDERING PENCIL. This type of soldering iron is less expensive and creates less heat than an electric soldering gun. A typical electric soldering pencil (iron) creates 30 to 60 watts of heat and is suitable for soldering smaller wires and connections.

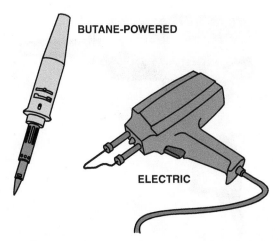

BUTANE-POWERED

ELECTRIC

FIGURE 1–53 Electric and butane-powered soldering guns used to make electrical repairs. Soldering guns are sold by the wattage rating. The higher the wattage, the greater amount of heat created. Most solder guns used for automotive electrical work usually fall within the 60 to 160 watt range.

BUTANE-POWERED SOLDERING IRON. A butane-powered soldering iron is portable and very useful for automotive service work because an electrical cord is not needed. Most butane-powered soldering irons produce about 60 watts of heat, which is enough for most automotive soldering. ● **SEE FIGURE 1–53.**

ELECTRICAL WORK HAND TOOLS In addition to a soldering iron, most service technicians who do electrical-related work should have the following:

- Wire cutters
- Wire strippers
- Wire crimpers
- Heat gun for heat shrink tubing

DIGITAL METER A digital meter is a necessary tool for any electrical diagnosis and troubleshooting. A digital multimeter, abbreviated DMM, is usually capable of measuring the following units of electricity:

- DC volts
- AC volts
- Ohms
- Amperes

HAND TOOL MAINTENANCE

Most hand tools are constructed of rust-resistant metals but they can still rust or corrode if not properly maintained. For best results and long tool life, the following steps should be taken:

FREQUENTLY ASKED QUESTION

What Is an "SST"?

Vehicle manufacturers often specify a **special service tool (SST)** to properly disassemble and assemble components, such as transmissions and other components. These tools are also called special tools and are available from the vehicle manufacturer or their tool supplier, such as Kent-Moore and Miller tools. Many service technicians do not have access to special service tools so they use generic versions that are available from aftermarket sources.

- Clean each tool before placing it back into the tool box.
- Keep tools separated. Moisture on metal tools will start to rust more readily if the tools are in contact with another metal tool.
- Line the drawers of the tool box with a material that will prevent the tools from moving as the drawers are opened and closed. This helps to quickly locate the proper tool and size.
- Release the tension on all "clicker-type" torque wrenches.
- Keep the tool box secure.

TROUBLE LIGHTS

INCANDESCENT *Incandescent lights* use a filament that produces light when electric current flows through the bulb. This was the standard **trouble light**, also called a *work light* for many years until safety issues caused most shops to switch to safer fluorescent or LED lights. If incandescent lightbulbs are used, try to locate bulbs that are rated "rough service," which is designed to withstand shock and vibration more than conventional lightbulbs.

 WARNING

Do not use incandescent trouble lights around gasoline or other flammable liquids. The liquids can cause the bulb to break and the hot filament can ignite the flammable liquid, which can cause personal injury or even death.

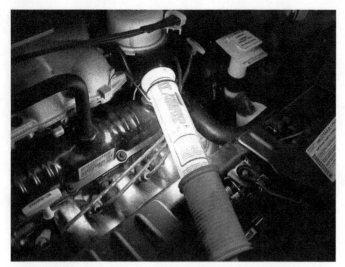

FIGURE 1–54 A fluorescent trouble light operates cooler and is safer to use in the shop because it is protected against accidental breakage where gasoline or other flammable liquids would happen to come in contact with the light.

FIGURE 1–55 A typical 1/2 inch drive air impact wrench. The direction of rotation can be changed to loosen or tighten a fastener.

FLUORESCENT   A trouble light is an essential piece of shop equipment, and for safety, should be fluorescent rather than incandescent. Incandescent lightbulbs can scatter or break if gasoline were to be splashed onto the bulb creating a serious fire hazard. Fluorescent light tubes are not as likely to be broken and are usually protected by a clear plastic enclosure. Trouble lights are usually attached to a retractor, which can hold 20 to 50 feet of electrical cord. ● **SEE FIGURE 1–54.**

LED TROUBLE LIGHT   **Light-emitting diode (LED)** trouble lights are excellent to use because they are shock resistant, are long lasting, and do not represent a fire hazard. Some trouble lights are battery powered and therefore can be used in places where an attached electrical cord could present problems.

FIGURE 1–56 A typical battery-powered 3/8 inch drive impact wrench.

AIR AND ELECTRICALLY OPERATED TOOLS

IMPACT WRENCH   An impact wrench, either air or electrically powered, is a tool that is used to remove and install fasteners. The air-operated 1/2 inch drive impact wrench is the most commonly used unit. ● **SEE FIGURE 1–55.**

Electrically powered impact wrenches commonly include:

- Battery-powered units. ● **SEE FIGURE 1–56.**
- 110 volt AC-powered units. This type of impact is very useful, especially if compressed air is not readily available.

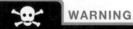

☠ **WARNING**

Always use impact sockets with impact wrenches, and always wear eye protection in case the socket or fastener shatters. Impact sockets are thicker walled and constructed with premium alloy steel. They are hardened with a black oxide finish to help prevent corrosion and distinguish them from regular sockets. ● SEE FIGURE 1–57.

FIGURE 1–57 A black impact socket. Always use an impact-type socket whenever using an impact wrench to avoid the possibility of shattering the socket, which could cause personal injury. If a socket is chrome plated, it is not to be used with an impact wrench.

AIR RATCHET An air ratchet is used to remove and install fasteners that would normally be removed or installed using a ratchet and a socket. ● **SEE FIGURE 1–58.**

DIE GRINDER A die grinder is a commonly used air-powered tool which can also be used to sand or remove gaskets and rust. ● **SEE FIGURE 1–59.**

BENCH- OR PEDESTAL-MOUNTED GRINDER These high-powered grinders can be equipped with a wire brush wheel and/or a stone wheel.

- **Wire brush wheel**—This type is used to clean threads of bolts as well as to remove gaskets from sheet metal engine parts.
- **Stone wheel**—This type is used to grind metal or to remove the mushroom from the top of punches or chisels. ● **SEE FIGURE 1–60.**

Most **bench grinders** are equipped with a grinder wheel (stone) on one end and a wire brush wheel on the other end. A bench grinder is a very useful piece of shop equipment and the wire wheel end can be used for the following:

- Cleaning threads of bolts
- Cleaning gaskets from sheet metal parts, such as steel valve covers

CAUTION: Only use a steel wire brush on steel or iron components. If a steel wire brush is used on aluminum or copper-based metal parts, it can remove metal from the part.

FIGURE 1–58 An air ratchet is a very useful tool that allows fast removal and installation of fasteners, especially in areas that are difficult to reach or do not have room enough to move a hand ratchet or wrench.

FIGURE 1–59 This typical die grinder surface preparation kit includes the air-operated die grinder as well as a variety of sanding disks for smoothing surfaces or removing rust.

FIGURE 1–60 A typical pedestal grinder with a wire wheel on the left side and a stone wheel on the right side. Even though this machine is equipped with guards, safety glasses or a face shield should always be worn whenever using a grinder or wire wheel.

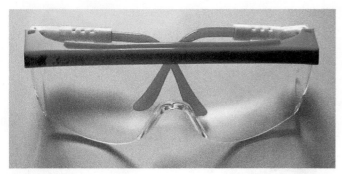

FIGURE 1–61 Safety glasses should be worn at all times when working on or around any vehicle or servicing any components.

The grinding stone end of the bench grinder can be used for the following:

- Sharpening blades and drill bits
- Grinding off the heads of rivets or parts
- Sharpening sheet metal parts for custom fitting

PERSONAL PROTECTIVE EQUIPMENT

Service technicians should wear **personal protective equipment (PPE)** to prevent personal injury. The personal protection devices include the following:

SAFETY GLASSES Wear safety glasses at all times while servicing any vehicle and be sure that they meet standard ANSI Z87.1. ● **SEE FIGURE 1–61.**

STEEL-TOED SAFETY SHOES ● **SEE FIGURE 1–62.** If steel-toed safety shoes are not available, then leather-topped shoes offer more protection than canvas or cloth covered shoes.

BUMP CAP Service technicians working under a vehicle should wear a **bump cap** to protect the head against under-vehicle objects and the pads of the lift. ● **SEE FIGURE 1–63.**

HEARING PROTECTION Hearing protection should be worn if the sound around you requires that you raise your voice (sound level higher than 90 dB). For example, a typical

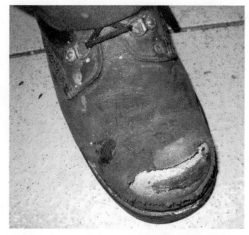

FIGURE 1–62 Steel-toed shoes are a worthwhile investment to help prevent foot injury due to falling objects. Even these well-worn shoes can protect the feet of this service technician.

FIGURE 1–63 One version of a bump cap is a molded plastic insert that is worn inside a regular cloth cap.

lawnmower produces noise at a level of about 110 dB. This means that everyone who uses a lawnmower or other lawn or garden equipment should wear ear protection.

GLOVES Many technicians wear gloves not only to help keep their hands clean but also to help protect their skin from the effects of dirty engine oil and other possibly hazardous materials.

Several types of gloves and their characteristics include:

- **Latex surgical gloves.** These gloves are relatively inexpensive, but tend to stretch, swell, and weaken when exposed to gas, oil, or solvents.
- **Vinyl gloves.** These gloves are also inexpensive and are not affected by gas, oil, or solvents.
- **Polyurethane gloves.** These gloves are more expensive, yet very strong. Even though these gloves are also not affected by gas, oil, or solvents, they do tend to be slippery.

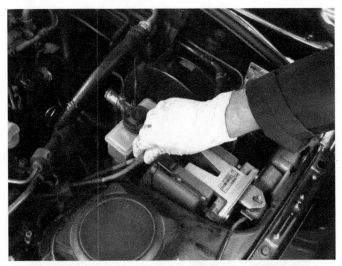

FIGURE 1–64 Protective gloves are available in several sizes and materials.

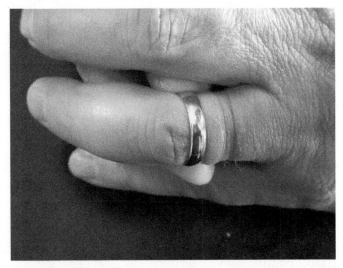

FIGURE 1–65 Remove all jewelry before performing service work on any vehicle.

- **Nitrile gloves.** These gloves are exactly like latex gloves, but are not affected by gas, oil, or solvents, yet they tend to be expensive.
- **Mechanic's gloves.** These gloves are usually made of synthetic leather and spandex and provide thermo protection, as well as protection from dirt and grime.

● **SEE FIGURE 1–64.**

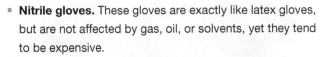
SAFETY PRECAUTIONS

FIGURE 1–66 Always connect an exhaust hose to the tailpipe of a vehicle to be run inside a building.

Besides wearing personal safety equipment, there are also many actions that should be performed to keep safe in the shop. These actions include:

- Remove jewelry that may get caught on something or act as a conductor to an exposed electrical circuit. ● **SEE FIGURE 1–65.**
- Take care of your hands. Keep your hands clean by washing with soap and hot water that is at least 110°F (43°C).
- Avoid loose or dangling clothing.
- When lifting any object, get a secure grip with solid footing. Keep the load close to your body to minimize the strain. Lift with your legs and arms, not your back.
- Do not twist your body when carrying a load. Instead, pivot your feet to help prevent strain on the spine.
- Ask for help when moving or lifting heavy objects.

- Push a heavy object rather than pull it. (This is opposite to the way you should work with tools—never push a wrench! If you do and a bolt or nut loosens, your entire weight is used to propel your hand(s) forward. This usually results in cuts, bruises, or other painful injury.)
- Always connect an exhaust hose to the tailpipe of any running vehicle to help prevent the buildup of carbon monoxide inside a closed garage space. ● **SEE FIGURE 1–66.**
- When standing, keep objects, parts, and tools with which you are working between chest height and waist height. If seated, work at tasks that are at elbow height.
- Always be sure the hood is securely held open.

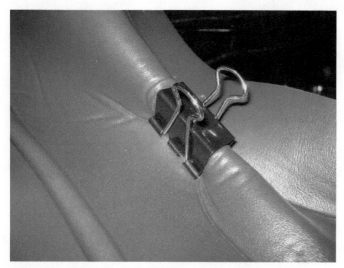

FIGURE 1–67 A binder clip being used to keep a fender cover from falling off.

FIGURE 1–68 Covering the interior as soon as the vehicle comes in for service helps improve customer satisfaction.

VEHICLE PROTECTION

FENDER COVERS Whenever working under the hood of any vehicle, be sure to use fender covers. They not only help protect the vehicle from possible damage but they also provide a clean surface to place parts and tools. The major problem with using fender covers is that they tend to move and often fall off the vehicle. To help prevent the fender covers from falling off secure them to a lip of the fender using a *binder clip* available at most office supply stores. ●**SEE FIGURE 1–67.**

INTERIOR PROTECTION Always protect the interior of the vehicle from accidental damage or dirt and grease by covering the seat, steering wheel, and floor with a protective covering. ●**SEE FIGURE 1–68.**

SAFETY LIFTING (HOISTING) A VEHICLE

Many chassis and underbody service procedures require that the vehicle be hoisted or lifted off the ground. The simplest methods involve the use of drive-on ramps or a floor jack and safety (jack) stands, whereas in-ground or surface-mounted lifts provide greater access.

✚ SAFETY TIP

Shop Cloth Disposal

Always dispose of oily shop cloths in an enclosed container to prevent a fire. ●**SEE FIGURE 1–69.** Whenever oily cloths are thrown together on the floor or workbench, a chemical reaction can occur, which can ignite the cloth even without an open flame. This process of ignition without an open flame is called **spontaneous combustion.**

Setting the pads is a critical part of this hoisting procedure. All vehicle service information, including service, shop, and owner's manuals, include recommended locations to be used when hoisting (lifting) a vehicle. Newer vehicles have a triangle decal on the driver's door indicating the recommended lift points. The recommended standards for the lift points and lifting procedures are found in SAE Standard JRP-2184. ● **SEE FIGURE 1–70.**

FIGURE 1–69 All oily shop cloths should be stored in a metal container equipped with a lid to help prevent spontaneous combustion.

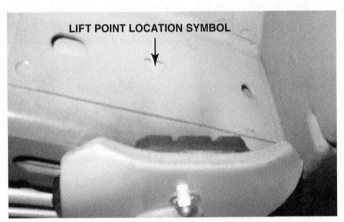

LIFT POINT LOCATION SYMBOL

FIGURE 1–70 Most newer vehicles have a triangle symbol indicating the recommended hoisting lift location.

These recommendations typically include the following points:

1. The vehicle should be centered on the lift or hoist so as not to overload one side or put too much force either forward or rearward. ●**SEE FIGURE 1–71.**

2. The pads of the lift should be spread as far apart as possible to provide a stable platform.

3. Each pad should be placed under a portion of the vehicle that is strong and capable of supporting the weight of the vehicle.

   a. Pinch welds at the bottom edge of the body are generally considered to be strong.

CAUTION: Even though **pinch weld seams** are the recommended location for hoisting many vehicles with unitized

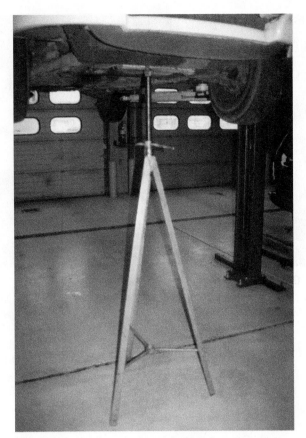

(a)

(b)

FIGURE 1–71 (a) Tall safety stands can be used to provide additional support for the vehicle while on the hoist. (b) A block of wood should be used to avoid the possibility of doing damage to components supported by the stand.

bodies (unit-body), care should be taken not to place the pad(s) too far forward or rearward. Incorrect placement of the vehicle on the lift could cause the vehicle to be imbalanced, and the vehicle could fall. This is exactly what happened to the vehicle in ●**FIGURE 1–72.**

   b. Boxed areas of the body are the best places to position the pads on a vehicle without a frame. Be careful to note whether the arms of the lift might come into

FIGURE 1–72 This training vehicle fell from the hoist because the pads were not set correctly. No one was hurt but the vehicle was damaged.

contact with other parts of the vehicle before the pad touches the intended location. Commonly damaged areas include the following:

(1) Rocker panel moldings

(2) Exhaust system (including catalytic converter)

(3) Tires or body panels (● **SEE FIGURES 1–73 AND 1–74.**)

4. The vehicle should be raised about a foot (30 centimeters [cm]) off the floor, then stopped and shaken to check for stability. If the vehicle seems to be stable when checked at a short distance from the floor, continue raising the vehicle and continue to view the vehicle until it has reached the desired height. The hoist should be lowered onto the mechanical locks, and then raised off of the locks before lowering.

CAUTION: Do not look away from the vehicle while it is being raised (or lowered) on a hoist. Often one side or one end of the hoist can stop or fail, resulting in the vehicle being slanted enough to slip or fall, creating physical damage not only to the vehicle and/or hoist but also to the technician or others who may be nearby.

HINT: Most hoists can be safely placed at any desired height. For ease while working, the area in which you are working should be at chest level. When working on brakes or suspension components, it is not necessary to work on them down near the floor or over your head. Raise the hoist so that the components are at chest level.

5. Before lowering the hoist, the safety latch(es) must be released and the direction of the controls reversed. The speed downward is often adjusted to be as slow as possible for additional safety.

JACKS AND SAFETY STANDS

Floor jacks properly rated for the weight of the vehicle being raised are a common vehicle lifting tool. Floor jacks are portable and relatively inexpensive and must be used with safety (jack) stands. The floor jack is used to raise the vehicle off the ground and safety stands should be placed under the frame on the body of the vehicle. The weight of the vehicle should never be kept on the hydraulic floor jack because a failure of the jack could cause the vehicle to fall. ● **SEE FIGURE 1–75.** The jack is then slowly released to allow the vehicle weight to be supported on the safety stands. If the front or rear of the vehicle is being raised, the opposite end of the vehicle must be blocked.

CAUTION: Safety stands should be rated higher than the weight they support.

DRIVE-ON RAMPS

Ramps are an inexpensive way to raise the front or rear of a vehicle. ● **SEE FIGURE 1–76.** Ramps are easy to store, but they can be dangerous because they can "kick out" when driving the vehicle onto the ramps.

CAUTION: Professional repair shops do not use ramps because they are dangerous to use. Use only with extreme care.

ELECTRICAL CORD SAFETY

Use correctly grounded three-prong sockets and extension cords to operate power tools. Some tools use only two-prong plugs. Make sure these are double insulated and repair or replace any electrical cords that are cut or damaged to prevent the possibility of an electrical shock. When not in use, keep electrical cords off the floor to prevent tripping over them. Tape the cords down if they are placed in high foot traffic areas.

(a)

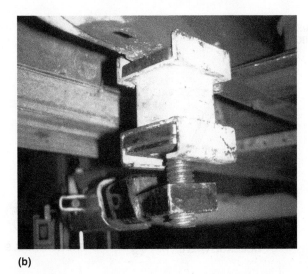
(b)

FIGURE 1–73 (a) An assortment of hoist pad adapters that are often needed to safely hoist many pickup trucks, vans, and sport utility vehicles (SUVs). (b) A view from underneath a Chevrolet pickup truck showing how the pad extensions are used to attach the hoist lifting pad to contact the frame.

(a)

(b)

FIGURE 1–74 (a) The pad arm is just contacting the rocker panel of the vehicle. (b) The pad arm has dented the rocker panel on this vehicle because the pad was set too far inward underneath the vehicle.

JUMP STARTING AND BATTERY SAFETY

To jump start another vehicle with a dead battery, connect good-quality copper jumper cables as indicated in ● **SEE FIGURE 1–77** or a jump box. The last connection made should always be on the engine block or an engine bracket as far from the battery as possible. It is normal for a spark to be created when the jumper cables finally complete the jumper cable connections, and this spark could cause an explosion of the gases around the battery. Many newer vehicles have special ground connections built away from the battery just for the purpose of jump starting. Check the owner's manual or service information for the exact location.

Batteries contain acid and should be handled with care to avoid tipping them greater than a 45-degree angle. Always remove jewelry when working around a battery to avoid the possibility of electrical shock or burns, which can occur when the metal comes in contact with a 12 volt circuit and ground, such as the body of the vehicle.

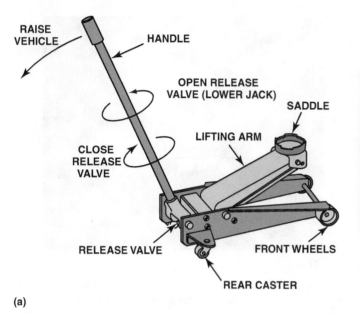

(a)

(b)

FIGURE 1–75 (a) A hydraulic hand-operated floor jack. (b) Whenever a vehicle is raised off the ground, a safety stand should be placed under the frame, axle, or body to support the weight of the vehicle.

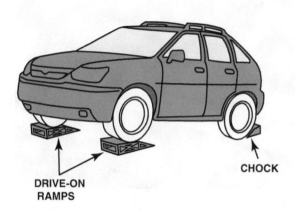

FIGURE 1–76 Drive-on-type ramps are dangerous to use. The wheels on the ground level must be chocked (blocked) to prevent accidental movement down the ramp.

SAFETY TIP

Air Hose Safety

Improper use of an air nozzle can cause blindness or deafness. Compressed air must be reduced to less than 30 psi (206 kPa). ●**SEE FIGURE 1–78.** If an air nozzle is used to dry and clean parts, make sure the airstream is directed away from anyone else in the immediate area. Coil and store air hoses when they are not in use.

FIRE EXTINGUISHERS

There are four **fire extinguisher classes**. Each class should be used on specific fires only:

- **Class A** is designed for use on general combustibles, such as cloth, paper, and wood.
- **Class B** is designed for use on flammable liquids and greases, including gasoline, oil, thinners, and solvents.
- **Class C** is used only on electrical fires.
- **Class D** is effective only on combustible metals such as powdered aluminum, sodium, or magnesium.

The class rating is clearly marked on the side of every fire extinguisher. Many extinguishers are good for multiple types of fires. ●**SEE FIGURE 1–79.**

When using a fire extinguisher, remember the word "PASS."

P = Pull the safety pin.

A = Aim the nozzle of the extinguisher at the base of the fire.

S = Squeeze the lever to actuate the extinguisher.

S = Sweep the nozzle from side-to-side.

● **SEE FIGURE 1–80.**

TYPES OF FIRE EXTINGUISHERS Types of fire extinguishers include the following:

- **Water.** A water fire extinguisher, usually in a pressurized container, is good to use on Class A fires by reducing

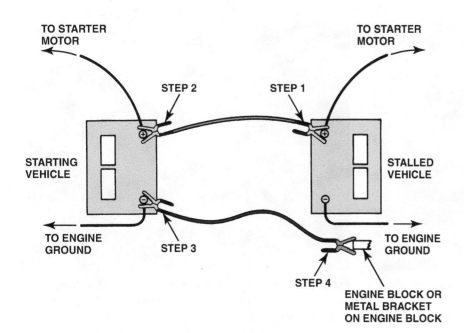

TO STARTER MOTOR

TO STARTER MOTOR

STEP 2

STEP 1

STARTING VEHICLE

STALLED VEHICLE

TO ENGINE GROUND

STEP 3

TO ENGINE GROUND

STEP 4

ENGINE BLOCK OR METAL BRACKET ON ENGINE BLOCK

FIGURE 1–77 Jumper cable usage guide. Follow the same connections if using a portable jump box.

FIGURE 1–78 The air pressure going to the nozzle should be reduced to 30 psi or less to help prevent personal injury.

the temperature to the point where a fire cannot be sustained.

- **Carbon dioxide (CO₂).** A carbon dioxide fire extinguisher is good for almost any type of fire, especially Class B and Class C materials. A CO_2 fire extinguisher works by removing the oxygen from the fire and the cold CO_2 also helps reduce the temperature of the fire.

- **Dry chemical (yellow).** A dry chemical fire extinguisher is good for Class A, B, and C fires. It acts by coating the flammable materials, which eliminates the oxygen from the fire. A dry chemical fire extinguisher tends to be very corrosive and will cause damage to electronic devices.

FIRE BLANKETS

Fire blankets are required to be available in the shop areas. If a person is on fire, a fire blanket should be removed from its storage bag and thrown over and around the victim to smother the fire. ● **SEE FIGURE 1–81** showing a typical fire blanket.

FIRST AID AND EYE WASH STATIONS

All shop areas must be equipped with a first aid kit and an eye wash station centrally located and kept stocked with emergency supplies. ● **SEE FIGURE 1–82.**

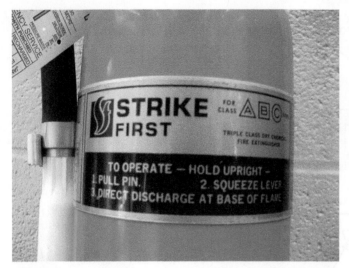

FIGURE 1–79 A typical fire extinguisher designed to be used on type A, B, or C fires.

FIGURE 1–81 A treated wool blanket is kept in an easy-to-open wall-mounted holder and should be placed in a central location in the shop.

FIGURE 1–80 A CO_2 fire extinguisher being used on a fire set in an open drum during a demonstration at a fire training center.

FIGURE 1–82 A first aid box should be centrally located in the shop and kept stocked with the recommended supplies.

FIRST AID KIT   A first aid kit should include:

- Bandages (variety)
- Gauze pads
- Roll gauze
- Iodine swab sticks
- Antibiotic ointment
- Hydrocortisone cream
- Burn gel packets
- Eye wash solution
- Scissors
- Tweezers
- Gloves
- First aid guide

Every shop should have a person trained in first aid. If there is an accident, call for help immediately.

EYE WASH STATION   An **eye wash station** should be centrally located and used whenever any liquid or chemical gets into the eyes. If such an emergency does occur, keep eyes in a constant stream of water and call for professional assistance. ●**SEE FIGURE 1–83.**

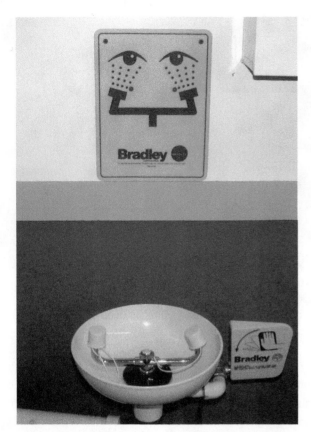

FIGURE 1–83 A typical eye wash station. Often a thorough flushing of the eyes with water is the first and often the best treatment in the event of eye contamination.

HYBRID ELECTRIC VEHICLE SAFETY ISSUES

Hybrid electric vehicles (HEVs) use a high-voltage battery pack and an electric motor(s) to help propel the vehicle. ● **SEE FIGURE 1–84** for an example of a typical warning label on a hybrid electric vehicle. The gasoline or diesel engine also is equipped with a generator or a combination starter and an integrated starter generator (ISG) or integrated starter alternator (ISA). To safely work around a hybrid electric vehicle, the high-voltage (HV) battery and circuits should be shut off following these steps:

> ☠ **WARNING**
>
> Some vehicle manufacturers specify that insulated rubber *lineman's gloves* be used whenever working around the high-voltage circuits to prevent the danger of electrical shock.

FIGURE 1–84 A warning label on a Honda hybrid warns that a person can be killed due to the high-voltage circuits under the cover.

> ✚ **SAFETY TIP**
>
> **Infection Control Precautions**
>
> Working on a vehicle can result in personal injury including the possibility of being cut or hurt enough to cause bleeding. Some infections such as hepatitis B, HIV (which can cause acquired immunodeficiency syndrome, or AIDS), and hepatitis C virus are transmitted through blood. These infections are commonly called blood-borne pathogens. Report any injury that involves blood to your supervisor and take the necessary precautions to avoid coming in contact with blood from another person.

STEP 1 Turn off the ignition key (if equipped) and remove the key from the ignition switch. (This will shut off all high-voltage circuits if the relay[s] is [are] working correctly.)

STEP 2 Disconnect the high-voltage circuits.

TOYOTA PRIUS The cutoff switch is located in the trunk. To gain access, remove three clips holding the upper left portion of the trunk side cover. To disconnect the high-voltage system, pull the orange handled plug while wearing insulated rubber lineman's gloves. ● **SEE FIGURE 1–85.**

FORD ESCAPE/MERCURY MARINER Ford and Mercury specify that the following steps should be included when working with the high-voltage (HV) systems of a hybrid vehicle:

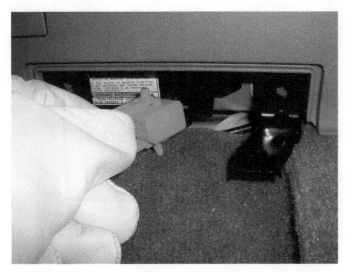

FIGURE 1–85 The high-voltage disconnect switch is in the trunk area on a Toyota Prius. Insulated rubber lineman's gloves should be worn when removing this plug.

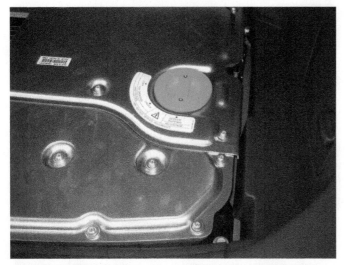

FIGURE 1–86 The high-voltage shut-off switch on a Ford Escape hybrid. The switch is located under the carpet at the rear of the vehicle.

- Four orange cones are to be placed at the four corners of the vehicle to create a buffer zone.
- High-voltage insulated gloves are to be worn with an outer leather glove to protect the inner rubber glove from possible damage.
- The service technician should also wear a face shield and a fiberglass hook should be in the area and used to move a technician in the event of electrocution.

The high-voltage shut-off switch is located in the rear of the vehicle under the right side carpet. ● **SEE FIGURE 1–86.**

FIGURE 1–87 The shut-off switch on a GM parallel hybrid truck is green because this system uses 42 volts instead of higher, and possibly fatal, voltages used in other hybrid vehicles.

Rotate the handle to the "service shipping" position, lift it out to disable the high-voltage circuit, and wait five minutes before removing high-voltage cables.

HONDA CIVIC To totally disable the high-voltage system on a Honda Civic, remove the main fuse (labeled number 1) from the driver's side underhood fuse panel. This should be all that is necessary to shut off the high-voltage circuit. If this is not possible, then remove the rear seat cushion and seat back. Remove the metal switch cover labeled "up" and remove the red locking cover. Move the "battery module switch" down to disable the high-voltage system.

CHEVROLET SILVERADO/GMC SIERRA PICKUP TRUCK The high-voltage shut-off switch is located under the rear passenger seat. Remove the cover marked "energy storage box" and turn the green service disconnect switch to the horizontal position to turn off the high-voltage circuits. ● **SEE FIGURE 1–87.**

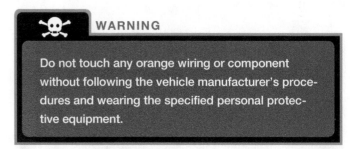

☠ **WARNING**

Do not touch any orange wiring or component without following the vehicle manufacturer's procedures and wearing the specified personal protective equipment.

1 The first step in hoisting a vehicle is to properly align the vehicle in the center of the stall.

2 Most vehicles will be correctly positioned when the left front tire is centered on the tire pad.

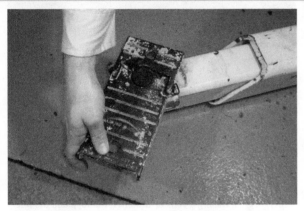

3 The arms can be moved in and out and most pads can be rotated to allow for many different types of vehicle construction.

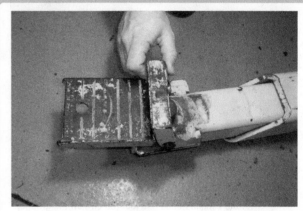

4 Most lifts are equipped with short pad extensions that are often necessary to use to allow the pad to contact the frame of a vehicle without causing the arm of the lift to hit and damage parts of the body.

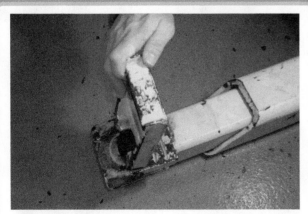

5 Tall pad extensions can also be used to gain access to the frame of a vehicle. This position is needed to safely hoist many pickup trucks, vans, and sport utility vehicles.

6 An additional extension may be necessary to hoist a truck or van equipped with running boards to give the necessary clearance.

CONTINUED ▶

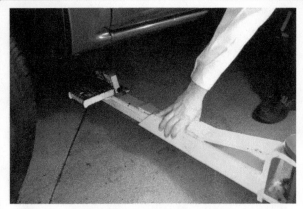

7 Position the pads under the vehicle under the recommended locations.

8 After being sure all pads are correctly positioned, use the electromechanical controls to raise the vehicle.

9 With the vehicle raised one foot (30 cm) off the ground, push down on the vehicle to check to see if it is stable on the pads. If the vehicle rocks, lower the vehicle and reset the pads. The vehicle can be raised to any desired working level. Be sure the safety is engaged before working on or under the vehicle.

10 If raising a vehicle without a frame, place the flat pads under the pinch weld seam to spread the load. If additional clearance is necessary, the pads can be raised as shown.

11 When the service work is completed, the hoist should be raised slightly and the safety released before using the hydraulic lever to lower the vehicle.

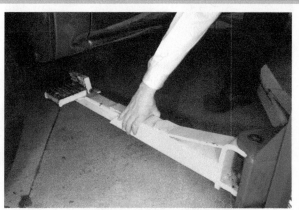

12 After lowering the vehicle, be sure all arms of the lift are moved out of the way before driving the vehicle out of the work stall.

1. Bolts, studs, and nuts are commonly used as fasteners in the chassis. The sizes for fractional and metric threads are different and are not interchangeable. The grade is the rating of the strength of a fastener.

2. Whenever a vehicle is raised above the ground, it must be supported at a substantial section of the body or frame.

3. Wrenches are available in open end, box end, and combination open and box end.

4. An adjustable wrench should only be used where the proper size is not available.

5. Line wrenches are also called flare-nut wrenches, fitting wrenches, or tube-nut wrenches and are used to remove fuel or refrigerant lines.

6. Sockets are rotated by a ratchet or breaker bar, also called a flex handle.

7. Torque wrenches measure the amount of torque applied to a fastener.

8. Screwdriver types include straight blade (flat tip) and Phillips.

9. Hammers and mallets come in a variety of sizes and weights.

10. Pliers are a useful tool and are available in many different types, including slip-joint, multigroove, linesman's, diagonal, needle-nose, and locking pliers.

11. Other common hand tools include snap-ring pliers, files, cutters, punches, chisels, and hacksaws.

12. Hybrid electric vehicles should be de-powered if any of the high-voltage components are going to be serviced.

REVIEW QUESTIONS

1. List three precautions that must be taken whenever hoisting (lifting) a vehicle.

2. Describe how to determine the grade of a fastener, including how the markings differ between fractional and metric bolts.

3. List four items that are personal protective equipment (PPE).

4. List the types of fire extinguishers and their usage.

5. Why are wrenches offset 15 degrees?

6. What are the other names for a line wrench?

7. What are the standard automotive drive sizes for sockets?

8. Which type of screwdriver requires the use of a hammer or mallet?

9. What is inside a dead-blow hammer?

10. What type of cutter is available in left and right cutters?

CHAPTER QUIZ

1. The correct location for the pads when hoisting or jacking the vehicle can often be found in the _____.
   a. Service manual
   b. Shop manual
   c. Owner's manual
   d. All of the above

2. For the best working position, the work should be _____.
   a. At neck or head level
   b. At knee or ankle level
   c. Overhead by about 1 foot
   d. At chest or elbow level

3. A high-strength bolt is identified by _____.
   a. A UNC symbol
   b. Lines on the head
   c. Strength letter codes
   d. The coarse threads

4. A fastener that uses threads on both ends is called a _____.
   a. Cap screw
   b. Stud
   c. Machine screw
   d. Crest fastener

5. When working with hand tools, always _____.
   a. Push the wrench—don't pull toward you
   b. Pull a wrench—don't push a wrench away from you

6. The proper term for Channel Locks is _____.
   a. Vise Grips
   b. Crescent wrench
   c. Locking pliers
   d. Multigroove adjustable pliers

7. The proper term for Vise Grips is _____.
   a. Locking pliers
   b. Slip-joint pliers
   c. Side cuts
   d. Multigroove adjustable pliers

8. Two technicians are discussing torque wrenches. Technician A says that a torque wrench is capable of tightening a fastener with more torque than a conventional breaker bar or ratchet. Technician B says that a torque wrench should be calibrated regularly for the most accurate results. Which technician is correct?
   a. Technician A only
   b. Technician B only
   c. Both Technicians A and B
   d. Neither Technician A nor B

9. What type of screwdriver should be used if there is very limited space above the head of the fastener?
   a. Offset screwdriver
   b. Standard screwdriver
   c. Impact screwdriver
   d. Robertson screwdriver

10. What type of hammer is plastic coated, has a metal casing inside, and is filled with small lead balls?
   a. Dead-blow hammer
   b. Soft-blow hammer
   c. Sledgehammer
   d. Plastic hammer

chapter 2
ENVIRONMENTAL AND HAZARDOUS MATERIALS

LEARNING OBJECTIVES

After studying this chapter, the reader will be able to:

1. Identify hazardous waste materials in accordance with state and federal regulations and follow proper safety precautions while handling hazardous materials.

2. Define the Occupational Safety and Health Act (OSHA).

3. Explain the term safety data sheets (SDS).

4. Define the steps required to safely handle and store automotive chemicals and waste.

KEY TERMS

Aboveground storage tank (AGST) 43
Asbestosis 42
BCI 46
CAA 41
CFR 40
EPA 40
Hazardous waste material 40
HEPA vacuum 42
Mercury 48
MSDS 40
OSHA 40
RCRA 41
Right-to-know laws 40
Solvent 42
Underground storage tank (UST) 43
Used oil 43
WHMIS 40

HAZARDOUS WASTE

DEFINITION OF HAZARDOUS WASTE

Hazardous waste materials are chemicals, or components, that the shop no longer needs and that pose a danger to the environment and people if they are disposed of in ordinary garbage cans or sewers. However, no material is considered hazardous waste until the shop has finished using it and is ready to dispose of it.

PERSONAL PROTECTIVE EQUIPMENT (PPE)

When handling hazardous waste material, one must always wear the proper protective clothing and equipment detailed in the right-to-know laws. This includes respirator equipment. All recommended procedures must be followed accurately. Personal injury may result from improper clothing, equipment, and procedures when handling hazardous materials.

FEDERAL AND STATE LAWS

OCCUPATIONAL SAFETY AND HEALTH ACT

The U.S. Congress passed the **Occupational Safety and Health Act (OSHA)** in 1970. This legislation was designed to assist and encourage the citizens of the United States in their efforts to assure:

- Safe and healthful working conditions by providing research, information, education, and training in the field of occupational safety and health.
- Safe and healthful working conditions for working men and women by authorizing enforcement of the standards developed under the act.

Because about 25% of workers are exposed to health and safety hazards on the job, OSHA standards are necessary to monitor, control, and educate workers regarding health and safety in the workplace.

EPA

The **Environmental Protection Agency (EPA)** publishes a list of hazardous materials that is included in the **Code of Federal Regulations (CFR)**. The EPA considers waste hazardous if it is included on the EPA list of hazardous materials, or it has one or more of the following characteristics:

- **Reactive**—Any material that reacts violently with water or other chemicals is considered hazardous.
- **Corrosive**—If a material burns the skin, or dissolves metals and other materials, a technician should consider

it hazardous. A pH scale is used, with number 7 indicating neutral. Pure water has a pH of 7. Lower numbers indicate an acidic solution and higher numbers indicate a caustic solution. If a material releases cyanide gas, hydrogen sulfide gas, or similar gases when exposed to low pH acid solutions, it is considered hazardous.

- **Toxic**—Materials are hazardous if they leak one or more of eight different heavy metals in concentrations greater than 100 times the primary drinking water standard.
- **Ignitable**—A liquid is hazardous if it has a flash point below 140°F (60°C), and a solid is hazardous if it ignites spontaneously.
- **Radioactive**—Any substance that emits measurable levels of radiation is radioactive. When individuals bring containers of a highly radioactive substance into the shop environment, qualified personnel with the appropriate equipment must test them.

☠ WARNING

Hazardous waste disposal laws include serious penalties for anyone responsible for breaking these laws.

RIGHT-TO-KNOW LAWS

The **right-to-know laws** state that employees have a right to know when the materials they use at work are hazardous. The right-to-know laws started with the Hazard Communication Standard published by the Occupational Safety and Health Administration (OSHA) in 1983. Originally, this document was intended for chemical companies and manufacturers that required employees to handle hazardous materials in their work situation but the federal courts have decided to apply these laws to all companies, including automotive service shops. Under the right-to-know laws, the employer has responsibilities regarding the handling of hazardous materials by their employees. All employees must be trained about the types of hazardous materials they will encounter in the workplace. The employees must be informed about their rights under legislation regarding the handling of hazardous materials.

MATERIAL SAFETY DATA SHEETS. All hazardous materials must be properly labeled, and information about each hazardous material must be posted on **material safety data sheets (MSDS)**, now called simply *safety data sheets (SDS)*, available from the manufacturer. In Canada, MSDS information is called **Workplace Hazardous Materials Information Systems (WHMIS)**.

FIGURE 2–1 Safety data sheets (SDS), formerly known as material safety data sheets (MSDS), should be readily available for use by anyone in the area who may come into contact with hazardous materials.

The employer has a responsibility to place MSDS (SDS) information where they are easily accessible by all employees. The data sheets provide the following information about the hazardous material: chemical name, physical characteristics, protective handling equipment, explosion/fire hazards, incompatible materials, health hazards, medical conditions aggravated by exposure, emergency and first-aid procedures, safe handling, and spill/leak procedures.

The employer also has a responsibility to make sure that all hazardous materials are properly labeled. The label information must include health, fire, and reactivity hazards posed by the material, as well as the protective equipment necessary to handle the material. The manufacturer must supply all warning and precautionary information about hazardous materials. This information must be read and understood by the employee before handling the material. ● **SEE FIGURE 2–1**.

RESOURCE CONSERVATION AND RECOVERY ACT

Federal and state laws control the disposal of hazardous waste materials and every shop employee must be familiar with these laws. Hazardous waste disposal laws include the **Resource Conservation and Recovery Act (RCRA)**. This law states that hazardous material users are responsible for hazardous materials from the time they become a waste until the proper disposal is completed. Many shops hire an independent hazardous waste hauler to dispose of hazardous waste material. The shop owner, or manager, should have a written contract with the hazardous waste hauler. Rather than have hazardous waste material hauled to an approved hazardous

FIGURE 2–2 Tag identifying that the power has been removed and service work is being done.

waste disposal site, a shop may choose to recycle the material in the shop. Therefore, the user must store hazardous waste material properly and safely, and be responsible for the transportation of this material until it arrives at an approved hazardous waste disposal site, where it can be processed according to the law. The RCRA controls the following types of automotive waste:

- Paint and body repair products waste
- Solvents for parts and equipment cleaning
- Batteries and battery acid
- Mild acids used for metal cleaning and preparation
- Waste oil and engine coolants or antifreeze
- Air-conditioning refrigerants and oils
- Engine oil filters

LOCKOUT/TAGOUT According to OSHA Title 29, code of Federal Regulations (CPR), part 1910.147, machinery must be locked out to prevent injury to employees when maintenance or repair work is being performed. Any piece of equipment that should not be used must be tagged and the electrical power disconnected to prevent it from being used. Always read, understand, and follow all safety warning tags. ● **SEE FIGURE 2–2**.

CLEAN AIR ACT Air-conditioning (A/C) systems and refrigerant are regulated by the **Clean Air Act (CAA)**, Title VI, Section 609. Technician certification and service equipment is also regulated. Any technician working on automotive A/C systems must be certified. A/C refrigerants must not be released or vented into the atmosphere, and used refrigerants must be recovered.

ASBESTOS HAZARDS

Friction materials such as brake and clutch linings often contain asbestos. While asbestos has been eliminated from most original equipment friction materials, the automotive service technician cannot know whether or not the vehicle being serviced is or is not equipped with friction materials containing asbestos. It is important that all friction materials be handled as if they do contain asbestos.

Asbestos exposure can cause scar tissue to form in the lungs. This condition is called **asbestosis**. It gradually causes increasing shortness of breath, and the scarring to the lungs is permanent.

Even low exposures to asbestos can cause *mesothelioma*, a type of fatal cancer of the lining of the chest or abdominal cavity. Asbestos exposure can also increase the risk of *lung cancer* as well as cancer of the voice box, stomach, and large intestine. It usually takes 15 to 30 years or more for cancer or asbestos lung scarring to show up after exposure. Scientists call this the *latency period*.

Government agencies recommend that asbestos exposure should be eliminated or controlled to the lowest level possible. These agencies have developed recommendations and standards that the automotive service technician and equipment manufacturer should follow. These U.S. federal agencies include the National Institute for Occupational Safety and Health (NIOSH), Occupational Safety and Health Administration (OSHA), and Environmental Protection Agency (EPA).

ASBESTOS OSHA STANDARDS The Occupational Safety and Health Administration has established three levels of asbestos exposure. Any vehicle service establishment that does either brake or clutch work must limit employee exposure to asbestos to less than 0.2 fibers per cubic centimeter (cc) as determined by an air sample.

If the level of exposure to employees is greater than specified, corrective measures must be performed and a large fine may be imposed.

NOTE: Research has found that worn asbestos fibers such as those from automotive brakes or clutches may not be as hazardous as first believed. Worn asbestos fibers do not have sharp flared ends that can latch onto tissue, but rather are worn down to a dust form that resembles talc. Grinding or sawing operations on unworn brake shoes or clutch discs however *will* contain *harmful* asbestos fibers. To limit health damage, always use proper handling procedures while working around any component that may contain asbestos.

FIGURE 2–3 All brakes should be moistened with water or solvent to help prevent brake dust from becoming airborne.

ASBESTOS EPA REGULATIONS The federal Environmental Protection Agency has established procedures for the removal and disposal of asbestos. The EPA procedures require that products containing asbestos be "wetted" to prevent the asbestos fibers from becoming airborne. According to the EPA, asbestos-containing materials can be disposed of as regular waste. Only when asbestos becomes airborne is it considered to be hazardous.

ASBESTOS HANDLING GUIDELINES The air in the shop area can be tested by a testing laboratory, but this can be expensive. Tests have determined that asbestos levels can easily be kept below the recommended levels by using a liquid, like water, or a special vacuum.

NOTE: Even though asbestos is being removed from brake and clutch lining materials, the service technician cannot tell whether or not the old brake pads, shoes, or clutch discs contain asbestos. Therefore, to be safe, the technician should assume that all brake pads, shoes, or clutch discs contain asbestos.

HEPA VACUUM. A special **high-efficiency particulate air (HEPA) vacuum** system has been proven to be effective in keeping asbestos exposure levels below 0.1 fibers per cubic centimeter.

SOLVENT SPRAY. Many technicians use an aerosol can of brake cleaning solvent to wet the brake dust and prevent it from becoming airborne. A **solvent** is a liquid that is used to dissolve dirt, grime, or solid particles. Commercial brake cleaners are available that use a concentrated cleaner that is mixed with water. ● **SEE FIGURE 2–3**. The waste liquid is filtered, and when dry, the filter can be disposed of as solid waste.

WARNING

Never use compressed air to blow brake dust. The fine talclike brake dust can create a health hazard even if asbestos is not present or is present in dust rather than fiber form.

DISPOSAL OF BRAKE DUST AND BRAKE SHOES. The hazard of asbestos occurs when asbestos fibers are airborne. Once the asbestos has been wetted down, it is then considered to be solid waste, rather than hazardous waste. Old brake shoes and pads should be enclosed, preferably in a plastic bag, to help prevent any of the brake material from becoming airborne. *Always follow current federal and local laws concerning disposal of all waste.*

USED BRAKE FLUID

Most brake fluid is made from polyglycol, is water soluble, and can be considered hazardous if it has absorbed metals from the brake system.

STORAGE AND DISPOSAL OF BRAKE FLUID

- Collect brake fluid in a container clearly marked to indicate that it is designated for that purpose.
- If the waste brake fluid is hazardous, be sure to manage it appropriately and use only an authorized waste receiver for its disposal.
- If the waste brake fluid is nonhazardous (such as old, but unused), determine from your local solid waste collection provider what should be done for its proper disposal.
- Do not mix brake fluid with used engine oil.
- Do not pour brake fluid down drains or onto the ground.
- Recycle brake fluid through a registered recycler.

USED OIL

Used oil is any petroleum-based or synthetic oil that has been used. During normal use, impurities such as dirt, metal scrapings, water, or chemicals can get mixed in with the oil. Eventually, this used oil must be replaced with virgin or re-refined oil. The EPA's used oil management standards include a three-pronged approach to determine if a substance meets the definition of *used oil*. To meet the EPA's definition of used oil, a substance must meet each of the following three criteria.

- **Origin.** The first criterion for identifying used oil is based on the oil's origin. Used oil must have been refined from crude oil or made from synthetic materials. Animal and vegetable oils are excluded from the EPA's definition of used oil.
- **Use.** The second criterion is based on whether and how the oil is used. Oils used as lubricants, hydraulic fluids, heat transfer fluids, and for other similar purposes are considered used oil. The EPA's definition also excludes products used as cleaning agents, as well as certain petroleum-derived products like antifreeze and kerosene.
- **Contaminants.** The third criterion is based on whether or not the oil is contaminated with either physical or chemical impurities. In other words, to meet the EPA's definition, used oil must become contaminated as a result of being used. This aspect of the EPA's definition includes residues and contaminants generated from handling, storing, and processing used oil.

NOTE: **The release of only one gallon of used oil (a typical oil change) can make a million gallons of fresh water undrinkable.**

If used oil is dumped down the drain and enters a sewage treatment plant, concentrations as small as 50 to 100 PPM (parts per million) in the waste water can foul sewage treatment processes. Never mix a listed hazardous waste, gasoline, waste water, halogenated solvent, antifreeze, or an unknown waste material with used oil. Adding any of these substances will cause the used oil to become contaminated, which classifies it as hazardous waste.

STORAGE AND DISPOSAL OF USED OIL Once oil has been used, it can be collected, recycled, and used over and over again. An estimated 380 million gallons of used oil are recycled each year. Recycled used oil can sometimes be used again for the same job or can take on a completely different task. For example, used engine oil can be re-refined and sold at some discount stores as engine oil or processed for furnace fuel oil. After collecting used oil in an appropriate container such as a 55-gallon steel drum, the material must be disposed of in one of two ways:

- Shipped offsite for recycling
- Burned in an onsite or offsite EPA-approved heater for energy recovery

Used oil must be stored in compliance with an existing **underground storage tank (UST)** or an **aboveground**

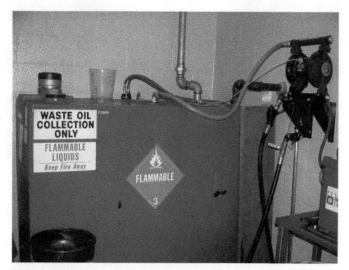

FIGURE 2–4 A typical aboveground oil storage tank.

storage tank (AGST) standard, or kept in separate containers. ● SEE FIGURE 2–4. Containers are portable receptacles, such as a 55-gallon steel drum.

KEEP USED OIL STORAGE DRUMS IN GOOD CONDITION. This means that they should be covered, secured from vandals, properly labeled, and maintained in compliance with local fire codes. Frequent inspections for leaks, corrosion, and spillage are an essential part of container maintenance.

NEVER STORE USED OIL IN ANYTHING OTHER THAN TANKS AND STORAGE CONTAINERS. Used oil may also be stored in units that are permitted to store regulated hazardous waste.

USED OIL FILTER DISPOSAL REGULATIONS. Used oil filters contain used engine oil that may be hazardous. Before an oil filter is placed into the trash or sent to be recycled, it must be drained using one of the following hot-draining methods approved by the EPA.

- Puncture the filter antidrainback valve or filter dome end and hot-drain for at least 12 hours
- Hot-drain and crushing
- Dismantling and hot draining
- Any other hot-draining method, which will remove all the used oil from the filter

After the oil has been drained from the oil filter, the filter housing can be disposed of in any of the following ways:

- Sent for recycling
- Picked up by a service contract company
- Disposed of in regular trash

The major sources of chemical danger are liquid and aerosol brake cleaning fluids that contain chlorinated hydrocarbon solvents. Several other chemicals that do not deplete the ozone, such as heptane, hexane, and xylene, are now being used in nonchlorinated brake cleaning solvents. Some manufacturers are also producing solvents they describe as environmentally responsible, which are biodegradable and noncarcinogenic (non-cancer-causing).

There is no specific standard for physical contact with chlorinated hydrocarbon solvents or the chemicals replacing them. All contact should be avoided whenever possible. The law requires an employer to provide appropriate protective equipment and ensure proper work practices by an employee handling these chemicals.

 SAFETY TIP

Hand Safety

Service technicians should wash their hands with soap and water after handling engine oil, differential oil, or transmission fluids or wear protective rubber gloves. Another safety tip is that the service technician should not wear watches, rings, or other jewelry that could come in contact with electrical or moving parts of a vehicle. ● SEE FIGURE 2–5.

EFFECTS OF CHEMICAL POISONING The effects of exposure to chlorinated hydrocarbon and other types of solvents can take many forms. Short-term exposure at low levels can cause symptoms such as:

- Headache
- Nausea
- Drowsiness
- Dizziness
- Lack of coordination
- Unconsciousness

It may also cause irritation of the eyes, nose, and throat, and flushing of the face and neck. Short-term exposure to higher concentrations can cause liver damage with symptoms such as yellow jaundice or dark urine. Liver damage may not become evident until several weeks after the exposure.

FIGURE 2–5 Washing hands and removing jewelry are two important safety habits all service technicians should practice.

FIGURE 2–6 Typical fireproof flammable storage cabinet.

HAZARDOUS SOLVENTS AND REGULATORY STATUS

Most solvents are classified as hazardous wastes. Other characteristics of solvents include the following:

- Solvents with flash points below 140 degrees F (60 degrees C) are considered flammable and, like gasoline, are federally regulated by the Department of Transportation (DOT).

- Solvents and oils with flash points above 60°C are considered combustible and, like engine oil, are also regulated by the DOT. All flammable items must be stored in a fireproof container. ● **SEE FIGURE 2–6.**

It is the responsibility of the repair shop to determine if its spent solvent is hazardous waste. Solvent reclaimers are available that clean and restore the solvent so it lasts indefinitely.

USED SOLVENTS Used or spent solvents are liquid materials that have been generated as waste and may contain xylene, methanol, ethyl ether, and methyl isobutyl ketone (MIBK). These materials must be stored in OSHA-approved safety containers with the lids or caps closed tightly. Additional requirements include the following:

- Containers should be clearly labeled "Hazardous Waste" and the date the material was first placed into the storage receptacle should be noted.

- Labeling is not required for solvents being used in a parts washer.

- Used solvents will not be counted toward a facility's monthly output of hazardous waste if the vendor under contract removes the material.

- Used solvents may be disposed of by recycling with a local vendor, like SafetyKleen®, to have the used solvent removed according to specific terms in the vendor agreement.

- Use aqueous-based (nonsolvent) cleaning systems to help avoid the problems associated with chemical solvents. ● **SEE FIGURE 2–7.**

COOLANT DISPOSAL

Coolant is a mixture of antifreeze and water. New antifreeze is not considered to be hazardous even though it can cause death if ingested. Used antifreeze may be hazardous due to dissolved metals from the engine and other components of the cooling system. These metals can include iron, steel, aluminum, copper, brass, and lead (from older radiators and

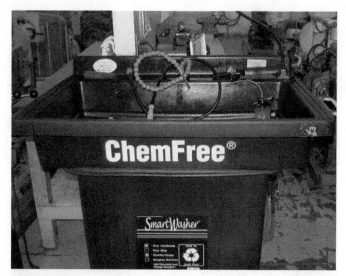

FIGURE 2–7 Using a water-based cleaning system helps reduce the hazards from using strong chemicals.

FIGURE 2–8 Used antifreeze coolant should be kept separate and stored in a leakproof container until it can be recycled or disposed of according to federal, state, and local laws. Note that the storage barrel is placed inside another container to catch any coolant that may spill out of the inside barrel.

heater cores). Coolant should be disposed of in one of the following ways:

- Coolant should be recycled either onsite or offsite.
- Used coolant should be stored in a sealed and labeled container. ●**SEE FIGURE 2–8**.
- Used coolant can often be disposed of into municipal sewers with a permit. Check with local authorities and obtain a permit before discharging used coolant into sanitary sewers.

LEAD-ACID BATTERY WASTE

About 70 million spent lead-acid batteries are generated each year in the United States alone. Lead is classified as a toxic metal, and the acid used in lead-acid batteries is highly corrosive. The vast majority (95% to 98%) of these batteries are recycled through lead reclamation operations and secondary lead smelters for use in the manufacture of new batteries.

BATTERY DISPOSAL Used lead-acid batteries must be reclaimed or recycled in order to be exempt from hazardous waste regulations. Leaking batteries must be stored and transported as hazardous waste. Some states have more strict regulations, which require special handling procedures and transportation. According to the **Battery Council International (BCI)**, battery laws usually include the following rules:

1. Lead-acid battery disposal is prohibited in landfills or incinerators. Batteries are required to be delivered to a battery retailer, wholesaler, recycling center, or lead smelter.

2. All retailers of automotive batteries are required to post a sign that displays the universal recycling symbol and indicates the retailer's specific requirements for accepting used batteries.

3. Battery electrolyte contains sulfuric acid, which is a very corrosive substance capable of causing serious personal injury, such as skin burns and eye damage. In addition, the battery plates contain lead, which is highly poisonous. For this reason, disposing of batteries improperly can cause environmental contamination and lead to severe health problems.

BATTERY HANDLING AND STORAGE Batteries, whether new or used, should be kept indoors if possible. The storage location should be an area specifically designated for battery storage and must be well ventilated (to the outside). If outdoor storage is the only alternative, a sheltered and secured area with acid-resistant secondary containment is strongly recommended. It is also advisable that acid-resistant secondary containment be used for indoor storage. In addition, batteries should be placed on acid-resistant pallets and never stacked.

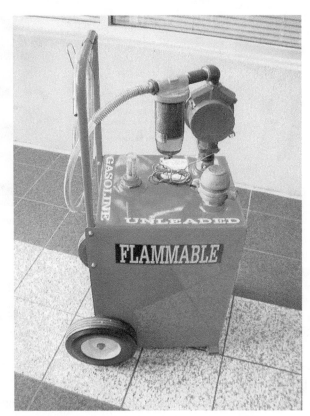

FIGURE 2-9 This red gasoline container holds about 30 gallons of gasoline and is used to fill vehicles used for training.

FUEL SAFETY AND STORAGE

Gasoline is a very explosive liquid. The expanding vapors that come from gasoline are extremely dangerous. These vapors are present even in cold temperatures. Vapors formed in gasoline tanks on many vehicles are controlled, but vapors from gasoline storage may escape from the can, resulting in a hazardous situation. Therefore, place gasoline storage containers in a well-ventilated space. Although diesel fuel is not as volatile as gasoline, the same basic rules apply to diesel fuel and gasoline storage. These rules include the following:

1. Use storage cans that have a flash-arresting screen at the outlet. These screens prevent external ignition sources from igniting the gasoline within the can when someone pours the gasoline or diesel fuel.

2. Use only a red approved gasoline container to allow for proper hazardous substance identification.
   ● **SEE FIGURE 2-9**.

3. Do not fill gasoline containers completely full. Always leave the level of gasoline at least one inch from the top of the container. This action allows expansion of the gasoline at higher temperatures. If gasoline containers are completely full, the gasoline will expand when the temperature increases. This expansion forces gasoline from the can and creates a dangerous spill. If gasoline or diesel fuel containers must be stored, place them in a designated storage locker or facility.

4. Never leave gasoline containers open, except while filling or pouring gasoline from the container.

5. Never use gasoline as a cleaning agent.

6. Always connect a ground strap to containers when filling or transferring fuel or other flammable products from one container to another to prevent static electricity that could result in explosion and fire. These ground wires prevent the buildup of a static electric charge, which could result in a spark and disastrous explosion.

AIRBAG HANDLING

Airbag modules are pyrotechnic devices that can be ignited if exposed to an electrical charge or if the body of the vehicle is subjected to a shock. Airbag safety should include the following precautions:

1. Disarm the airbag(s) if you will be working in the area where a discharged bag could make contact with any part of your body. Consult service information for the exact procedure to follow for the vehicle being serviced. The usual procedure is to deploy the airbag using a 12 volt power supply, such as a jump start box, using long wires to connect to the module to ensure a safe deployment.

2. Do not expose an airbag to extreme heat or fire.

3. Always carry an airbag pointing away from your body.

4. Place an airbag module facing upward.

5. Always follow the manufacturer's recommended procedure for airbag disposal or recycling, including the proper packaging to use during shipment.

6. Wear protective gloves if handling a deployed airbag.

7. Always wash your hands or body well if exposed to a deployed airbag. The chemicals involved can cause skin irritation and possible rash development.

FIGURE 2–10 Air-conditioning refrigerant oil must be kept separated from other oils because it contains traces of refrigerant and must be treated as hazardous waste.

FIGURE 2–11 Placard near driver's door, including what devices in the vehicle contain mercury.

USED TIRE DISPOSAL

Used tires are an environmental concern because of several reasons, including the following:

1. In a landfill, they tend to "float" up through the other trash and rise to the surface.

2. The inside of tires traps and holds rainwater, which is a breeding ground for mosquitoes. Mosquito-borne diseases include encephalitis and dengue fever.

3. Used tires present a fire hazard and, when burned, create a large amount of black smoke that contaminates the air.

Used tires should be disposed of in one of the following ways:

1. Used tires can be reused until the end of their useful life.

2. Tires can be retreaded.

3. Tires can be recycled or shredded for use in asphalt.

4. Tires removed from the rims can be sent to a landfill (most landfill operators will shred the tires because it is illegal in many states to landfill whole tires).

5. Tires can be burned in cement kilns or other power plants where the smoke can be controlled.

6. A registered scrap tire handler should be used to transport tires for disposal or recycling.

AIR-CONDITIONING REFRIGERANT OIL DISPOSAL

Air-conditioning refrigerant oil contains dissolved refrigerant and is therefore considered to be hazardous waste. This oil must be kept separated from other waste oil or the entire amount of oil must be treated as hazardous. Used refrigerant oil must be sent to a licensed hazardous waste disposal company for recycling or disposal. ● **SEE FIGURE 2–10**.

WASTE CHART All automotive service facilities create some waste and while most of it is handled properly, it is important that all hazardous and nonhazardous waste be accounted for and properly disposed. ● **SEE CHART 2–1** for a list of typical wastes generated at automotive shops, plus a checklist for keeping track of how these wastes are handled.

🔧 **TECH TIP**

Remove Components that Contain Mercury

Some vehicles have a placard near the driver's side door that lists the components that contain the heavy metal, mercury. **Mercury** can be absorbed through the skin and is a heavy metal that once absorbed by the body does not leave. ● **SEE FIGURE 2–11**.

These components should be removed from the vehicle before being sent to be recycled to help prevent releasing mercury into the environment.

WASTE STREAM	TYPICAL CATEGORY IF NOT MIXED WITH OTHER HAZARDOUS WASTE	IF DISPOSED IN LANDFILL AND NOT MIXED WITH A HAZARDOUS WASTE	IF RECYCLED
Used oil	Used oil	Hazardous waste	Used oil
Used oil filters	Nonhazardous solid waste, if completely drained	Nonhazardous solid waste, if completely drained	Used oil, if not drained
Used transmission fluid	Used oil	Hazardous waste	Used oil
Used brake fluid	Used oil	Hazardous waste	Used oil
Used antifreeze	Depends on characterization	Depends on characterization	Depends on characterization
Used solvents	Hazardous waste	Hazardous waste	Hazardous waste
Used citric solvents	Nonhazardous solid waste	Nonhazardous solid waste	Hazardous waste
Lead-acid automotive batteries	Not a solid waste if returned to supplier	Hazardous waste	Hazardous waste
Shop rags used for oil	Used oil	Depends on used oil characterization	Used oil
Shop rags used for solvent or gasoline spills	Hazardous waste	Hazardous waste	Hazardous waste
Oil spill absorbent material	Used oil	Depends on used oil characterization	Used oil
Spill material for solvent and gasoline	Hazardous waste	Hazardous waste	Hazardous waste
Catalytic converter	Not a solid waste if returned to supplier	Nonhazardous solid waste	Nonhazardous solid waste
Spilled or unused fuels	Hazardous waste	Hazardous waste	Hazardous waste
Spilled or unusable paints and thinners	Hazardous waste	Hazardous waste	Hazardous waste
Used tires	Nonhazardous solid waste	Nonhazardous solid waste	Nonhazardous solid waste

CHART 2–1

Typical wastes generated at auto repair shops and typical category (hazardous or nonhazardous) by disposal method.

 TECH TIP

What Every Technician Should Know

OSHA has adopted new hazardous chemical labeling requirements making it agree with global labeling standards established by the United Nations. As a result, workers will have better information available on the safe handling and use of hazardous chemicals, allowing them to avoid injuries and possible illnesses related to exposures to hazardous chemicals. ● **SEE FIGURE 2–12.**

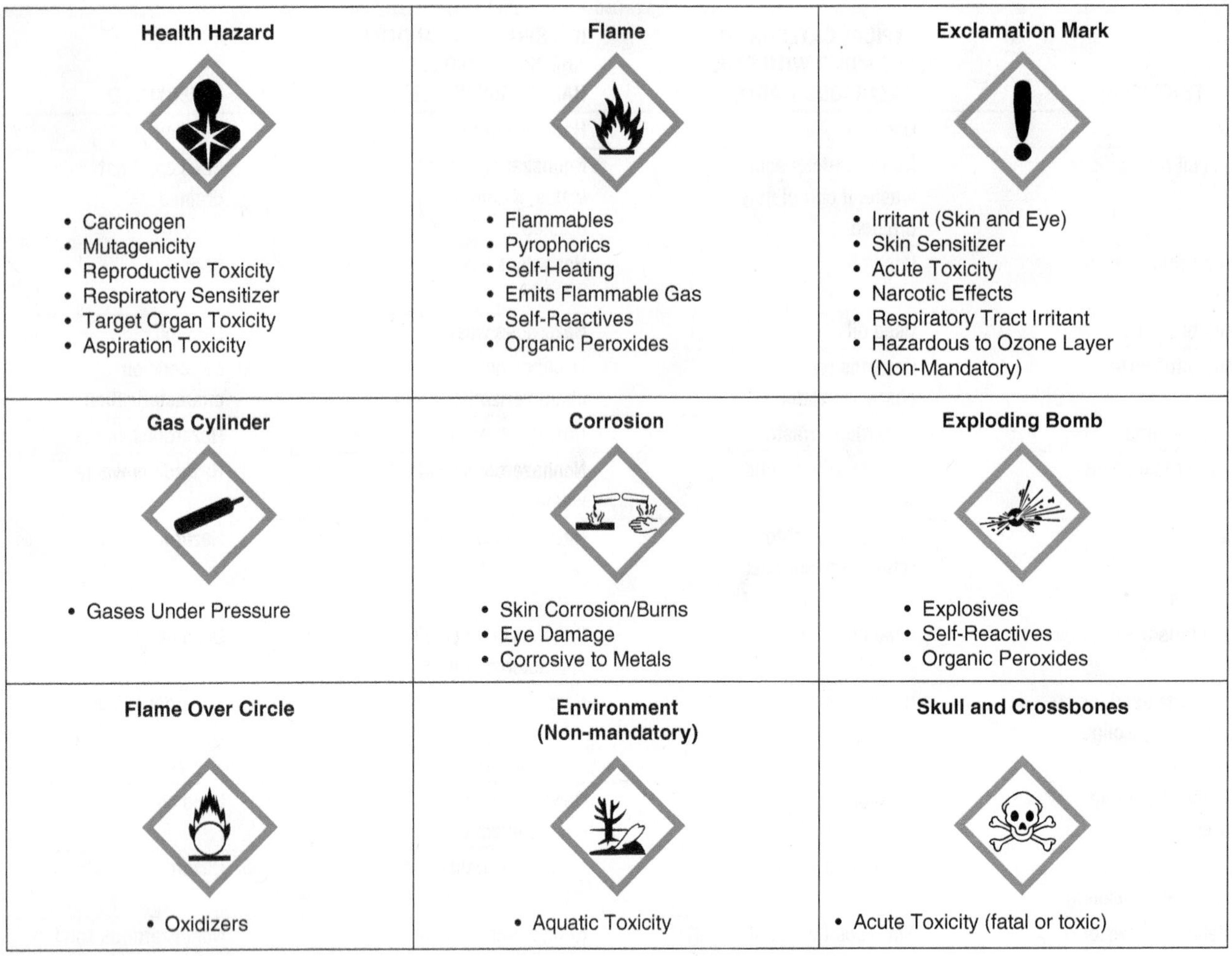

Health Hazard	Flame	Exclamation Mark
• Carcinogen • Mutagenicity • Reproductive Toxicity • Respiratory Sensitizer • Target Organ Toxicity • Aspiration Toxicity	• Flammables • Pyrophorics • Self-Heating • Emits Flammable Gas • Self-Reactives • Organic Peroxides	• Irritant (Skin and Eye) • Skin Sensitizer • Acute Toxicity • Narcotic Effects • Respiratory Tract Irritant • Hazardous to Ozone Layer (Non-Mandatory)
Gas Cylinder	Corrosion	Exploding Bomb
• Gases Under Pressure	• Skin Corrosion/Burns • Eye Damage • Corrosive to Metals	• Explosives • Self-Reactives • Organic Peroxides
Flame Over Circle	Environment (Non-mandatory)	Skull and Crossbones
• Oxidizers	• Aquatic Toxicity	• Acute Toxicity (fatal or toxic)

FIGURE 2–12 The OSHA global hazardous materials labels.

SUMMARY

1. Hazardous materials include common automotive chemicals, liquids, and lubricants, especially those whose ingredients contain *chlor* or *fluor* in their name.

2. Right-to-know laws require that all workers have access to material safety data sheets (MSDS).

3. Asbestos fibers should be avoided and removed according to current laws and regulations.

4. Used engine oil contains metals worn from parts and should be handled and disposed of properly.

5. Solvents represent a serious health risk and should be avoided as much as possible.

6. Coolant should be disposed of properly or recycled.

7. Batteries are considered to be hazardous waste and should be discarded to a recycling facility.

REVIEW QUESTIONS

1. List five common automotive chemicals or products that may be considered hazardous.

2. Describe the labels used to identify flammables and explosive materials used by OSHA.

1. Hazardous materials include all of the following *except* _____.
   a. Engine oil
   b. Asbestos
   c. Water
   d. Brake cleaner

2. To determine if a product or substance being used is hazardous, consult _____.
   a. A dictionary
   b. An MSDS
   c. SAE standards
   d. EPA guidelines

3. Exposure to asbestos dust can cause what condition?
   a. Asbestosis
   b. Mesothelioma
   c. Lung cancer
   d. All of the above

4. Wetted asbestos dust is considered to be _____.
   a. Solid waste
   b. Hazardous waste
   c. Toxic
   d. Poisonous

5. An oil filter should be hot drained for how long before disposing of the filter?
   a. 30 to 60 minutes
   b. 4 hours
   c. 8 hours
   d. 12 hours

6. Used engine oil should be disposed of by all *except* the following methods.
   a. Disposed of in regular trash
   b. Shipped offsite for recycling
   c. Burned onsite in a waste oil-approved heater
   d. Burned offsite in a waste oil-approved heater

7. All of the following are the proper ways to dispose of a drained oil filter *except* _____.
   a. Sent for recycling
   b. Picked up by a service contract company
   c. Disposed of in regular trash
   d. Considered to be hazardous waste and disposed of accordingly

8. Which act or organization regulates air-conditioning refrigerant?
   a. Clean Air Act (CAA)
   b. MSDS
   c. WHMIS
   d. Code of Federal Regulations (CFR)

9. Gasoline should be stored in approved containers that include what color(s)?
   a. A red container with yellow lettering
   b. A red container
   c. A yellow container
   d. A yellow container with red lettering

10. What automotive devices may contain mercury?
    a. Rear seat video displays
    b. Navigation displays
    c. HID headlights
    d. All of the above

chapter 3

INTRODUCTION TO DRIVETRAINS

LEARNING OBJECTIVES

After studying this chapter, the reader should be able to:

1. Define torque, and explain the relationship between torque and horsepower.
2. Describe the various gear types and their effect on speed, torque and direction of rotation.
3. Explain gear ratios and their effect on vehicle operation.
4. Discuss the types of manual transmissions and transaxles that are currently in use.
5. Discuss automatic transmissions and the planetary gear sets used for automatic transmissions.
6. Compare rear-wheel drive, front-wheel drive, four-wheel drive, and all-wheel drive systems.
7. Explain the characteristics of drive shafts and drive axle assemblies.

KEY TERMS

All-wheel drive (AWD) 67
Automatic transmission 60
Bevel gear 57
Clutch 59
Constant-velocity (CV) joint 65
Differential 65
Dynamometer 55
Drive axle 65
Driveshaft 65
Final drive 64
Four-wheel drive (4WD) 67
Front-wheel drive (FWD) 64
Gear ratio 58
Half shaft 64
Helical gear 56
Horsepower 55
Hypoid gear 57
Manual transmission 59
Overdrive 58
Pinion gear 59
Pitch diameter 55
Planet carrier 62
Planetary gear set 62
Power transfer unit 67
Rear-wheel drive (RWD) 64
Ring gear 62
Spiral bevel gear 57
Spur gear 56
Sun gear 62
Torque 53
Torque converter 62
Transaxle 64
Transfer case 67
Transmission 59
Universal joint (U-joint) 65
Worm gear 57

DRIVETRAINS

PURPOSE AND FUNCTION

The purpose of a vehicle drivetrain is to transfer power from the engine to the drive wheels. The drivetrain, also called a powertrain, serves the following functions:

- It allows the driver to control the power flow.
- It multiplies the engine torque.
- It controls the engine speed.

TORQUE

DEFINITION

Torque is a rotating or twisting force that may or may not result in motion. A vehicle moves because of the torque the drive axle exerts on the wheels and tires to make them rotate. Being a form of mechanical energy, torque cannot be created or destroyed—it is converted from one form of energy to another form of energy.

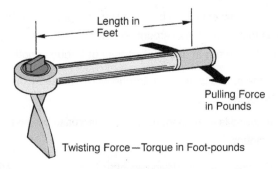

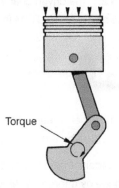

FIGURE 3–1 Torque, a twisting force, is produced when you pull on a wrench. An engine produces torque at the crankshaft as combustion pressure pushes the piston downward.

? **FREQUENTLY ASKED QUESTION**

Is It Lb-Ft or Ft-Lb of Torque?

The unit for torque is expressed as a force times the distance (leverage) from the object. Therefore, the official unit for torque is lb-ft (pound-feet) or Newton-meters (a force times a distance). However, it is commonly expressed in ft-lb and most torque wrenches are labeled with this unit.

UNITS OF TORQUE

Engine torque is developed when combustion pressure pushes a piston downward to rotate the crankshaft. ● **SEE FIGURE 3–1.**

The amount of torque produced will vary depending on the size and design of the engine and the throttle opening. Torque is measured in pounds-feet (lb-ft) or Newton-meters (N-m). One Newton-meter of torque is equal to 0.737 lb-ft. A factor that greatly affects drivetrain design is that very little or no torque is developed at engine speeds below 1000 RPM (revolutions per minute). An engine begins producing usable torque at about 1200 RPM and peak torque at about 2500 to 4000 RPM, with an upper usable speed limit of 5000 to 7000 RPM. The gear ratios in the transmission and drive axle are used to match the engine speed and torque output to the vehicle speed and torque requirements. ● **SEE FIGURE 3–2.**

DRIVE VS. DRIVEN GEARS

The *drive* gear is the gear that is the source of the engine torque and rotation. The *driven* gear is the gear that is driven or rotated by the drive gear. Two gears meshed together are used to transmit torque and rotational motion. The driven gear can then rotate yet another gear. In this case, the second gear becomes the drive gear and the third gear is the driven gear.

TORQUE MULTIPLICATION

The gear teeth are cut proportional to the diameter of the gear. If one of two mating gears were twice as large as the other, it would have twice as many teeth. For example, if the smaller gear has 10 teeth, a gear twice as large will have 20 teeth. If the teeth of these gears are intermeshed, 10 teeth of each gear will come into contact when the smaller gear rotates one revolution. This will require one revolution of the small gear and one-half revolution of the larger gear. It will take two revolutions of the small gear to produce one revolution of the larger gear. This is a gear ratio of 2:1, assuming that the small gear is the drive gear. To determine a gear ratio, divide the driven gear by the driving gear. ● **SEE FIGURE 3–3.**

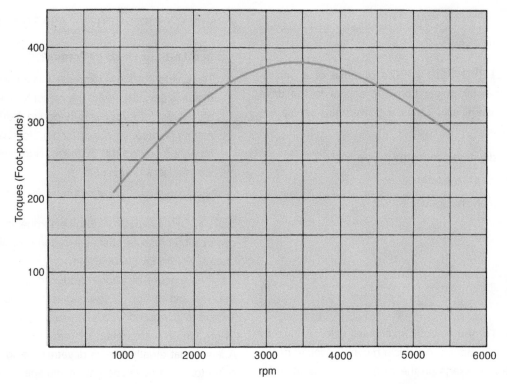

FIGURE 3–2 The torque produced by a 5.7 L engine as plotted on a graph. Note that the engine begins producing usable torque at 1000 to 1200 RPM and a maximum torque (381 ft-lb) at 3500 RPM. The torque produced by the engine decreases at higher RPM due to a decrease in volumetric efficiency.

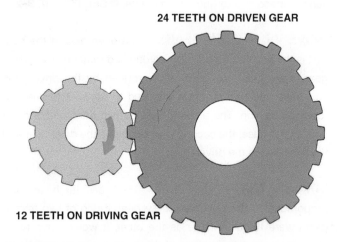

24 TEETH ON DRIVEN GEAR

12 TEETH ON DRIVING GEAR

FIGURE 3–3 Gear ratio is determined by dividing the number of teeth of the driven (output) gear (24 teeth) by the number of teeth on the driving (input) gear (12 teeth). The ratio illustrated is 2:1.

GEARS ARE LEVERS Torque is increased because of the length of the gear lever, as measured from the center of the gear. Think of each tooth as a lever, with the fulcrum being the center of the gear. The lever lengths of the two gears can provide leverage much like that of a simple lever. Physics does not allow energy to become lost in a gear set, other than what is lost as heat in overcoming friction. Therefore, whatever power that comes in one shaft, goes out through another.

- If the speed is reduced, torque will increase by the same amount.
- If speed is increased, torque will decrease by the same amount.

For example, if the driving gear has 20 lb-ft (27 N-m) of torque at 500 RPM and the ratio is 2:1, the driven gear will have 40 lb-ft (54 N-m) of torque (twice as much) at 250 RPM (half the speed).

HORSEPOWER

DEFINITION The term power means the rate of doing work. Power equals work divided by time.

- Work is done when a certain amount of mass (weight) is moved a certain distance by a force. Whether the object is moved in 10 seconds or 10 minutes does not make a difference in the amount of work accomplished, but it does affect the amount of power needed. ● **SEE FIGURE 3–4.**

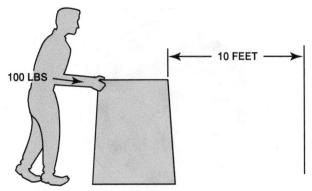

FIGURE 3–4 Work is calculated by multiplying force times distance. If you push 100 pounds 10 feet, you have done 1,000 foot-pounds of work.

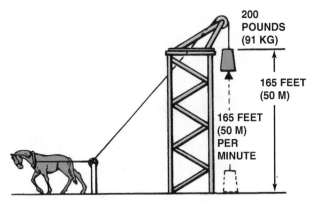

FIGURE 3–5 One horsepower is equal to 33,000 foot-pounds (200 lbs × 165 ft) of work per minute.

- Power is expressed in units of foot-pounds per minute. One **horsepower** is the power required to move 550 pounds one foot in one second, or 33,000 pounds one foot in one minute (550 lb × 60 sec = 33,000 lb). This is expressed as 550 foot-pounds (ft-lb) per second or 33,000 foot-pounds per minute. ● **SEE FIGURE 3–5**.

HORSEPOWER AND TORQUE RELATIONSHIP To determine horsepower, a **dynamometer** is used to measure the amount of torque an engine can produce at various points through its operating range. The formula used to convert torque at a certain revolution per minute (RPM) into a horsepower reading is

$$\text{Horsepower} = \text{Torque} \times \text{RPM}/5{,}252$$

The various readings are then plotted into a curve. A typical horsepower and torque curve shows us that an engine does not produce very much torque at low RPM. The most usable torque is produced in the mid-RPM range. Torque decreases with an increase in horsepower at a higher RPM.

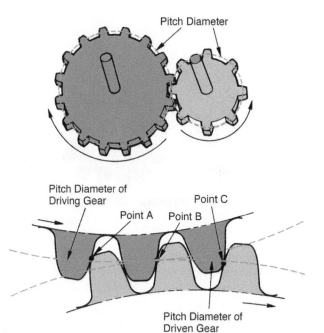

FIGURE 3–6 The pitch diameter is the effective diameter of the gear. Note how the contact points slide on the gear teeth as they move in and out of contact.

The torque from an engine can be increased or decreased through the use of gears, belts, and chains. Gears, belts, or chains cannot increase horsepower; they can only modify its effect. A gear set can increase torque, but it will decrease speed by the same amount.

GEARS

TERMINOLOGY The effective diameter of a gear is the **pitch diameter** (or *pitch line*). ● **SEE FIGURE 3–6**.

The pitch diameter is the diameter of the gear at the point where the teeth of the two gears meet and transfer power. The gear teeth are shaped to be able to slide in and out of mesh with a minimum amount of friction and wear. Major points include:

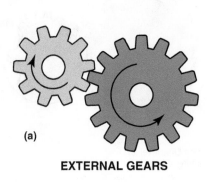

(a)

EXTERNAL GEARS

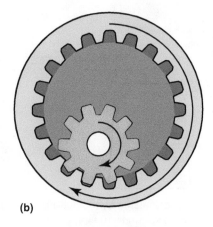

(b)

**INTERNAL AND
EXTERNAL GEARS**

FIGURE 3–7 (a) When one external gear drives another, the direction of rotation is always reversed. (b) When an external gear drives an internal gear, the two gears will rotate in the same direction.

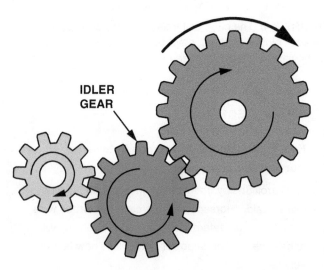

IDLER
GEAR

EXTERNAL GEARS

FIGURE 3–8 An idler gear reverses the direction of rotation so that the driving and driven gears rotate in the same direction.

- Driven and driving gears will rotate in opposite directions.
- External gears will always reverse shaft motion.
- If same-direction motion is required, the power will be routed through two gear sets.
- When power goes through a series of gears, an even number of gears (2, 4, 6, and 8) will cause a reversal in direction and an odd number of gears (3, 5, 7, and 9) will produce same-direction of rotation.

● **SEE FIGURE 3–7.**

REVERSING DIRECTION OF ROTATION   External gears reverse the direction of rotation when the drive gear transfers power to the driven gear. When it is necessary to change the

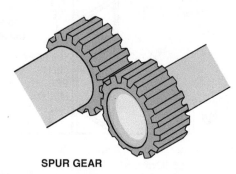

SPUR GEAR

FIGURE 3–9 The teeth of a spur gear are cut parallel to the shaft, and this produces a straight pressure between the driving and the driven gear teeth.

ratio without changing the direction of power flow, an idler gear is added. An idler gear changes the rotational direction but does not affect the ratio. ● **SEE FIGURE 3–8.**

GEAR TYPES   Gears come in different types depending on the cut and relationship of the teeth to the shafts.

- **Spur gears**—Spur gears, the simplest gears, are on parallel shafts with teeth cut straight or parallel to the shaft. ● **SEE FIGURE 3–9.**
- **Helical gear**—Helical gears are the most used of all gears used in transmissions. These gears have teeth cut in a spiral or helix shape. ● **SEE FIGURE 3–10.**

Helical gears are quieter than spur gears, but generate axial or end thrust under a load. A helical gear is stronger than a comparable-sized spur gear and has an almost continuous power flow because of the angled teeth. ● **SEE FIGURE 3–10.**

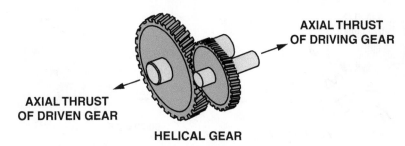

FIGURE 3–10 The teeth of a helical gear are cut on a slant, and this produces an axial or side thrust.

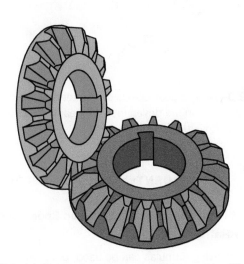

FIGURE 3–11 Bevel gears are commonly used in differentials.

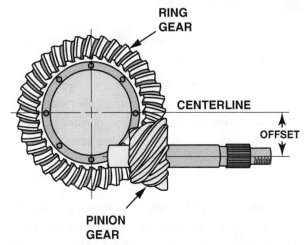

FIGURE 3–12 A hypoid gear set uses a pinion gear that is located below the centerline of the ring gear and is commonly used in drive axles.

NOTE: When discussing gears, a pinion gear is the smaller gear of a pair.

- **Bevel gears**—Bevel gears are used on nonparallel shafts. The outer edge of the gear must be cut on the angle that bisects the angle of the two shafts. In other words, if the two shafts meet at an angle of 90° and the two gears are the same size, the outer edge of the gears will be cut at 45°. The simplest bevel gears have teeth cut straight and are called spur bevel gears. They are inexpensive but noisy. ● **SEE FIGURE 3–11.**

- **Spiral bevel gears**—Spiral bevel gears, like helical gears, have curved teeth for quieter operation.

- **Hypoid gear**—A variation of the spiral bevel gear is the hypoid gear, also called an *offset-bevel gear*. Hypoid gears are used in most drive axles and transaxles that have longitudinal mounted engines. The hypoid gear

design places the drive pinion gear lower in the housing (below the centerline) of the ring gear and axle shafts. ● **SEE FIGURE 3–12.**

- **Worm gear**—A gear set used with shafts that cross each other but do not intersect is the worm gear. The worm gear or drive pinion is cut in a rather severe helix, much like a bolt thread, and the ring gear or wheel is cut almost like a spur gear. Worm gears are used in vehicle speed sensor drives. To determine the ratio of a worm gear, divide the number of teeth on the wheel by the pitch of the worm gear. For example, a single-pitch worm gear tooth driving a 20-tooth ring gear will have a ratio of 20:1, a very low ratio, and the wheel does not have to be 20 times larger than the worm gear. A 20:1 ratio in most gear sets requires the driven gear to be 20 times larger than the driving gear. ● **SEE FIGURE 3–13.**

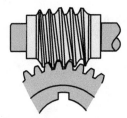

FIGURE 3–13 A worm gear set is also used to transmit power between angled shafts.

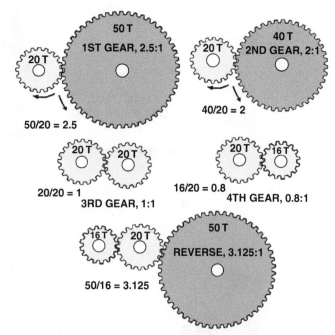

FIGURE 3–14 The gear ratio is determined by dividing the number of teeth on the driven (output) gear by the number of teeth on the driving (input) gear.

GEAR RATIOS

TERMINOLOGY **Gear ratios** are determined by the following methods:

- Dividing the number of teeth on the driven gear (output) by the number of teeth on the driving gear (input). Most of the time, this means dividing a larger number, such as 20, by a smaller number, such as 5. In this case, 20 ÷ 5 = 4, so the ratio will be 4:1.

- Gear ratio = driven gear/drive gear

- The driving gear will turn four times for each revolution of the driven gear. This results in a speed reduction and a torque increase. The speed of the output will be 4 times slower than the input speed but, the output torque will be four times more than the input torque. The higher the ratio number, the lower the gear ratio. A 5:1 ratio is higher numerically, but, in terms of speed of the driven gear, it is a lower ratio than 4:1. ● **SEE FIGURE 3–14.**

Most of the time, the ratio will not end up as whole numbers. It will be something like an 11-tooth driving gear and a 19-tooth driven gear, which results in a ratio of 19 divided by 11, which equals 1.7272727 and can be rounded off to 1.73.

COMMONLY USED RATIOS The automotive industry commonly rounds off gear ratios to two decimal points. Drivetrain engineers usually do not use even ratios like 3:1 or 4:1 but instead use ratios that are at least 10 percent greater or less than even numbers. An even ratio, like 3:1, repeats the same gear tooth contacts every third revolution. If there is a damaged tooth, a noise will be repeated continuously, and most drivers will not like the noise. A gear set with a ratio such as 3.23:1 is called a hunting gear set, and a tooth of one gear contacts all of the other gear teeth, which produces quieter operation.

? FREQUENTLY ASKED QUESTION

What Is the Relationship between Speed and Gear Ratio?

The following formulas can be used to determine the vehicle speed based on the gear ratio and engine speed, or the engine speed based on the gear ratio and MPH:

- MPH = (RPM × tire diameter) ÷ (gear ratio × 336)
- Engine RPM = (MPH × gear ratio × 336) ÷ tire diameter

NOTE: Use the loaded tire radius times two for the tire diameter.

OVERDRIVE If the driving gear has more teeth (20) than the driven gear (5), there will be an increase in speed and a reduction in torque. This is called an **overdrive**. The ratio is computed by dividing 5 by 20, 5 ÷ 20 = 0.25, so the ratio would be expressed as 0.25:1. The driving gear will turn 0.25 or one-fourth of a revolution for each turn of the driven gear. Note that a gear ratio is always written with the number 1 to the right of the colon. This represents one turn of the output gear, while the number to the left represents the revolutions of the input gear.

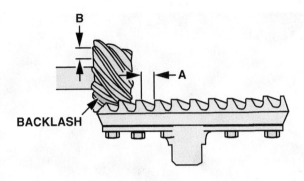

BACKLASH

A–B = BACKLASH

FIGURE 3–15 Backlash is the clearance between the teeth of two meshing gears. There has to be some clearance (backlash) to prevent the gears from getting into a bind condition when they are transmitting torque.

CALCULATING OVERALL RATIOS When power goes through more than one gear set, two or more ratios are involved. In most cases, the simplest way to handle this is to figure the ratio of each set and then multiply the ratios. An example of this is a vehicle with a first-gear ratio of 2.68:1 and a rear axle ratio of 3.45:1. The overall ratio in first gear is 2.68 × 3.45 or 9.246:1.

- At the same time there will be 9.246 times as much torque at the rear wheels than the engine produced.
- The engine will rotate at a speed that is 9.246 times faster than the rear axle shafts. The overall ratios for the other transmission gears would be figured in the same manner.

GEAR SET SUMMARY Typical rules about gear sets include the following:

- Two mated external gears will always rotate in opposite directions.
- Gear sets will multiply torque but at a reduced speed.
- An idler gear allows the drive and driven gears to rotate in the same direction.
- To find the ratio, divide the driven gear by the drive gear.
- When power transfers through an even number (two or four) of gears, the input and output gears will rotate in opposite directions.
- When power transfers through an uneven number (one, three, or five) of gears, the input and output gears will rotate in the same direction.
- To find the overall ratio of multiple gear sets, multiply the ratios of the gear sets.

- Two gears transferring power push away from each other in an action called *gear separation*. The gear separation force (thrust) is proportional to the torque being transferred.
- The smaller gear(s) in a gear set may also be called a **pinion gear**.
- All gear sets *must* have backlash to prevent binding. ● **SEE FIGURE 3–15.**

TRANSMISSIONS

PURPOSE AND FUNCTION The purpose and function of gears in a **transmission** include the following:

- Low/first gear must provide enough torque to get the vehicle moving.
- High gear should provide an engine speed for fuel-efficient operation at highway speeds.
- The intermediate ratios should be spaced to provide adequate acceleration while minimizing the potential of overrevving the engine before the shift or lugging the engine after the shift.

TRENDS The majority of vehicles up to the 1970s used three-speed transmissions while some added an overdrive unit for a fourth gear ratio to lower engine RPM at cruise speeds. As the need to improve fuel economy and reduce exhaust emissions has improved, four-, five-, and six-speed transmissions have been introduced to provide lower first gears, overdrive, and/or smaller steps between gear ratios.

MANUAL TRANSMISSIONS

PURPOSE AND FUNCTION A **manual transmission**, also called a *standard transmission*, is constructed with a group of paths through which power can flow with each path used being a different gear ratio. ● **SEE FIGURE 3–16.**

Synchronizer assemblies or sliding gears and the shift linkage are used to control or engage the power paths.

CLUTCH Engine power must be stopped when making a shift in a manual transmission. The **clutch** is used to stop the power flow to allow the transmission to be shifted. It is also

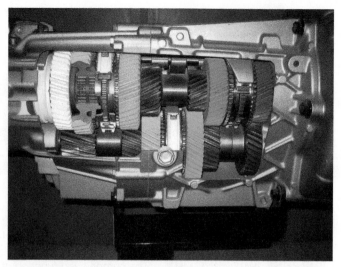

FIGURE 3–16 A manual transmission provides several gear ratios and a method to shift them.

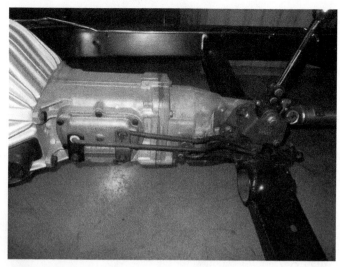

FIGURE 3–17 A Muncie four-speed manual transmission on a restored muscle car.

FREQUENTLY ASKED QUESTION

What Is a "Close-Ratio" Transmission?

Gear ratio spread (GRS), is the difference between the lowest and highest ratios or, in other words, the overall range of the transmission gear ratios. In transmissions, it is fairly easy to visualize the difference between a 3.59:1 first gear and a 0.83:1 fifth gear. Gear ratio spread is determined by dividing the low gear ratio by the high gear ratio. The GRS for the gear transmission is $3.59 \div 0.83 = 4.33$.

RPM change/drop is fairly easy to determine:

- Subtract the higher ratio from the lower ratio and divide the product by the lower ratio.
- A close-ratio Muncie four-speed has ratios spaced fairly close together (25% or less), closer than the wide-ratio version. ● **SEE FIGURE 3–17.**

FREQUENTLY ASKED QUESTION

What Is an Automated Manual Transmission?

An automated manual transmission is a type of automatic transmission/transaxle that uses two clutches and a manual transmission-type gears and is shifted hydraulically by computer-controlled solenoids. This type of transmission is commonly called a *dual clutch* or an *electronically controlled manual transmission*.

used to ease the engagement of the power flow when the vehicle starts from a standstill. The slight slippage as the clutch engages allows the engine speed to stay up where it produces usable torque as the vehicle begins moving.

Most vehicles use a foot-pedal-operated single-plate clutch assembly that is mounted on the engine flywheel. When the pedal is pushed down, the power flow is disengaged and when the pedal is released, power can flow from the engine to the transmission through the engaged clutch. ● **SEE FIGURE 3–18.**

AUTOMATIC TRANSMISSIONS

PURPOSE AND FUNCTION The purpose and function of an **automatic transmission** is to provide the forward and reverse gear ratios needed without requiring the driver to make the change in gearing as with a manual transmission. An automatic transmission has various gear ratios, but the paths of power flow are different from those of a manual transmission.

SHIFT MODES The transmission provides the various gear ratios for forward and reverse operations as well as two methods for the engine to run without moving the vehicle. Most automatic transmissions and transaxles include the following shift modes. ● **SEE FIGURE 13–19.**

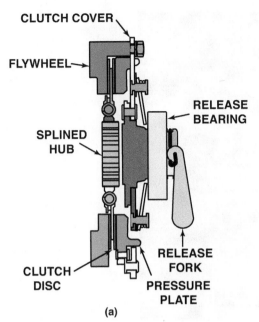

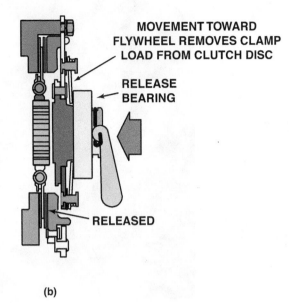

FIGURE 3–18 (a) A clutch cover (pressure plate assembly) is bolted onto the flywheel with the clutch disc between them. The release bearing and fork provide a method to release (disengage) the clutch. (b) When the clutch is engaged, the disc is squeezed against the flywheel by the pressure plate. Releasing the clutch separates the disc from the flywheel and pressure plate.

FIGURE 3–19 The gear selector is often called the "PRNDL," pronounced "prindle," regardless of the actual letters or numbers used.

- **Park.** In the park position, the output shaft is locked to the case of the transmission/transaxle which keeps the vehicle from moving. No power is transmitted through the unit so the engine can remain running while the vehicle is held stationary. In the park position

1. The engine can be started by the driver.

2. To move the shifter out of the park position on a late model vehicle, the brake pedal must be depressed to release the transmission shift interlock.

- **Reverse.** The reverse gear selector position is used to move the vehicle in reverse. Reverse usually uses a gear ratio similar to first gear.

- **Neutral.** In the neutral position no torque is being transmitted through the automatic transmission/transaxle. In this position the engine can be started by the driver.

CAUTION: The vehicle is free to roll when the gear selector is placed in the neutral position unless the brake pedal is depressed to prevent the vehicle from moving.

- **Overdrive (OD).** The OD is the normal position for the shift selector for most driving conditions. This position allows the transmission or transaxle to shift through all forward gears as needed for the best fuel economy and lowest exhaust emissions.

NOTE: The overdrive button used on many automatic transmissions is used to turn off overdrive and is used while towing or when driving in city traffic to prevent the transmission from shifting in and out of overdrive.

- **Drive (D).** The D position includes the overdrive ratios in most vehicles. If there is an overdrive shift mode, however, then D is used to provide all forward gears except overdrive. Use this position when driving on the highway.

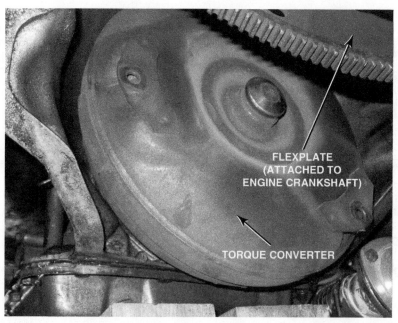

FIGURE 3–20 A torque converter is attached to the engine crankshaft and the other end is splined to the input shaft of the automatic transmission. The torque converter is used to transmit engine torque to the transmission yet slip when the engine is at idle speed.

- **Third (3).** In third position the transmission/transaxle will upshift normally to third gear but will not upshift to a higher gear. When the third position is selected while driving in a higher gear, the transmission will downshift into third if the vehicle speed is low enough to prevent the engine from being overrevved. This gear selection is used for gentle grades at a moderate vehicle speed when engine braking is needed.

- **Second (2).** The second position is used for slowing the vehicle while descending long grades. In this gear selection, the vehicle speed is controlled and the engine speed is increased to provide engine braking. This gear selection is used for the gentle grades at a moderate vehicle speed.

- **First (1 or Low).** The first (or low) position is used for slowing the vehicle while descending steep grades. In this gear selection, the vehicle speed is controlled and engine braking is used to slow the vehicle. This gear selection is used for the steepest grades at the lowest possible speed.

TORQUE CONVERTERS

A **torque converter** replaces the manual transmission clutch. It is a type of fluid coupling that can release the power flow at slow engine speeds and also multiply the engine torque during acceleration. Torque converters in newer vehicles include a friction clutch that locks up to eliminate slippage at cruising speeds, improving fuel economy and reducing exhaust emissions. ●**SEE FIGURE 3–20.**

PLANETARY GEAR SETS

Most automatic transmissions use **planetary gear sets**, which are a combination of gears. When the gear set is assembled, the sun gear is in the center and meshed with the planet gears, which are located around it, somewhat like the planets in our solar system. The ring gear is meshed around the outside of the planet gears. The three main members of the planetary gear set include the following:

1. **Sun gear**—It is the gear in the center.
2. **Ring gear**—It is also called an *annulus gear* or *internal gear*.
3. **Planet carrier**—It holds the planet gears (also called *pinions*) in position. ●**SEE FIGURE 3–21.**

Each of these gears can have two possible actions: They can rotate or stand still.

The planet gears/pinions have the following three possible actions.

1. They can rotate on their shafts in a stationary carrier and act like idler gears.
2. They can rotate on their shafts in a rotating carrier; the planet gears are walking.
3. They can stand still on their shafts and rotate with the carrier.

Planetary gear sets are used and combined in a complex manner so that transmissions with seven or eight speeds forward plus reverse are possible. Shifts are made by engaging or releasing one or more internal clutches that drive a gear set member, or by engaging or releasing other clutches or bands that hold a gear set member stationary. An automatic transmission might have as many as seven of these power control units

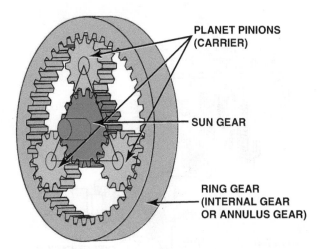

FIGURE 3–21 A typical planetary gear set showing the terms that are used to describe each member.

(clutches or bands). One-way clutches are also used that self-release and overrun when the next gear is engaged. The control units can operate without the interruption of the power flow.

PLANETARY GEAR SET OPERATION
Planetary gear sets are so arranged that power enters through one of the members and leaves through one of the other members while the third member is held stationary in reaction. Power flow through a planetary gear set is controlled by clutches, bands, and one-way clutches. One or more clutches will control the power coming to a planetary member and one or more reaction members can hold a gear set member stationary. The third planetary member will be the output. ● SEE FIGURE 3–22.

PLANETARY GEAR SET RATIOS
A simple planetary gear set can produce one of the following:

- A neutral if either the input clutch or reaction member is not applied
- Two reduction ratios
- Two overdrive ratios
- Two reverse ratios, one a reduction and one an overdrive
- The reduction, overdrive, and reverse ratios will require one driving member, one output member, and one reaction member in the gear set.

NOTE: A 1:1, direct-drive ratio is achieved if two gear set members are driven.

ADVANTAGES OF PLANETARY GEAR SETS
Planetary gear sets offer several advantages over conventional gear sets.

1. Because there is more than one gear transferring power, the torque load is spread over several gear teeth.

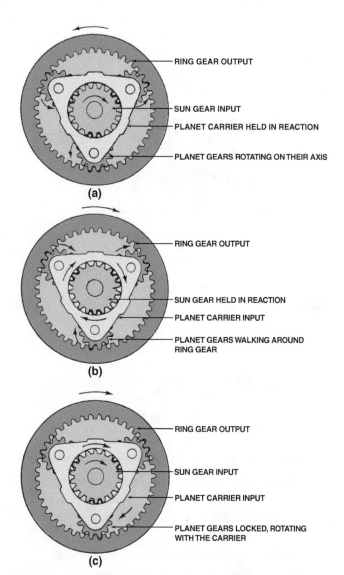

(a)

(b)

(c)

FIGURE 3–22 (a) If the planet carrier is held with the sun gear rotating, the planet gears simply rotate in the carrier and act as idler gears between the sun and ring gears. (b) If the sun or ring is held, the planet gears will walk around that stationary gear; they rotate on their shafts as the carrier rotates. (c) If two parts are driven and no parts are held, the planet gears are stationary on their shafts, and the whole assembly rotates as a unit.

2. Also, any gear separation forces (as gears transfer power, they tend to push away from each other) are contained within the planetary gear set, preventing this load from being transmitted to the transmission case.

3. Another advantage is the small relative size of the planetary gear set. Conventional gears are normally side by side, and for a 2:1 gear ratio, one gear has to be twice the size of the other. A planetary gear set can easily produce this same ratio in a smaller package.

4. Also, planetary gear sets are in constant mesh and no coupling or uncoupling of the gears is required.

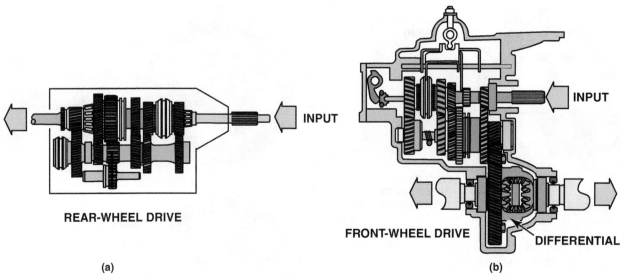

FIGURE 3–23 A RWD drivetrain uses a transmission to provide the necessary gear ratio and a single driveshaft to transfer power to the rear axle (a). A FWD drivetrain uses a transaxle that combines the transmission's final drive, and differential (b). A driveshaft is used for each front drive wheel.

? FREQUENTLY ASKED QUESTION

What Do All the Letters and Numbers Mean in Transmission Designations?

The numbers and letters usually mean the following:

- **Number of forward speeds.** The number of forward speeds may include four, five, or six such as the GM 4T60-E four-speed unit and the ZF 5HP24 five-speed unit.
- **Front-wheel drive or rear-wheel drive.** The letter **T** usually means *transverse* (front-wheel-drive transaxle) such as the Chrysler 41-TE; the **L** means *longitudinal* (rear-wheel-drive transmission) such as the General Motors 6L80; and the **R** means *rear-wheel drive* such as the Ford 5R55E.
- **Electronically controlled.** The letter **E** is often used to indicate that the unit is electronically controlled, and **M** or **H** is used to designate older mechanically (hydraulically) controlled units. Most automatic transmissions built since the early 1990s are electronically controlled and therefore the **E** is often included in the designation of newer designs of transmission or transaxles.
- **Torque rating.** The torque rating is usually designated by a number where the higher the number, the higher the amount of torque load the unit is designed to handle. In a GM 6L80-E, the torque rating is 80. Always check service information for the exact transmission designation for the vehicle being studied.

REAR-WHEEL DRIVE VS. FRONT-WHEEL DRIVE

At one time, most vehicles had the transmission mounted behind the engine and used a driveshaft to transfer power to the rear axle and driving wheels. This drivetrain is called **rear-wheel drive (RWD)**.

Many vehicles use a transaxle to drive the front wheels, called **front-wheel drive (FWD)**. Most FWD vehicles have the engine mounted in a transverse position, crosswise in the vehicle. Some are longitudinally mounted, in a lengthwise position as in RWD vehicles.

Two short driveshafts, called **half shafts**, are used to connect the transaxle to the front wheels. Driving only two wheels is adequate for most driving conditions. When the roads are slippery or driving off-road, driving all four wheels provides better vehicle control. ● **SEE FIGURE 3–23.**

TRANSAXLES

TERMINOLOGY A **transaxle** is a compact combination of a transmission, the **final drive** gear reduction, and the differential. It can be either a manual, automatic, or continuously variable transaxle. Transaxles are used in nearly all front-wheel-drive vehicles, some mid-engine vehicles, rear engine, and even a few rear-wheel-drive vehicles. ● **SEE FIGURE 3–24.**

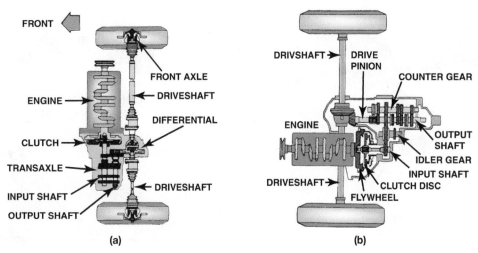

FRONT

FRONT AXLE

DRIVESHAFT

ENGINE

DIFFERENTIAL

CLUTCH

TRANSAXLE

INPUT SHAFT

DRIVESHAFT

OUTPUT SHAFT

(a)

DRIVSHAFT

DRIVE PINION

COUNTER GEAR

ENGINE

OUTPUT SHAFT

IDLER GEAR

INPUT SHAFT

DRIVESHAFT

CLUTCH DISC

FLYWHEEL

(b)

FIGURE 3–24 Transverse (a) and longitudinal (b) mounted front-wheel-drive (FWD) drivetrains.

OPERATION A transmission normally has one output shaft that couples to the rear axle through the driveshaft. A transaxle has two output shafts that couple to the two front wheels through a pair of driveshafts. The **differential** used in transaxles or drive axles is a torque-splitting device that allows the two axle shafts to operate at different speeds so that a vehicle can turn corners. When a vehicle turns a corner, the wheel on the outer side of the turning radius must travel farther than the inner wheel, but it must do this in the same period of time. Therefore, it must rotate faster while turning. Most differentials are composed of a group of four or more gears. One gear is coupled to each axle and two are mounted on the differential pinion shaft.

DRIVESHAFTS

TERMINOLOGY **Driveshafts**, also called a *propeller shaft* or *prop shaft*, transfer power from one component to another. Rear-wheel-drive vehicle driveshafts are usually made from steel tubing, and normally have either a **universal joint (U-joint)** or a **constant-velocity (CV) joint** at each end. Most front-wheel-drive vehicles use driveshafts that are a solid shaft or hollow steel tubing. A U-joint allows the shaft to change angle as the drive axle moves up and down when the wheels travel over bumps. Speed fluctuations occur in the driveshaft as the U-joints transfer power at an angle, but these fluctuations are

canceled out or eliminated by the position of the U-joint at the other end of the driveshaft.

A front-wheel-drive vehicle driveshaft must use a CV joint at its ends because the front wheels must be steered at sharp angles. The short driveshafts used with transaxles and independent rear suspension drive axles are often called half shafts. ● **SEE FIGURE 3–25.**

DRIVE AXLE ASSEMBLIES

TERMINOLOGY Rear-wheel-drive vehicles use a drive axle assembly at the rear. A **drive axle** performs four functions:

1. It supports the weight of the rear of the vehicle.
2. It contains the final drive reduction gears.
3. It contains the differential, which transfers torque to both drive wheels and allows the wheels to rotate at different speeds when cornering.
4. It allows the power to turn 90 degrees.

Most axle assemblies use strong axle shafts to transfer the torque from the differential gears to the wheels and tires. A bearing at the outer end of the axle housing serves to transfer vehicle weight to the axle and then to the wheels and tires while allowing the shaft to rotate.

The term final drive refers to the last set of reduction gears in a gear train. The torque that is applied to the drive wheels, and cruising speed engine RPM, is determined by the reduction gears and the drive wheel diameter. ● **SEE FIGURE 3–26.**

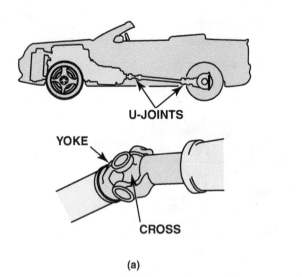

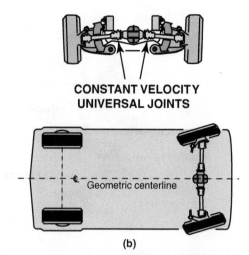

FIGURE 3–25 (a) A rear-wheel-drive (RWD) driveshaft uses a pair of universal joints to allow the rear axle to move up and down. (b) A front-wheel-drive (FWD) driveshaft uses a pair of constant-velocity joints to allow the front wheels to move up and down and steer.

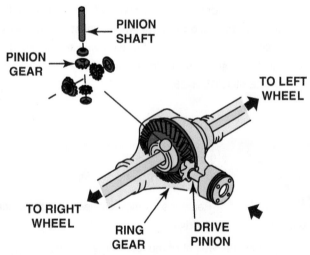

FIGURE 3–26 A drive axle includes a ring and pinion gear to produce a lower gear ratio as it turns the power flow 90° and a differential (differential pinion and side gears) to allow the drive wheels to rotate at different speeds.

TOWING CAPABILITY

DRIVETRAIN REQUIREMENTS Trucks are often used to tow trailers or heavy loads. In order for a vehicle to tow a heavy load, the vehicle must have the following features:

- An engine that can produce the needed torque and horsepower.
- A strong frame to withstand the forces involved.
- A strong trailer hitch properly installed and attached to the frame of the vehicle.

What Must the Powertrain Overcome to Move the Vehicle?

To propel the vehicle, the engine and drivetrain must overcome the following:

- Rolling friction, which is the drag of the tires on the road, and bearing friction. These frictions increase at a constant rate, doubling as the speed is doubled.
- Aerodynamic drag, which is the wind resistance of air moving over the size and shape of the vehicle. It increases at a rapid rate, roughly four times as the speed is doubled (actually, velocity squared).
- Grade resistance, which is equal to 0.01 times the vehicle weight times the angle of the grade in percent.

- A strong drivetrain (transmission, driveshaft, and drive axle(s)) that can transmit the engine torque to the drive wheels.
- Heavy-duty brakes so that the heavy load can be slowed and stopped safely.

SAE J2807 STANDARD Starting in 2013, the Society of Automotive Engineers (SAE) established a standardized test procedure to determine the tow rating for vehicles. The standard includes three vehicle performance standards including:

1. **Climbing test** During the climbing test, the vehicle with the loaded trailer (at the specified rating that the vehicle

manufacture states is the capacity of the vehicle) has 12 seconds to climb a hill that rises 3,000 feet (900 m) over a length of 11.4 miles (18 km) without dropping below 40 MPH (64 km/h). This test is based on the Davis Dam grade, a stretch of road in Arizona southeast of Las Vegas.

2. **Acceleration test** During this test, the vehicle with loaded trailer must accelerate from 0 to 30 MPH (48 km/h) in 12 seconds and less than 30 seconds to reach 60 MPH (100 km/h).

3. **Launching** This test is used to test the vehicle and loaded trailer in both forward and reverse. The test places the vehicle at the base of a long hill with a 12% grade. The vehicle must be able to climb the grade 16 feet (5 m) from a stop five times within five minutes.

These tests not only test the power of the vehicle but also that the engine and transmission can be kept at the proper temperature, meaning that the engine and transmission (if automatic) be equipped with a cooler.

NOTE: Not all vehicle manufactures adhere to the SAE standard when reporting their recommended tow rating, because while while standardized, the use of the SAE J2807 is voluntary.

FOUR-WHEEL DRIVE

TERMINOLOGY **Four-wheel drive (4WD)** is often designated as "4 × 4" and refers to a vehicle that has four driven wheels.

- The first 4 indicates that the vehicle has four wheels.
- The second 4 indicates that all four wheels are driven.

A vehicle will have more pulling power and traction if all of its wheels are driven. This requires a drive axle at each end of the vehicle, another driveshaft, and a **transfer case** or **power transfer unit** to drive the additional driveshaft and drive axle. The transfer case is normally attached to the rear of the transmission. It has a single input shaft from the transmission and two output shafts, one to the front drive axle and one to the rear drive axle. Some transfer cases are two-speed and include a set of reduction gears for lower-speed, higher-torque operation.

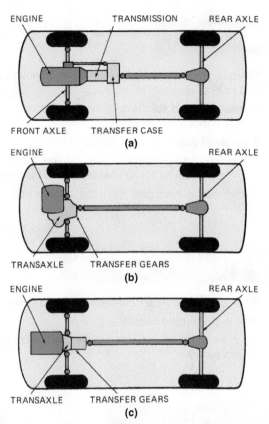

FIGURE 3–27 Three major 4WD configurations. The traditional form (a) uses a transfer case to split the torque for the front and rear drive axles. Both (b) and (c) are typical AWD configurations.

Four-wheel drive can be built into

- A front-engine rear-wheel drive
- A front-engine front-wheel drive
- A rear-engine rear-wheel drive

● **SEE FIGURE 3–27.**

ALL-WHEEL DRIVE **All-wheel-drive (AWD),** also called full-time four-wheel drive, vehicles are four-wheel-drive vehicles equipped with a center (inner-axle) differential so they can be operated on pavement in four-wheel drive. Full-time four-wheel drive is another name for all-wheel drive. All-wheel-drive vehicles are designed for improved on-road handling. There will be one differential in each drive axle assembly plus a differential between the two drive axles. The inter-axle differential allows the front-to-rear wheel speed differential. Because all wheels are driven, these vehicles are excellent for use in rain and snow where added control is needed.

1. Vehicles are built as rear-wheel drive, front-wheel drive, and four- or all-wheel drive.
2. Engines develop torque and the drivetrains modify that torque to move the vehicle.
3. A variety of gears are used to modify torque.
4. The gear ratio is determined by dividing the number of driven gear teeth by the number of teeth on the driving gear.
5. Transmissions have gear ratios that a driver can select.
6. Manual transmissions use a clutch and automatic transmissions use a torque converter.
7. Transaxles combine the final drive gears and differential with the transmission.
8. Driveshafts and the drive axle complete the drivetrain.
9. Four-wheel-drive and all-wheel-drive vehicles have a transfer case or transfer gears and a second drive axle.

REVIEW QUESTIONS

1. What is the difference between torque and horsepower?
2. How is a gear ratio calculated?
3. What are the common shift modes used in an automatic transmission?
4. What is an inter-axle differential?

CHAPTER QUIZ

1. Torque is _____.
   a. A twisting force
   b. The rate of doing work
   c. Results in motion
   d. The gear ratio

2. Gears can be used to _____.
   a. Increase speed
   b. Increase torque
   c. Reverse direction
   d. All of the above

3. If a gear with 20 teeth is driving a gear with 60 teeth, the gear ratio is _____.
   a. 2:6
   b. 3:1
   c. 1:3
   d. 0.33:1

4. Technician A says a helical gear is stronger than a spur gear. Technician B says a helical gear is noisier than a spur gear. Which technician is correct?
   a. Technician A only
   b. Technician B only
   c. Both Technicians A and B
   d. Neither Technician A nor B

5. Which type of gear may be found in a rear-wheel-drive axle?
   a. Hypoid
   b. Spiral Bevel
   c. Spur
   d. Helical

6. The transmission is in first gear, which has a 2.5:1 ratio, and the rear axle has a ratio of 2:1. What is the overall ratio?
   a. 2:1
   b. 2.5:1
   c. 4.5:1
   d. 5:1

7. The type of gear set used in most automatic transmissions is _____.
   a. Spur gears
   b. Planetary gears
   c. Helical gears
   d. Any of the above

8. What shift mode should be used when descending a steep hill?
   a. Drive (D)
   b. Second (2)
   c. Neutral (N)
   d. Low (L)

9. Full-time four-wheel-drive vehicles use _____.
   a. Transfer case
   b. Spiral bevel drive axles
   c. Three differentials
   d. Both a and c

10. What is used to transfer engine torque to all four wheels?
    a. Four driveshafts
    b. A transfer case or power transfer unit
    c. Four differentials
    d. All of the above

chapter 4

HYDRAULIC SYSTEM PARTS AND OPERATION

LEARNING OBJECTIVES

After studying this chapter, the reader will be able to:

1. Prepare for ASE Automatic Transmissions (A2) certification test content area "A" (General Transmission and Transaxle Diagnosis).

2. Discuss the specifications and types of automatic transmission fluids (ATF).

3. Discuss hydraulic principles and Pascal's Law.

4. Describe the types and operation of automatic transmission/transaxle pumps.

5. Explain the different methods for controlling fluid flow and regulating pressure.

6. Identify the types of hydraulic seals.

7. Discuss ATF filters, heaters, and coolers.

KEY TERMS

Automatic transmission fluid (ATF) 70

Balance valve 79

Depth filter 77

Fluid power 70

Gerotor 74

Hydraulics 70

Internal–external gear 74

Land 78

Mainline pressure 75

Micron 77

Paper filter 76

Positive displacement pump 75

Pressure regulator valve 78

Pump 74

Static seal 79

Spool valve 77

Surface filter 76

Supply pressure 75

Turbulator 83

Vane pump 74

Variable displacement pump 76

THE HYDRAULIC SYSTEM

PURPOSE AND FUNCTION The automatic transmission's hydraulic system has several important functions. It must be able to

- Apply the clutches and bands and therefore control the transmission's power flow
- Transmit sufficient force and motion to completely apply the control units to prevent slippage
- Maintain fluid flow through the torque converter for its proper operation
- Maintain fluid flow to lubricate and cool the moving parts of the gear train

HYDRAULIC PRINCIPLES

DEFINITION **Hydraulics**, often called **fluid power**, is a method of transmitting motion and/or force using a fluid. Hydraulics is based on the principle that liquids can flow easily through complicated paths, but they cannot be compressed. All the components in a hydraulic system are interconnected so that fluid pressure can be transmitted to all parts to work as designed. ● **SEE FIGURE 4–1.**

AUTOMATIC TRANSMISSION FLUID

PURPOSE AND FUNCTION **Automatic transmission fluid (ATF)** is highly refined oil with a viscosity similar to SAE 20W-20 oil, and is specially designed for use in automatic transmissions. Newer ATFs are lower in viscosity and are similar to SAE 0W-10 oil.

The purpose and function of ATF includes the following:

- Transfers power in torque converters
- Provides hydraulic pressure in clutches and band servos
- Lubricates bearings, bushings, and gears
- Transfers heat to cool transmission parts
- Provides the correct friction for clutch and band application
- Acts as the medium to control transmission shifting by traveling through passageways, acting on valves, and being directed by solenoids.

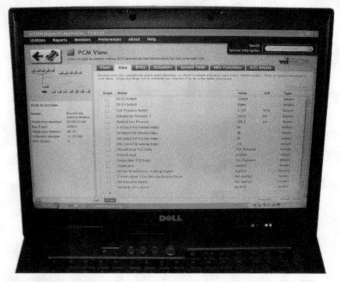

FIGURE 4–1 Fluid pressure is used to apply clutches and bands. The pressure and calculated volume index readings of the fluid in the unit can be monitored using a scan tool.

BACKGROUND Early automatic transmissions used engine oil for a transmission fluid. Since internal operating conditions in engines and automatic transmissions are significantly different, a special transmission fluid was developed in the late 1940s. At first, the ATF was simply a mineral oil similar to engine oil, but dyed red.

ADDITIVES Transmission fluid is formulated with various additives to produce favorable operating characteristics. Automatic transmission fluid contains about 10% to 15% additives. These additives are chemical compounds, and the reasons for their use are as follows:

- **Detergents-dispersants.** Keep the transmission clean and the valves free from sticking by keeping foreign items in suspension until they are removed by the filter or by draining.
- **Oxidation inhibitors.** Reduce oxidation and decomposition of the fluid, which can produce varnish and sludge.
- **Viscosity index improvers.** Change the fluid viscosity with change in temperature so that fluid thickness and shift characteristics remain stable during a range of changing temperatures.
- **Friction modifiers.** Change the fluid's coefficient of friction.
- **Foam inhibitors.** Prevent formation of air bubbles and foam in the fluid.
- **Seal swelling agents.** Produce a slight swelling of the elastomers (seals) to compensate for any wear that occurs.
- **Anti-wear agents.** Reduce friction and prevent scoring and seizure of metal parts running against each other.

- **Rust inhibitors.** Prevent rust from forming on the iron and steel parts.
- **Corrosion inhibitors.** Prevent corrosion of the nonferrous parts.
- **Metal deactivators.** Form a protective film to inhibit oxidation of metal surfaces.
- **Dye.** Dye is added to make ATF red except for the fluid used in most continuously variable transmissions or dual clutch automatics which is often dyed green.

SYNTHETIC ATF Synthetic engine oils have been available for years for military, commercial, and general public use. The term synthetic means that it is a manufactured product and not refined from a naturally occurring substance, as engine oil (petroleum base) is refined from crude oil. Synthetic oil is processed from several different base stocks using several different methods.

According to the American Petroleum Institute, oils are classified into the following groups.

- **Group I.** Mineral, non-synthetic base oil with few, if any, additives.
- **Group II.** Mineral oil with quality additive packages; includes most friction-modified automatic transmission fluids.
- **Group III.** Hydrogenated (hydroisomerized) synthetic compounds, commonly referred to as hydrowaxes or hydrocracked oil and is the lowest cost synthetic ATF. Most "fill-for life" ATF is made from Group III base stock.
- **Group IV.** Synthetic oils made from mineral oil and monomolecular oil called polyalpholefin (POA) and include Mobil 1 ATF.
- **Group V.** Non-mineral sources such as alcohol from corn, called diesters or polyolesters; includes Red Line and Royal Purple ATF.

Groups III, IV, and V are considered to be synthetic because the molecular structure of the finished product does not occur naturally, but is man-made through chemical processes. These are man-made oils.

- The major advantage of using synthetic ATF is its ability to remain fluid at very low temperatures, which results in consistent transmission operation regardless of operating temperature.
- The major disadvantage is cost. The cost of synthetic automatic transmission fluid can be four to five times the cost of petroleum-based fluids. A synthetic blend indicates that some synthetic fluid is mixed with petroleum base oil but the percentage of synthetic used in the blend is unknown.

TYPES The three basic types of ATF include

1. **Non-friction modified.** The first ATF did not have friction reducing additives. This type of fluid was used in early band-type automatics. Type F ATF is an example of a non-friction-modified ATF.
2. **Friction modified.** Friction-modified ATF types include Dexron.
3. **Highly friction modified.** All current original equipment manufacturers use automatic transmission fluids that are highly friction modified. These include Dexron VI, Mercon V, ATF +4, and ATF WS.

ATF EXAMPLES

GENERAL MOTORS The first transmission fluid was developed by General Motors and was labeled *Type A* transmission fluid. As transmission fluid was improved, Type A was replaced with *Type A, Suffix A; Dexron;* and then *Dexron II, Dexron IIE,* and *Dexron III.* The Dexron fluids are compatible, and Dexron III can be used in older transmissions that specify one of the older fluid types.

General Motors introduced Dexron® VI in 2005 for use in the then new six speed transmissions/transaxles. It is superior to the older versions of Dexron and is the recommended fluid for all General Motors automatic transmissions/transaxles. It has a more consistent viscosity to produce more consistent shift performance during extreme conditions and less degradation over time. This fluid has more than twice the durability and stability in tests compared to previous ATFs.

TOYOTA Toyota uses world standard (WS) fluid. It is formulated to provide lower viscosity at normal operating temperatures, which helps improve fuel economy. At higher temperatures, this ATF provides greater durability.

FORD Ford Motor Company has developed fluids for use in its vehicles. *Types F, CJ, Mercon,* and *Mercon V* and Mercon LV (low viscosity) are required for various Ford transmission models. Mercon can be used in place of older Ford fluids but Mercon V should be used only in transmissions that specify its use. Ford introduced Mercon SP fluid, which has the same characteristics as Dexron® VI and Toyota WS, and although these fluids are similar, they are not interchangeable.

TYPICAL ATF APPLICATIONS Automatic transmission fluid is formulated to work in specific transmissions. Using the

GENERAL MOTORS	DESCRIPTION
Type A	1949
Type A, Suffix A	1957 (friction modified)
Dexron	1967 (lower viscosity)
Dexron II	1978 (lower viscosity)
Dexron II-E	1990 (improved low temperature fluidity)
Dexron III	1993–2005 (improved low temperature fluidity)
Dexron VI	2005 (improved viscosity stability)

FORD/JAGUAR	DESCRIPTION
Type F	1967 (non-friction modified; designed for older band-type automatic transmissions)
Mercon	1987 (friction modified)
Mercon V	1997 (highly friction modified)
Mercon SP	Used in the Ford six speeds such as the 6R60 6HP 26 and also the 2003 and up Torque Shift
Idemitsu K-17	Jaguar X-type

CHRYSLER	DESCRIPTION
Chrysler 7176	Designed for front-wheel-drive transaxles
ATF + 2	1997 (improved cold temperature flow)
ATF + 3	1997 (designed for four-speed automatics)
ATF + 4	Used in most 2000 and newer Chrysler vehicles

HONDA/TOYOTA	DESCRIPTION
Honda Z-1	For use in all Honda automatic transaxles
Toyota Type III	Specific vehicles and years
Toyota Type IV	Specific vehicles and years
Toyota WS	Lower viscosity than Type IV; used in specific vehicles and years

MAZDA/NISSAN/SUBARU	DESCRIPTION
Mazda ATF-III	Specific vehicles and years
Mazda ATF-MV	Specific vehicles and years
Nissan Matic D	Specific vehicles and years
Nissan Matic J	Specific vehicles and years
Nissan Matic K	Specific vehicles and years
Subaru ATF	Specific vehicles and years
Subaru ATF-HP	Specific vehicles and years

AUDI/BMW/MERCEDES/ VOLVO	DESCRIPTION
Audi G-052-025-A2	Specific vehicles and years
Audi G-052-162-A1	Specific vehicles and years
BMW LA2634	Specific vehicles and years
BMW LT1141	Lifetime fill (BMW warns to not use any other type of fluid)
Mercedes 236.1	Specific vehicles and years
Mercedes 236.2	Specific vehicles and years
Mercedes 236.5	Specific vehicles and years
Mercedes 236.6	Specific vehicles and years
Mercedes 236.7	Specific vehicles and years
Mercedes 236.9	Specific vehicles and years
Mercedes 236.10	Specific vehicles and years
Volvo 97340	Specific vehicles and years
Volvo JWS 3309	Specific vehicles and years

MITSUBISHI/HYUNDAI/KIA	DESCRIPTION
Diamond SP II	Specific vehicles and years
Diamond SP III	Specific vehicles and years

CHART 4–1

Selected samples of automatic transmission fluid and some applications. Always check service information for proper specified fluid when servicing automatic transmissions/transaxles.

specified fluid is the key to proper operation. ● **SEE CHART 4–1** for examples of the types and applications of selected vehicles and fluids.

ATF OPTIONS The shop has three options when filling or replacing automatic transmission fluid:

Option 1. Use the exact specified fluid as recommended by the vehicle manufacturer for the particular transmission/transaxle. This is the preferred option because it has been recommend by the vehicle manufacturer. The major disadvantage of this option is that some fluids are hard to find at local parts suppliers and may have to be purchased from a dealer. ● **SEE FIGURE 4–2.**

Option 2. Use a multi-vehicle fluid, also called *universal ATF,* which is designed to meet the specifications of several different makes. This is commonly used by many shops and can be successfully used if the fluid is within the specified viscosity and the fluid manufacturer

FIGURE 4–2 The use of the factory-specific fluid is the recommend fluid to insure the best possible shifting and transmission operation.

FIGURE 4–3 Multi-vehicle, or universal fluid, is designed to meet the specifications of many types of fluids, making it popular with independent shops that service many makes and models of vehicles.

states that it meets the original equipment (OE) requirement for friction coefficient. ● SEE FIGURE 4–3.

Option 3. Use a standard ATF with a "top treatment" additive to meet the friction characteristics of the OE fluid. This option is popular with shops that do not

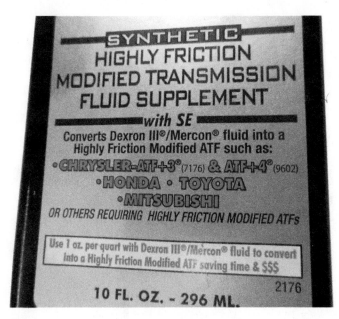

FIGURE 4–4 Aftermarket additives are available that can convert friction-modified ATF into highly friction-modified ATF.

want to stock more than a few types of fluids. A bottle of additive can change the coefficient of the fluid but it cannot make the viscosity of the fluid lower (thinner). If using a top treatment additive, always follow the instructions on the bottle and do not exceed the specified amount. For additional information on top treatments, visit these websites:

http://www.lubegard.com

http://www.lifeautomotive.com/ ● SEE FIGURE 4–4.

HYDRAULIC PRINCIPLES

PASCAL'S LAW DEFINITION Pascal's law, formulated by Blaise Pascal (1623–1662), a French mathematician, states:

"When force is applied to a liquid confined in a container or an enclosure, the pressure is transmitted equally and undiminished in every direction." To help understand this principle, assume that a force of 10 lb is exerted on a piston with a surface area of 1 square inch (sq. in.). Since this force, measured in lb or Newton (N), is applied to a piston with an area measured in square inches (sq. in.), the pressure is the force divided by the area, that is, "10 pounds per square inch (PSI)." It is this "pressure" that is transmitted, without loss, throughout the hydraulic system. ● SEE FIGURE 4–5.

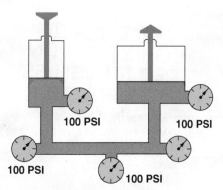

FIGURE 4–5 Fluid pressure is transmitted undiminished in all directions. Note that the pressure is equal throughout the system.

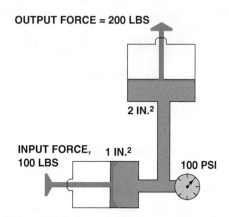

FIGURE 4–6 A 100 lb force applied on an input piston that has an area of 1 sq. in. will produce a fluid pressure of 100 PSI.

PASCAL'S LAW FORMULA

$F = P \times A$ (force is equal to pressure multiplied by area)

$P = F \div A$ (pressure is equal to force divided by area)

$A = F \div P$ (area is equal to force divided by pressure)

where

F = force (lb) or (Newton)

P = pressure in pounds per sq. in. or (kPa)

A = area in sq. in. or (sq.cm)

When fluid pressure or force is computed, use the area of the piston and not its diameter. The area of a piston or any circle can be determined using the following formula

$$A = \pi r^2$$

where

$\pi = 3.1416$

r = one-half the diameter

The pressure in a hydraulic system becomes a force to produce work, and the amount of force can be determined by multiplying the area of the output piston by the system

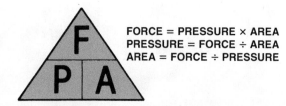

FIGURE 4–7 A simple memory triangle can be used to help remember the commonly used hydraulic formulas.

pressure. A force of 100 pounds pushing on a piston that has an area of two square inches produces a force of 200 Lb. (200 x1) on a piston that has an area of two square inches. ● **SEE FIGURE 4–6**.

Application force is multiplied whenever the output piston is larger than the input piston. Automatic transmissions contain valves that are moved based on which valve has the largest diameter and therefore the greater area. Force will decrease if the input piston is larger than the output piston. A simple memory triangle can be used as an aid to determine area, force, or pressure. ● **SEE FIGURE 4–7**.

PUMPS

PURPOSE AND FUNCTION Every hydraulic system requires a **pump** to maintain fluid flow and to pressurize the fluid in the system. However, the pump itself does not develop pressure but instead pressure occurs when there is a resistance to flow. Initially, fluid flows freely when a hydraulic circuit is empty or partially filled. Once the circuit is completely full, there is a resistance to further flow. At this point, pressure begins to build up in the circuit as the pump continues the fluid flow.

PARTS AND OPERATION The torque converter housing is bolted to the engine flywheel, or flexplate, and rotates whenever the engine is running. The torque converter hub is keyed to the pump tangs located inside the pump housing of the transmission.

Three common types of rotary pumps are used to produce the fluid flow and resulting pressure in an automatic transmission. They include:

1. The **internal–external gear** with *crescent (or gear) pump*

2. The **Gerotor** (rotor) pump

3. The **vane pump**

   ● **SEE FIGURE 4–8**.

The pumping action in each of these pump types is essentially the same. The inner pumping member (external gear or inner

(a)

(b)

PRIMING SPRING

(c)

FIGURE 4–8 (a) Gear-type pump. (b) Gerotor-type pump. (c) Vane-type pump.

rotor) is driven by the torque converter hub or a driveshaft, and the outer pumping member (the internal gear, outer rotor, or vane housing) is offset or eccentric relative to the inner gear or rotor As the inner member rotates, a series of chambers

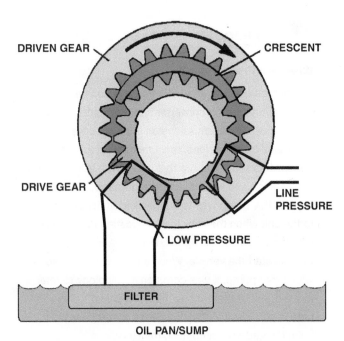

DRIVEN GEAR · CRESCENT · DRIVE GEAR · LINE PRESSURE · LOW PRESSURE · FILTER

OIL PAN/SUMP

FIGURE 4–9 As a pump rotates, a low pressure (vacuum) is created as the pumping members move apart in one area, and atmospheric pressure will force fluid into this area. Pressure is created where the pumping members move together.

(between the gear teeth, the rotor lobes, or vanes) increase in volume in one area and decrease in another. A low-pressure area is created in the void area where the chamber volume increases. This area is connected to a passage leading to the filter that is submerged in fluid near the bottom of the sump. Atmospheric pressure inside the transmission pushes fluid into the filter, through the intake passage, and into the pump inlet. ● **SEE FIGURE 4–9.**

As the pump rotates, fluid fills the chambers just as fast as they enlarge. On the other side of the pump the chambers get smaller and the outlet port of the pump is positioned in this area. Here the fluid is forced out of the pump and into the passage leading to the pressure control valve and the rest of the hydraulic system. The parts in a pump must fit together with very little clearance to prevent the fluid from leaking across the pump from the high-pressure area to areas of lower pressure. The fit provides just enough clearance for the parts to move without excess drag. The pressure-regulated fluid is often called **supply pressure** or **mainline pressure**.

FIXED DISPLACEMENT PUMPS Many automatic transmissions use a fixed-size **positive displacement pump**. Every revolution of the pump will move the same volume of fluid. The faster the pump is turned, the more fluid will be pumped during a given time period. Both the gear pump and the rotor pump are positive displacement pumps.

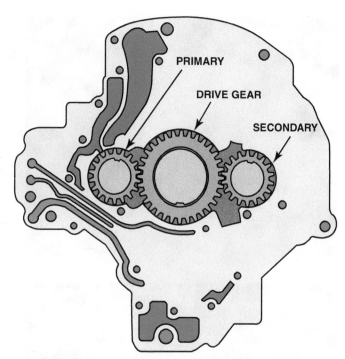

FREQUENTLY ASKED QUESTION

What Is a Front Pump?

The pumps used in automatic transmissions are driven by the torque converter and are located at the front of the transmissions. In the early days of automatic transmissions, manufacturers equipped the transmission with a pump that was driven from the output shaft and was called the rear pump. The purpose of this pump was to supply fluid under pressure to the unit when the vehicle was coasting down a hill with the engine at idle speed. It also made it possible to push start the vehicle. When a unit was equipped with a rear pump, it was common terminology to refer to the pump at the front as the "front pump." This term is still heard today long after the rear pump has been deleted from automatic transmissions.

FIGURE 4–11 A dual-stage, external gear pump. Both stages are used at low engine speeds to produce enough fluid for the transmission's needs. At higher engine speeds, the output of secondary stage is vented.

DUAL-STAGE PUMPS Some transmissions use a dual-stage gear pump, which is a combination of two positive displacement pumps. Both pumps supply fluid when demands are high. The output of the second stage pump is released or vented when the primary stage can supply the needed flow and pressure. This system provides the volume of a large displacement pump at low speeds plus the economy of a small displacement pump at higher, cruising speeds. ●SEE FIGURE 4–11.

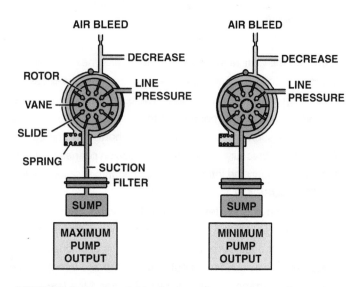

FIGURE 4–10 A variable displacement vane pump in maximum and minimum output positions. The slide is moved to the high output position by a spring. Decreased pressure comes from the pressure regulator valve.

VARIABLE DISPLACEMENT PUMPS **Variable displacement pumps** are also positive displacement in that they will pump a certain volume on each revolution, but the displacement, and therefore the fluid volume, can be changed.

This is done by moving the vane housing to reduce the size of the pumping chambers. ●SEE FIGURE 4–10.

Variable displacement pumps allow a large output to produce the fluid volume needed for shifts and lubrication and a reduced output when it is not needed.

ATF FILTERS

PURPOSE AND FUNCTION A filter is located at the pump inlet to trap dirt, metal, and other foreign particles that might cause wear in the pump, bearings, bushings, and gear train or cause sticking of the various valves.

TYPES OF FILTERS

- A **surface filter** traps the foreign particles at the outer surface. ●SEE FIGURE 4–12.

This filter can be a woven screen of metal or synthetic material such as dacron or polyester. Some sources consider a **paper filter** to be a surface filter. With a metal or synthetic screen, the size of the openings varies from rather large to very fine, in the range of 50 to 100 microns

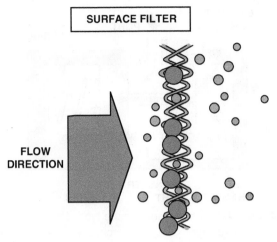

FLOW DIRECTION

FIGURE 4–12 A surface filter traps particles that are too big to pass through the openings in the screen.

OPENING SIZE

SCREEN MATERIAL DIAMETER

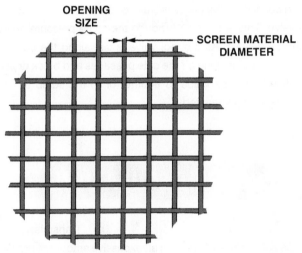

FIGURE 4–13 The surface area of a surface filter is reduced somewhat by the material that makes up the screen. The size of the screen openings determines how small of a particle can be filtered.

(or micrometers). A **micron** is 1 millionth of a meter or 39 millionths of an inch. The symbol for micron is μm. The disadvantage of a surface filter is its limited surface area, which in turn limits its capacity. The mesh openings are the usable area. A large portion of a filter's surface is the fiber or wire that makes up the filter, with the remainder being the openings. ● **SEE FIGURE 4–13**.

■ A **depth filter** traps particles as they try to pass through the filter material. Depth filters are made of felt or a synthetic material of various thickness. The thickness of the material allows room to trap particles as well as room for fluid flow. It also has the ability to trap smaller particles, has more capacity to trap particles, and can function for a longer period of time. ● **SEE FIGURE 4–14**.

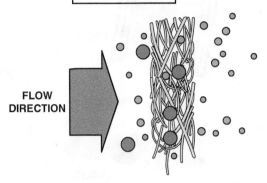

FLOW DIRECTION

FIGURE 4–14 A depth filter is a group of woven fibers of a certain thickness. Foreign particles are trapped at different levels as they try to flow through.

? FREQUENTLY ASKED QUESTION

How Large Are Dirt Particles?

Some depth filters trap particles as small as 10 μm. The space between a bushing and the shaft is about 0.001 to 0.003 inch (0.025 to 0.076 mm), but if the shaft is loaded to one side by gear pressure, this clearance might be only the width of two or three oil molecules. A hard, abrasive particle in this area will produce wear that, in turn, will produce small metal particles that cause more wear. Dirt or other particles that enter the valve body may cause a valve to stick in its bore. This can cause a no-shift problem or a partial shift with low pressure. A recent study of the fluid from eight different transmissions used for less than 3,000 miles (4,800 km) showed the following:

• 1 to 20 particles in the 50-μm size
• 800 to 8,000 particles in the 15-μm size
• More than 50,000 particles in the 5-μm size

CONTROLLING FLUID FLOW

TERMINOLOGY The fluid flow from the pressure regulator valve to the manual valve and into the control circuit is called *mainline, line,* or *control pressure.*

SPOOL VALVES Flow to and from a transmission hydraulic actuator is controlled by one or more valves. Spool valves sliding in a round bore are used to control fluid flow. A **spool valve** gets its name because it looks similar to the spool that holds thread. ● **FIGURE 4–15**.

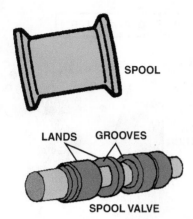

FIGURE 4–15 A spool valve resembles a spool for thread (top).

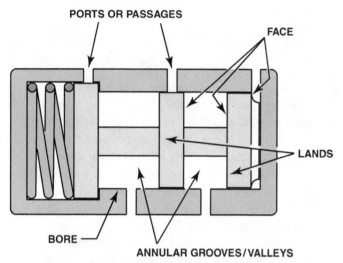

FIGURE 4–16 A spool valve and its bore. Note the names of the various parts.

A spool valve can have two or more **lands** that fit the valve bore tightly enough so that fluid cannot escape past the valve land but also loosely enough so that the valve can slide freely in the bore. ●**SEE FIGURE 4–16**.

The annular grooves (valleys) between the lands are where the fluid flows through the valve. Typically, the valve-to-bore clearance is about 0.003 to 0.004 inch (80 to 100 μm). The close fit requires the valve to expand and contract at the same rate as the valve body. This prevents the valve from sticking or having excessive leakage. The outer edges of the lands have sharp corners to help prevent debris from wedging between the land and the valve bore. The valleys or grooves between the lands serve as fluid passages. The faces serve as pressure surfaces, called *reaction surfaces*, to produce valve movement. Some valves are relatively long with a series of lands and grooves so fluid flow through two or more passages are controlled at the same time. The lands of a spool valve often have different diameters in order to provide different size reaction areas. A

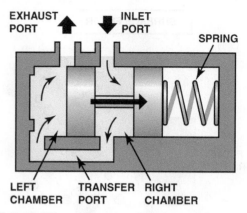

FIGURE 4–17 When pressure on the face of the pressure regulator valve overcomes spring force, the valve moves to open the exhaust port.

spool valve bore has fluid passages entering from the sides, which connect to the grooves (valleys) that extend clear around the valve. This is done to produce the same pressure entirely around the valve. As a spool valve is slid along the bore, the lands open up or close off the side passages and block or allow fluid flow from one place to another or to the sump to allow pressure to be exhausted.

PRESSURE REGULATION

PRESSURE REGULATOR VALVE Transmission oil pumps are capable of creating an excessive amount of pressure quickly and therefore, every transmission uses a **pressure regulator valve**, or *pressure control valve*, to control hydraulic pressure. This is usually a spool valve and spring combination. This regulated pressure, commonly known as *mainline pressure, line,* or *control pressure,* is the working pressure for the entire hydraulic system. Most pressure regulator valves balance pump pressure on one side of the valve against a preset spring force acting on the other side of the valve. When hydraulic pressure is greater than the spring force, the valve moves in its bore far enough to uncover an exhaust port. ●**SEE FIGURE 4–17**.

The exhaust port provides a low-pressure path to the transmission oil pan (sump) where excess ATF is stored. Excess pressurized fluid flowing through this port reduces system pressure. When hydraulic pressure drops below spring pressure, the regulator valve closes the port and pressure begins to build up again. In operation, the opening and closing of the exhaust port occurs many times per second. This sequence of events achieves a steady pressure as the valve balances both

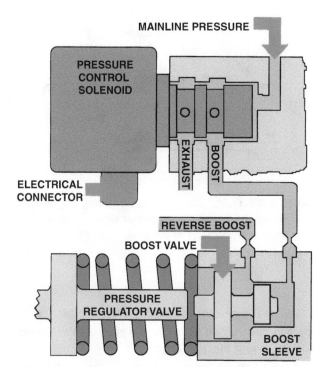

FIGURE 4–18 The pressure control solenoid controls the mainline pressure, which is in turn controlled by the powertrain control module (PCM) or the transmission control module (TCM), by applying pressure to the spring side of the pressure regulator valve.

the spring pressure and the hydraulic pressure. Because of this action, this type of valve is sometimes called a **balance valve**.

ELECTRONIC PRESSURE REGULATION Electronic automatic transmissions/transaxles often regulate hydraulic system pressure using computer-controlled solenoids called by any of the following names:

- **Pressure control solenoids (PCS)**
- **Electronic pressure control (EPC)**
- **Pressure control (PC)**
- **Variable force solenoids (VFS)**
- **Force motors**

An onboard computer switches the solenoids on and off very quickly using pulse-width modulation (PWM). The solenoid pushes against an internal valve which opens and closes the hydraulic circuit it regulates. Electronic pressure control allows precise hydraulic system pressure regulation and can also be used to modify the timing and feel of transmission shifting. ● **SEE FIGURE 4–18.**

TYPICAL PRESSURES Line pressure is controlled by the powertrain control module (PCM) or the transmission control

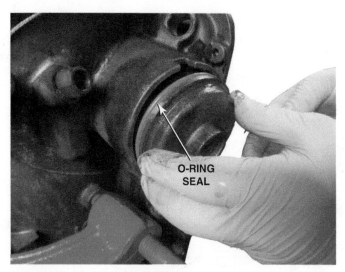

FIGURE 4–19 A new O-ring seal being installed on a cover.

module (TCM) to provide the specific pressure needed by the system based on input from the sensors such as vehicle speed and engine load. Line pressure is reduced to improve fuel economy because lowering pressure reduces draw on the engine that is driving the pump.

Typical line pressures include:

- Normal line pressure—60 to 120 PSI (414 to 830 kPa)
- The accelerator pedal pressed to wide open throttle (WOT)—90 to 150 PSI (620 to 1,034 kPa)
- The gear selector in reverse or manual low (1) —150 to 300 PSI (1,034 to 2,068 kPa)

HYDRAULIC SEALS

TYPES OF SEALS Gaskets and seals are used to keep the pressure from escaping where fluid flows between parts. Seals are of two types:

1. **Static**—A **static seal** is used to seal the space between two parts that are stationary relative to each other. Static seals include gaskets and O rings that are placed between the two parts and squeezed tightly as the parts are fastened together. A static seal must provide enough compression to fill any possible voids between the two surfaces. ● **SEE FIGURE 4–19.**

2. **Dynamic**—A dynamic seal has a more difficult job because one of the surfaces to be sealed is moving relative to the seal. The movement can be rotating, such as when the torque converter enters the front of the transmission or the fluid flows from the pump housing into a clutch

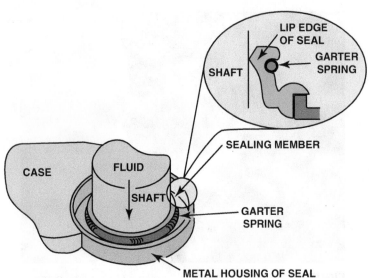

FIGURE 4–20 The sealing member of a metal-clad lip seal makes a dynamic seal with the rotating shaft while the metal case forms a static seal with the transmission case.

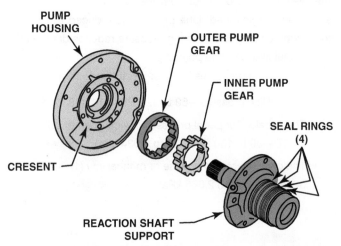

FIGURE 4–21 Sealing rings are used to seal the passages between stationary and rotating members. For example, the seal rings at the right keep the fluid flows from the pump to the front clutch from escaping.

assembly, or sliding. At each end of the transmission, a rotating shaft enters or leaves the transmission, and the opening through which the shaft runs must be sealed to keep the fluid in and the dirt and water out. In both cases, a metal-clad lip seal is used. A lip seal has a flexible rubber sealing lip that rubs against the revolving shaft with enough pressure so fluid cannot flow between the shaft and the seal lip. A garter spring is often used to increase this sealing pressure. ● SEE FIGURE 4–20.

SEALING RINGS   Another type of seal are sealing rings used to seal the fluid passages where fluid leaves a stationary member and transfers to a rotating member. ● SEE FIGURE 4–21.

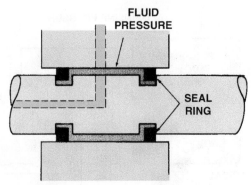

FIGURE 4–22 Fluid pressure forces a sealing ring outward in both directions to make firm contact with the side of the groove and outer diameter of the bore.

This seal is a metal, plastic, or Teflon ring that fits tight in its bore to make a seal while the side seals against the side of its groove. ● SEE FIGURE 4–22.

A seal with a small leak is sometimes desirable to lubricate a bearing area close to the sealing ring. Metal and plastic sealing rings can be a *full-circle, hook ring,* or a *butt-cut ring* with a small gap. Teflon rings can be *scarf cut* (have the ends cut at an angle so they overlap), *butt cut,* or *uncut.* ● SEE FIGURE 4–23.

Teflon seals can change size. When a Teflon ring is stretched over a shaft, it must be resized to fit into the groove and bore. Special installing and resizing tools are recommended when installing Teflon sealing rings. The sliding seals for the clutch and band servo pistons are made of rubber in an O-ring, D-ring, lathe-cut seal, or lip seal shape. An O-ring is a rubber ring with a round cross section. A D-ring is rounded on the sealing side and square on the side where it is retained; the square portion prevents the seal from rotating. A lathe-cut seal, also called a *square-cut seal,* is a rubber ring with a square cross section. ● SEE FIGURE 4–24.

ATF HEATERS AND COOLERS

TEMPERATURES   Transmissions are expected to perform over a wide range of temperatures. Cold fluids are much thicker than hot fluids. On a cold day, the first shifts tend to be sluggish because the fluid moves slowly through the orifices and small openings. The best operating temperature for an automatic transmission is in the range of 170°F to 180°F (77°C to 82°C). This produces good fluid viscosity without excessive

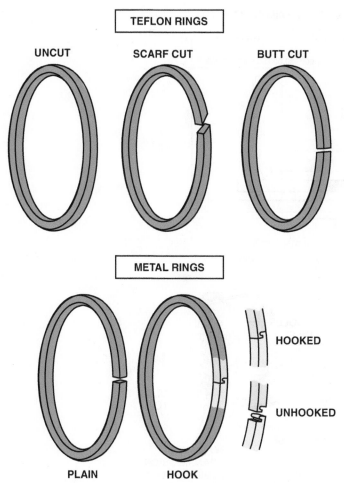

TEFLON RINGS

UNCUT   SCARF CUT   BUTT CUT

METAL RINGS

HOOKED

UNHOOKED

PLAIN   HOOK

FIGURE 4–23 Metal seal rings (bottom) have plain or hooked ends. Teflon rings (top) are either uncut, scarf cut, or butt cut.

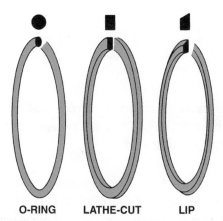

O-RING   LATHE-CUT   LIP

FIGURE 4–24 Clutch and servo piston seals are usually O-rings, lathe-cut rings, or lip seals

fluid degradation. Some transmissions use fluid heaters to improve cold operation. ● **SEE FIGURE 4–25.**

Probably the greatest problem for transmission fluid is heat. Excess heat significantly shortens the life of ATF. Excess temperatures cause the fluid to break down and

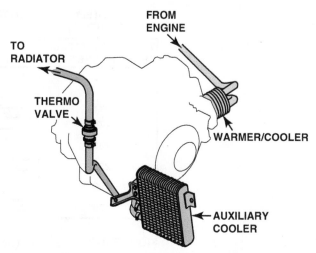

FROM ENGINE

TO RADIATOR

THERMO VALVE

WARMER/COOLER

AUXILIARY COOLER

FIGURE 4–25 Engine coolant from the engine block flows through the passages in the warmer/cooler, and then out through the thermo valve to the upper radiator tank. The thermostatic valve uses a wax element–type valve to control the flow of engine coolant through the case-mounted cooler/warmer. The thermostatic valve improves the ATF warm-up times and maintains ATF temperature within the optimum operating range between 170°F and 180°F (77°C and 82°C).

form gum or varnish. This in turn can cause valve sticking or reduce the fluid flow in certain circuits. All transmissions use a cooler to help remove excess heat. The fluid should be changed more frequently than normal if the vehicle is driven under conditions such as towing that could result in fluid temperatures above 180°F (82°C). Adverse driving conditions that produce higher fluid temperatures are trailer towing, driving on hills, and stop-and-go driving. The torque converter is the primary source of heat in an automatic transmission. For example,

- A temperature of 195°F (90°C) will double the rate of fluid oxidation and cut the fluid life to half or about 50,000 miles (80,000 km).

- A transmission operating at 235°F (113°C) will reduce fluid life to about 25,000 miles (40,000 km).

- The same transmission operating at a temperature of 255°F (124°C) will reduce fluid life to less than 12,000 miles (19,000 km). ● **SEE FIGURE 4–26.**

OIL COOLER CIRCUITS The cooler oil flow begins as soon as the pump begins to rotate. Cooler oil flow then exits the pump and enters the converter. As soon as the supply circuit begins to develop pressure, the regulator valve moves slightly

APPROXIMATELY MILEAGE TO TRANSMISSION FAILURE AT AVERAGE TEMPERATURE

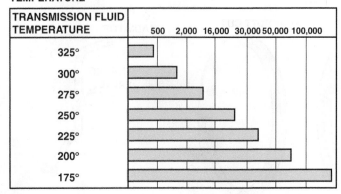

TRANSMISSION FLUID TEMPERATURE	500	2,000	16,000	30,000	50,000	100,000
325°						
300°						
275°						
250°						
225°						
200°						
175°						

FIGURE 4–26 The life of automatic transmission fluid drops drastically when the temperature increases above normal.

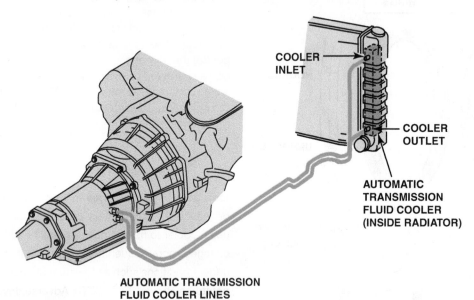

COOLER INLET

COOLER OUTLET

AUTOMATIC TRANSMISSION FLUID COOLER (INSIDE RADIATOR)

AUTOMATIC TRANSMISSION FLUID COOLER LINES

FIGURE 4–27 Automatic transmission fluid is routed from the torque converter, where most of the heat is generated, to the radiator where it is cooled. The fluid then returns to the transmission/transaxle to lubricate the bearings and bushings.

and opens a passage to the torque converter. This fluid flow serves several purposes including the following:

- It ensures that the torque converter is filled so it can transmit engine torque to the transmission input shaft.
- It helps control converter fluid temperature.
- It provides lubrication to the moving parts inside the transmission.

COOLER FLOW The fluid leaving the torque converter is routed out of the transmission case and through a steel line to the *transmission cooler.* The cooler is positioned in the colder (outlet) tank of the radiator. Another steel line is used to return the fluid to the transmission. A cooler is often called a *heat*

exchanger because it moves heat from one location to another. Heat from the transmission fluid is transferred to the engine coolant. ● **SEE FIGURE 4–27.**

AUXILIARY FILTERS The transmission cooler tends to trap foreign particles and can become plugged, especially when the fluid is extremely dirty, contains metal particles, or there is a torque converter clutch mechanical failure. At least one aftermarket manufacturer markets a filter that can be installed in the transmission-to-cooler line. This filter provides added protection by removing foreign particles from the fluid and preventing cooler blockage. Many filters contain a magnet to remove iron particles. If the filter gets plugged, fluid flow will be restricted or blocked completely, which then shuts

What Is a "Turbulator"?

A plain-tube cooler is not very effective for cooling fluid because fluid tends to increase its viscosity and slow down as it cools. The cooler oil then tends to become stationary on the outer, cooler areas of the cooler while the hotter, thinner-viscosity fluid flows through the center. The **turbulator** in well-designed oil coolers continuously mixes the fluid. The ATF in contact with the outer part of the cooler tubes are in contact with the relatively cool coolant in the radiator tank. The screen-like turbulator causes turbulence in the fluid flow to ensure constant mixing and thorough cooling of all the fluid. ● SEE FIGURE 4–28.

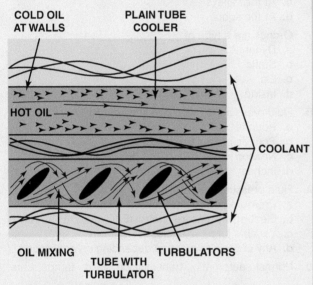

FIGURE 4–28 Cold fluid tends to stick to the walls of a plain tube cooler (top). The turbulator causes fluid turbulence to promote mixing so all of the fluid cools (bottom).

Don't Tow a Vehicle with the Drive Wheels on the Ground

A vehicle with an automatic transmission should not be towed or pushed very far because there will be no lubricating fluid flow when the engine is not running. The gear sets and bushings will run dry, wear, and overheat or burn out without a constant flow of lubricating oil. Most manufacturers recommend towing only when absolutely necessary. They caution that towing should be limited to a few miles with a maximum speed of 20 to 25 mph (32 to 40 km/h). If possible, the drive wheels should be lifted off the ground or the driveshaft removed from a rear-wheel-drive (RWD) vehicle. Special cautions also should be taken when towing an all-wheel-drive (AWD) vehicle.

off transmission lubrication. To prevent this from happening, many supplementary filters include a bypass valve to maintain fluid flow when the filter becomes plugged.

LUBRICATION FLOW In most transmissions, the fluid returning from the torque converter and cooler lubricates the transmission. The fluid from the cooler enters the lubrication passages at the case. It flows through holes drilled in the case to the main shaft bushings, where it passes into holes drilled in the input or output shaft. From there, it flows through the shaft to side holes that align with support bushings, thrust washers, planetary gear sets, clutch drum bushings, and clutch packs. Most transaxle final drive gears and differentials are also lubricated by this circuit.

SUMMARY

1. The hydraulic system applies the band and clutches, transmits force and motion, maintains fluid flow to the torque converter, and provides lubrication and cooling to the moving parts of the transmission.

2. Pumps produce the fluid flow in a transmission and the restriction to the flow results in the system pressure.

3. The mainline pressure is controlled by a variable pressure regulator.

4. Seals are used to confine the fluid to the appropriate passages.

5. Automatic transmission fluid is the lifeblood of an automatic transmission, and only the specified fluid should be used.

1. What are the functions of ATF?
2. What are the three options that a technician or shop can use when selecting the ATF for a vehicle?
3. How does a variable displacement pump work?
5. How does a filter trap particles?
6. Why do some vehicles use a transmission fluid warmer and a cooler?

CHAPTER QUIZ

1. Which fluid is highly friction modified?
   a. Type A
   b. Type F
   c. ATF+4
   d. Dexron

2. What is the color of ATF?
   a. Red
   b. Yellow
   c. Blue
   d. Green

3. Using an additive to convert friction-modified ATF into highly friction-modified ATF is often called _____.
   a. ATF+
   b. Top treatment
   c. Friction treatment
   d. Conversion fluid

4. Which is NOT a type of pump used in automatic transmissions or transaxles?
   a. Gear-type pump
   b. Gerotor-type pump
   c. Vane-type pump
   d. Cupped-wheel type pump

5. The two types of automatic transmission filters are _____ and _____.
   a. Micron and paper
   b. Surface and depth
   c. Paper and cloth
   d. Nylon and rayon

6. Using a spool valve to control fluid flow, where is the fluid blocked?
   a. At the lands
   b. At the grooves
   c. At the valleys
   d. At the spool

7. O-rings are a type of _____ seal.
   a. Dynamic
   b. Static
   c. Lip
   d. Inside

8. Fluid pressure is measured in what unit?
   a. Pounds
   b. Pounds per square inch (PSI)
   c. Newton
   d. Inches

9. Fluid pressure is controlled by _____
   a. Pressure control solenoids (PCS)
   b. Electronic pressure control (EPC)
   c. Variable force solenoids (VFS)
   d. Any of the above terms depending on application

10. Normal automatic transmission fluid temperature is _____.
    a. Between 170°F and 180°F (77°C and 82°C)
    b. 195°F (90°C)
    c. 235°F (113°C)
    d. 255°F (124°C)

chapter 5
TORQUE CONVERTERS

After studying this chapter, the reader will be able to:

1. Prepare for ASE Automatic Transmissions (A2) certification test content area "A" (General Transmission and Transaxle Diagnosis).

2. Identify and describe the components of a torque converter.

3. Explain torque converter operation.

4. Discuss the parts and operation of torque converter clutches.

5. Describe the purpose and procedure of a stall test.

6. Discuss the service of torque converters.

Coupling phase 89

Creep 89

Damper assembly 90

Flexplate 86

Impeller 86

Rotary flow 88

Stall speed 89

Stator 87

Torque converter clutch (TCC) 89

Torsional vibrations 90

Turbine 86

Vortex flow 88

FIGURE 5–1 A cutaway of a Chrysler PowerFlite two-speed automatic transmission used in the 1950s showing the large torque converter and a front and rear pump.

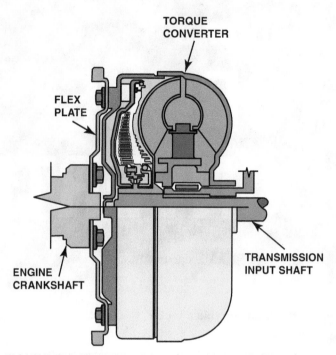

FIGURE 5–2 The torque converter bolts to the flexplate which is attached to the engine crankshaft and rotates at engine speed.

TORQUE CONVERTER TERMINOLOGY

PURPOSE AND FUNCTION The torque converter is located between the engine and the transmission/transaxle and performs the following functions.

1. Transmits and multiplies engine torque

2. Acts as a clutch between the engine and the transmission/transaxle

3. Allows slippage, which makes it possible for the transmission to be engaged even when the vehicle and wheels are stopped. ● **SEE FIGURE 5–1.**

LOCATION The torque converter is bolted to a thin metal disc called a **flexplate**. The center of the flexplate often has a pilot indentation for the nose of the converter, and the flexplate itself is bolted to the rear flange of the engine crankshaft.

The flexplate replaces the heavy flywheel used with a manual transmission. An important function of a flywheel is to smooth out engine pulsations and dampen vibrations. An automatic transmission does not require a conventional flywheel because the weight of the torque converter provides enough mass to dampen engine vibrations. An external ring gear generally attaches to the outer rim of the flexplate, while on some applications the ring gear may be welded to the outside of the torque converter cover. This ring gear engages the starter motor pinion gear to turn the engine during starting. ● **SEE FIGURE 5–2.**

ELEMENTS The three major parts of the torque converter are

▪ **Impeller.** The impeller is the driving member and rotates with the engine, and is located on the transmission side of the converter. When the engine is running, the flexplate and converter rotate with the crankshaft. The flexplate is flexible enough to allow the front of the converter to move forward or backward if the converter expands or contracts slightly from heat or pressure. The impeller inside the torque converter is also called the pump (not to be confused with the pump used to supply fluid under pressure to the entire transmission/transaxle). The impeller is the input to the converter. The vanes/fins inside the converter are attached to the rear of the impeller, transmission end, of the converter housing or cover. ● **SEE FIGURE 5–3.**

▪ **Turbine.** The turbine is located on the engine side of the converter. The impeller vanes pick up fluid in the converter housing and direct it toward the turbine. Fluid flow drives the turbine, and when the flow between the impeller and the turbine is adequate, the turbine rotates and turns the transmission input shaft. The turbine is the converter's output member. The center hub of the turbine is splined to the transmission input shaft. The turbine is positioned in the front, engine end, of the converter housing so the turbine vanes face the impeller vanes. ● **SEE FIGURE 5–4.**

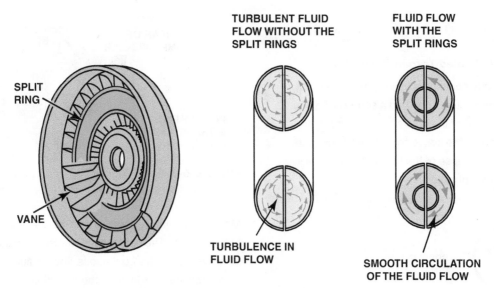

TURBULENT FLUID FLOW WITHOUT THE SPLIT RINGS

FLUID FLOW WITH THE SPLIT RINGS

SPLIT RING

VANE

TURBULENCE IN FLUID FLOW

SMOOTH CIRCULATION OF THE FLUID FLOW

FIGURE 5–3 The split rings in the impeller and turbine help to direct the flow of fluid and improve the efficiency of the torque converter by reducing turbulence.

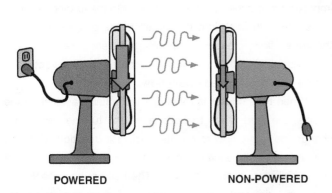

POWERED   NON-POWERED

FIGURE 5–4 Two fans can be used to show how fluid, or air in the case of fans instead of automatic transmission fluid, can be used to transfer energy. If one fan is operating, which represents the impeller, and the blades of a second fan (turbine) will be rotated by the flow of air past the fan that is unplugged, causing the blades to rotate.

- **Stator.** A torque converter also contains the stator, or reactor, which is mounted on a one-way clutch. The stator is the reaction member of the torque converter. The stator assembly is about one-half the diameter of the impeller or turbine. The outer edge of the stator vanes forms the inner edge of the three-piece fluid guide ring that is also part of the impeller and turbine vanes. The stator is mounted on a one-way clutch that is attached to the stationary reaction shaft splines. The reaction shaft is made as part of the transmission front pump housing and is fixed and does not rotate. The one-way clutch allows the stator to rotate clockwise but blocks counterclockwise rotation. ●**SEE FIGURE 5–5**.

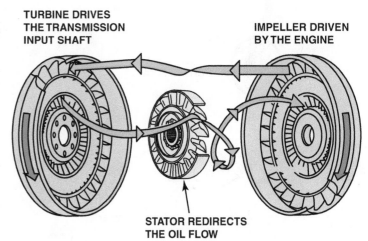

TURBINE DRIVES THE TRANSMISSION INPUT SHAFT

IMPELLER DRIVEN BY THE ENGINE

STATOR REDIRECTS THE OIL FLOW

FIGURE 5–5 A torque converter is made from three parts: The impeller is located at the transmission end, attached to the housing, and is driven by the engine. The turbine is located at the engine side and is driven by the fluid flow from the impeller and drives the input shaft of the transmission. The stator redirects the flow to improve efficiency and multiply torque.

TORQUE CONVERTER OPERATION

TORQUE TRANSFER A torque converter is a *hydrodynamic* unit because it transfers power through the dynamic motion of the fluid. Most other hydraulic units transfer power through the static pressure of the fluid. When the engine is running, the converter impeller acts as a centrifugal pump. Fluid is thrown from the outer edge of the impeller vanes, and because of the curved shape of the converter cover, the fluid is thrown

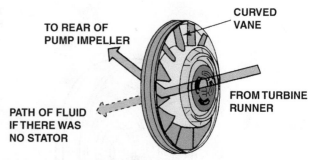

FIGURE 5–7 The fluid flow from the turbine is turned in the same direction as the impeller by the stator vanes.

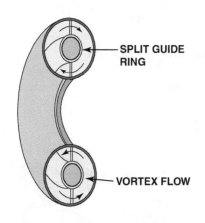

(a)

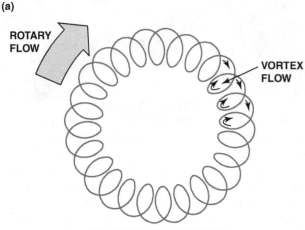

(b)

FIGURE 5–6 (a) The fluid flowing around the guide ring is called vortex flow. (b) The fluid flow around the converter is called rotary flow.

forward into the turbine. The impeller is turning in a clockwise direction, and the fluid also rotates in a clockwise direction as it leaves the impeller vanes. The mechanical power entering the converter is transformed in the fluid as fluid motion.

VORTEX FLOW The rotating fluid in the impeller tries to turn the turbine in a clockwise direction. If the turbine is stationary or turning at a speed substantially slower than the impeller, only part of the energy leaves the fluid to drive the turbine.

Most of the fluid energy is lost as the fluid bounces off the turbine vanes. The fluid moves toward the center of the turbine, driven there by the continuous flow of fluid from the impeller. As energy leaves the fluid, the flow slows down and returns to the center of the impeller vanes, where the impeller will pick it up and keep it circulating. This flow is called a **vortex flow**. The vortex flow is a continuous circulation of fluid outward from the impeller, around the guide ring, inward into the turbine, through the stator, and back into the impeller. The guide ring directs the vortex flow, creating a smooth, turbulence-free flow. The clockwise flow of fluid leaving the impeller, in the direction of engine rotation, is called **rotary flow**.

When the impeller is rotating substantially faster than the turbine, the fluid tends to bounce off the turbine vanes and change the rotary flow to counterclockwise direction. The fluid flow still has quite a bit of energy. It can be compared with a tennis ball thrown against a wall. The ball bounces back and travels in a different direction, but it still has most of its energy of motion. A strong counterclockwise fluid flow from the turbine would tend to work against the clockwise rotation of the impeller. ●**SEE FIGURE 5–6.**

TORQUE MULTIPLICATION The stator redirects the fluid flow in the torque converter. It returns the fluid from the turbine back to the impeller in a clockwise direction. This action helps recover any energy remaining in the fluid. The curved shape of the stator vanes and a one-way clutch make this possible. Fluid leaving the turbine in a counterclockwise direction tries to turn the stator counterclockwise. This causes the stator one-way clutch to lock up and hold the stator stationary. The smooth, curved shape of the stator vanes redirects the fluid flow in a clockwise direction. ●**SEE FIGURE 5–7.**

Torque multiplication occurs because the stator redirects the fluid flow. This occurs only when the impeller is rotating faster than the turbine. As the turbine speed increases, the direction of flow becomes more rotary. The stator clutch overruns and the converter becomes more of a coupling, transferring power from the engine to the transmission. ●**SEE FIGURE 5–8.**

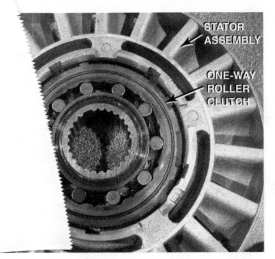

FIGURE 5–8 A stator contains a one-way roller clutch which locks it from rotating in one direction and allows it to rotate freely in the opposite direction.

An engineering term used for torque converters is the *stall torque ratio (STR),* which is the torque converter's ability to multiply torque. Most passenger vehicle torque converters have a STR between 1.68:1 and 2.1:1. For most converters, this means that the torque converter is able to double the torque of the engine at the stall speed of the converter.

COUPLING PHASE When the turbine speed reaches 90% to 95% of impeller speed, *coupling* occurs. The **coupling phase** occurs when the speeds of the impeller and turbine are nearly equal. Centrifugal force acting on the fluid in the spinning turbine is high enough to stop the vortex flow. At this point, there is no torque multiplication. It should be noted that this coupling speed is a relative point between the speeds of the impeller and turbine. Therefore, the coupling phase occurs at various vehicle speeds depending on throttle position and speed.

Some slippage occurs during the coupling phase. If power and load demands require, the converter can return to the torque multiplication phase. In a nonlock-up converter, the turbine almost never turns at the same speed as the engine and impeller, a condition commonly referred to as *converter slippage.* The converter's efficiency steadily improves during torque multiplication and the coupling phases to about 90% to 95%.

STALL SPEED **Stall speed** is the fastest RPM that an engine can reach while the turbine is held stationary. Stall is when the turbine is held stationary while the converter housing and impeller are spinning. This is done by shifting the transmission into gear and applying the brakes to hold the drive wheels stationary. The importance of stall speed is that an engine must be able to reach an RPM where enough torque is available to accelerate the vehicle, but not running so fast that

there is poor fuel economy and excessive noise. Stall occurs to some degree each time a vehicle starts moving, either forward or backward, and each time a vehicle stops at a stop sign.

CREEP When the transmission selector is moved from park (P) or neutral (N) into a drive gear, some engine torque is transferred to the input shaft of the transmission or transaxle. The vehicle will move slightly if the brakes are released. This slight movement of the vehicle when the engine is at idle speed and the brakes are released is called **creep**. Therefore, a slight movement is normal for a vehicle equipped with an automatic transmission.

NOTE: Vehicle creep is more noticeable when the engine is cold due to the higher idle speed.

TORQUE CONVERTER CLUTCHES

PURPOSE AND FUNCTION The **torque converter clutch (TCC)** is applied to eliminate the slippage during the coupling phase, which improves fuel economy. When the TCC applies, the converter locks up, connecting the transmission

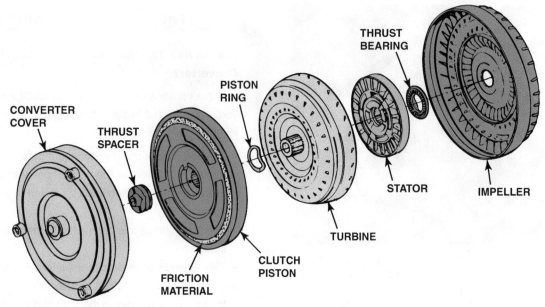

FIGURE 5–9 An expanded view of a typical torque converter assembly showing the torque converter clutch (TCC).

input shaft directly to the engine, much like a vehicle with a manual transmission and clutch.

PARTS AND OPERATION   The converter clutch is a large clutch disc called a *pressure plate* or *clutch disc*. It has friction material and a damper assembly attached to it and it is splined to the turbine. When the friction material is forced against the torque converter cover, the turbine is driven mechanically by the engine. ● **SEE FIGURE 5–9**.

The torque converter clutch is controlled by a solenoid which is controlled by the powertrain control module (PCM) or the transmission control module (TCM). The TCC is applied and released when the fluid entering the converter changes from the rear or front.

- Normal torque converter action occurs when the TCC is released, and the fluid flows from the front to the rear, past the clutch plate.

- TCC lockup occurs when the fluid enters the rear of the torque converter and forces the clutch plate against the front cover.

- TCC apply forces the fluid in front of the clutch outward, and this fluid acts like an accumulator to soften clutch application.

- When fluid is flowing into the back (turbine) side of the torque converter, pressure is applied to the back side of the clutch piston, which forces it to come in contact with the torque converter cover. This locks the turbine to the cover and all the elements of the torque converter rotate as one unit.

- In order to release the TCC, the flow of fluid in the torque converter housing is reversed. This causes the clutch piston to move away from the torque converter cover and the turbine is thus released. ● **SEE FIGURE 5–10**.

TCC fluid flow is controlled by a TCC control valve that is in turn controlled by a solenoid. TCC apply blocks the flow of fluid through the torque converter and cooler. The torque converter does not generate heat when TCC is applied, but some heat is generated by the rest of the transmission. Some fluid will be directed past the TCC control valve to provide cool fluid for transmission lubrication.

FRICTION MATERIALS USED   Most TCCs use paper friction material. It can be secured to the front of the clutch disc, to the inside of the converter cover, or left free between the two. Some vehicles use a modulated or pulsed TCC apply pressure to smooth out TCC apply. This produces a lot of slipping that can burn out paper clutch lining fairly rapidly. These converters use synthetic materials for greater endurance under more severe operating conditions. ● **SEE FIGURE 5–11**.

TCC DAMPER ASSEMBLY   Clutch discs include a **damper assembly** that transfers the power through a group of coil springs. In most converters, the damper springs are grouped at the center; in others they are grouped around the outer edge. These springs are used to dampen **torsional vibrations** from the engine. All automotive engines produce torsional vibration at some operating speed. Torsional vibrations are small speed increases and slowdowns as the crankshaft revolves between engine cylinder firing pulses.

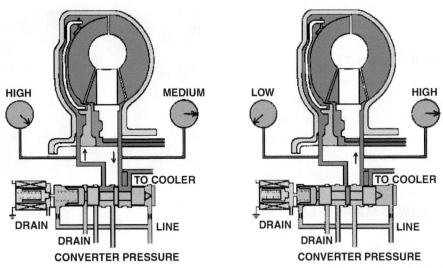

HIGH MEDIUM LOW HIGH

TO COOLER TO COOLER

DRAIN LINE DRAIN LINE
DRAIN DRAIN
CONVERTER PRESSURE CONVERTER PRESSURE

FIGURE 5–10 TCC releases fluid flows through the center of the turbine shaft to the front of the clutch disc (left). Pressure to apply the clutch enters between the converter hub and the stator support (right).

PAPER

KEVLAR®

CARBON FIBER

FIGURE 5–11 Torque converter clutch friction material is determined by the vehicle manufacturer to provide the needed coefficient of friction needed. For example, many older units use a paper-type friction material because they are fully applied or released, whereas most newer units use a synthetic material such as Kevlar ® or carbon fiber because the torque converter clutch is pulsed on and off, therefore requiring a more robust material for long service life.

These vibrations can produce gear noise in the transmission and drivetrain as well as a noticeable vibration and harshness in the vehicle. ● **SEE FIGURE 5–12**.

STALL TEST

PURPOSE OF THE TEST A stall test is used to check the stator one-way clutch inside the torque converter and the strength of the apply devices inside the transmission/transaxle. A stall test measures stall speed of the torque converter in

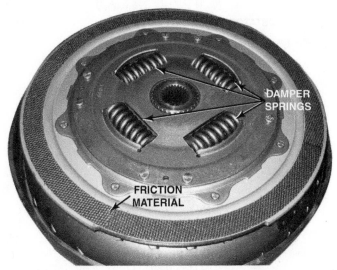

DAMPER SPRINGS

FRICTION MATERIAL

FIGURE 5–12 The damper springs used in many torque converter clutches are similar to the damper springs used in clutch discs used with a manual transmission.

each of the gear positions. It is an important diagnostic test to determine transmission and torque converter condition. This test should be performed with caution because it operates the vehicle in a potentially dangerous situation: The vehicle is in gear with the throttle wide open. It is recommended that both the parking brake and the service brake be firmly applied, the wheels blocked, and the throttle be held open for a maximum of 5 seconds.

A stall test can severely damage the transmission if done incorrectly. During a stall test, the dynamic fluid pressure inside a converter becomes very high, because there is a lot of turbulence. Fluid temperature also becomes very high. All of the power the engine is producing is going into the converter, and no mechanical power is being delivered to the transmission. The

FIGURE 5–14 This 4-cylinder General Motors vehicle has a stall speed of about 2350 RPM. Notice that the gear selector is in drive and the speedometer is reading zero.

STALL TEST PROCEDURE To conduct a stall test, perform the following steps:

STEP 1 Connect a scan tool to monitor engine speed (RPM).

STEP 2 Position the vehicle with all four wheels firm on the ground and place blocks at the front and back of the drive wheels.

STEP 3 Start the engine and note the RPM reading. ● **SEE FIGURE 5–14**.

STEP 4 Apply the brakes firmly, move the gear selector to reverse, move the throttle to wide open, and watch the tachometer. The speed should increase to somewhere between 1500 and 3000 RPM. As soon as the speed stops increasing or goes higher than 3500 RPM, quickly note the reading and close the throttle. Record the speed.

STEP 5 Shift to neutral, and run the engine at fast idle for 30 to 60 seconds to cool the converter.

STEP 6 Repeat steps 4 and 5 with the gear selector in drive.

STEP 7 Repeat steps 4 and 5 with the gear selector in low.

CAUTION: Direct any bystanders away from the front or rear of the vehicle.

INTERPRETING STALL TEST READINGS

- **If all of the stall speeds were within the specification range.** The apply devices for the three gear ranges are all sound and in good shape. The apply devices for some gear(s) cannot be applied with the vehicle at rest so they cannot be stall tested.

- **If all of the stall speeds were equal but low.** The engine is weak, out of tune, or the stator one-way clutch is slipping. Checking engine performance should indicate which is at fault.

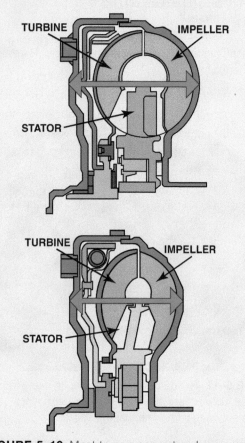
natural law of energy conservation states that energy can neither be created nor destroyed. The energy going into the converter must go somewhere and it is converted to heat. Because so much heat is generated, stall tests should not be conducted for more than 5 seconds, followed by a cooling period.

CAUTION: Exercise caution when performing a stall test for several reasons: personal safety, and the chance of possible damage to the vehicle and transmission.

What Is a High-Stall Speed Converter?

A high stall speed converter is called a *loose converter*. A low stall speed converter is called a *tight converter*. When a vehicle is standing still, the turbine is not rotating. As the vehicle accelerates, the engine RPM increases quickly to the torque capacity of the converter (stall speed) and then it stabilizes. As the turbine speed increases, the engine speed also increases. A loose converter allows a higher engine RPM relative to the turbine RPM.

The actual stall speed of a torque converter is determined by the following factors.

- Amount of engine torque
- Diameter of the converter
- Angle of the impeller vanes
- Angle of the stator vanes

A high-torque engine has the ability to turn the impeller faster against a stalled turbine than a small or weak engine. A low-torque engine is normally equipped with a looser converter.

- If the converter is too tight, the engine RPM cannot increase to the point of usable power and the vehicle would lose acceleration and overall performance.
- A converter that is too loose will cause the engine to operate at excessive speed. The result will be poor fuel economy, excessive noise, and reduced performance because of the excessive slippage.

In production, the torque converter capacity/stall speed is matched to the engine size and vehicle weight to produce the best vehicle performance and fuel economy. Depending on the engine, different converters are used with a transmission model. One manufacturer uses eight different converters with one transmission model. The technician must ensure that the correct replacement converter is used.

- **If the stall speeds are normal, but the vehicle has normal acceleration and has reduced performance at higher speeds.** The stator one-way clutch could be seized in a locked-up condition.
- **If the stall speed is high in one or two of the gear ranges.** One or more of the apply devices is slipping. Consult a clutch and band application chart to determine which apply devices are at fault.

TORQUE CONVERTER SERVICE

REPLACEMENT A torque converter is considered to be part of the transmission and should be serviced or replaced when a transmission is overhauled. A torque converter is always replaced with a new or rebuilt unit if it has an internal failure. Most shops do not rebuild torque converters. There are companies that specialize in torque converter overhaul.

Torque converters tend to collect the metal, dirt, and other debris that enter with the fluid. It is impossible to thoroughly check a torque converter without cutting it open. The internal shape and the centrifugal force inside a torque converter can pack dirt and debris around the outer diameter. Foreign material can also lodge in the clutch lining of a lock-up torque converter. Some shops flush and check the torque converter during every transmission overhaul. Other shops install a rebuilt torque converter as standard practice. High-mileage transmissions, ones that show a lot of metal wear, and units with lock-up torque converters are candidates for replacement.

TORQUE CONVERTER CHECKS The torque converter should be checked to make sure it is in usable condition when the transmission is removed. These checks include:

1. **Visual inspection.** It includes the following steps:
   - Check the outer side (especially at the welds) for wetness, which might indicate a leak.
   - Check the mounting drive studs or threaded holes and lugs for physical damage.
   - Check the pilot area for damage.
   - Check the hub for signs of seal or bushing area wear.
   - Check the pump drive tangs or lugs for wear or damage. ● SEE FIGURE 5–15.
   - Check the starter ring gear, if used, for wear or damage.

2. **Stator one-way clutch operation.** It includes the following steps:
   - Place the converter flat on a bench.
   - Reach into the hub so one finger contacts the splines. ● SEE FIGURE 5–16.
   - Rotate the splines in a clockwise direction. If they rotate, the clutch is probably locked.
   - Try to rotate the splines counterclockwise. If they rotate, the clutch is slipping.

FIGURE 5–15 Visually check the pump drive notches or tangs for damage and the hub sealing surface for wear.

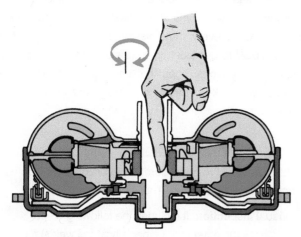

FIGURE 5–16 A stator clutch can be checked by reaching into the hub so a finger contacts the splines. The splines should rotate in one direction but not in the other.

NOTE: A commercial stator-holding tool may be used to check a one-way clutch. This tool can be inserted into a groove in the thrust washer on some stators to keep it and the stator from rotating. Next, a special one-way clutch-tool is inserted into the stator splines, and a torque wrench is used to apply torque to the tool and one-way clutch inner race. The one-way clutch should turn freely in a clockwise direction, and it should lock and hold at least 10 foot pound (14 N-m) of torque in a counterclockwise direction. Do not apply any more torque than this because the special tool can break. A torque converter with a faulty one-way clutch must be replaced.

3. **Turbine end play.** End play is normally measured using a dial indicator. Two styles of dial indicator fixtures are commonly used to measure end play.

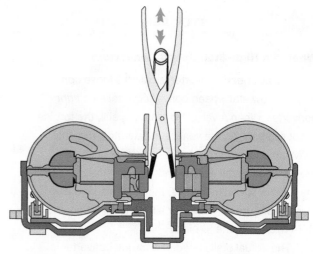

FIGURE 5–17 A quick end-play check can be made by gripping the turbine or stator splines and trying to move the turbine or stator in and out.

- One fixture uses an expandable stem that fits into the turbine splines and is expanded to lock into the splines. The dial indicator is positioned and adjusted so the measuring stylus is against the fixture and the dial reads zero. The fixture and turbine are lifted as far as they will go. The travel (end play) is read on the dial indicator.
- Another fixture for checking end play is designed so the torque converter sits on top of it. The measuring stem is moved upward to contact the turbine splines, and the dial indicator is adjusted to zero. Then the turbine is lifted as far as possible. The end play is read on the dial indicator.

The end-play can be felt as the turbine or stator is lifted and then lowered. Some manufacturers publish torque converter end-play specifications. If no specifications are available, use the rule of thumb that 0.030 inch (0.8 mm) is normal and 0.050 inch (1.3 mm) is the maximum allowable end play. A torque converter with excess end play (more than 0.050 inch) should be rebuilt or replaced. ● **SEE FIGURE 5–17**.

4. **Internal interference.** Torque converter interference should be checked twice, first with the turbine and stator toward the front and a second time with these toward the rear. To check a converter for internal interference, perform the following steps:
   - Set the torque converter on a bench with the hub up. Gravity will move the turbine and stator toward the front of the torque converter.
   - Insert the transmission pump stator support into the torque converter so the support splines engage the stator clutch splines.

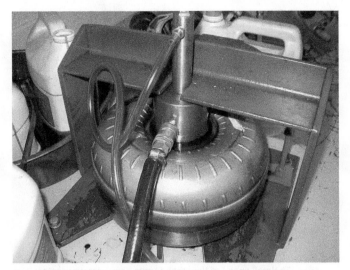

FIGURE 5–18 A leak-test fixture has been placed on the torque converter. It will be filled with ATF and then inspected for leaks.

- Insert the transmission input shaft into the torque converter so its splines enter the turbine splines.
- Rotate the pump and input shaft in both clockwise and counterclockwise directions, one at a time and together. If there is any sign of contact or rubbing, either a rubbing or grating sound or rough feel, the torque converter needs to be replaced.
- Turn the whole assembly over so the turbine and stator move toward the rear of the torque converter.
- Repeat step 4. Again, any sign of internal contact indicates a torque converter that should be rebuilt or replaced.

5. **Lock-up clutch operation.** Two styles of testers are available for checking torque converter clutches.
   - One type uses adapters that replace the turbine shaft and allow a vacuum to be exerted on the front side of the clutch plate assembly. If this chamber can hold a vacuum, the center seal and the clutch lining (which forms the outer seal) are good.
   - The second tester style uses adapters that attach to the turbine, which uses air pressure to apply the clutch. With the clutch applied, torque is exerted to try to turn the turbine. A good torque converter clutch locks the turbine and prevents it from turning.

6. **External leakage.** The torque converter must be pressurized to test for a leak. A special tool with an expandable plug that fits into the hub and a device to keep the plug in place is used. The plug is equipped with an air chuck to allow pressure to be added. ● **SEE FIGURE 5–18**.

A torque converter that passes inspection is reusable. One that fails one or more of the checks should be replaced with

 REAL WORLD FIX

The Case of the Blue Torque Converter

A 2005 Acura (85,000 mi) runs good in park and neutral, but the engine dies as soon as it is shifted into gear. Tests reveal no problems outside of the transmission.

When the transmission was removed, the torque converter was found to be blue from overheating and seized up internally. It had also sent metal particles throughout the transmission. The root cause of the problem was never discovered but rebuilding the transmission along with a replacement torque converter fixed this transmission.

 **TECH TIP**

Converter Drain-Back Test

If the fluid leaves the torque converter when the engine is off, the vehicle will not move when the engine is restarted until the torque converter is refilled by the pump, which causes a delay. If torque converter drain back is suspected, operate the vehicle until it is at normal operating temperature, and drive the vehicle through several full-shift cycles. Check and adjust the fluid level if it is low, and shut off the engine. Allow the vehicle to sit for 30 to 60 minutes, then recheck the fluid level and mark it on the dipstick. Allow the vehicle to sit for 24 hours and then recheck the fluid level. If the level has risen by 1 inch (25 mm) or more, converter drain back has occurred. This means that the sealing rings around the torque converter are not able to seal properly and this means that the transmission or transaxle has to be removed to correct this condition.

a new or rebuilt unit. A torque converter that has turned blue from overheating has failed internally and should be replaced.

NOTE: All torque converters are balanced but a service technician is not able to verify that it is balanced. To avoid possible balance issues, purchase torque converters from a known company that checks the balance of all converters before they are packaged and sent out for sale.

INSTALLING A HIGHER STALL SPEED TORQUE CONVERTER

1 A restored 1971 Chevrolet Camaro has an aftermarket high-lift camshaft and does not idle correctly in drive with the stock torque converter.

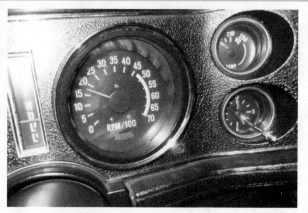

2 The stall speed of the stock torque converter was tested at 1850 RPM, which is normal for a stock engine but not for an engine equipped with a high-performance camshaft.

3 The inspection cover is removed.

4 The torque converter retaining bolts are removed requiring the engine be rotated using a flywheel turning tool.

5 The speedometer cable was removed.

6 The vacuum hose to the modulator valve was removed.

7 The cooling lines and the dip stick tube are removed.

8 After removing the driveshaft, the cross member was unbolted and removed after supporting the transmission using a transmission jack.

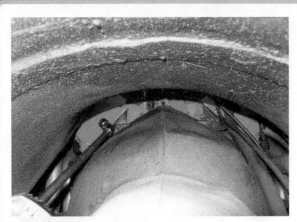

9 The bell housing bolts were removed using a long extension and a swivel socket.

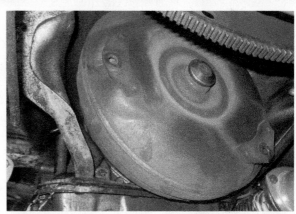

10 The transmission is removed from the engine with the torque converter still in place.

11 The flexplate was inspected for cracks or worn ring gear teeth and found to be normal.

12 The torque converter was removed and the front seal was found to be leaking. All seals were replaced on this transmission before it was returned to the customer.

CONTINUED ▶

13 The new replacement higher stall speed converter is on the left, which is noticeably smaller in diameter than the stock converter.

14 The new torque converter is filled with ATF before being installed.

15 The torque converter is wiggled back and forth to ensure that all of the splines are engaged.

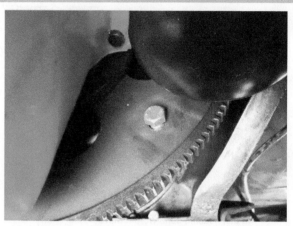

16 The holes in the flexplate were enlarged so that the new larger torque converter bolts would fit.

17 The transmission was installed and all parts reconnected, then the transmission was filled to the proper level with the specified ATF.

18 The stall speed was retested and the new converter is at 2350 RPM, which worked perfectly well for this engine. The customer was very happy with the results.

1. The torque converter is located between the engine and the transmission/transaxle and performs the following functions:
   a. Transmits and multiplies engine torque
   b. Acts as a clutch between the engine and the transmission/transaxle
   c. Allows slippage, which makes it possible for the transmission to be engaged in gear even when the vehicle and wheels are stopped.
2. The three major parts of the torque converter are the turbine, impeller, and stator.
3. A torque converter is a hydrodynamic unit because it transfers power through the dynamic motion of the fluid.
4. The flow of fluid inside a torque converter is both rotary and vortex flow.

5. When the turbine speed reaches 90% to 95% of impeller speed, coupling occurs.
6. Stall speed is the fastest RPM that an engine can reach while the turbine is held stationary.
7. The torque converter clutch is applied to eliminate slippage, thereby improving fuel economy.
8. A stall test is used to check the stator one-way clutch and the strength of the apply devices inside the transmission/transaxle.
9. A torque converter is considered to be part of the transmission and should be serviced or replaced when a transmission is overhauled.

REVIEW QUESTIONS

1. What are the three elements inside a torque converter?
2. What is the difference between rotary flow and vortex flow?
3. What is the purpose and function of a torque converter?
4. How much torque is a torque converter able to multiply?
5. What precautions are needed to be adhered to when performing a stall test?

CHAPTER QUIZ

1. The parts of a torque converter include _____.
   a. Flexplate, housing, and turbine
   b. Turbine, impeller, and stator
   c. Impeller, flexplate, and housing
   d. Stator, turbine, and housing
2. When the impeller and turbine are rotating at about the same speed, this is called _____.
   a. Coupling
   b. Stall speed
   c. Torque multiplication
   d. Vortex flow
3. Creep is _____.
   a. Normal operation
   b. Caused by slippage inside the torque converter
   c. Causes the vehicle to move slightly when the engine is at idle speed and the transmission is in drive gear.
   d. All of the above

4. A stall test is used to check the _____.
   a. Stator
   b. Impeller
   c. Turbine
   d. Torque converter clutch
5. A modified engine may need a torque converter that is _____.
   a. Looser
   b. Smaller in diameter
   c. Has a higher stall speed
   d. All of the above
6. The torque converter clutch circuit is controlled by the _____.
   a. Driver
   b. Fluid temperature
   c. Command from the PCM/TCM
   d. Fluid pressure

7. A torque converter should be checked by a technician for all of the following *except* _____.
   a. Leaks
   b. Proper balance
   c. Stator one-way clutch operation
   d. Turbine end play

8. If the stall speed is lower than specified, what could be the cause?
   a. Incorrect ATF was used in the automatic transmission/transaxle
   b. A slipping stator clutch
   c. Defective turbine
   d. Slipping torque converter clutch

9. A torque converter can multiply engine torque at the stall speed by about _____.
   a. Double
   b. Three times
   c. 10 times
   d. 100 times

10. A vehicle creeps faster than normal when the engine is cold. What is the most likely cause?
    a. Normal operation
    b. A TCC stuck in the applied position
    c. A defective stator one-way clutch
    d. Incorrect ATF

After studying this chapter, the reader will be able to:

1. Prepare for ASE Automatic Transmissions (A2) certification test content area "A" (General Transmission and Transaxle Diagnosis).
2. Explain how power can be transferred through planetary gear sets to produce the various ratios.
3. Discuss the Simpson gear set and identify the different types of Simpson gear trains.
4. Discuss the Ravigneaux gear set.
5. Explain the operation of the LePelletier gear train.

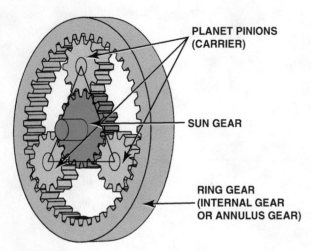

FIGURE 6–1 A typical planetary gear set showing the terms that are used to describe each member.

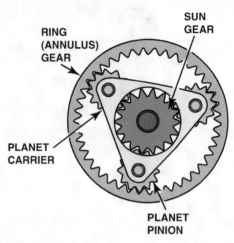

FIGURE 6–2 A typical planetary gear set showing the planet carrier which supports all of the pinion gears (also called planet pinion gears).

PLANETARY GEAR SETS

RATIOS Planetary gear sets are able to provide the following conditions:

- neutral
- one or more gear reductions
- direct-drive ratio (1:1)
- reverse
- overdrive

The exact ratio for reduction and overdrive are achieved by varying the number of teeth on the sun and ring gears.

SIMPLE PLANETARY GEAR SET A simple planetary gear set consists of three primary components.

- Sun gear
- Planet carrier (including planet pinion gears)
- Ring (annulus) gear

The **sun gear** gets its name from its position at the center of the gear set. The **planet carrier** holds the pinion gears, also known as planet gears, which revolve around the sun gear. The planet carrier assembly is commonly referred to simply as "the carrier." The outermost member of the gear set is the **ring gear**, an internal gear with teeth on the inside. The ring gear is sometimes called an annulus or internal gear. The pinion gears are in constant mesh with both the sun gear and the ring gear. ● **SEE FIGURE 6–1**.

The pinion gears are free to rotate on pins that are part of the carrier, and the entire assembly rotates to direct torque flow. Most transmission gear sets use three, four, or even five planet pinions. The pinions are fully meshed with both the sun gear and internal ring gear *at all times.*

The planetary gears never disengage to change gear ratios but torque is redirected. Both input and output torque flow through a planetary gear set occurs along a single axis.

PLANETARY GEAR SET TORQUE FLOW In a planetary gear set, the following operations are executed in order to achieve the various gear ratios and reverse.

- One of the members is being driven (input).
- One of the members is being held (reaction member).
- One of the members is the output.

Therefore, driving one element will cause all of the other gears to rotate as well. This allows the gear set to provide different gear ratios, depending upon how torque is transmitted through the assembly. ● **SEE FIGURE 6–2**.

Each member of a planetary gear set can play any one of these three roles (drive, held, or driven) to transmit torque. The various combinations of drive, held, and driven members result in the number of gear ratios available and change the direction of rotation as well for reverse.

NOTE: The held member can also be allowed to move in one direction or another as it is being held and does not necessarily need to be held to zero RPM to create a variable gear ratio. This is done in hybrid electric vehicle transmissions.

NEUTRAL, FORWARD, OR REVERSE	REDUCTION, OVERDRIVE, OR DIRECT DRIVE	PLANETARY GEAR ACTION
Neutral		When there is no driving member or reaction member, neutral results.
Forward	Direct drive, 1:1	When there are two driving members, direct drive occurs.
Forward	Reduction	When the carrier is the output, a forward reduction occurs.
Forward	Overdrive	When the carrier is the input, an overdrive occurs.
Reverse	Reduction or OD	When the carrier is the reaction member, a reverse occurs.
F or R	OD	When the sun gear is the output, an overdrive occurs.
F or R	Reduction	When the sun gear is the input, a reduction occurs.
Reverse	Reduction or OD	When one external gear drives another, reverse rotation occurs.
Forward	Any	When an external gear drives an internal gear or vice versa, same-direction rotation occurs.

CHART 6–1

Planetary gear set fundamentals.

Torque flows through a planetary gear set in several steps to get from the drive action of the first member to the driven action of the last member.

- The terms "*drive*" and "*driven*" describe how any two gears work together.

- When three or more gears are involved, the second gear is a *driven* gear in relation to the first, but it becomes a *drive* gear in relation to the third gear. ● SEE CHART 6–1.

COMPOUND GEAR SETS There are several different designs of planetary gear sets. The most popular compound planetary design is the **Simpson gear set.** This gear set was named for its inventor, Howard Woodworth Simpson (1892–1963), who was an American automotive engineer. ● SEE FIGURE 6–3.

- **Simpson gear set.** Combines one sun gear with two carriers with planet gears and two ring gears. A simple planetary gear set and a Simpson gear set can be combined to provide four- and five-speed transmissions.

- **Ravigneaux gear set.** Combines one carrier that has two sets of planet gears with two sun gears, and one ring gear. ● SEE FIGURE 6–4.

- **LePelletier gear set.** A Ravigneaux gear set and a simple planetary gear set can be combined to get six, seven, and eight speeds and is known as the **LePelletier gear set** (pronounced "la-plet-e-ay").

CALCULATING GEAR RATIOS A simple planetary gear set can produce seven different gear ratios, plus neutral. The gear ratio is changed by changing the input (driving) and the

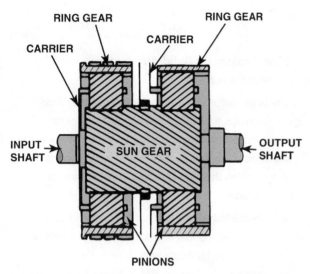

FIGURE 6–3 A Simpson planet gear set is composed of two ring gears and two planet carrier assemblies that share one sun gear.

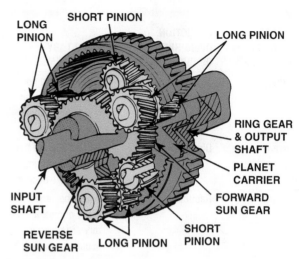

FIGURE 6–4 A Ravigneaux gear set is composed of two sun gears, one planet carrier that supports two sets of pinion gears, and a single ring gear.

reaction (held) members. The various conditions that can be achieved are as follows:

A. If the ring gear is held and the sun gear is driven, the planet gears are forced to rotate as they move around inside the ring gear. The result is an increase in torque and a decrease in speed. The formula for calculating the gear ratio is (sun + ring) ÷ sun.

B. If the ring gear is held and the carrier is driven, the planet gears are forced to rotate as they move around inside the ring gear. This is the reciprocal, or inverse (opposite), of A. The opposite of a reduction ratio is an overdrive ratio. The formula for calculating the gear ratio is sun ÷ (sun + ring).

C. If the sun gear is held in reaction and the ring gear is driven, the planet gears are forced to rotate as they move around the sun gear. The result is an increase in torque and decrease in speed. The formula for calculating the gear ratio is (sun + ring) ÷ ring.

D. If the sun gear is held and the carrier is driven, the planet gears are forced to rotate as they move around the sun

gear. The result is an increase in speed and a decrease in torque. The formula for calculating the gear ratio is ring ÷ (sun + ring). This ratio is the reciprocal of C.

E. If the carrier is held and the sun gear is driven, the planet gears will rotate and act as idlers and the planet gears drive the ring gear in a direction opposite to the sun gear. The result is a reverse with an increase in torque and a decrease in speed. The formula for calculating the gear ratio is ring ÷ sun.

F. If the carrier is held and the ring gear is driven, the planet gears will rotate and act as idlers, driving the sun gear in a direction opposite to the ring. The result is a reverse with an increase in speed and a decrease in torque. The formula for calculating the gear ratio is sun ÷ ring. This ratio is the reciprocal of "E" above.

NOTE: A technician rarely needs to calculate planetary gear set ratios. The gear ratio formulas are shown here for those who are interested or for reference. ● **SEE FIGURE 6–5.** ● **SEE CHART 6–2.**

Sun Gear	Planet Carrier	Ring Gear	Speed	Torque	Direction
Input (Drive)	Output (Driven)	Held	Maximum reduction	Increase	Same as input
Held	Output (Driven)	Input (Drive)	Minimum reduction	Increase	Same as input
Output (Driven)	Input (Drive)	Held	Maximum Increase	Reduction	Same as input
Held	Input (Drive)	Output (Driven)	Minimum Increase	Reduction	Same as input
Input (Drive)	Held	Output (Driven)	Reduction	Increase	Reverse of input
Output (Driven)	Held	Input (Drive)	Increase	Reduction	Reverse of input

CHART 6–2

If any two members are locked together, then the resulting output is 1:1 ratio in the same direction as the input. If no member is held (locked), then there is no output (neutral).

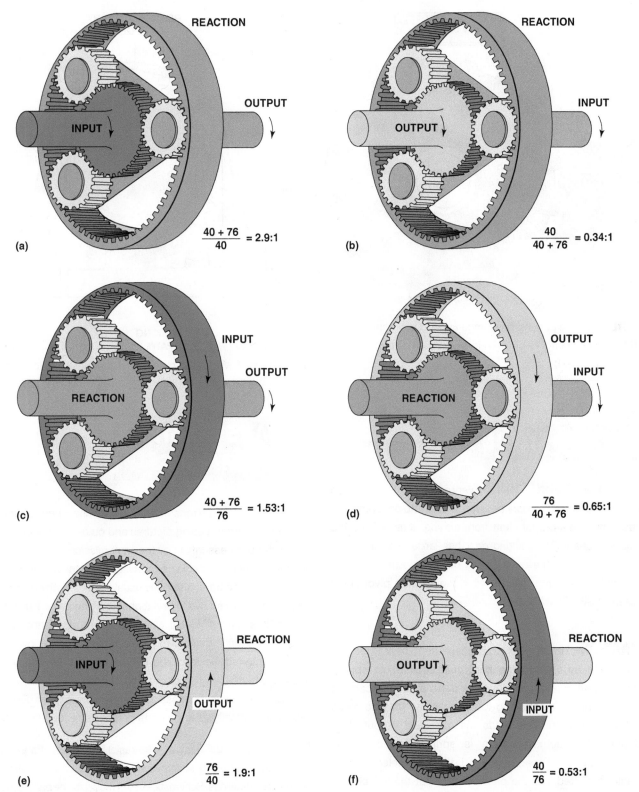

FIGURE 6–5 The gear ratio through a planetary gear set depends on which part is driven, which part is held, and which part is the output. The formula used to calculate the ratio is included with each illustration. Each gear set uses a 40-tooth sun gear and a 77-tooth ring gear.

Manufacturers usually provide clutch and band application charts for their transmissions, and these charts show which apply devices are used for each gear range. Each apply device drives a particular gear set member or holds it in reaction. Clutch and band charts are very helpful in understanding the power flow through a transmission. They are also very helpful when diagnosing transmission failures.

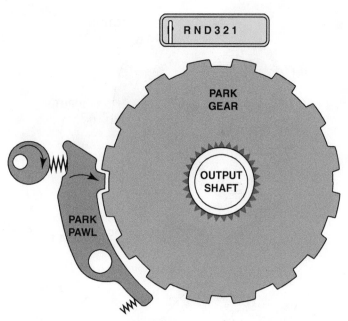

FIGURE 6–6 The parking pawl engages and locks the output shaft to the transmission case.

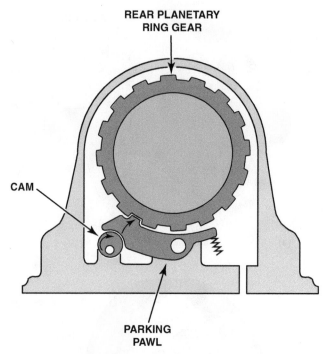

FIGURE 6–7 When the control rod is moved, the locking cam pushes the pawl into engagement with the parking gear.

PARK POSITION

PURPOSE AND FUNCTION Every automatic transmission and transaxle includes a park position. A shift into park prevents the transmission's output shaft from turning, thus holding the vehicle stationary. The parking gear has large gear-like teeth and is mounted on the output shaft of the transmission. The **park pawl** (sometimes called a lever) moves on a pivot pin in the case. ● **SEE FIGURE 6–6**.

OPERATION In all gear positions except park, the park pawl is held away from the park gear teeth by a spring. When the gear selector is moved to park, a circular cam on the end of the park actuating rod pushes the pawl to mesh with the gear teeth. This holds the gear and output shaft stationary. The actuating cam is spring loaded. If the gear teeth and pawl are not aligned, the gear selector lever can still be shifted into the park position but the vehicle will not be held until the output shaft rotates slightly, then the spring moves the cam, which in turn moves the pawl into engagement.

The shift into park is a mechanical connection that should be made with the driveshaft stopped. ● **SEE FIGURE 6–7**.

TRANSMISSION SCHEMATICS

DESCRIPTION Transmission parts and their operations are often illustrated using pictures and cutaway drawings. They show the bare essentials of the transmission gear train in the simplest way possible. When viewing a typical cutaway view of a gear train, the transmission is usually split lengthwise through the middle. This shows the relationship of the parts, but in many cases, it is difficult to tell where one part stops and another begins, making it difficult to trace the path of the power flow. Many exploded views of the internal parts show the front or back of a clutch, carrier, or gear, but it is difficult to tell what the backside connects to unless a separate view is given. Exploded views are typically used by parts personnel to identify parts.

READING SCHEMATICS An easier way to view transmission operation is by using schematics. Transmission schematics resemble stick drawings. Schematics use symbols for the parts and a line shows the link between the parts. Similar to electrical schematics, the major objective is to simplify the transmission as much as possible. A schematic is most useful when tracing the power flow. At present, there is no industry-wide standard for automatic transmission symbols and manufactures can use different formats for their transmission schematics. ● **SEE FIGURE 6–8**.

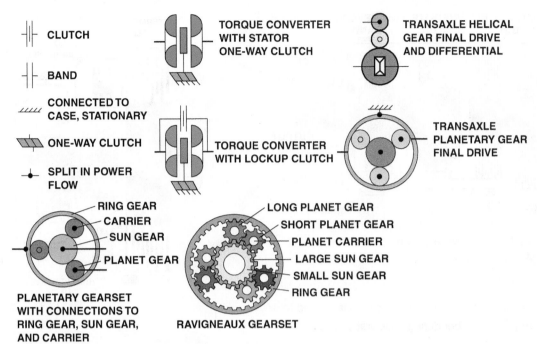

FIGURE 6–8 Common symbols used in the transmission schematics to illustrate the various parts.

SIMPSON GEAR TRAIN TYPES

BACKGROUND The Simpson gear set consists of a double sun gear that is meshed with the planet gears of the two carriers and is a compound gear set commonly used in many three-speed transmissions/transaxles. Most of the automatic transmissions used in domestic vehicles during the 1960s and 1970s used this gear train. The better-known Simpson gear train transmissions are as follows:

Aisin-Warner: Three-speed models

Chrysler Corporation: 36 and 37 RH (Torqueflite A-727 and A-904) transmissions and the 31TH (A-404, A-413, A-415, and A470) transaxles

Ford Motor Company: Cruisomatic C3, C4, C5, and C6 and JATCO transmissions

General Motors: The 3L80 (THM 400), THM 200, 250, 350, 375, and 425 transmissions and 3T40 (THM 125) and THM 325 transaxles

JATCO: Three-speed models

Toyota: A40, A41, A130, A131, and A132

Although transmissions using a Simpson gear train are similar, they are not identical. The power flow through the gear set is essentially the same. They all have two input or driving clutches and a one-way reaction clutch, but the reaction members vary.

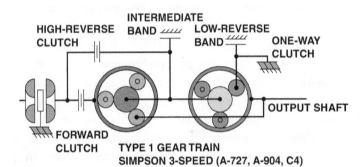

FIGURE 6–9 Type 1 gear set is a three-speed Simpson gear train that uses bands to hold the sun gear and reaction carrier. Note that the reaction carrier can also be held by a one-way clutch.

GEAR SET TYPES 1, 2, 3, AND 4 The major difference between these transmissions is the type of reaction member. A multiple-disc clutch can handle more torque than a band. It has a much larger friction area and multiple case connections. A clutch is more complex than a band and requires more space. To help understand these different arrangements, they will be grouped into similar types, as follows:

- **Type 1**—transmissions use a band for both reaction members. ● **SEE FIGURE 6–9.**

- **Type 2**—transmissions use a multiple-disc clutch for the reaction carrier and a band to hold the sun gear.

- **Type 3**—transmissions use a multiple-disc clutch, a one-way clutch, and an overrun band for the sun gear reaction member and a multiple-disc clutch to hold the reaction carrier. (When a one-way clutch is used for a

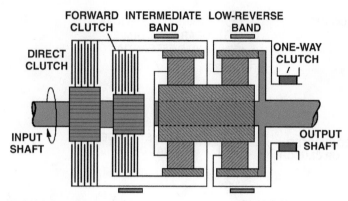

FIGURE 6–10 The one-way clutch of this type 1 gear set serves as the reaction member in first gear with the gear selector in Drive (D1). The low-reverse band is applied in manual first (M1) to allow engine compression braking.

reaction member, an overrun band or clutch is applied to hold the reaction member during deceleration.)

- **Type 4**—transmissions use a multiple-disc clutch, a one-way clutch, and an overrun band for the sun gear reaction member and a band to hold the reaction carrier.

NONSYNCHRONOUS AND SYNCHRONOUS DESIGNS

Type 3 and 4 units are **nonsynchronous** (asynchronous) designs. A nonsynchronous transmission is a unit that uses a one-way clutch to allow an upshift that requires only the application of the next driving or reaction member. All four types use a nonsynchronous 1–2 shift in drive. The 2–3 upshift timing is less critical because the disc clutch is used with a one-way clutch and the clutch stays applied while the one-way clutch simply overruns as the upshift occurs. A **synchronous** design transmission means that during an upshift, the new driving or reaction member must be timed or synchronized with the release of a driving or reaction member. The band used in synchronous designs must be released at an exact time for the upshift, and it must reapply at the exact time during a downshift. ● **SEE FIGURE 6–10.**

The nonsynchronous arrangement is great for upshifts, but is ineffective during deceleration. Similar to the one-way clutch in first gear, the one-way clutch overruns during deceleration.

NEUTRAL Neutral is achieved by not applying the input clutches. Power enters the transmission from the torque converter but travels only as far as the released clutches. When shifted into neutral, some transmissions apply one of the clutches needed for first or reverse to prevent a harsh engagement when the vehicle is shifted into gear.

FIRST GEAR The Simpson gear set has two slightly different first gears—drive-1 and manual-1—the difference

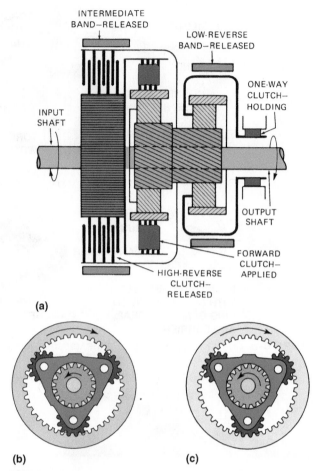

(a)

(b)   (c)

FIGURE 6–11 (a) In drive low (D1), the front ring gear is driven while the rear carrier is held by the one-way clutch. A reverse reduction occurs in both (b) the front unit and (c) the rear unit.

being in how the reaction carrier is held. In both gear ranges, power flows through the gear set when the front ring gear is driven and the reaction carrier is held. All Simpson gear sets use a clutch to drive the front (input) ring gear. Transmission types 1 and 4 use a one-way clutch and a band and types 2 and 3 use a one-way clutch and a holding clutch to hold the reaction carrier. In drive-1, the one-way clutch is used and it provides self-application and release. In manual-1, a band or holding clutch is applied to provide engine compression braking during deceleration. ● **SEE FIGURE 6–11.**

When manual-1 (low) is selected, the one-way clutch is assisted by either a band (types 1 and 4) or a multiple-disc clutch (types 2 and 3). The band is called the *low and reverse* or **low-reverse band**. The multiple-disc clutch is called a **low-reverse clutch**. The power flow is exactly the same as in drive-1 except that power can be transmitted from the drive shaft to the engine during deceleration. This provides engine (compression) braking as the vehicle slows. Engine braking is easily noticed by comparing the deceleration of a vehicle in drive-1 and manual-1.

FIGURE 6–12 In second gear, the ring gear is driven while the sun gear is held, and the planet gears walk around the sun gear and force the carrier to revolve at a reduced speed.

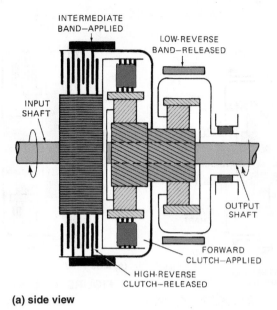

INTERMEDIATE BAND—APPLIED

LOW-REVERSE BAND—RELEASED

INPUT SHAFT

OUTPUT SHAFT

FORWARD CLUTCH—APPLIED

HIGH-REVERSE CLUTCH—RELEASED

(a) side view

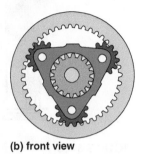

(b) front view

For simplicity, this holding member will be called either a low-reverse band or a low-reverse clutch in this text.

In drive-1 (low), the following occur.

- The **forward clutch** is applied to drive the input ring gear in a clockwise direction.

- The output/front carrier will not rotate because it is connected to the driveshaft.

- The front planet gears are driven clockwise.

- The sun gear is driven in the reverse direction (counterclockwise) at a reduced speed.

- The reaction carrier is held from turning counterclockwise by the one-way clutch (or the low-reverse band or clutch in manual-1).

- The rear planet gears are driven clockwise.

- The rear ring gear is driven clockwise at a reduced speed.

- The output shaft and driveshaft are driven clockwise at a reduced speed.

The gear set is producing two reverse reduction ratios, and the result is a forward (clockwise) rotation of the driveshaft. The overall ratio will be about 2.45:1 to 2.74:1 depending on the size of the gears used in a specific transmission.

SECOND GEAR The sun gear must be held stationary in second gear. This is done by a band in type 1 and 2 transmissions or a multiple-disc clutch plus a one-way clutch in type 3 and 4 transmissions. Type 3 and 4 transmissions use an **intermediate clutch** and an *intermediate one-way clutch*. When the intermediate clutch is applied, it holds the outer race of the intermediate roller clutch stationary. The

one-way clutch locks, holding the sun gear from rotating counterclockwise. Because the one-way clutch will only hold in one direction, these units have two slightly different power flows in second gear: **drive-2** and **manual-2**. Manual-2 applies an intermediate overrun band to provide engine compression braking during deceleration. For simplicity, we will call this reaction member either an intermediate band or intermediate clutch in this text.

In drive-2 (intermediate), the following occur.

- The forward clutch stays applied to drive the input ring gear clockwise. ● **SEE FIGURE 6–12**.

- The intermediate band or clutch applies to hold the sun gear stationary (reaction member).

- The front planet gears are driven clockwise and walk around the sun gear.

- The front carrier is driven clockwise.

- The front carrier drives the output shaft clockwise at about a 1.5:1 ratio.

THIRD GEAR Third gear in this gear set is direct drive with a 1:1 ratio. It is produced by applying both driving clutches (forward and high-reverse) and either releasing the intermediate band in synchronous transmissions (types 1 and 2) or allowing the intermediate roller clutch to overrun in nonsynchronous transmissions (types 3 and 4). The gear set locks up because the ring gear is trying to turn the planet pinions clockwise while the sun gear is trying to turn them counterclockwise.

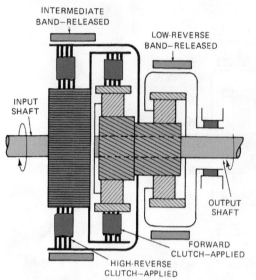

FIGURE 6–13 In third gear, both driving clutches are applied so two members (the ring and sun gears) of the same gear set are driven. This locks the gears and produces a 1:1 gear ratio.

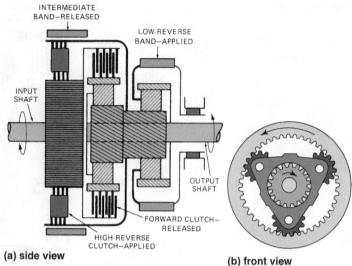

(a) side view　　　　　**(b) front view**

FIGURE 6–14 In reverse, the sun gear is driven while the carrier is held. The planet gears act as idlers and cause the ring gear to revolve in a reverse direction at a reduced speed.

In drive-3 (high), the following occur.

- The forward clutch stays applied to drive the input ring gear clockwise.

- The **high-reverse clutch** applies to drive the sun gear clockwise.

- The front planet gears become locked in the carrier.

- The front carrier is driven clockwise at the same speed as the ring and sun gears.

- The front carrier drives the output shaft clockwise at a 1:1 ratio. ● **SEE FIGURE 6–13.**

REVERSE Reverse in a Simpson gear train occurs when the high-reverse clutch and the low-reverse band or clutch are applied. The high-reverse clutch drives the sun gear (input member) while the carrier (reaction member) in the rear gear set is held stationary by the low-reverse band or clutch. The planet gears act as idlers, reversing the power flow as they transfer power from the smaller sun gear to the larger ring gear. A reverse reduction is produced at the output ring gear of about 2.07:1 to 2.22:1. ● **SEE FIGURE 6–14.**

SHIFT TIMING EXAMPLE As a vehicle accelerates from a stop to cruising speed, the driving and reaction members have to apply and release in an exact operating sequence. When they apply, they must come on at a precise rate. To illustrate this, we will follow an upshift sequence during a hard acceleration with shift points occurring at 4800 RPM.

In first gear, the ratio will be 2.5:1, so the vehicle driveshaft will be revolving at 1920 RPM (4800 ÷ 2.5) when the 1–2 upshift occurs. Second gear has a ratio of 1.5:1, so the engine speed will drop from 4800 to 2800 RPM (1920 × 1.5) during the shift. ● **SEE FIGURE 6–15.**

FOURTH GEAR MADE POSSIBLE The Simpson gear train with an additional simple planetary gear set is used to produce a four-speed overdrive transmission or transaxle. The overdrive planetary gear set provides two speeds: direct 1:1 and overdrive. When the overdrive planetary gear set is in direct drive it turns the Simpson planetary gear set input at engine speed. When the overdrive gear train is in direct drive 1:1, the Simpson gear train will shift from first to second and then to third. If the overdrive planetary gear set is in overdrive, it will turn the Simpson planetary gear set input faster than engine speed. The three-speed Simpson gear train will operate as described earlier. To get overdrive, the overdrive planetary gear set will be in overdrive and the Simpson gear set will be in direct 1:1. To get reverse, the overdrive gear set will be in direct and the Simpson will be in reverse. The more common transmissions using this gear set are as follows:

- Chrysler 42RH (A-500), 46RH (A-518)

- Ford 4R44E (A4LD), 5R55E, and E4OD

- GM 4T80-E, THM-200-4R, and 325–4L

- Jeep AW-4

- Nissan E4N7IB

- Toyota A40 and A340 series

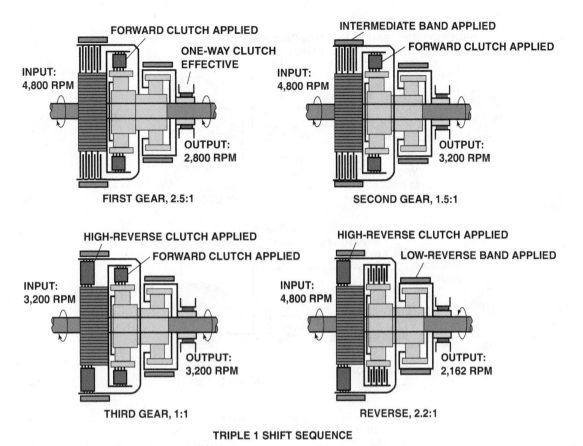

FIRST GEAR, 2.5:1

FORWARD CLUTCH APPLIED
ONE-WAY CLUTCH EFFECTIVE
INPUT: 4,800 RPM
OUTPUT: 2,800 RPM

SECOND GEAR, 1.5:1

INTERMEDIATE BAND APPLIED
FORWARD CLUTCH APPLIED
INPUT: 4,800 RPM
OUTPUT: 3,200 RPM

THIRD GEAR, 1:1

HIGH-REVERSE CLUTCH APPLIED
FORWARD CLUTCH APPLIED
INPUT: 3,200 RPM
OUTPUT: 3,200 RPM

REVERSE, 2.2:1

HIGH-REVERSE CLUTCH APPLIED
LOW-REVERSE BAND APPLIED
INPUT: 4,800 RPM
OUTPUT: 2,162 RPM

TRIPLE 1 SHIFT SEQUENCE

FIGURE 6–15 The full-throttle shift sequence for a type 1 transmission showing the apply devices and the output shaft speed at the 1–2 and 2–3 upshifts. Reverse is also shown.

OVERDRIVE In most of these transmissions, the overdrive gear set is built into the area at the front of the case between the torque converter and the main gear set. The input shaft from the torque converter is connected to the carrier of the overdrive gear set, and the ring gear of the overdrive gear set is arranged so it becomes the input of the main gear set. The Chrysler 42RH and 46RH have the overdrive gear set built into the transmission extension housing to cause a speed increase between the main gear set and the output shaft.

GEAR SET TYPES 5, 6, 7, AND 8 For examples of types 5, 6, 7, and 8 that use the Simpson gear train. ● **SEE FIGURE 6–16.**

The Chrysler 42RH and 46RH are a little unusual in that one hydraulic piston and return spring is used for both the direct clutch and the overdrive clutch (type 5 gear train). The very strong return spring is used to release the overdrive clutch and apply the direct clutch. Hydraulic pressure at the piston releases the direct clutch and then almost immediately applies the overdrive clutch. With this arrangement, the gear set is locked in either direct drive or overdrive with the overrunning clutch transferring power while the upshift or downshift is made.

In the 4R44E/5R55E (type 6), the power is transferred directly from the carrier to the ring gear. In the GM 200-4R (type 7), the gear set is locked because the one-way clutch does not allow the sun gear to overrun the carrier. The type 8 gear train describes the power flow through a Jeep AW-4 transmission.

Like other power flows using a one-way clutch, these gear sets overrun during deceleration and do not produce engine (compression) braking. To prevent this in manual-1, M2, or M3, the overdrive clutch in the Ford 4R44E/5R55E, overrun clutch in the 200-4R, or the O/D direct clutch in the AW-4 are applied. This locks the overdrive gear assembly so it operates in direct drive in both acceleration and deceleration. ● **SEE FIGURE 6–17.**

RAVIGNEAUX GEAR SETS

DESCRIPTION The Ravigneaux gear set uses

- a single carrier that has two sets of intermeshed planet gears,
- two sun gears, and
- a single ring gear.

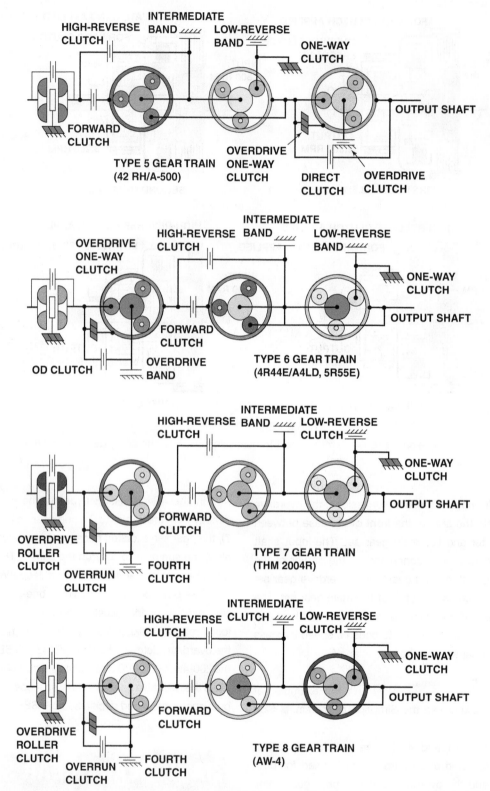

FIGURE 6–16 Types 5, 6, 7, and 8 gear sets illustrate the different four-speed gear train arrangements that combine a Simpson three-speed gear set with an overdrive unit.

The planet gears are different lengths. The two sun gears have different diameters and are independent of each other. On one side of the Ravigneaux gear set, the sun gear meshes with the short pinion gears, which in turn mesh with the longer pinion gears which are meshed with one of the ring gears. On the other side of the gear set, the long pinion gears mesh with the other ring gear and sun gear. In some transmissions, the ring gear is in mesh with the short pinions.

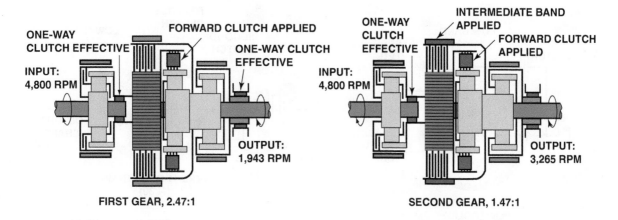

ONE-WAY CLUTCH EFFECTIVE

INPUT: 4,800 RPM

FORWARD CLUTCH APPLIED

ONE-WAY CLUTCH EFFECTIVE

OUTPUT: 1,943 RPM

FIRST GEAR, 2.47:1

ONE-WAY CLUTCH EFFECTIVE

INPUT: 4,800 RPM

INTERMEDIATE BAND APPLIED

FORWARD CLUTCH APPLIED

OUTPUT: 3,265 RPM

SECOND GEAR, 1.47:1

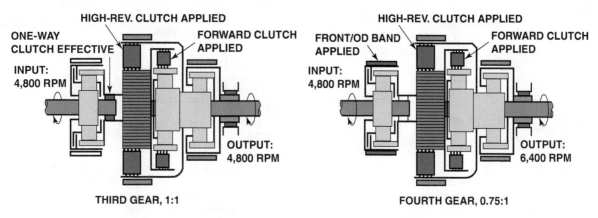

HIGH-REV. CLUTCH APPLIED

ONE-WAY CLUTCH EFFECTIVE

FORWARD CLUTCH APPLIED

INPUT: 4,800 RPM

OUTPUT: 4,800 RPM

THIRD GEAR, 1:1

HIGH-REV. CLUTCH APPLIED

FRONT/OD BAND APPLIED

FORWARD CLUTCH APPLIED

INPUT: 4,800 RPM

OUTPUT: 6,400 RPM

FOURTH GEAR, 0.75:1

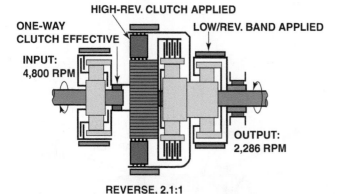

HIGH-REV. CLUTCH APPLIED

ONE-WAY CLUTCH EFFECTIVE

LOW/REV. BAND APPLIED

INPUT: 4,800 RPM

OUTPUT: 2,286 RPM

REVERSE, 2.1:1

FIGURE 6–17 The full-throttle shift sequence for a type 6 transmission showing the apply devices and the output shaft speed at the 1–2, 2–3, and 3–4 upshifts, plus reverse.

EXAMPLES The Ravigneaux gear set is used in the following.

- **Two-speed transmissions**—Chrysler Powerflite, the Ford two-speed, and the General Motors Powerglide, and THM 300

- **Three-speed transmissions**—Ford FMX and General Motors 3L30 (THM 180)

- **Three-speed transaxles**—Ford ATX, KM 171 to 175 versions

- **Four-speed transmission**—Ford 4R70W (AOD)

- **Four-speed transaxles**—Ford 4EAT, KM 175 to 177, and ZF-4

The exact arrangement of the gear set varies depending on the usage. ● **SEE FIGURE 6–18.**

FOUR-SPEED RAVIGNEAUX ARRANGEMENT AND OPERATION

The Ford 4R70W (AOD) (type 12 gear set) uses a four-speed version of the Ravigneaux gear train. The first version of this transmission, the AOD, has an additional input shaft (the direct driveshaft) and an additional clutch (the direct clutch). These are arranged so the carrier can be an input member in third and fourth gears as well as a reaction member in first and reverse. The direct driveshaft is driven by a damper assembly at the front of the torque converter so it is a

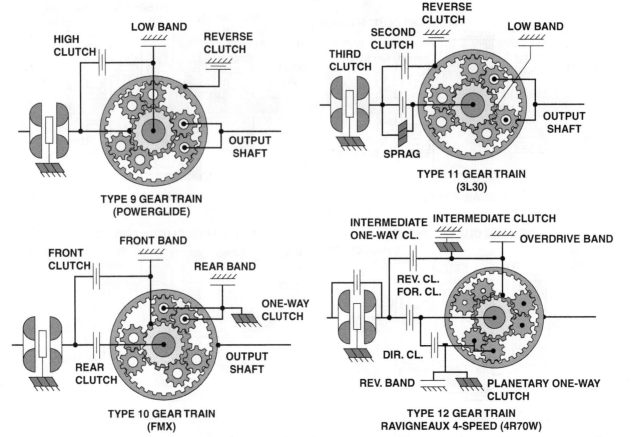

FIGURE 6–18 Types 9, 10, 11, and 12 gear sets illustrate the different three- and four-speed gear train arrangements that use a single Ravigneaux gear set.

? FREQUENTLY ASKED QUESTION

How Was the Powerglide Different?

Two-speed transmissions were used in the 1950s and 1960s and are still a popular transmission used in racing. They are no longer in production, but so many were produced that they are still encountered. The most common was the Chevrolet Powerglide (type 9 gear set).

In two-speed Ravigneaux transmissions, the small **primary sun gear** is attached to the input shaft so it is always an input. The large sun gear, called the **secondary sun gear,** is either a reaction member or an input member. The carrier is the output member, and the ring gear can be a reaction member. A driving clutch is placed on the input shaft so the secondary sun gear can be driven, and a band, is placed around the clutch drum so the secondary sun gear can be held in reaction. The clutch is often called the *high clutch*, and the band is called a *low band*. The ring gear is held by either a band (first version) or a multiple-disc clutch (second version), called either a *reverse clutch* or a *reverse band*. ● **SEE FIGURE 6–19**.

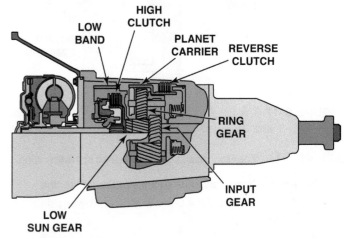

FIGURE 6–19 When a Powerglide is in low gear, the low band is applied to hold the low sun gear stationary. At this time, the long pinions will be driven by the input sun gear and walk around the low sun gear to drive the carrier.

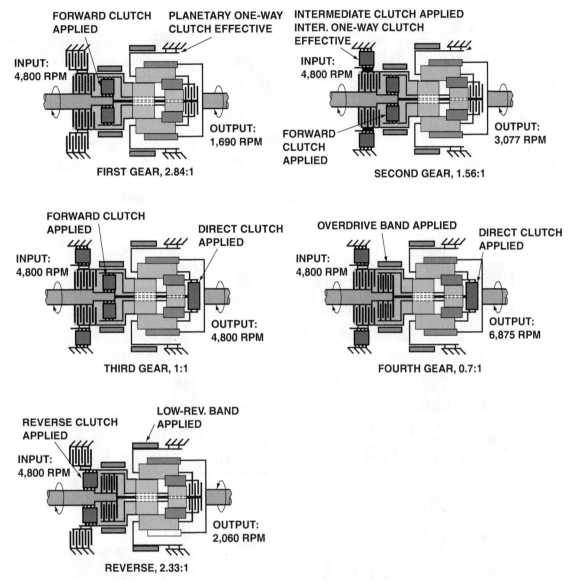

FORWARD CLUTCH APPLIED   PLANETARY ONE-WAY CLUTCH EFFECTIVE

INPUT: 4,800 RPM

OUTPUT: 1,690 RPM

FIRST GEAR, 2.84:1

INTERMEDIATE CLUTCH APPLIED INTER. ONE-WAY CLUTCH EFFECTIVE

INPUT: 4,800 RPM

FORWARD CLUTCH APPLIED

OUTPUT: 3,077 RPM

SECOND GEAR, 1.56:1

FORWARD CLUTCH APPLIED   DIRECT CLUTCH APPLIED

INPUT: 4,800 RPM

OUTPUT: 4,800 RPM

THIRD GEAR, 1:1

OVERDRIVE BAND APPLIED   DIRECT CLUTCH APPLIED

INPUT: 4,800 RPM

OUTPUT: 6,875 RPM

FOURTH GEAR, 0.7:1

REVERSE CLUTCH APPLIED   LOW-REV. BAND APPLIED

INPUT: 4,800 RPM

OUTPUT: 2,060 RPM

REVERSE, 2.33:1

FIGURE 6–20 The full-throttle shift sequence for a type 12 transmission showing the apply devices and the output shaft speed at the 1–2, 2–3, and 3–4 upshifts and reverse.

purely mechanical input into the gear set. Newer versions use a more conventional torque converter with a converter clutch and connect the direct clutch to the forward clutch by a short stub shaft.

The first-, second-, and reverse-gear power flows in the 4R70W are the same as those in the old FMX unit used by Ford, with the exception that the intermediate clutch is used to hold the carrier for a reaction member in second gear. In third gear, the direct-drive clutch is applied to drive the carrier while the forward clutch remains applied to drive the small, forward sun gear. This locks the planet gears and drives the ring gear in direct drive. The intermediate clutch remains applied, but it becomes ineffective because the intermediate one-way clutch overruns. ● **SEE FIGURE 6–20**.

LEPELLETIER GEAR TRAIN

OPERATION   The LePelletier gear train combines a simple planetary gear set with a Ravigneaux gear set providing six forward speeds. The combination is fairly simple, using only five multiplate clutches and, in some transmissions, a one-way clutch. Three of the clutches are driving members and the other two are used in reaction. This gear set is used in the Ford 6R60 and 6R80 and General Motors 6L80E transmissions, and transmissions produced by Aisin and ZF. ● **SEE FIGURE 6–21**.

Because the ring gear is always an input and the sun gear is always a reaction member (it is splined to the back of the pump), the simple gear set is always in reduction. The C1 and C3

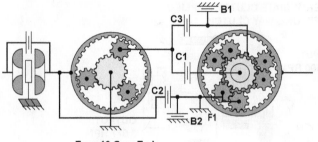

Lepelletier Gear Ranges						
Range	C1	C2	C3	B1	B2	F1	Ratio
1	X					X	4.15:1
Manual 1	X				X		4.15:1
2	X			X			2.37:1
3	X		X				1.56:1
4	X	X					1.15:1
5		X	X				0.86:1
6		X		X			0.69:1
Reverse			X		X		3.39:1

FIGURE 6–21 (a) A schematic view of a type 13, LePelletier six-speed gear set (b) and a clutch application chart.

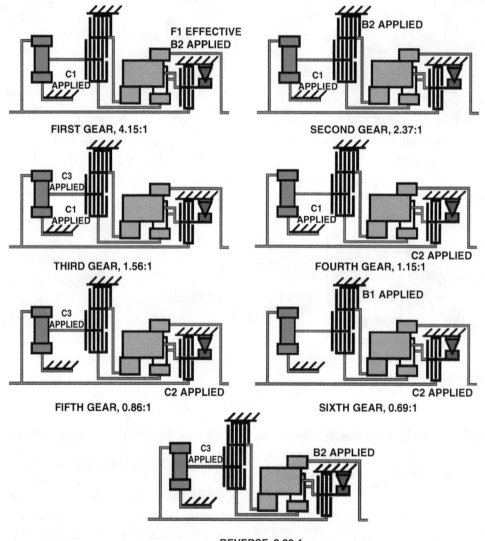

FIGURE 6–22 A type 13 shift sequence.

clutches can provide a reduced speed input to the Ravigneaux gear set. The Ravigneaux gear set is arranged like a type 12 gear set, with three possible inputs and two reaction members.

This gear set has four reduction ratios and two overdrive ratios, with a gear ratio spread of over 6:1. Compared to current five-speed transmissions, these six-speed transmissions have fewer control devices and weigh about 13% less. Because of the close gear ratios and lighter weight, they also promise fuel mileage increases of 5% to 7%, and provide faster acceleration. ● **SEE FIGURE 6–22.**

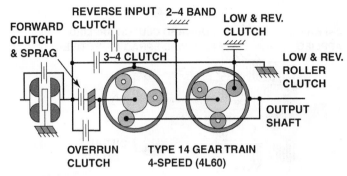

FIGURE 6–23 A schematic view of a type 14, GM 4L60-E four-speed gear set.

GM 4L60-E AND OTHERS

A four-speed gear set was developed by General Motors and introduced in the 4L60-E (THM 700-R4) rear-wheel-drive transmission. It has two simple planetary gear sets that have the ring gears interconnected with the carriers of the other set. A second version of this gear set is used in the following units:

- Chrysler 41TE (A-604) (front-wheel-drive unit) and 42LE (rear-wheel-drive unit)
- Ford AX4N, AX4S (AXOD), and CD4E units.
- General Motors uses this type of gear set in the 4T60-E, 4T65-E, and 4T80-E transaxles.

The 4L60-E (THM 7004R) rear-wheel-drive unit is a type 14 gear train and uses four multiple-disc clutches plus a one-way clutch as driving members and one multiple-disc clutch, a one-way clutch, and a band for holding members. ● SEE **FIGURE 6–23**.

The driving clutches are arranged so they can drive the sun gear and ring gear in the front gear set, called the **input gear set**, and the sun gear and carrier in the rear gear set, called the **reaction gear set**. The input housing contains three of the driving clutches and the hub for the fourth. There are two ways that the front sun gear can be driven. One way is through the *forward clutch* and forward one-way clutch, called a **forward sprag**, and the other way is through the *overrun clutch*. The overrun clutch is used in manual first (M1), M2, and M3 to provide engine braking during deceleration.

The rear carrier (and front ring gear) can be held by the one-way clutch, *low-roller clutch*, or the multiple-disc *low and reverse clutch*. The rear sun gear can be held by the *2–4 band* to serve as a reaction member as well as a driving member.

In neutral, all clutches are released so the power flows no farther than the input housing. ● **FIGURE 6–24**.

41TE/42LE The 41TE (A-604) and 42LE (Type 15) use a similar gear set to the 4L60 (THM 700R4), with different input and output members and a reversal of the gear set so the front ring gear and the rear carrier are the output members. This produces slightly different power flows.

NOTE: The 41TE transmission is also unique in that no bands or one-way clutches are used. This type of transmission/transaxle is called a *clutch-to-clutch* transmission.

Three of the multiple-disc clutches used in the 41TE are driving members and the other two clutches are holding members. The driving clutches are arranged so they can drive the front sun gear (closest to the engine), the front carrier, or the rear sun gear. Driving the carrier in the front gear set also drives the ring gear in the rear gear set. The holding clutches are arranged so one clutch can hold the sun gear in the front gear set. The other clutch can hold the ring gear in the rear gear set as well as the carrier in the front set.

Clutch application is controlled by the manual valve and four solenoid valves. The solenoid valves are controlled by the transaxle electronic control module, and they are opened and closed to produce the automatic upshifts and downshifts. They are also operated at the exact rate to produce the proper clutch application and release for good shift quality. In neutral, the three driving clutches are released. The low-reverse clutch is applied to hold the reaction member as soon as the transmission is shifted into first or reverse gear. ● **SEE FIGURE 6–25**.

A clutch and band chart is shown in ● **CHART 6–3**.

4T60/AX4N

The General Motors 4T60-E (THM 440), 4T65-E, and 4T80-E and the Ford AX4N (AXOD), AX4S, and CD4E transaxles use gear sets that are very similar to the arrangement in the 41TE. These transaxles have the front carrier and the rear ring gears combined and are the output members. The rear carrier and the front ring gear can be a driving member, a reaction, or neither. The rear sun gear can only be a reaction member. The 4T60 is illustrated as a type 16 gear train. ● **SEE FIGURE 6–26**.

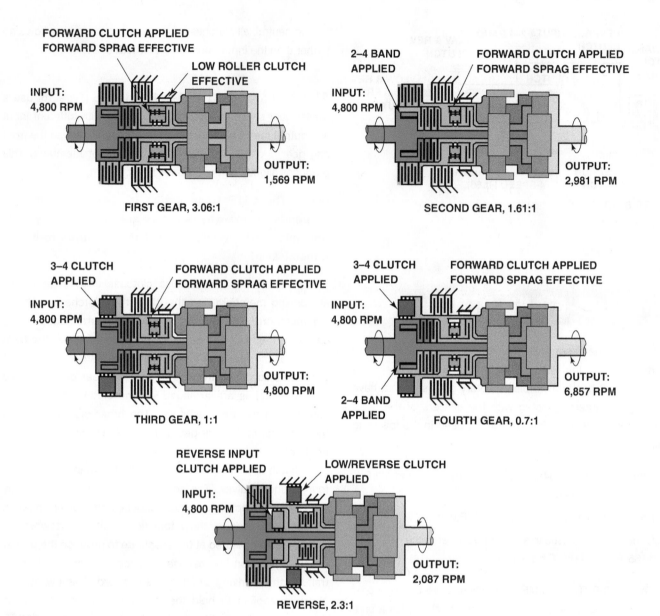

FIGURE 6–24 The full-throttle shift sequence for a type 14, 4L60 transmission showing the apply devices and the output shaft speed at the 1–2, 2–3, and 3–4 upshifts and reverse.

FORD CD4E

The Ford CD4E is another version of the four-speed gear set and is a type 17 gear train. It is a compact transaxle with a chain drive between the transmission gear set and the planetary reduction gears and differential of the final drive. The power flows through this gear set are quite similar. ● SEE **FIGURE 6–27**.

GM 6T70/FORD 6F50

OPERATION   The type 18 gear set was developed jointly by Ford (6F50) and General Motors (6T70 and 6T75). It uses three simple planetary gear sets and has each carrier connected to the ring gear of another set. The sun gear of the center gear set is connected to the input shaft, so it is always driven. It uses two driving clutches, three reaction clutches (brakes), and one

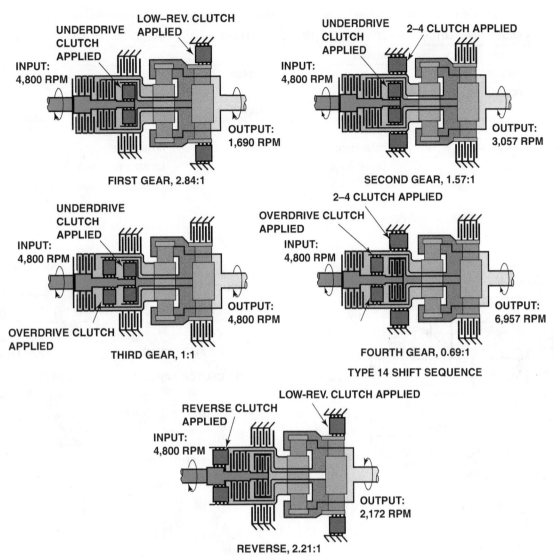

FIRST GEAR, 2.84:1

SECOND GEAR, 1.57:1

THIRD GEAR, 1:1

FOURTH GEAR, 0.69:1

TYPE 14 SHIFT SEQUENCE

REVERSE, 2.21:1

FIGURE 6–25 The full-throttle shift sequence for a type 15, 41TE transmission showing the apply devices and the output shaft speed at the 1–2, 2–3, and 3–4 upshifts and reverse.

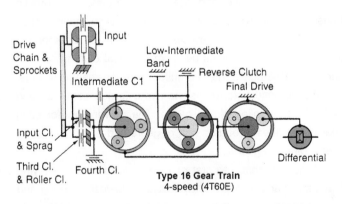

FIGURE 6–26 A schematic view of a type 16, GM 4T60 four-speed gear set. The Ford AX4N gear set is similar.

mechanical diode (one-way clutch). The front carrier and rear ring gear are the output. Except for first gear with the one-way clutch, it uses clutch-to-clutch shifts. It has a low 4.48:1 first gear, and an overdrive 0.74:1:1 sixth gear. ● **SEE FIGURE 6–28.**

NONPLANETARY GEAR SETS

Several automatic transmission designs do not use planetary gear sets. These designs are attempts to produce a smaller, simpler, lighter, and less expensive transmission that will produce better fuel mileage with lower exhaust emissions.

GEAR	UNDERDRIVE CLUTCH	LOW-REV. CLUTCH	2–4 CLUTCH	OVERDRIVE CLUTCH	REVERSE CLUTCH
D1	Applied	Applied			
D2	Applied		Applied		
D3	Applied			Applied	
D4			Applied	Applied	
R		Applied			Applied
Planetary	Drives Rear	Holds Front	Holds	Drives Front	Drives
Member	Sun	Carrier & Rear Ring	Front Sun	Carrier & Rear Ring	Front Sun

CHART 6–3

Four-Speed Gear Train Band and Clutch Application, Type 15.

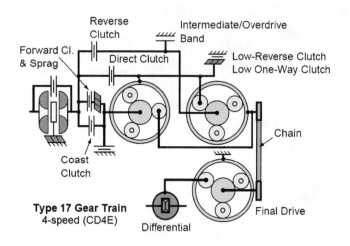

FIGURE 6–27 A schematic view of a type 17, Ford CD4E four-speed gear set.

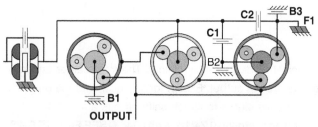

JOINT VENTURE 6-SPEED GEARSET

(a)

Joint Venture Gearset						
Range	C1	C2	B1	B2	B3	F1	Ratio
1			X			X	4.48:1
Manual 1			X		X		4.48:1
2			X	X			2.87:1
3	X		X				1.84:1
4		X	X				1.41:1
5	X	X					1:1
6		X		X			0.74:1
Reverse	X				X		2.88:1

(b)

FIGURE 6–28 (a) A schematic view of (a) a type 18, joint venture six-speed gear set and (b) a clutch application chart.

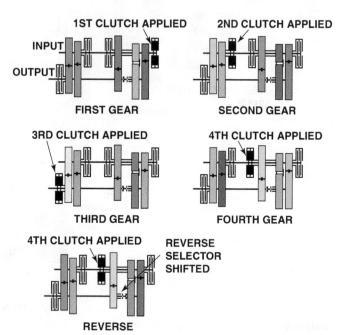

FIGURE 6–29 The shift sequence for a type 19, four-speed transmission showing the apply devices.

The Hondamatic and the Saturn transaxle automatic transmission (TAAT) use constant-mesh helical gears, much like those in a manual transmission. The major difference is that manual transmissions use a mechanical clutch and synchronizer assemblies that are shifted through manual linkage, and the automatic transmissions use a torque converter and hydraulically applied clutch packs. The power flow for each gear range goes through a pair of gears and each gear range uses a different gear set.

A garage shift into first or reverse is made by applying that particular clutch pack. Upshift and downshift timing and ratio changes are made by applying the next clutch pack while releasing the previous one. All shifts, with one exception, occur with the application of a single clutch pack. The exception is reverse, which requires the movement of the reverse selector and the engagement of the fourth clutch. ● **SEE FIGURE 6–29.**

1. The gear set in an automatic transmission must provide a
   - neutral
   - one or more gear reductions
   - direct-drive ratio (1:1)
   - reverse
   - overdrive

2. In a planetary gear set, the following is done to achieve the various gear ratios and reverse.
   - One of the members is being driven (input).
   - One of the members is being held (reaction member).
   - One of the members is the output.

3. A synchronous design transmission means that during an upshift, the new driving or reaction member must be timed or synchronized with the release of a driving or reaction member.

4. A nonsynchronous transmission is a unit that uses a one-way clutch to allow an upshift that requires only the application of the next driving or reaction member

5. There are three basic types of planetary gear sets used: Simpson, Ravigneaux, and LePelletier.

6. Combinations of Simpson or Ravigneaux gear sets with a simple planetary gear set will produce four, five, six, eight, or more gear ratios.

1. In a planetary gear set, what needs to be done to achieve the various gear ratios and reverse?

2. How is a 1:1 ratio achieved using a planetary gear set?

3. What needs to be done with a planetary gear set to achieve neutral?

4. What is the difference between a nonsynchronous and a synchronous design?

5. What type of gears do the Hondamatic and the Saturn transaxle automatic transmission (TAAT) use?

1. How many planet pinions are used in a planetary gear set?
   a. Two
   b. Three
   c. Four
   d. Three, four, or five

2. When are the planet gears fully meshed with the sun gear and ring gear?
   a. All the time
   b. During torque multiplication
   c. During gear reduction
   d. When overdrive is occurring

3. A Simpson gear train consists of _____.
   a. Two sun gears, one planet carrier, and one ring gear
   b. One sun gear, two planet carriers, and one ring gear
   c. One sun gear with two carriers with planet gears and two ring gears
   d. Two sun gears with two planet carriers and one ring gear

4. A Ravigneaux gear set _____.
   a. Uses two carriers that have three sets of planet gears with one sun gear and one ring gear
   b. Combines one carrier that has two sets of planet gears with two sun gears, and one ring gear
   c. Combines one carrier that has one set of planet gears with two sun gears, and two ring gears
   d. Uses two carriers that have two sets of planet gears with two sun gears, and two ring gears

5. LePelletier gear train uses _____.
   a. A Ravigneaux gear set and a simple planetary gear set
   b. Two Simpson gear sets tied together
   c. A Simpson gear set and a simple planetary gear set combined
   d. Two Ravigneaux gear sets combined

6. A Nonsynchronous design _____.
   a. Requires that a clutch or band be released before another clutch is applied
   b. Allows an upshift that requires only the application of the next driving or reaction member
   c. Uses a Simpson gear set only
   d. Uses a Ravigneaux gear set only

7. A synchronous design _____.
   a. Requires that a clutch or band be released before another clutch is applied
   b. Allows an upshift that requires only the application of the next driving or reaction member
   c. Uses a Simpson gear set only
   d. Uses a Ravigneaux gear set only

8. A clutch-to-clutch automatic transmission, such as the Chrysler 41TE, does not use _____.
   a. Roller clutches
   b. Sprags
   c. Bands
   d. All of the above

9. Which transmission is a rear-wheel-drive unit?
   a. 4L60-E
   b. 41TE
   c. 6F60
   d. 4T80-E

10. What type of gears do the Hondamatic and the Saturn transaxle automatic transmission (TAAT) use?
   a. Simpson gear sets
   b. Ravigneaux gear set
   c. Helical cut constant mesh
   d. LePelletier gear set

chapter 7
CLUTCHES AND BANDS

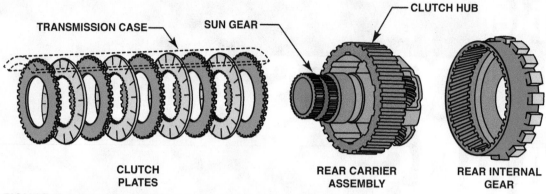

TRANSMISSION CASE — SUN GEAR — CLUTCH HUB

CLUTCH
PLATES

REAR CARRIER
ASSEMBLY

REAR INTERNAL
GEAR

FIGURE 7–1 A multiple-disc clutch can hold, or drive a member of a gear set.

INTRODUCTION

There are several paths for power to flow through an automatic transmission, and each path provides a different gear ratio. These power paths are controlled by clutches and bands, also called driving and reaction members. The **driving devices** connect the turbine shaft from the torque converter to the elements of the planetary gear train. The **reaction devices** connect (lock) a member of the gear train to the transmission case. ● SEE **FIGURE 7–1**.

DRIVING DEVICES

PURPOSE AND FUNCTION   The driving devices provide the input to the planetary gear set. The turbine shaft (which transfers power into the transmission) is normally built as part of or splined to one or more of the driving devices.

TERMINOLOGY   Driving devices are usually multiple-plate disc clutches. In most cases, they will be at the front of the transmission, just behind the pump. Although the parts perform the same job, the driving clutches are often given different names by different manufacturers. An example of this involves the two clutches in front of a Simpson gear train transmission.

- Chrysler Corporation calls the first clutch the **front clutch**.
- Ford Motor Company calls it a **high-reverse clutch**.
- General Motors Corporation and Toyota call it a **direct clutch**.
- Toyota commonly calls it C2.

SYNCHRONIZING SHIFTS   Automatic shifts must be timed to happen quickly without the possibility of being in two gears at the same time. A gear set will lock up if it has two ratios at the same time. In order to prevent this from happening, transmission manufacturers adopt the following two strategies:

1. First strategy is **synchronous**, *overlap*, or **clutch-to-clutch** shifting. This requires that one apply device be timed or synchronized with the application of the apply device for the next gear range.

2. The second strategy is called *nonsynchronous, asynchronous*, or *freewheel shifts*. Nonsynchronous shifts use one or more one-way clutches as driving or reaction devices. A one-way clutch will self-release during a shift as soon as the next clutch applies, eliminating the need to synchronize the shifts.

MULTIPLE-DISC DRIVING CLUTCHES

PARTS INVOLVED   The parts of a clutch assembly include:

- drum
- hub
- lined plates (discs)
- unlined discs (steels)
- pressure plate
- apply piston
- piston return springs.

The **drum**, also called the *housing*, has internal splines that mate with external splines on the steel plates for the externally lugged discs, usually the unlined discs (steels). The

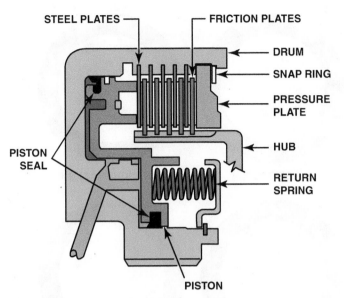

FIGURE 7–2 A sectioned view of a multiple-disc clutch. Note the piston to apply the clutch and the spring(s) to release it.

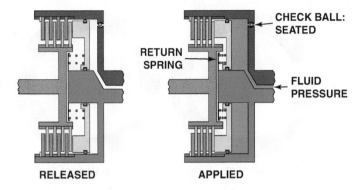

FIGURE 7–3 The apply piston is released (left) by the coil springs. Fluid pressure moves the piston to apply the clutch (right).

inner diameter of the drum is machined for the apply piston and its inner and outer seals. The drum of the forward clutch is usually built as part of or splined to the input or turbine shaft. A clutch can be built as a single unit or combined with another drum or hub of a second clutch assembly. ● SEE FIGURES 7–2 AND 7–3.

CLUTCH PLATES

- The unlined plates are called **steels**, or **separator plates**. They are flat pieces of steel stamped into the desired shape. A steel plate is usually about 0.070 to 0.100 inch (1.78 to 2.54 mm) thick. After being stamped, the plate is carefully flattened. An out-of-flat plate will take up clutch clearance and cause drag while released. An unlined steel plate usually has lugs on its outer diameter to engage with the clutch drum/housing or transmission case. The steel plates used in current automatic transmissions are very smooth and often have a polished appearance with a surface roughness of 12 to 15 microinches. Steel plates have a secondary purpose of serving as heat sinks to help remove heat from the lined friction plates.

- Plates lined with friction material are called **friction plates**, *friction disc,* or simply *frictions*. These plates are also made from stamped steel with lining material bonded to each side. The engagement lugs are usually on the inner diameter. A friction plate is about 0.063 to 0.086 inch (1.6 to 2.2 mm) thick, and the friction material is about 0.015 to 0.030 inch (0.4 to 0.8 mm) thick.

LINING SURFACE
The lining material can have a plain, smooth, flat, or a grooved friction surface. A grooved plate can have one of several grooving patterns cut or stamped into the friction material. The grooves help fluid leave or enter between the unlined and lined plates during a shift. The different grooving patterns help control the speed with which the fluid leaves the friction area to produce different shift-quality characteristics. The faster the oil leaves, the faster the clutch can apply. However, the longer the oil stays between the plates, the more heat can be absorbed by the oil. Different clutch packs for the same transmission will often use lined plates with different grooving patterns. Clutches that apply with the vehicle at rest can be smooth because apply rate is not important. Clutches that are used for upshifts will often have a groove pattern. Some new clutch designs use friction plates with **directional grooving**. These are a slanted groove that must face the proper direction. Some have an inner spline shape that allows the plate to be installed only in the proper direction. ● SEE FIGURE 7–4.

FRICTION LINING MATERIALS
Clutch lining material is a mix of natural and man-made fibers, fillers, and binders. The exact mixture is selected to provide the desired clutch apply duration and heat resistance characteristics. Clutch friction material includes the following:

- **Paper**—Paper-based friction material is the most commonly used material and offers smooth and chatter-free performance. ● SEE FIGURE 7–5.

- **Aramid (Kevlar)**—This synthetic material is used in clutches that are under heavy stress, such as in heavy-duty vehicle transmissions.

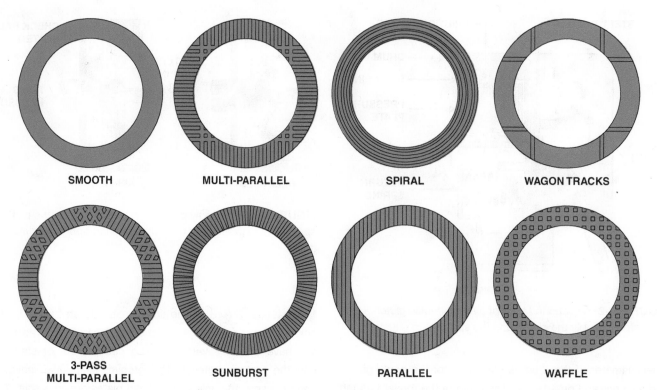

SMOOTH   MULTI-PARALLEL   SPIRAL   WAGON TRACKS

3-PASS MULTI-PARALLEL   SUNBURST   PARALLEL   WAFFLE

FIGURE 7–4 Friction plates often have a groove pattern to help wipe fluid away, dissipate heat, eliminate clutch noise, and change friction qualities during apply and release. A smooth plate is the coolest and slowest to apply and the waffle plate will apply the fastest.

FIGURE 7–5 Most clutches included in overhaul kits use paper as the basis for the lining material.

Fillers help determine the density, porosity, and flexibility. Some commonly used filler materials include:

- diatomaceous earth
- graphite/carbon
- friction particles

Binders hold the mix together and the most common binder is thermosetting phenolic resin.

CLUTCH OPERATION

CLUTCH PACK APPLY An automatic transmission shifts when hydraulic pressure applies or releases a clutch. Hydraulic pressure causes the clutch or servo piston to move, taking up the clearance, and then squeezes the parts together. The force that a clutch piston exerts on the clutch plates is a product of piston area multiplied by hydraulic pressure. A rotating, driving clutch has a piston with an outside diameter (OD) of about 6 inches (152 mm) and an inner diameter (ID) that can vary from 2 to 5 inches (102 to 127 mm). ●**SEE FIGURE 7–6**.

Most bands use fairly small servo pistons, which generate less force than a clutch piston. Some transmissions are designed so that several different servo piston diameters can be used. ●**SEE FIGURE 7–7**.

PRESSURE BALANCED RELEASE Traditionally, clutches are released by the spring(s), but this might be too slow in recent clutch-to-clutch transmissions. ●**SEE FIGURE 7–8**.

The clutch is applied when fluid pressure is sent to the apply side of the piston. Releasing pressure from the apply side

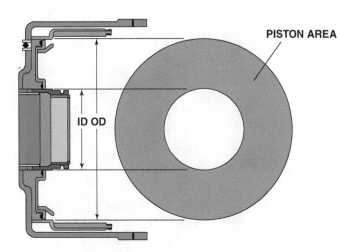

PISTON AREA

ID OD

PISTON AREA: 6" OD = 28.27 in.²   (3 × 3 × 3.1416)
              3" ID = −7 in.²   (1.5 × 1.5 × 3.1416)
              AREA = 21.27 in.²

FIGURE 7–6 A typical clutch piston area is determined by subtracting the area of the inner diameter from the area of the outer-circle diameter.

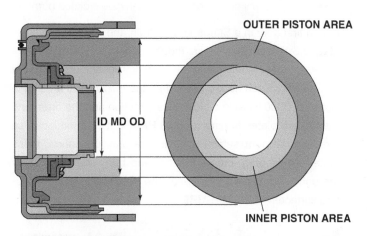

OUTER PISTON AREA

ID MD OD

INNER PISTON AREA

OUTER PISTON AREA: INNER PISTON AREA:
6" OD = 28.27 in.²   4" MD = 12.56 in.²
4" MD = −12.56 in.²   3" ID = −7 in.²
AREA = 15.71 in.²   AREA = 5.56 in.²

FIGURE 7–7 Some clutch pistons use a middle seal so the piston will have two working areas.

and sending fluid pressure, also called *compensator* or cancel pressure, to the release side produces a precisely controlled clutch release. ● **SEE FIGURE 7–9**.

CLUTCH PACK RELEASE The clutches are flooded with transmission fluid while released, and during application this fluid prevents any heat generated by friction from overheating the lining. Theoretically, there will always be a film of fluid between the friction and steel plates.

Manufacturers often provide some means of adjusting the released clearance in a clutch pack. There must be sufficient

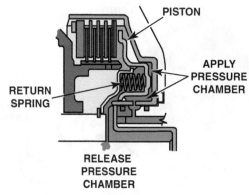

PISTON

RETURN
SPRING

APPLY
PRESSURE
CHAMBER

RELEASE
PRESSURE
CHAMBER

FIGURE 7–8 The baffle that supports the return springs also forms a chamber for release pressure. The clutch is released when fluid pressure enters this chamber as pressure is released from the apply side of the piston.

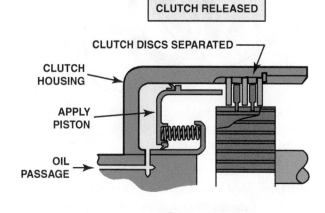

CLUTCH RELEASED

CLUTCH DISCS SEPARATED

CLUTCH
HOUSING

APPLY
PISTON

OIL
PASSAGE

CLUTCH APPLIED

ALL CLUTCH DISCS ARE FORCED TOGETHER

OIL FORCES
PISTON TO
APPLY CLUTCH

PRESSURIZED
OIL FOR APPLY

FIGURE 7–9 Pressurized oil is sent to the apply side of the piston to force the clutch discs together.

clearance between the plates to ensure that there is no drag when released. This clearance should be about 0.010 to 0.015 inch (0.25 to 0.38 mm) between each friction surface-lined and unlined plate. Clutch pack clearance is also called *piston travel*. Common methods of adjusting clutch pack clearance are selective size retaining rings, pressure plates, and steel plates. A selective part is available in several thicknesses, and when a clutch is assembled, the correct width or thickness is selected. ● **SEE FIGURE 7–10**.

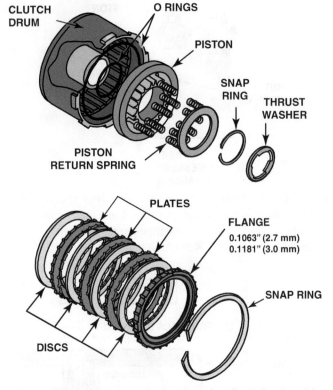

FIGURE 7–10 Clutch stack clearance is adjusted using either the large or the small flange (backing plate). Other clutches may use a selective snap ring.

DOUBLE- AND SINGLE-SIDED FRICTION PLATES

Single-sided plates have friction material on one side only, and half of the plates have lugs on the inner diameter while the other half have them on the outer diameter. Single-sided plates run cooler than two-sided plates, a feature that allows for more power transfer. The plates can be made thinner so that more plates can be put into a clutch pack. Single-sided plates have encountered problems of uneven heating because one side gets hotter, and the plate tends to deform into a conical shape. This problem has been solved by mechanically distorting the plates slightly or by specially designed grooves cut in the end plates.

FORCES INVOLVED

When a clutch is applied, the plates are squeezed together and torque is transferred from the friction plates to the steel plates. The amount of torque that can be transferred is determined by the following factors: diameter and width of the friction surfaces, number of friction surfaces (two per lined plate), and the amount of force being applied (hydraulic pressure times the piston area). The greater the plate area, number of plates, piston size, or hydraulic pressure, the greater the torque capacity.

When a clutch is released, there must be clearance between the plates. There is often a considerable speed differential between the friction and steel plates. For example,

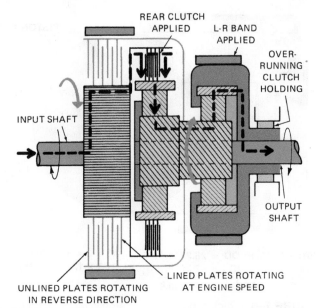

FIGURE 7–11 When this transmission is in first gear, the sun gear and unlined plates of the front clutch rotate counterclockwise while the hub and lined plates of this clutch rotate clockwise. Any drag will produce heat that can cause clutch burnout.

during first gear in a Simpson gear train, the sun gear revolves at a 2.5:1 ratio in reverse (counterclockwise). Imagine the speed difference between a released high-gear clutch with the input shaft, clutch hub, and lined plates revolving at an engine speed of 3000 RPM in a clockwise direction and the drum and the unlined plates turning at 7500 RPM in a counterclockwise direction. Without sufficient clearance and lubrication, these plates would drag, create friction, and burn up. The oil flow through the grooves and between the plates helps cool the friction surfaces. ● SEE FIGURE 7–11.

STATIC AND DYNAMIC FRICTION

A transmission engineer is concerned with three different friction conditions in a clutch:

1. While the clutch is released, there should be no friction or drag.

2. While applied, there should be sufficient **static friction** to transfer torque without slippage.

3. While applying, there should be the proper **dynamic friction** to get a good, smooth shift.

The amount of friction between two objects or surfaces is commonly expressed as a value called the *coefficient of friction* and is represented by the Greek letter μ (mu). The coefficient of friction, also referred to as the friction coefficient, is determined by dividing tensile force by weight force. The tensile force is the pulling force required to slide one of the surfaces across the other. The weight force is the force pushing down on the object being pulled. ● SEE FIGURE 7–12.

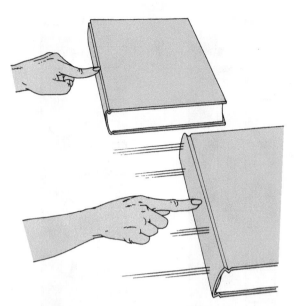

FIGURE 7–12 When pushing against a stationary book, the static friction resists motion. Pushing against the same book while it is sliding is easier because the dynamic friction is less.

The friction characteristics of a clutch are designed to work with the friction characteristics of the transmission fluid.

GARAGE SHIFTS Some clutches in an automatic transmission are applied while the vehicle is at rest. The neutral-to-drive and neutral-to-reverse shifts are called **garage shifts**.

- The clutches for first or reverse gear need a high amount of static friction because of the amount of torque required to get the vehicle moving. The garage shifts can occur slowly so they are usually less severe than the 1–2, 2–3, or 3–4 shifts; they may take 3 or 4 seconds to apply.

- Clutches that are applied while the vehicle is in motion are called *power shift* elements. They are applied under power and have to transfer substantial torque as they are applied. These clutches must have a high dynamic coefficient of friction.

ONE-WAY DRIVING CLUTCHES

PURPOSE AND FUNCTION In most transmissions, a one-way clutch allows rotation in a clockwise direction but blocks counterclockwise rotation.

- Applying and holding in a one-way clutch is often referred to as holding or being *effective*

- Releasing it is called ineffective or *noneffective*.

? FREQUENTLY ASKED QUESTION

What Is Wet Friction?

Wet friction occurs because ATF fills the space between the clutch plates. This ATF film transmits torque between the clutch plates as the clutch is being applied. The action of the film of fluid is called *fluid shear*.

As the clutch is applied, the clutch plate clearance is reduced as the fluid is squeezed from between the plates, leaving a film of fluid. This hydrodynamic film begins transferring torque. Fluid shear, which is the resistance to motion, is the primary torque transmitting force at the start of a shift. As the plate clearance is reduced, fluid viscosity increases and its resistance to shear increases. The clutch plates make physical contact at the end of application. Since there is no movement between the plates at this time, friction lining wear is minimized.

ROLLER CLUTCH A roller clutch is made up of a smooth inner race, a ramped outer race, a series of rollers and energizing springs, and a cage or guide to contain the springs. Some roller clutches are made with a ramped inner race and a smooth outer race. Each roller fits in the ramp or cam section of the race. An energizing spring pushes the roller so there is a light contact between the roller, the ramp, and the smooth race. Counterclockwise rotation of the hub will wedge the rollers so they become locked between the inner and outer races. When locked, they will block any further rotation in that direction. Clockwise rotation will unwedge the rollers, and each roller will simply rotate, much like a roller bearing. The inner hub will rotate freely or overrun in a clockwise direction. ● **SEE FIGURE 7–13.**

SPRAG CLUTCHES A sprag clutch uses smooth, hardened inner and outer races and a series of sprags that are mounted in a special cage. A sprag is an odd-shaped part that somewhat resembles an hourglass or fat letter *S* when viewed from the end. A sprag has two effective diameters. The major diameter is greater than the space between the inner and outer races, and the minor diameter is smaller than this space. The sprags are mounted in a cage that spring loads each sprag in a direction to "stand up" or wedge the major diameter between the two races. A clockwise rotation of the inner race causes the sprags to rotate in the stand-up direction. This causes them to wedge firmly between the two races and lock the races together. A counterclockwise rotation of the inner race rotates

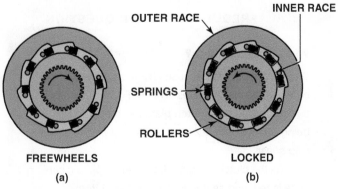

FIGURE 7–13 (a) Roller one-way clutch in released (free) position. When the inner roller clutch race rotates faster than the outer support, the rollers move out of the wedge and are free to rotate, thereby unlocking the one-way clutch. (b) Roller one-way clutch in the locked (held) position. Note how the rollers are wedged into the ramp that is machined into the outer support.

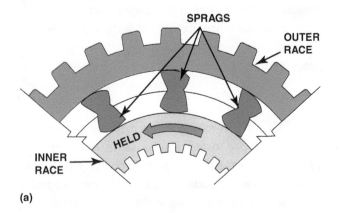

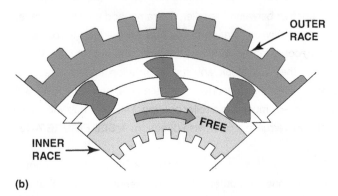

FIGURE 7–14 (a) The sprag in the holding (locked) position. Note how the long portion of the sprag is wedged between the inner and outer race. (b) The sprag in the released position. The inner race is free to rotate faster than the outer race.

the sprags in the opposite (laydown) direction. Each sprag tends to lie down so its minor diameter is between the races, and the inner race rotates freely. ● SEE FIGURE 7–14.

MECHANICAL DIODE   A **mechanical diode** is a type of one-way clutch. It uses spring-loaded, rectangular struts in the face of one clutch ring, the pocket plate that can engage

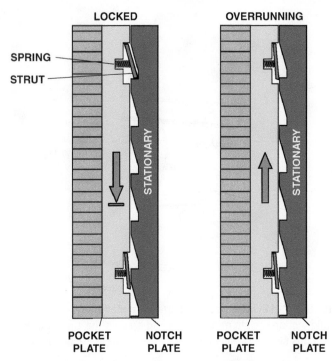

FIGURE 7–15 A mechanical diode. The struts can move out of the pocket plate to engage the notch plate, and this will lock the pocket plate. The pocket plate can overrun in the opposite direction.

notches in the face of another ring, the notch plate. The struts are pushed into their pockets when the clutch is overrunning, and they can move outward, about 15 degrees, to engage the notch plate to lock up. Because the compressive forces through the strut are in the load direction, only one or two of the struts need to engage. A mechanical diode is much stronger than a roller or sprag clutch. ● SEE FIGURE 7–15.

ONE-WAY CLUTCH OPERATION   A one-way clutch can be placed as an input to a gear set. In transmissions like the Ford 5R55E, a one-way clutch is always driving the forward planetary gear set at input shaft speed. In other transmissions, such as the General Motors 4T65-E, one-way clutches are driven through multiple-disc clutches to become effective in first and third gears. One-way clutches will overrun as the transmission shifts into the next higher gear. ● SEE FIGURE 7–16.

HOLDING/REACTION DEVICES

PURPOSE AND FUNCTION   A holding member acts as a brake to hold a planetary gear set member in reaction. Three types of holding devices are used: multiple-disc clutches, bands, and one-way clutches. Multiple-disc clutches and

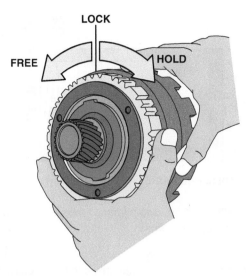

FIGURE 7–16 This clutch hub and sprag clutch should rotate freely in a counterclockwise direction but should lock up in the opposite direction.

bands are applied by hydraulic pressure and are controlled by the valve body. A one-way clutch is mechanically controlled; it allows rotation in one direction only.

HOLDING CLUTCHES

PURPOSE AND FUNCTION A multiple-disc holding clutch is quite similar to a driving clutch. The difference is that the transmission case is the clutch drum, and the clutch plates splined to it do not rotate. Some manufacturers call these clutches a *brake*.

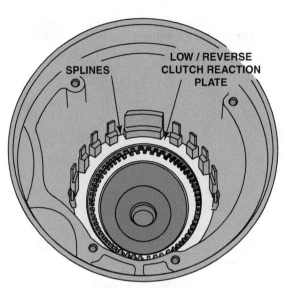

FIGURE 7–17 The 41TE transaxle low/reverse clutch is a holding clutch. Note the splines in the case for the clutch plates.

PARTS AND OPERATION The lugs on the outside of the unlined plates fit into slots built into the case. ● **SEE FIGURE 7–17**.

Like a driving clutch, the lugs on the inner diameter of the lined plates fit over the hub, which is often a part of the planetary gear train or the outer race of a one-way clutch.

The hydraulic piston can be built into the case, at the back of the front pump assembly, or in a center support. The stationary position of the piston and cylinder makes it relatively easy to provide fluid to it. Like a driving clutch, the piston is normally returned to a released position by springs.

ONE-WAY HOLDING CLUTCHES One-way clutches are commonly used as reaction devices. The outer race is often secured directly to the transmission case so it cannot rotate.

BANDS

PURPOSE AND FUNCTION The purpose of a band is to prevent rotation of the drum it is wrapped around. The drum can be a member of the planetary gear train.

TYPES A band is a circular strip of metal that has lining bonded to the inner surface. It wraps around the smooth surface of a drum. There are three types of bands:

1. A single thick, heavy band, also called a **rigid band**.

2. A single thin, light band, also called a *flexible* or **flex band**.

3. A split, **double-wrap**, heavy band. ● **SEE FIGURE 7–18**.

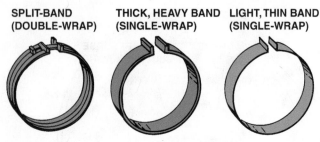

SPLIT-BAND (DOUBLE-WRAP) THICK, HEAVY BAND (SINGLE-WRAP) LIGHT, THIN BAND (SINGLE-WRAP)

FIGURE 7–18 Transmission bands come in several designs and thicknesses.

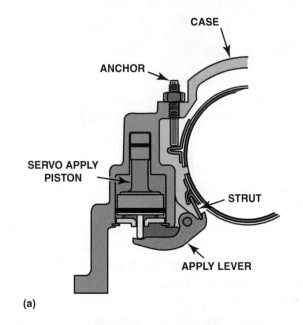

CASE

ANCHOR

SERVO APPLY PISTON

STRUT

APPLY LEVER

(a)

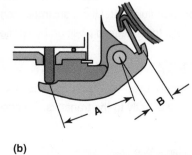

(b)

FIGURE 7–19 (a) This band uses an adjustable anchor that allows the clearance to be easily adjusted. (b) Note that the apply lever will increase apply force.

A rigid band is strong and provides a good heat sink to absorb some of the friction heat during application. The disadvantage with a rigid band is that it is relatively expensive and does not always conform to the shape of the drum. A flex band is less expensive and, because of its flexibility, can easily conform to the shape of the drum. Double-wrap bands give more holding power, and are often used for reverse or manual first gears. Each band type has end lugs so it can be attached to

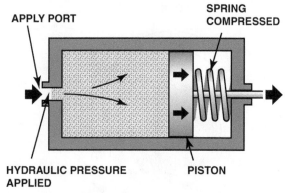

APPLY PORT   SPRING COMPRESSED

HYDRAULIC PRESSURE APPLIED   PISTON

FIGURE 7–20 A servo uses hydraulic pressure to move a piston, which applies a band.

the anchor and the servo. A small link, commonly called a *strut*, is often used to connect the lugs of the band to the anchor or the servo piston rod. ● **SEE FIGURE 7–19**.

FRICTION MATERIALS ON BANDS The friction material used on a band is similar to that used on clutch plates. Paper- and cloth-based materials are normally used. The drum must be a smooth cylinder with straight sides in order to have complete contact with the band lining. The lining surface of the band is often grooved to help control fluid flow during apply and release operations. Similar to a clutch, band friction material and grooving are designed to operate with a specified fluid to ensure good shift quality and long life.

SERVOS The servo is the hydraulic assembly that applies the band. Its main components include a

- cylinder
- piston
- piston rod/pin
- return spring

● **SEE FIGURE 7–20**.

The piston rod pushes directly on the end of the band on most servos. Some servo pistons are connected to the band through a lever or linkage attached to the band strut.

A band lever provides a force increase because of the lever ratio. The ratio will require more piston travel to apply the band but increases the application force acting on the end of the band. Some manufacturers incorporate a band adjustment screw in the apply lever. Other manufacturers use selective-size servo piston rods for band adjustment. ● **SEE FIGURE 7–21**.

ADJUSTMENT The anchor for the band can be a fixed or adjustable point in the transmission case. Some bands have

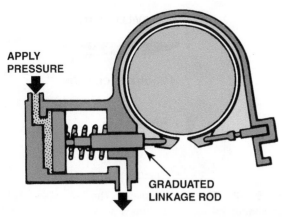

FIGURE 7–21 One end of a band is held stationary and the other end is attached to the servo.

an adjustable anchor, which provides a method of adjusting the clearance between the band and the drum. The bands that are adjustable are usually the rigid bands that have thick lining. Most bands use thin linings and are not adjustable. There must be enough clearance to ensure there is no band-to-drum contact with the band released, but too much clearance might cause slippage if the band does not apply completely. A band that is too loose or too tight has an adverse effect on shift timing.

BAND OPERATION   When fluid pressure enters the servo, the servo piston moves, tightening the band around the drum. The amount of torque that a band can absorb before slipping is determined by the band-to-drum contact area, type of band, drum diameter, fluid type, and the force squeezing the band onto the drum.

When a band releases, the servo piston backs off, and the springy, elastic nature of the band causes it to move away from the drum. A servo piston can be released by either spring pressure and/or hydraulic pressure.

- When the shift has to be made to neutral, the release speed is not important. Normally, servos use only a release spring.
- During an upshift, the band release must be fast and carefully timed. The release of many bands is done by using fluid pressure from the clutch being applied. For example, in a Simpson gear train transmission during a 2–3 shift, the fluid pressure to apply the third-gear clutch is also used to release the second-gear band.
- During a downshift, band apply must be quick and firm.
  ● **SEE FIGURE 7–22**.

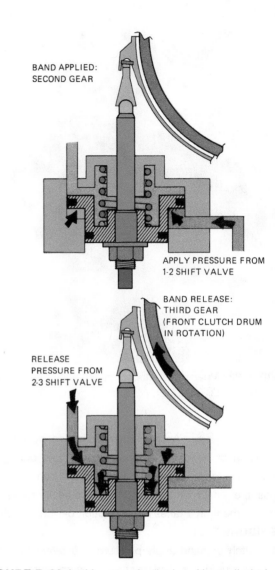

FIGURE 7–22 In this example, the band is applied when 1–2 shift valve pressure pushes upward on the servo piston (top). It will release when 2–3 shift valve pressure pushes the piston downward (bottom). Note the larger area above the piston.

SHIFT QUALITY

TERMINOLOGY   As a power shift occurs, there must be a smooth transition from one apply device to the next. The smoothness of the shift is referred to as shift quality or **shift feel**.

A shift should be smooth without any unusual noises. In order for this to occur, the clutches and bands must apply smoothly and quietly. The timing of the band releasing from second gear and the clutch applying for third gear must be precise. Any improper noises such as squeaks, squawks, or shrieks or operations such as engine RPM flare, jerks, bumps, or harsh application are considered faults that need to be corrected.

FIGURE 7–23 A band accumulator piston and spring being removed from a GM 4T65-E.

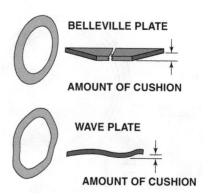

FIGURE 7–24 Two cushion plates: The Belleville plate has a coned shape; the wave plate has a wavy shape. Both of them will flatten slightly as the clutch is applied.

ACCUMULATORS

An **accumulator** is tied hydraulically to the clutch or band servo, and absorbs fluid during the pressure buildup stage when a clutch or band applies. This has the effect of slowing the pressure increase and lengthening the time it takes for the friction device to lock up. ● **SEE FIGURE 7–23**.

As clutch or band apply pressure is entering the apply side of the accumulator, fluid must leave the opposite, exhaust side of the accumulator piston. The pressure on the apply side and rate of stroke depends on how easily the fluid leaves the exhaust side. An accumulator valve or shift control valve is often placed in the accumulator exhaust passage. The shift must be completed before the accumulator completes its stroke. If the accumulator piston reaches the bottom before the shift is complete, there will be a sudden pressure increase that will cause a *slide-bump shift*. This is a shift with poor quality that starts smooth, but ends harsh.

WAVE PLATE

Clutch shift quality is controlled by the type of lining material and grooving, the use of wave or Belleville plates, the type of fluid used, and the speed at which fluid moves the piston.

A **wave plate** is an unlined plate that is wavy, not flat. A **Belleville plate**, like a Belleville spring, is also not flat. These are often called **cushion plates**. ● **SEE FIGURE 7–24**.

If either plate is used in a clutch pack, it will be placed between the piston and the first unlined plate or between the last unlined plate and the pressure plate. Both plates are designed to compress slightly under pressure during clutch application. The result is to slightly prolong the clutch apply time.

Many transmissions do not use Belleville or wave plates. Hydraulic controls (accumulators and orifices) are used to control piston movement and produce the desired shift quality. Electronically controlled transmissions have even greater ability to alter shift quality. The shift solenoids and hydraulic pressure control solenoids can be turned off and on, or cycled to produce the desired shifts.

SHIFTS INVOLVING ONE-WAY CLUTCHES

A one-way clutch is an ideal driving or reaction member for automatic shifts. It applies or holds when it is needed and self-releases or overruns when it is not needed. Its operation is controlled by the load direction on the inner or outer race so shift timing is automatic. When the transmission upshifts, the reaction or driving member for the next gear is applied, and the one-way clutch simply overruns. This is called a nonsynchronous or asynchronous shift and the shift elements do not need to be synchronized. It is also called a **freewheel shift**.

DECELERATION WITH ONE-WAY CLUTCHES

When the throttle is released while in a gear that uses a one-way clutch, the transmission will go into neutral as the one-way clutch overruns. This action is good if the vehicle is coasting to a stop, but can be a problem if going down a steep hill.

1. The power flow through a gear set is controlled by driving and reaction devices.

2. The driving and reaction devices are multiple-disc clutches, one-way clutches, and bands.

3. Multiple-disc clutches are the primary driving devices and are also used to hold planetary members in reaction.

4. One-way clutches are primarily used to hold planetary members in reaction, but can be used with a multiple-disc clutch as a driving device.

5. Bands are used to hold a planetary member in reaction.

6. The timing of the apply devices has a direct effect on shift quality.

REVIEW QUESTIONS

1. What is the difference between a driving device and a reaction device?

2. What is the difference between synchronous and nonsynchronous shifts?

3. What parts are included in a typical clutch pack assembly?

4. Why do some clutch discs use friction material on only one side?

5. What is the purpose and function of an accumulator?

CHAPTER QUIZ

1. The _____ connects the turbine shaft from the torque converter to the elements of the planetary gear train.
   a. Reaction devices
   b. Accumulator
   c. Driving devices
   d. Servo

2. The _____ connect (lock) a member of the gear train to the transmission case.
   a. Reaction devices
   b. Accumulator
   c. Driving devices
   d. Servo

3. The apply device that is most commonly used as a driving member is a _____.
   a. Cone clutch
   b. Multiple-disc clutch
   c. One-way clutch
   d. Band

4. Plates lined with friction material are called _____.
   a. Friction disc
   b. Simply frictions
   c. Friction plates
   d. Any of the above

5. Some clutches in an automatic transmission are applied while the vehicle is at rest. This application of the clutch(es) is often called a _____ shift.
   a. Static
   b. Garage
   c. Synchronous
   d. Nonsynchronous

6. The lining material most often used is made from _____.
   a. Paper
   b. Asbestos
   c. Inorganic fibers
   d. Any of the above depending on application

7. Typical clearance should be about _____ between each friction surface-lined and unlined plate.
   a. 0.001 to 0.005 inch (0.025 to 0.012 mm)
   b. 0.010 to 0.015 inch (0.25 to 0.38 mm)
   c. 0.020 to 0.035 inch (0.050 to 0.090 mm)
   d. 0.050 to 0.075 inch (1.3 to 1.9 mm)

8. What is an example of a one-way clutch?
   a. Multi-clutch pack
   b. Band
   c. Roller clutch
   d. Accumulator

9. The torque-carrying capacity of a clutch is determined by the _____.
   a. Number of plates
   b. Amount of lining area on the plates
   c. Amount of pressure squeezing the plates together
   d. All of the above

10. How does an accumulator work?
    a. Slows the application of the clutch or band
    b. Includes a solenoid to apply a clutch
    c. Supplies high-pressure ATF to a band so it applies quickly
    d. Accumulates extra ATF for use when it is low in the case of a leak

chapter 8
DRIVETRAIN ELECTRICITY AND ELECTRONICS

LEARNING OBJECTIVES

After studying this chapter, the reader should be able to:

1. Explain the characteristics of electricity.
2. Differentiate between conductors, insulators, and semiconductors.
3. Explain the units of electrical measurement.
4. List the parts of a complete circuit.
5. Discuss the types of electrical circuit faults.
6. Explain how to detect and measure electrical voltage, current, and resistance.
7. Discuss the purpose and function of terminals, connectors, relays, and switches.
8. Explain the operation of speed sensors and throttle position (TP) sensors.
9. State the need for networks and discuss network classifications.

KEY TERMS

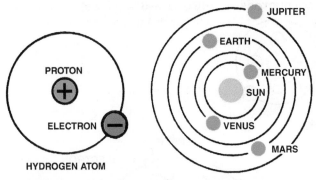

FIGURE 8–1 In an atom (left), electrons orbit protons in the nucleus just as planets orbit the sun in our solar system (right).

INTRODUCTION

The electrical system is one of the most important systems in a vehicle today. Every year more and more vehicle components and systems use electricity.

Electricity may be difficult for some people to learn for the following reasons.

- It cannot be seen.
- Only the results of electricity can be seen.
- It has to be detected and measured.

ELECTRICITY

BACKGROUND Our universe is composed of matter, which is anything that has mass and occupies space. All matter is made from slightly over 100 individual components called elements. The smallest particle that an element can be broken into and still retain the properties of that element is known as an atom. ● **SEE FIGURE 8–1**.

DEFINITION **Electricity** is the movement of electrons from one atom to another. The dense center of each atom is called the nucleus. The nucleus contains

- Protons, which have a positive charge
- Neutrons, which are electrically neutral (have no charge)
- Electrons, which have a negative charge, orbit the nucleus. Each atom contains an equal number of electrons and protons.

NOTE: As an example of the relative sizes of the parts of an atom, consider that if an atom were magnified so that the nucleus were the size of the period at the end of this sentence, the whole atom would be bigger than a house.

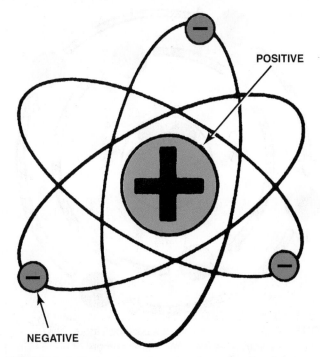

FIGURE 8–2 The nucleus of an atom has a positive (+) charge and the surrounding electrons have a negative (–) charge.

POSITIVE AND NEGATIVE CHARGES The parts of an atom have different charges. The orbiting electrons are negatively charged, while the protons are positively charged. Positive charges are indicated by the "plus" sign (+), and negative charges by the "minus" sign (–). ● **SEE FIGURE 8–2**.

These same + and – signs are used to identify parts of an electrical circuit. Neutrons have no charge at all. They are neutral. In a normal or balanced atom, the number of negative particles equals the number of positive particles. That is, there are as many electrons as there are protons. ● **SEE FIGURE 8–3**.

MAGNETS AND ELECTRICAL CHARGE An ordinary magnet has two ends, or poles. One end is called the south pole, and the other is called the north pole. If two magnets are brought close to each other with like poles together (south to south or north to north), the magnets will push each other apart, because like poles repel each other. If the opposite poles of the magnets are brought close to each other, south to north, the magnets will snap together, because unlike poles attract each other. The positive and negative charges within an atom are like the north and south poles of a magnet. Charges that are alike will repel each other, similar to the poles of a magnet. ● **SEE FIGURE 8–4**.

That is why the negative electrons continue to orbit around the positive protons. They are attracted and held by the opposite charge of the protons. The electrons keep moving in orbit because they repel each other.

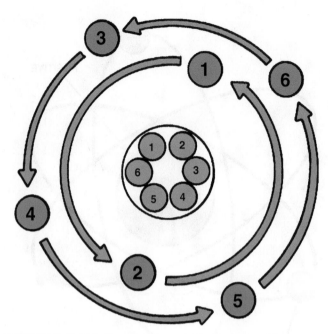

FIGURE 8–3 This figure shows a balanced atom. The number of electrons is the same as the number of protons in the nucleus.

FIGURE 8–4 Unlike charges attract and like charges repel.

ELECTRON ORBITS

Electrons orbit around the nucleus in rings and the outermost ring is called the "valence ring." Whether a material is a conductor or an insulator strictly depends on how many electrons are in the outer ring.

CONDUCTORS

Conductors are materials with fewer than four electrons in their atom's outer orbit. ●**SEE FIGURE 8–5**.

Copper is an excellent conductor because it has only one electron in its outer orbit. This orbit is far enough away from the nucleus of the copper atom that the pull or force holding the outermost electron in orbit is relatively weak. ●**SEE FIGURE 8–6**.

Copper is the conductor most used in vehicles because the price of copper is reasonable compared to the relative cost of other conductors with similar properties. Examples of commonly used conductors include:

- Silver
- Copper
- Gold
- Aluminum
- Steel
- Cast iron

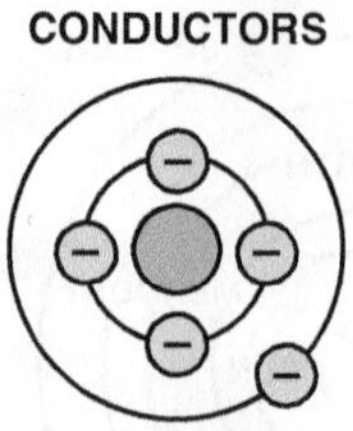

CONDUCTORS

FIGURE 8–5 A conductor is any element that has one to three electrons in its outer orbit.

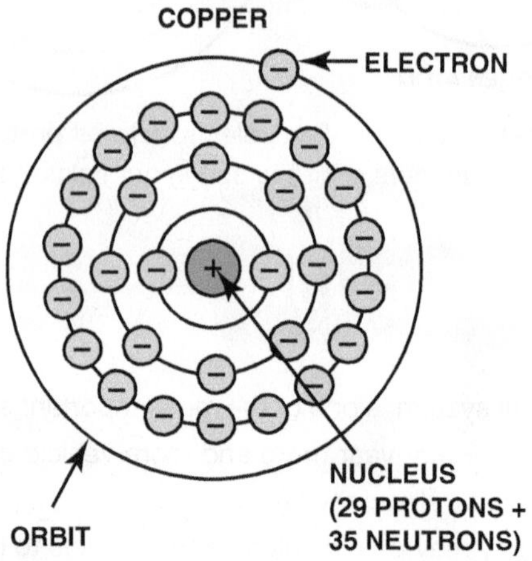

COPPER

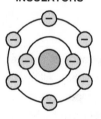

← ELECTRON

NUCLEUS
(29 PROTONS +
35 NEUTRONS)

ORBIT

FIGURE 8–6 Copper is an excellent conductor of electricity because it has just one electron in its outer orbit, making it easy to be knocked out of its orbit and flow to other nearby atoms. This causes electron flow, which is the definition of electricity.

INSULATORS

FIGURE 8–7 Insulators are elements with five to eight electrons in the outer orbit.

INSULATORS

Some materials hold their electrons tightly and, as a result, electrons do not move through them very well. These materials are called insulators. **Insulators** are materials with more than four electrons in their atom's outer orbit. Because they have more than four electrons in their outer orbit, it becomes easier for these materials to acquire (gain) electrons than to release electrons. ●**SEE FIGURE 8–7**.

Examples of insulators include:

- Rubber
- Plastic
- Nylon
- Porcelain
- Ceramic
- Fiberglass

FIGURE 8–8 Semiconductor elements contain exactly four electrons in the outer orbit.

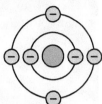

SEMICONDUCTORS

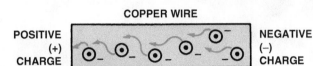

COPPER WIRE

POSITIVE (+) CHARGE

NEGATIVE (–) CHARGE

FIGURE 8–9 Current electricity is the movement of electrons through a conductor.

SEMICONDUCTORS
Materials with exactly four electrons in their outer orbit are neither conductors nor insulators, but are called **semiconductors**. Semiconductors can be either an insulator or a conductor in different design applications. ● **SEE FIGURE 8–8.**

Examples of semiconductors include:

- Silicon
- Germanium
- Carbon

Semiconductors are used mostly in transistors, computers, and other electronic devices.

HOW ELECTRONS MOVE THROUGH A CONDUCTOR

CURRENT FLOW The following events occur if a source of power, such as a battery, is connected to the ends of a conductor—a positive charge (lack of electrons) is placed on one end of the conductor and a negative charge (excess of electrons) is placed on the opposite end of the conductor. For current to flow, there must be an imbalance of excess electrons at one end of the circuit and a deficiency of electrons at the opposite end. ● **SEE FIGURE 8–9.**

CONVENTIONAL THEORY VERSUS ELECTRON THEORY

- **Conventional theory**: It was once thought that electricity had only one charge and moved from positive to negative. This theory of the flow of electricity through a conductor is called the conventional theory of current flow. Most automotive applications use the conventional theory. ● **SEE FIGURE 8–10.**

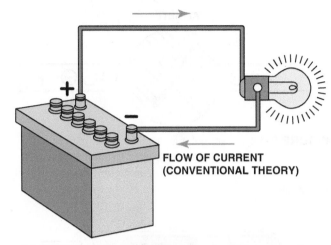

FLOW OF CURRENT (CONVENTIONAL THEORY)

FIGURE 8–10 Conventional theory states that current flows through a circuit from positive (+) to negative (–). Automotive electricity uses the conventional theory in all electrical diagrams and schematics.

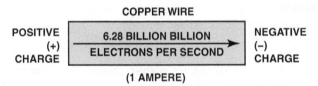

COPPER WIRE

POSITIVE (+) CHARGE

6.28 BILLION BILLION ELECTRONS PER SECOND

NEGATIVE (–) CHARGE

(1 AMPERE)

FIGURE 8–11 One ampere is the movement of 1 coulomb (6.28 billion billion electrons) past a point in 1 second.

- **Electron theory**: The discovery of the electron and its negative charge led to the electron theory, which states that there is electron flow from negative to positive.

UNITS OF ELECTRICITY

Electricity is measured using meters or other test equipment. The three fundamentals of electricity-related units include the ampere, volt, and ohm.

AMPERE The **ampere** is the unit used throughout the world to measure current flow. When 6.28 billion billion electrons (the name for this large number of electrons is called a coulomb) move past a certain point in 1 second, this represents 1 ampere of current. ● **SEE FIGURE 8–11.**

The ampere is the electrical unit for the amount of electron flow, just as "gallons per minute" is the unit that can be used to measure the quantity of water flow. It is named for the French electrician Andrè Marie Ampére (1775–1836). The conventional abbreviations and measurement for amperes are as follows:

1. The ampere is the unit of measurement for the amount of current flow.

2. A and amps are acceptable abbreviations for amperes.

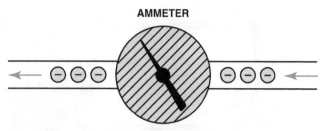

FIGURE 8–12 An ammeter is installed in the path of the electrons similar to a water meter used to measure the flow of water in gallons per minute. The ammeter displays current flow in amperes.

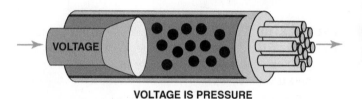

FIGURE 8–13 Voltage is the electrical pressure that causes the electrons to flow through a conductor.

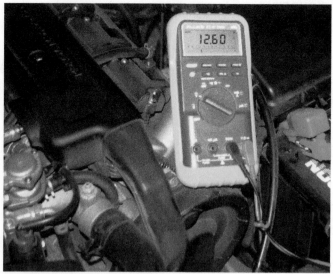

FIGURE 8–14 This digital multimeter set to read DC volts is being used to test the voltage of a vehicle battery. Most multimeters can also measure resistance (ohms) and current flow (amperes).

3. The capital letter I, for intensity, is used in mathematical calculations to represent amperes.

4. Amperes do the actual work in the circuit. It is the movement of the electrons through a light bulb or motor that actually makes the electrical device work. Without amperage through a device, it will not work at all.

5. Amperes are measured by an ammeter (not ampmeter). ● **SEE FIGURE 8–12**.

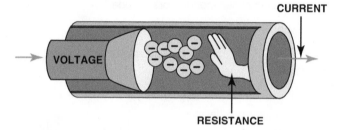

FIGURE 8–15 Resistance to the flow of electrons through a conductor is measured in ohms.

VOLTS The **volt** is the unit of measurement for electrical pressure. It is named for an Italian physicist, Alessandro Volta (1745–1827). The comparable unit using water pressure as an example would be pounds per square inch (PSI). It is possible to have very high pressures (volts) and low water flow (amperes). It is also possible to have high water flow (amperes) and low pressures (volts). Voltage is also called electrical potential, because if there is voltage present in a conductor, there is a potential (possibility) for current flow. ● **SEE FIGURE 8–13**.

The conventional abbreviations and measurement for voltage are as follows:

1. The volt is the unit of measurement for the amount of electrical pressure.

2. Electromotive force, abbreviated EMF, is another way of indicating voltage.

3. V is the generally accepted abbreviation for volts.

4. The symbol used in calculations is E, for electromotive force.

5. Volts are measured by a voltmeter. ● **SEE FIGURE 8–14**.

OHMS Resistance to the flow of current through a conductor is measured in units called **ohms**, named after the German physicist George Simon Ohm (1787–1854). The resistance to the flow of free electrons through a conductor results from the countless collisions the electrons cause within the atoms of the conductor. ● **SEE FIGURE 8–15**.

Resistance can be:

▪ Desirable when it is part of how a circuit works, such as the resistance of a filament in a light bulb.

▪ Undesirable, such as corrosion in a connection restricting the amount of current flow in a circuit.

The conventional abbreviations and measurement for resistance are as follows:

1. The ohm is the unit of measurement for electrical resistance.

2. The symbol for ohms is Ω (Greek capital letter omega), the last letter of the Greek alphabet.

3. The symbol used in calculations is R, for resistance.

4. Ohms are measured by an ohmmeter.

5. Resistance to electron flow depends on the material used.

ELECTRICAL CIRCUITS

DEFINITION A circuit is a complete path that electrons travel from a power source (such as a battery) through a load such as a light bulb and back to the power source. It is called a circuit because the current must start and finish at the same place (power source). For any electrical circuit to work at all, it must be continuous from the battery (power), through all the wires and components, and back to the battery (ground). A circuit that is continuous throughout is said to have continuity.

PARTS OF A COMPLETE CIRCUIT Every complete circuit contains the following parts

1. A power source, such as a vehicle's battery.

2. Protection from harmful overloads (excessive current flow). (Fuses, circuit breakers, and fusible links are examples of electrical circuit protection devices.)

3. The power path for the current to flow through, from the power source to the resistance. (This path from a power source to the load—a light bulb in this example—is usually an insulated copper wire.)

4. The electrical load or resistance, which converts electrical energy into heat, light, or motion.

5. A return path (ground) for the electrical current from the load back to the power source so that there is a complete circuit. (This return, or ground, path is usually the metal body, frame, ground wires, and engine block of the vehicle.) ● **SEE FIGURE 8–16**.

6. Switches and controls that turn the circuit on and off. ● **SEE FIGURE 8–17**.

ELECTRICAL SCHEMATICS

TERMINOLOGY Automotive manufacturer's service information includes wiring schematics of every electrical circuit in a vehicle. A wiring **schematic**, sometimes called a *diagram,* shows electrical components and wiring using symbols and lines to represent components and wires. A typical wiring schematic may include all of the circuits combined, or they may be broken down to show individual circuits. All circuit schematics or diagrams include:

- Power-side wiring of the circuit
- All splices
- Connectors
- Wire size
- Wire color
- Trace color (if any)
- Circuit number
- Electrical components
- Ground return paths
- Fuses and switches

CIRCUIT INFORMATION Many wiring schematics include numbers and letters near components and wires that may confuse readers of the schematic. Most letters used near or on a wire identify the color or colors of the wire.

- The first color or color abbreviation is the color of the wire insulation.
- The second color (if mentioned) is the color of the stripe or tracer on the base color. ● **SEE FIGURE 8–18**.

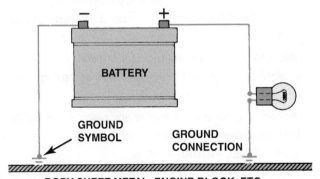

FIGURE 8–16 The return path back to the battery can be any electrical conductor, such as a copper wire or the metal frame or body of the vehicle.

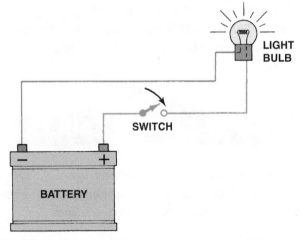

FIGURE 8–17 An electrical switch opens the circuit and no current flows. The switch could also be on the return (ground) path wire.

FIGURE 8–18 The center wire is a solid color wire, meaning that the wire has no other identifying tracer or stripe color. The two end wires could be labeled "BRN/WHT," indicating a brown wire with a white tracer or stripe.

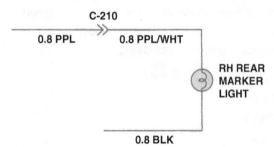

FIGURE 8–19 Typical section of a wiring diagram. Notice that the wire color changes at connection C210. The ".8" represents the metric wire size in square millimeters.

Wires with different color tracers are indicated by both colors with a slash (/) between them. For example, BRN/WHT means a brown wire with a white stripe or tracer.

WIRE SIZE Wire size is shown on all schematics. For example, ●**FIGURE 8–19** illustrates a rear side-marker bulb circuit diagram where ".8" indicates the metric wire gauge size in square millimeters (mm 2) and "PPL" indicates a solid purple wire.

The wire diagram also shows that the color of the wire changes at the number C210. This stands for "connector #210" and is used for reference purposes. The symbol for the connection can vary depending on the manufacturer. The color change from purple (PPL) to purple with a white tracer (PPL/WHT). The ground circuit is the ".8 BLK" wire.

●**SEE FIGURE 8–20**, which shows many of the electrical and electronic symbols that are used in wiring and circuit diagrams.

TYPES OF CIRCUIT FAULTS

Circuits can experience several different types of faults or problems, which often result in improper operation. The types of faults include opens, shorts, and high resistance.

OPEN CIRCUITS An **open circuit** is any circuit that is not complete, or that lacks continuity, such as a broken wire. ●**SEE FIGURE 8–21**.

Open circuits have the following features.

1. No current will flow through an open circuit.

2. An open circuit may be created by a break in the circuit or by a switch that opens (turns off) the circuit and prevents the flow of current.

3. In any circuit containing a power load and ground, an opening anywhere in the circuit will cause the circuit not to work.

4. A light switch in a home and the headlight switch in a vehicle are examples of devices that open a circuit to control its operation.

NOTE: A blown fuse opens the circuit to prevent damage to the components or wiring in the circuit in the event of an overload caused by a fault in the circuit.

SHORT-TO-VOLTAGE If a wire (conductor) or component is shorted to voltage, it is commonly referred to as being shorted. A **short-to-voltage** occurs when the power side of one circuit is electrically connected to the power side of another circuit. ●**SEE FIGURE 8–22**.

A short circuit has the following features:

1. It is a complete circuit in which the current usually bypasses some or all of the resistance in the circuit.

2. It involves the power side of the circuit.

3. It involves a copper-to-copper connection (two power side wires touching together).

4. It is also called a short-to-voltage.

5. It usually affects more than one circuit. In this case, if one circuit is electrically connected to another circuit, one of the circuits may operate when it is not supposed to because it is being supplied power from another circuit.

6. It may or may not blow a fuse. ●**SEE FIGURE 8–23**.

SHORT-TO-GROUND A **short-to-ground** is a type of short circuit that occurs when the current bypasses part of the normal circuit and flows directly to ground. A short-to-ground has the following features.

1. Because the ground return circuit is metal (vehicle frame, engine, or body), it is often identified as having current flowing from copper to steel.

2. A short-to-ground can occur at any place where a power path wire accidentally touches a return path wire or conductor. ●**SEE FIGURE 8–24**.

3. A defective component or circuit that is shorted to ground is commonly called grounded.

4. A short-to-ground almost always results in a blown fuse, damaged connectors, or melted wires.

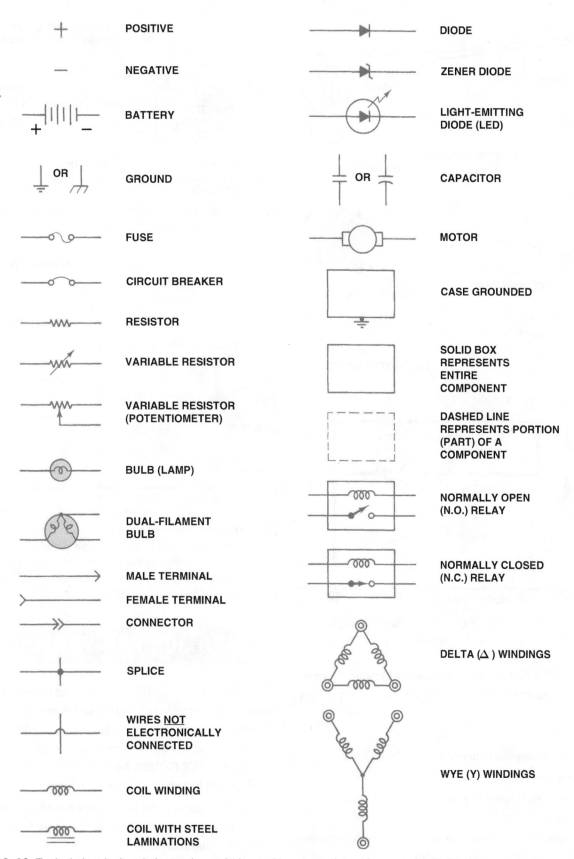

FIGURE 8–20 Typical electrical and electronic symbols used in automotive wiring and circuit diagrams.

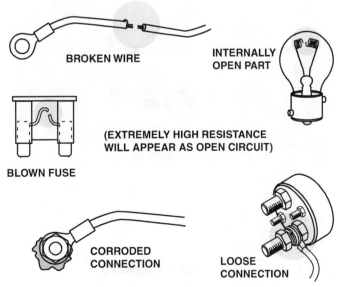

BROKEN WIRE

INTERNALLY OPEN PART

(EXTREMELY HIGH RESISTANCE WILL APPEAR AS OPEN CIRCUIT)

BLOWN FUSE

CORRODED CONNECTION

LOOSE CONNECTION

FIGURE 8–21 Examples of common causes of open circuits. Some of these causes are often difficult to find.

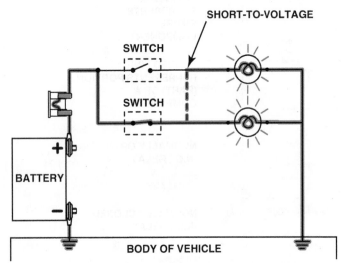

SHORT-TO-VOLTAGE

SWITCH

SWITCH

BATTERY

BODY OF VEHICLE

FIGURE 8–22 A short circuit permits electrical current to by-pass some or all of the resistance in the circuit.

HIGH RESISTANCE

High resistance is resistance higher than normal circuit resistance usually caused by any of the following:

- Corroded connections or sockets
- Loose terminals in a connector
- Loose ground connections

If there is high resistance anywhere in a circuit, it may cause the following problems:

1. Slow operation of a motor-driven unit, such as when the transfer case makes a range change.
2. Dim lights
3. "Clicking" of relays or solenoids
4. No operation of a circuit or electrical component

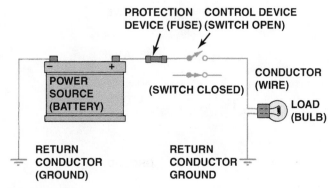

PROTECTION DEVICE (FUSE)   CONTROL DEVICE (SWITCH OPEN)

POWER SOURCE (BATTERY)

(SWITCH CLOSED)

CONDUCTOR (WIRE)

LOAD (BULB)

RETURN CONDUCTOR (GROUND)

RETURN CONDUCTOR GROUND

FIGURE 8–23 A fuse or circuit breaker opens the circuit to prevent possible overheating damage in the event of a short circuit.

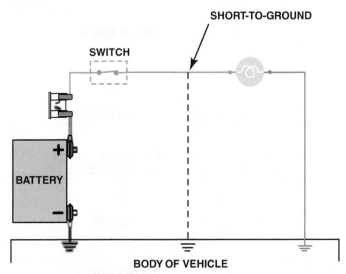

SHORT-TO-GROUND

SWITCH

BATTERY

BODY OF VEHICLE

FIGURE 8–24 A short-to-ground affects the power side of the circuit. Current flows directly to the ground return, bypassing some or all of the electrical loads in the circuit. There is no current in the circuit past the short. A short-to-ground will also cause the fuse to blow.

FUSED JUMPER WIRE

PURPOSE AND FUNCTION A fused jumper wire is used to check a circuit by bypassing the switch or to provide a power or ground to a component. A fused jumper wire, also called a fused test lead, can be purchased or made by the service technician. ● **SEE FIGURE 8–25**.

It should include the following features:

- *Fuse*: A typical fused jumper wire has a blade-type fuse that can be easily replaced. A 10 ampere fuse (red color) is often the value used.
- *Alligator clip ends*: Alligator clips on the ends allow the fused jumper wire to be clipped to a ground or power source while the other end is attached to the power side or ground side of the unit being tested.

FIGURE 8–25 A technician-made fused jumper lead, which is equipped with a red 10 ampere fuse. This fused jumper wire uses terminals for testing circuits at a connector instead of alligator clips.

- *Good-quality insulated wire:* Most purchased jumper wire is about 14 gauge stranded copper wire with a flexible rubberized insulation to allow it to move easily even in cold weather.

CAUTION: Never use a fused jumper wire to bypass any resistance or load in the circuit. The increased current flow could damage the wiring and could blow the fuse on the jumper lead. Be very cautious when working on or around any computer circuit. Permanent damage to the computer or electronic module could result if power or ground goes to the wrong circuit.

TEST LIGHT

NON-POWERED TEST LIGHT
A 12-volt test light is one of the simplest testers that can be used to detect electricity. A test light is simply a light bulb with a probe and a ground wire attached. ● **SEE FIGURE 8–26**.

A test light is used to detect battery voltage potential at various test points. Battery voltage cannot be seen or felt, and can be detected only with test equipment. The ground clip is connected to a clean ground on either the negative terminal of the battery or a clean metal part of the body and the

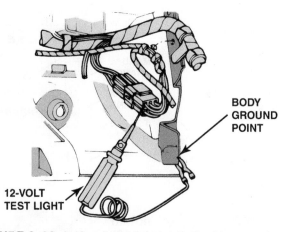

FIGURE 8–26 A 12-volt test light is attached to a good ground while probing for power.

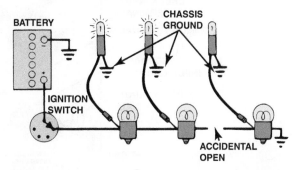

FIGURE 8–27 A test light can be used to locate an open in a circuit. Note that the test light is grounded at a different location than the circuit itself.

probe touched to terminals or components. If the test light comes on, this indicates that voltage is available. ● **SEE FIGURE 8–27**.

A purchased test light should be labeled as "12-volt test light." Do not purchase a test light designed for household current (110 or 220 volts), as it will not light with 12 to 14 volts.

USES OF A 12-VOLT TEST LIGHT
A 12-volt test light can be used to check the following:

- *Electrical power:* If the test light lights, then there is power available. It will not, however, indicate the voltage level or if there is enough current available to operate an electrical load. It only indicates that there is enough voltage and current to light the test light (about 0.25 A).

- *Grounds:* A test light can be used to check for grounds by attaching the clip of the test light to the positive terminal of the battery or any positive 12-volt electrical terminal. The tip of the test light can then be used to touch the ground wire. If there is a ground connection, the test light will light.

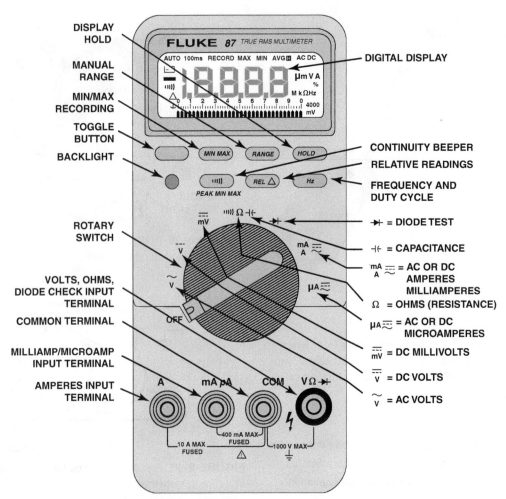

FIGURE 8–28 Typical digital multimeter. The black meter lead always is placed in the COM terminal. The red meter test lead should be in the volt-ohm terminal except when measuring current in amperes.

DIGITAL METERS

TERMINOLOGY Digital multimeter (DMM) and **digital volt-ohm-meter (DVOM)** are terms commonly used to describe digital meters. ● **SEE FIGURE 8–28**.

The common abbreviations for the units that many meters can measure are often confusing. ● **SEE CHART 8–1** for the most commonly used symbols and their meanings.

MEASURING VOLTAGE A **voltmeter** measures the pressure or potential of electricity in units of volts. A voltmeter is connected to a circuit in parallel. Voltage can be measured by selecting either AC or DC volts.

- *DC volts (DCV)*. This setting is the most common for automotive testing. Use this setting to measure battery voltage and voltage to all lighting and accessory circuits.

SYMBOL	MEANING
AC	Alternating current or voltage
DC	Direct current or voltage
V	Volts
mV	Millivolts (1/1,000 volts)
A	Ampere (amps), current
mA	Milliampere (1/1,000 amps)
%	Percent (for duty cycle readings only)
Ω	Ohms, resistance
kΩ	Kilohm (1,000 ohms), resistance
MΩ	Megohm (1,000,000 ohms), resistance
Hz	Hertz (cycles per second), frequency
kHz	Kilohertz (1,000 cycles/sec.), frequency
Ms	Milliseconds (1/1,000 sec.) for pulse width measurements

CHART 8–1

Common symbols and abbreviations used on digital meters.

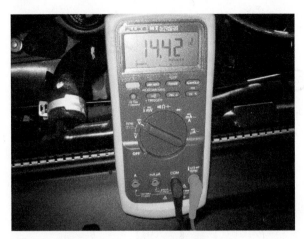

FIGURE 8–29 Typical digital multimeter (DMM) set to read DC volts.

- *AC volts (ACV).* This setting is used to check some computer sensors and to check for unwanted AC voltage from alternators.
- *Range.* The range is automatically set for most meters but can be manually adjusted if needed. ● **SEE FIGURES 8–29 AND 8–30.**

MEASURING RESISTANCE An **ohmmeter** measures the resistance in ohms of a component or circuit section when no current is flowing through the circuit. An ohmmeter contains a battery (or other power source) and is connected in series with the component or wire being measured. Note the following facts about using an ohmmeter.

- Zero ohms on the scale means that there is no resistance between the test leads, thus indicating continuity or a continuous path for the current to flow in a closed circuit.
- Infinity means no connection, as in an open circuit.
- Ohmmeters have no required polarity even though red and black test leads are used for resistance measurement.

Different meters have different ways of indicating infinity resistance, or a reading higher than the scale allows. Examples of an over-limit display include the following:

- OL, meaning over limit or overload
- Flashing or solid number 1
- Flashing or solid number 3 on the left side of the display

Check the meter instructions for the exact display used to indicate an open circuit or over-range reading. ● **SEE FIGURE 8–31 AND 8–32.**

To summarize, open and zero readings are as follows:

0.00 Ω = Zero resistance (component or circuit has continuity)

OL = An open circuit (no current flows) or the reading is higher than the scale selected.

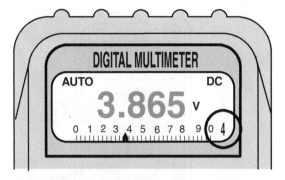

BECAUSE THE SIGNAL READING IS BELOW 4 VOLTS, THE METER AUTORANGES TO THE 4-VOLT SCALE. IN THE 4-VOLT SCALE, THIS METER PROVIDES THREE DECIMAL PLACES.

(a)

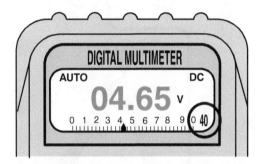

WHEN THE VOLTAGE EXCEEDED 4 VOLTS, THE METER AUTORANGES INTO THE 40-VOLT SCALE. THE DECIMAL POINT MOVES ONE PLACE TO THE RIGHT LEAVING ONLY TWO DECIMAL PLACES.

(b)

FIGURE 8–30 A typical autoranging digital multimeter automatically selects the proper scale to read the voltage being tested. The scale selected is usually displayed on the meter face. (a) Note that the display indicates "4," meaning that this range can read up to 4 volts. (b) The range is now set to the 40-volt scale, meaning that the meter can read up to 40 volts on the scale. Any reading above this level will cause the meter to reset to a higher scale. If not set on autoranging, the meter display would indicate OL if a reading exceeds the limit of the scale selected.

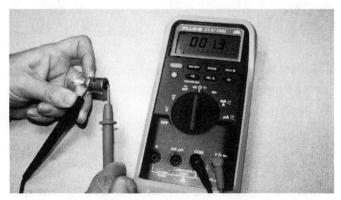

FIGURE 8–31 Using a digital multimeter set to read ohms (Ω) to test this light bulb. The meter reads the resistance of the filament.

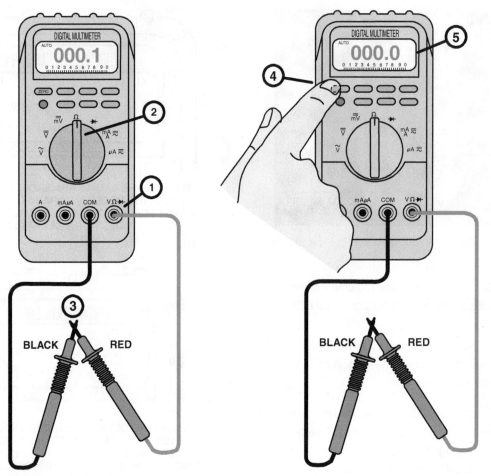

FIGURE 8–32 Many digital multimeters can have the display indicate zero to compensate for test lead resistance. (1) Connect leads in the V Ω and COM meter terminals. (2) Select the Ω scale. (3) Touch the two meter leads together. (4) Push the "zero" or "relative" button on the meter. (5) The meter display will now indicate zero ohms of resistance.

MEASURING AMPERES An **ammeter** measures the flow of current through a complete circuit in units of amperes or milliamperes (1/1,000 of an ampere). The ammeter has to be installed in the circuit (in series) so that it can measure all the current flow in that circuit, just as a water flow meter would measure the amount of water flow (cubic feet per minute, for example). ● **SEE FIGURE 8–33**.

CAUTION: An ammeter must be installed in series with the circuit to measure the current flow in the circuit. If a meter set to read amperes is connected in parallel, such as across a battery, the meter or the leads may be destroyed, or the fuse will blow, by the current available across the battery. Some DMMs beep if the unit selection does not match the test lead connection on the meter. However, in a noisy shop, this beep sound may be inaudible.

Digital meters require that the meter leads be moved to the ammeter terminals. Most digital meters have an ampere scale that can accommodate a maximum of 10 amperes. See the Tech Tip "Fuse Your Meter Leads!"

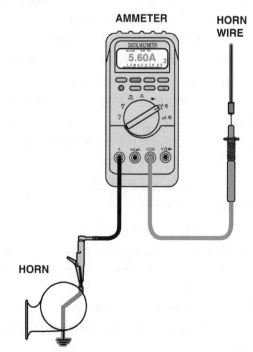

FIGURE 8–33 Measuring the current flow required by a horn requires that the ammeter be connected to the circuit in series and the horn button be depressed by an assistant.

FIGURE 8–34 Note the blade-type fuse holder soldered in series with one of the meter leads. A 10 ampere fuse helps protect the internal meter fuse (if equipped) and the meter itself from damage that may result from excessive current flow if accidentally used incorrectly.

 TECH TIP

Fuse Your Meter Leads!

Most digital meters include an ammeter capability. When reading amperes, the leads of the meter must be changed from volts or ohms (V or Ω) to amperes (A) or milliamperes (mA). A common problem may then occur the next time voltage is measured.

Although the technician may switch the selector to read volts, often the leads are not switched back to the volt or ohm position. Because the ammeter lead position results in zero ohms of resistance to current flow through the meter, the meter or the fuse inside the meter will be destroyed if the meter is connected to a battery. Many meter fuses are expensive and difficult to find. To avoid this problem, simply solder an inline 10 ampere blade-fuse holder into one meter lead. ● **SEE FIGURE 8–34**.

Do not think that this technique is for beginners only. Experienced technicians often get in a hurry and forget to switch the lead. A blade fuse is faster, easier, and less expensive to replace than a meter fuse or the meter itself. Also, if the soldering is done properly, the addition of an inline fuse holder and fuse does not increase the resistance of the meter leads. All meter leads have some resistance. If the meter is measuring very low resistance, touch the two leads together and read the resistance (usually no more than 0.2 ohm). Simply subtract the resistance of the leads from the resistance of the component being measured.

FIGURE 8–35 An inductive ammeter clamp is used with all starting and charging testers to measure the current flow through the battery cables.

FIGURE 8–36 A typical mini clamp-on-type digital multimeter. This meter is capable of measuring alternating current (AC) and direct current (DC) without requiring that the circuit be disconnected to install the meter in series. The jaws are simply placed over the wire and current flow through the circuit is displayed.

INDUCTIVE AMMETERS

OPERATION Inductive ammeters do not make physical contact with the circuit. Inductive ammeters have the advantage of being able to read much higher amperages than 10 amperes. A sensor is used to detect the strength of the magnetic field surrounding the wire carrying the current. The ammeter then uses the strength of the magnetic field to measure the electrical current. ● **SEE FIGURE 8–35**.

AC/DC CLAMP-ON DIGITAL MULTIMETERS An AC/DC clamp-on digital multimeter is a useful meter for automotive diagnostic work. ● **SEE FIGURE 8–36**.

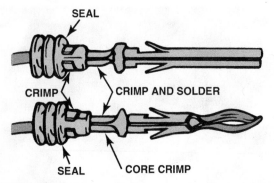

SEAL

CRIMP

CRIMP AND SOLDER

SEAL

CORE CRIMP

FIGURE 8–37 Some terminals have seals attached to help seal the electrical connections.

The major advantage of the clamp-on-type meter is that there is no need to break the circuit to measure current (amperes). Simply clamp the jaws of the meter around the power lead(s) or ground lead(s) of the component being measured and read the display. Most clamp-on meters can also measure alternating current, which is helpful in the diagnosis of an alternator problem. Volts, ohms, frequency, and temperature can also be measured with the typical clamp-on DMM, but conventional meter leads should be used. The inductive clamp is used to measure only amperes.

THINK OF MONEY Digital meter displays can often be confusing. The display for a battery measured as 12 1/2 volts would be 12.50 V, just as $12.50 is 12 dollars and 50 cents. A 1/2 volt reading on a digital meter will be displayed as 0.50 V, just as $0.50 is half of a dollar. It is more confusing when low values are displayed. For example, if a voltage reading is 0.063 volt, an auto-ranging meter will display 63 millivolts (63 mV), or 63/1,000 of a volt, or $63 of $1,000. (It takes 1,000 mV to equal 1 volt.) Think of millivolts as one-tenth of a cent, with 1 volt being $1.00. Therefore, 630 millivolts are equal to $0.63 of $1.00 (630 tenths of a cent, or 63 cents). To avoid confusion, try to manually range the meter to read base units (whole volts).

If the meter is ranged to base unit volts, 63 millivolts would be displayed as 0.063 or maybe just 0.06, depending on the display capabilities of the meter.

TERMINALS AND CONNECTORS

TERMINOLOGY A **terminal** is a metal fastener attached to the end of a wire, which makes the electrical connection. The term **connector** usually refers to the plastic portion that snaps or connects together, thereby making the mechanical connection. Wire terminal ends usually snap into and are held

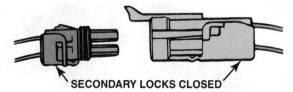

SECONDARY LOCKS CLOSED

FIGURE 8–38 Separate a connector by opening the lock and pulling the two apart.

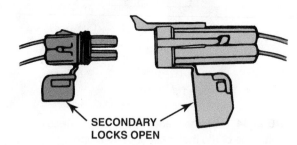

SECONDARY LOCKS OPEN

FIGURE 8–39 The secondary locks help retain the terminals in the connector.

by a connector. Male and female connectors can then be snapped together, thereby completing an electrical connection. Connectors exposed to the environment are also equipped with a weather-tight seal. ● **SEE FIGURE 8–37.**

SERVICING TERMINALS Terminals are retained in connectors by the use of a lock tang. Removing a terminal from a connector includes the following steps.

STEP 1 Release the connector position assurance (CPA), if equipped, that keeps the latch of the connector from releasing accidentally.

STEP 2 Separate the male and female connector by opening the lock. ● **SEE FIGURE 8–38.**

STEP 3 Release the secondary lock, if equipped. ● **SEE FIGURE 8–39.**

STEP 4 Using a pick, look for the slot in the plastic connector where the lock tang is located, depress the lock tang, and gently remove the terminal from the connector. ● **SEE FIGURE 8–40.**

WIRE REPAIR

SOLDERING Many manufacturers recommend that all wiring repairs be soldered. Solder is an alloy of tin and lead used to make a good electrical contact between two wires or connections in an electrical circuit. However, a flux must be used to help clean the area and to help make the solder flow. Therefore, solder is made with a resin (rosin) contained in the center, called *rosin-core solder*.

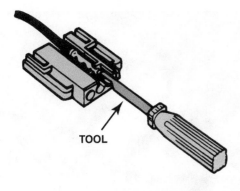

TOOL

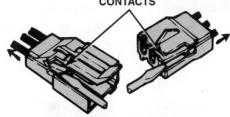

RAISING RETAINING
FINGERS TO REMOVE
CONTACTS

LOCKING WEDGE CONNECTOR

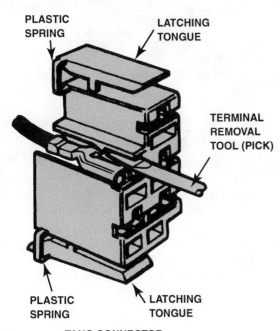

PLASTIC
SPRING

LATCHING
TONGUE

TERMINAL
REMOVAL
TOOL (PICK)

PLASTIC
SPRING

LATCHING
TONGUE

TANG CONNECTOR

FIGURE 8–40 Use a small removal tool, sometimes called a pick, to release terminals from the connector.

CAUTION: Never use acid-core solder to repair electrical wiring as the acid will cause corrosion. ● SEE FIGURE 8–41.

Solder is available with various percentages of tin and lead in the alloy. Ratios are used to identify these various types of solder, with the first number denoting the percentage of tin in the alloy and the second number giving the percentage of lead.

FIGURE 8–41 Always use rosin-core solder for electrical or electronic soldering. Also, use small-diameter solder for small soldering irons. Use large-diameter solder only for large-diameter (large-gauge) wire and higher-wattage soldering irons (guns).

The most commonly used solder is 50/50, which means that 50% of the solder is tin and the other 50 % is lead. The percentages of each alloy primarily determine the melting point of the solder.

- 60/40 solder (60% tin/40% lead) melts at 361°F (183°C).
- 50/50 solder (50% tin/50% lead) melts at 421°F (216°C).
- 40/60 solder (40% tin/60% lead) melts at 460°F (238°C).

SOLDERING PROCEDURE Soldering a wiring splice includes the following steps:

STEP 1 While touching the soldering gun to the splice, apply solder to the junction of the gun and the wire.

STEP 2 The solder will start to flow. Do not move the soldering gun.

STEP 3 Just keep feeding more solder into the splice as it flows into and around the strands of the wire.

STEP 4 After the solder has flowed throughout the splice, remove the soldering gun and the solder from the splice and allow the solder to cool slowly.

The solder should have a shiny appearance. Dull-looking solder may be caused by not reaching a high enough temperature, which results in a cold solder joint. Reheating the splice and allowing it to cool often restores the shiny appearance.

CRIMPING TERMINALS Terminals can be crimped to create a good electrical connection if the proper type of crimping tool is used. Most vehicle manufacturers recommend

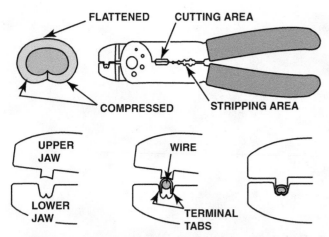

FIGURE 8–42 Notice that to create a good crimp, the open part of the terminal is placed in the jaws of the crimping tool toward the anvil or the W-shape part.

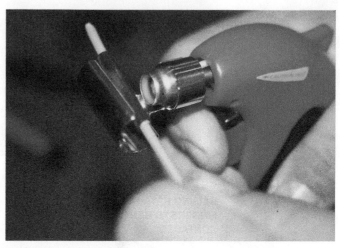

FIGURE 8–44 A butane torch especially designed for use on heat shrink applies heat without an open flame, which could cause damage.

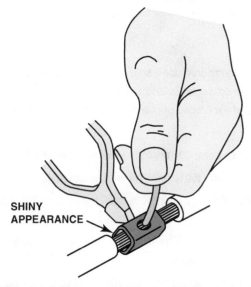

FIGURE 8–43 All hand-crimped splices or terminals should be soldered to be assured of a good electrical connection.

FIGURE 8–45 A typical crimp-and-seal connector. This type of connector is first lightly crimped to retain the ends of the wires and then it is heated. The tubing shrinks around the wire splice, and thermoplastic glue melts on the inside to provide an effective weather-resistant seal.

that a W-shaped crimp be used to force the strands of the wire into a tight space. ●SEE FIGURE 8–42.

Most vehicle manufacturers also specify that all hand-crimped terminals or splices be soldered. ●SEE FIGURE 8–43.

HEAT SHRINK TUBING Heat shrink tubing is usually made from polyvinyl chloride (PVC) or polyolefin and shrinks to about half of its original diameter when heated; this is usually called a 2:1 shrink ratio. Heat shrink by itself does not provide protection against corrosion, because the ends of the tubing are not sealed against moisture. Chrysler Corporation recommends that all wire repairs that may be exposed to the elements be repaired and sealed using adhesive-lined heat shrink tubing. The tubing is usually made from flame-retardant flexible polyolefin with an internal layer of special thermoplastic adhesive. When heated, this tubing shrinks to one-third of its original diameter (3:1 shrink ratio) and the adhesive melts and seals the ends of the tubing. ●SEE FIGURE 8–44.

CRIMP-AND-SEAL CONNECTORS Several vehicle manufacturers recommend the use of crimp-and-seal connectors as the method for wire repair. **Crimp-and-seal connectors** contain a sealant and shrink tubing in one piece and are not simply butt connectors. ●SEE FIGURE 8–45.

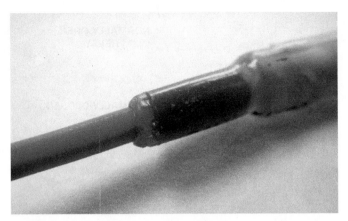

FIGURE 8–46 Heating the crimp-and-seal connector melts the glue and forms an effective seal against moisture.

The usual procedure specified for making a wire repair using a crimp-and-seal connector is as follows:

STEP 1 Strip the insulation from the ends of the wire (about 5/16 inch or 8 mm).

STEP 2 Select the proper size of crimp-and-seal connector for the gauge of wire being repaired. Insert the wires into the splice sleeve and crimp.

> **NOTE: Use only the specified crimping tool to help prevent the pliers from creating a hole in the cover.**

STEP 3 Apply heat to the connector until the sleeve shrinks down around the wire and a small amount of sealant is observed around the ends of the sleeve, as shown in ● **FIGURE 8–46**.

RELAYS

DEFINITION A **relay** is a magnetic switch that uses a movable armature to control a high-amperage circuit by using a low-amperage electrical switch.

TERMINAL IDENTIFICATION Most automotive relays adhere to common terminal identification. The primary source for this common identification comes from the standards established by the International Standards Organization (ISO). Knowing this terminal information will help in the correct diagnosis and troubleshooting of any circuit containing a relay. ● **SEE FIGURES 8–47 AND 8–48**.

Relays are found in many circuits because they are capable of being controlled by computers, yet are able to handle enough current to power motors and accessories. Relays include the following components and terminals:

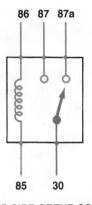

86 - POWER SIDE OF THE COIL
85 - GROUND SIDE OF THE COIL

(MOST RELAY COILS HAVE BETWEEN 60–100 OHMS OF RESISTANCE)

30 - COMMON POWER FOR RELAY CONTACTS
87 - NORMALLY OPEN OUTPUT (N.O.)
87a - NORMALLY CLOSED OUTPUT (N.C.)

FIGURE 8–47 A relay uses a movable arm to complete a circuit whenever there is a power at terminal 86 and a ground at terminal 85. A typical relay only requires about 1/10 ampere through the relay coil. The movable arm then closes the contacts (#30 to #87) and can often handle 30 amperes or more.

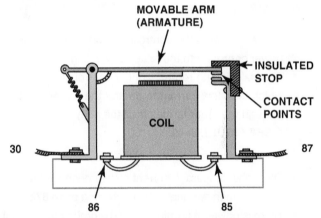

FIGURE 8–48 A cross-sectional view of a typical four-terminal relay. Current flowing through the coil (terminals 86 and 85) causes the movable arm (called the armature) to be drawn toward the coil magnet. The contact points complete the electrical circuit connected to terminals 30 and 87.

1. Coil (terminals 85 and 86)
   - A coil provides the magnetic pull to a movable armature (arm).
   - The resistance of most relay coils is usually between 60 ohms and 100 ohms.
   - The ISO identification of the coil terminals are 86 and 85. The terminal number 86 represents the power to the relay coil and the terminal labeled 85 represents the ground side of the relay coil.

FIGURE 8–49 A typical relay showing the schematic of the wiring in the relay.

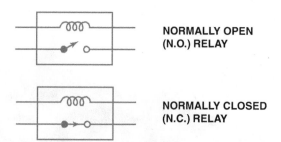

NORMALLY OPEN (N.O.) RELAY

NORMALLY CLOSED (N.C.) RELAY

FIGURE 8–50 All schematics are shown in their normal, non-energized position.

- The relay coil can be controlled by supplying either power or ground to the relay coil winding.
- The coil winding represents the control circuit, which uses low current to control the higher current through the other terminals of the relay. ● **SEE FIGURE 8–49.**

2. Other terminals used to control the load current

- The higher amperage current flow through a relay flows through terminals 30 and 87, and often 87a.
- There is power at terminal 86 and a ground at terminal 85 of the relay, a magnetic field is created in the coil winding, which draws the armature of the relay toward the coil. The armature, when energized electrically, connects terminals 30 and 87.

The maximum current through the relay is determined by the resistance of the circuit, and relays are designed to safely handle the designed current flow. ● **SEE FIGURES 8–50 AND 8–51.**

SWITCHES

OHMMETER CHECKS A control switch can be checked by removing it from the circuit and checking it with an ohmmeter.

🔧 **TECH TIP**

Divide the Circuit in Half

When diagnosing any circuit that has a relay, start testing at the relay and divide the circuit in half.

- **High current portion**: Remove the relay and check that there are 12 volts at the terminal 30 socket. If there is, then the power side is okay. Use an ohmmeter and check between terminal 87 socket and ground. If the load circuit has continuity, there should be some resistance. If OL, the circuit is electrically open.

- **Control circuit (low current):** With the relay removed from the socket, check that there is 12 volts to terminal 86 with the ignition on and the control switch on. If not, check service information to see if power should be applied to terminal 86, then continue troubleshooting the switch power and related circuit.

- **Check the relay itself**: Use an ohmmeter and measure for continuity and resistance.

- Between terminals 85 and 86 (coil), there should be 60 to 100 ohms. If not, replace the relay.

- Between terminals 30 and 87 (high-amperage switch controls), there should be continuity (low ohms) when there is power applied to terminal 86 and a ground applied to terminal 85 that operates the relay. If "OL" is displayed on the meter set to read ohms, the circuit is open which requires that the reply be replaced.

- Between terminals 30 and 87a (if equipped), with the relay turned off, there should be low resistance (less than 5 ohms).

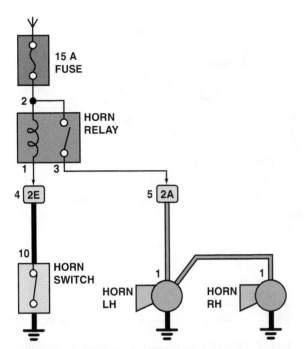

FIGURE 8–51 A typical horn circuit. Note that the relay contacts supply the heavy current to operate the horn when the horn switch simply completes a low-current circuit to ground, causing the relay contacts to close.

- The meter leads are connected to the two terminals of the switch. If there is only one terminal, one meter lead is connected to it, and the other lead is connected to the switch body. Some switches are normally open, and the reading should be high or infinite (OL). Some switches are normally closed, and the reading should be zero or nearly zero ohms.

- When the switch is operated, the reading should change to the opposite value.

- A pressure switch can usually be operated using a specialized tester or by applying air pressure with a rubber-tipped air gun.

The *transmission range (TR)* switch, also called the *manual lever position (MLP)* switch, or neutral start switch, has several circuits and terminals. This switch is checked using service information to determine which terminals should have continuity as the switch is moved through its travel. ● **SEE FIGURE 8–52.**

VOLTMETER CHECKS
A mechanically operated switch can also be checked on the vehicle using a voltmeter.

To test a switch, perform the following steps:

STEP 1 Connect the negative meter lead to a good ground or the switch body and the positive lead to the B+ wire entering the switch. Voltage should be available to the switch.

STEP 2 Move the positive meter lead to the second switch terminal, and operate the switch. As the switch is

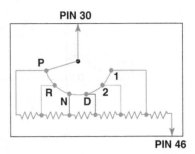

FIGURE 8–52 A typical transmission range switch is also similar to the circuit used for electronic transfer case switches. In this example, power, usually 12 volts, is applied at pin 30 and pin 46 is an input to the PCM. The change in voltage at pin 46 indicates how much resistance the circuit has, which is used to detect the gear selected.

operated, the output voltage should change from zero to the same as the input voltage or vice versa. If the voltage readings are not close to the same, there is a voltage drop, and high resistance in the switch is indicated.

SPEED SENSORS

OPERATION Speed sensors can be either magnetic or Hall-effect-type sensors. A magnetic sensor consists of a notched wheel and a coil consisting of an iron core wrapped with fine wire. The notched wheel causes magnetic strength changes enough to create a usable varying AC voltage signal. ● **SEE FIGURE 8–53.**

The voltage-generating speed sensor normally uses a two-wire connector and is checked using both an ohmmeter and a voltmeter.

SPEED SENSOR TESTS To test a speed sensor, perform the following steps:

STEP 1 Disconnect the sensor, and connect the two ohmmeter leads to the two sensor terminals.

STEP 2 There should be a complete circuit through the unit, and the resistance reading should fall within the specified range. Excessive or infinite resistance indicates a high resistance or open circuit; too low of a reading indicates a short circuit.

STEP 3 Attach the two leads of a voltmeter to the two sensor connectors, set the meter to AC volts.

STEP 4 Rotate the transmission shaft. As the shaft rotates, the voltmeter should show a fluctuating AC voltage reading, first + and then – of the same value.

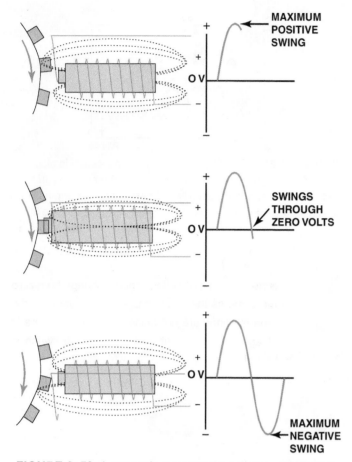

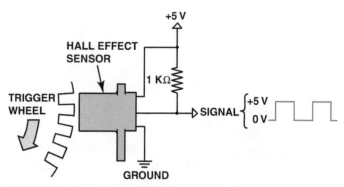

FIGURE 8-54 A Hall-Effect sensor produces an on-off voltage signal whether it is used with a blade or a notched wheel.

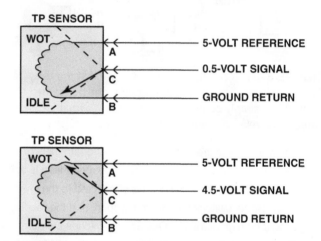

FIGURE 8-55 The signal voltage from a throttle position increases as the throttle is opened because the wiper arm is closer to the 5-volt reference. At idle, the resistance of the sensor winding effectively reduces the signal voltage output to the powertrain control module (PCM).

FIGURE 8-53 A magnetic sensor uses a permanent magnet surrounded by a coil of wire. The notches on the rotating shaft create a variable magnetic field strength around the coil. When a metallic section is close to the sensor, the magnetic field is stronger because metal is a better conductor of magnetic lines of force than air.

Unlike the magnetic pulse generator, the Hall-Effect switch requires a small input voltage to generate an output or signal voltage. **Hall Effect** has the ability to generate a voltage signal in semiconductor material (gallium arsenate crystal) by passing current through it in one direction and applying a magnetic field to it at a right angle to its surface. If the input current is held steady and the magnetic field fluctuates, an output voltage is produced that changes in proportion to field strength. ● **SEE FIGURE 8-54.**

THROTTLE POSITION (TP) SENSOR

PURPOSE AND FUNCTION The powertrain control module (PCM) uses TP sensor input to determine the amount of throttle opening and the rate of change to determine shift points of an automatic transmission and for engine management.

PARTS AND OPERATION The TP sensor consists of a **potentiometer,** a type of variable resistor. A potentiometer is a variable-resistance sensor with three terminals. One end of the resistor receives reference voltage, while the other end is grounded. The third terminal is attached to a movable contact that slides across the resistor to vary its resistance. Depending on whether the contact is near the supply end or the ground end of the resistor, return voltage is high or low.

A typical sensor has three wires:

- A 5-volt reference feed wire from the computer
- Signal return
- A ground wire back to the computer

● **SEE FIGURE 8-55.**

TESTING A TP SENSOR A throttle position (TP) sensor can be checked using a voltmeter.

To test a TP sensor, perform the following steps:

STEP 1 Leave the TP sensor connector connected. Turn the ignition "ON."

STEP 2 Connect the negative lead to a good ground, and use the positive lead to probe the input voltage at the connector. It should be the specified voltage indicated in the service information.

STEP 3 Move the positive voltmeter lead to the TP output voltage lead, and measure the voltage as the throttle opens and closes. The output voltage should increase and decrease smoothly as the throttle is opened and closed.

NEED FOR NETWORK Since the 1990s, vehicles have used modules to control the operation of most electrical components. A typical vehicle will have 10 or more modules and they communicate with each other over data lines or hard wiring, depending on the application. ●**SEE FIGURE 8–56**.

MODULES AND NODES Each module, also called a **node**, must communicate to other modules. For example, if the driver depresses the window-down switch, the power window switch sends a window-down message to the body control module. The body control module then sends the request to the driver's side window module. This module

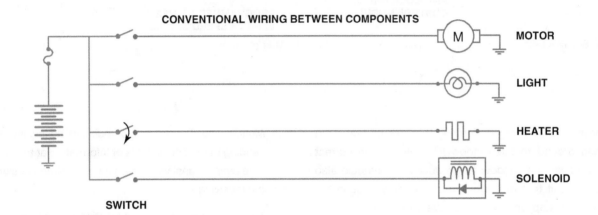

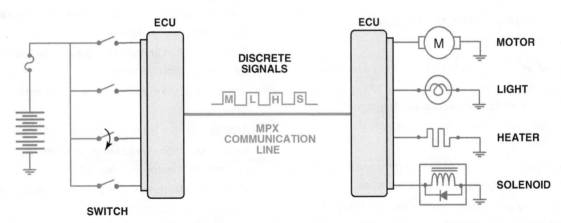

FIGURE 8–56 Module communications makes controlling multiple electrical devices and accessories easier by using simple low-current switches to signal another electronic control module (ECM), which does the actual switching of the current to the device.

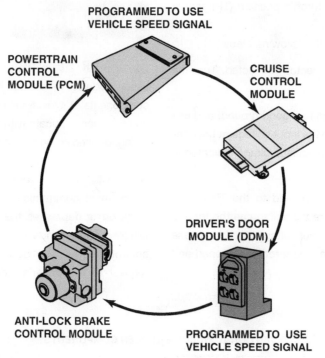

PROGRAMMED TO USE
VEHICLE SPEED SIGNAL

POWERTRAIN
CONTROL
MODULE (PCM)

CRUISE
CONTROL
MODULE

DRIVER'S DOOR
MODULE (DDM)

ANTI-LOCK BRAKE
CONTROL MODULE

PROGRAMMED TO USE
VEHICLE SPEED SIGNAL

FIGURE 8–57 A network allows all modules to communicate with other modules.

is responsible for actually performing the task by supplying power and ground to the window lift motor in the current polarity to cause the window to go down. The module also contains a circuit that monitors the current flow through the motor and will stop and/or reverse the window motor if an obstruction causes the window motor to draw more than the normal amount of current.

TYPES OF COMMUNICATION
The types of communications include the following:

- *Differential*. In the differential form of BUS communication, a difference in voltage is applied to two wires, which are twisted to help reduce electromagnetic interference (EMI). These transfer wires are called a twisted pair.
- *Parallel*. In the parallel type of BUS communication, the send and receive signals are on different wires.
- *Serial data*. The serial data is data transmitted by a series of rapidly changing voltage signals pulsed from low to high or from high to low.

- *Multiplexing*. The process of multiplexing involves the sending of multiple signals of information at the same time over a signal wire and then separating the signals at the receiving end.

This system of intercommunication of computers or processors is referred to as a network. ● **SEE FIGURE 8–57.**

By connecting the computers together on a communications network, they can easily share information back and forth. This multiplexing has the following advantages.

- Elimination of redundant sensors and dedicated wiring for these multiple sensors
- Reduction of the number of wires, connectors, and circuits
- Addition of more features and options to new vehicles
- Weight reduction due to fewer components, wires, and connectors, thereby increasing fuel economy
- Changeable features with software upgrades versus component replacement

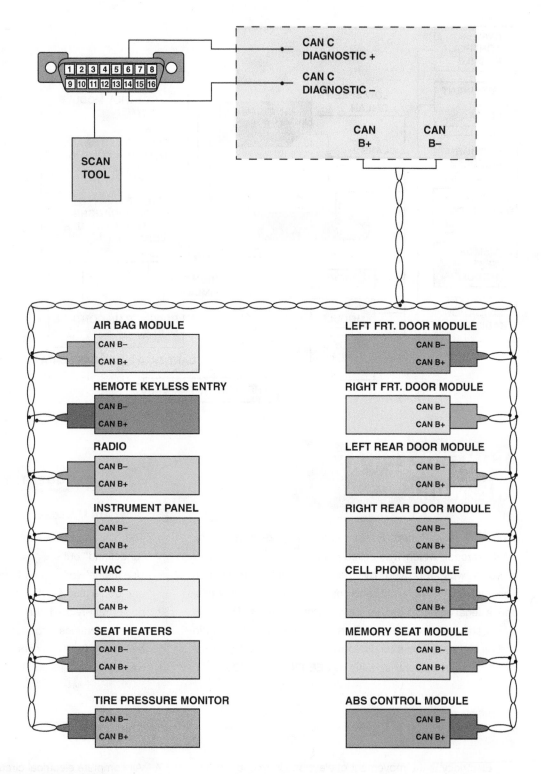

FIGURE 8–58 A typical BUS system showing module CAN communications and twisted pairs of wire.

CAN C DIAGNOSTIC +

CAN C DIAGNOSTIC –

CAN B+

CAN B–

SCAN TOOL

AIR BAG MODULE
CAN B–
CAN B+

REMOTE KEYLESS ENTRY
CAN B–
CAN B+

RADIO
CAN B–
CAN B+

INSTRUMENT PANEL
CAN B–
CAN B+

HVAC
CAN B–
CAN B+

SEAT HEATERS
CAN B–
CAN B+

TIRE PRESSURE MONITOR
CAN B–
CAN B+

LEFT FRT. DOOR MODULE
CAN B–
CAN B+

RIGHT FRT. DOOR MODULE
CAN B–
CAN B+

LEFT REAR DOOR MODULE
CAN B–
CAN B+

RIGHT REAR DOOR MODULE
CAN B–
CAN B+

CELL PHONE MODULE
CAN B–
CAN B+

MEMORY SEAT MODULE
CAN B–
CAN B+

ABS CONTROL MODULE
CAN B–
CAN B+

NETWORK CLASSIFICATIONS

The Society of Automotive Engineers (SAE) standards include the following three categories of in-vehicle network communications.

Class A Low-speed networks, meaning less than 10,000 bits per second (bps, or 10 Kbs), are generally used for trip computers, entertainment, and other convenience features.

Class B Medium-speed networks, meaning 10,000 bps to 125,000 bps (10 Kbs to 125 Kbs), are generally used for information transfer among modules, such as instrument clusters, temperature sensor data, and other general uses.

Class C High-speed networks, meaning 125,000 bps to 1,000,000 bps, are generally used for real-time powertrain and vehicle dynamic control. High-speed BUS communication systems now use a controller area network (CAN). ● **SEE FIGURE 8–58.**

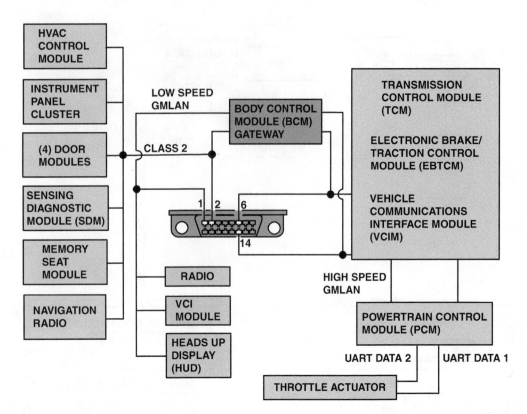

FIGURE 8–59 A schematic of a Chevrolet Equinox shows that the vehicle uses a GMLAN BUS (DLC pins 6 and 14), plus a Class 2 (pin 2). A scan tool can therefore communicate to the transmission control module (TCM) through the high-speed network. Pin 1 connects to the low-speed GMLAN network.

CONTROLLER AREA NETWORK

STANDARD Robert Bosch Corporation developed the CAN protocol, which was called CAN 1.2, in 1993. The CAN protocol was approved by the Environmental Protection Agency (EPA) for 2003 and newer vehicle diagnostics, and a legal requirement for all vehicles by 2008. The CAN diagnostic systems use pins 6 and 14 in the standard 16 pin OBD-II (J-1962) connector. Before CAN, the scan tool protocol had been manufacturer specific. ● **SEE FIGURE 8–59**.

? FREQUENTLY ASKED QUESTION

What Are U Codes?

The "U" diagnostic trouble codes were at first "undefined" but are now network-related codes. Use the network codes to help pinpoint the circuit or module that is not working correctly. Some powertrain-related faults are due to network communications errors and therefore can be detected by looking for "U" diagnostic trouble codes (DTCs).

SUMMARY

1. Electricity is the movement of electrons from one atom to another.

2. In order for current to flow in a circuit or wire, there must be an excess of electrons at one end and a deficiency of electrons at the other end.

3. Automotive electricity uses the conventional theory that electricity flows from positive to negative.

4. The ampere is the measure of the amount of current flow.

5. Voltage is the unit of electrical pressure.

6. The ohm is the unit of electrical resistance.

7. All complete electrical circuits have a power source (such as a battery), a circuit protection device (such as a fuse), a power-side wire or path, an electrical load, a ground return path, and a switch or a control device.

8. A short-to-voltage involves a copper-to-copper connection and usually affects more than one circuit.

9. A short-to-ground usually involves a power path conductor coming in contact with a return (ground) path conductor and usually causes the fuse to blow.

10. An open is a break in the circuit resulting in absolutely no current flow through the circuit.

11. Circuit testers include test lights and fused jumper leads.

12. Digital multimeter (DMM) and digital volt-ohm-meter (DVOM) are terms commonly used for electronic test meters.

13. Ammeters measure current and must be connected in series in the circuit.

14. Voltmeters measure voltage and are connected in parallel.

15. Ohmmeters measure resistance of a component and must be connected in parallel with the circuit or component disconnected from power.

16. A terminal is the metal end of a wire, whereas a connector is the plastic housing for the terminal.

17. All wire repair should use either soldering or a crimp-and-seal connector.

18. All switches and relays on a schematic are shown in their normal position, either normally closed (N.C.) or normally open (N.O.).

19. A typical relay uses a small current through a coil (terminals 85 and 86) to operate the higher current part (terminals 30 and 87).

20. The use of a network for module communications reduces the number of wires and connections needed.

21. The SAE communication classifications for vehicle communications systems include Class A (low speed), Class B (medium speed), and Class C (high speed).

REVIEW QUESTIONS

1. What are ampere, volt, and ohm?
2. What is included in a complete electrical circuit?
3. Why must an ohmmeter be connected to a disconnected circuit or component?
4. List and identify the terminals of a typical ISO type relay.
5. Why is a communication network used?

CHAPTER QUIZ

1. An electrical conductor is an element with _____ electrons in its outer orbit.
   a. Less than 2
   b. Less than 4
   c. Exactly 4
   d. More than 4

2. Like charges _____.
   a. Attract each other
   b. Repel each other
   c. Neutralize each other
   d. Add

3. If an insulated wire gets rubbed through a part of the insulation and the wire conductor touches the steel body of a vehicle, the type of failure would be called a(n) _____.
   a. Short-to-voltage
   b. Short-to-ground
   c. Open
   d. Chassis ground

4. High resistance in an electrical circuit can cause _____.
   a. Dim lights
   b. Slow motor operation
   c. Clicking of relays or solenoids
   d. All of the above

5. If two power-side insulated wires were to melt together at the point where the copper conductors touched each other, the type of failure would be called a(n) _____.
   a. Short-to-voltage
   b. Short-to-ground
   c. Open
   d. Floating ground

6. When testing a relay using an ohmmeter, which two terminals should be touched to measure the coil resistance?
   a. 87 and 30
   b. 86 and 85
   c. 87a and 87
   d. 86 and 87

7. Technician A says that a good relay should measure between 60 ohms and 100 ohms across the coil terminals. Technician B says that OL should be displayed on an ohmmeter when touching terminals 30 and 87. Which technician is correct?
   a. Technician A only
   b. Technician B only
   c. Both Technicians A and B
   d. Neither Technician A nor B

8. If a wire repair, such as that made under the hood or under the vehicle, is exposed to the elements, which type of repair should be used?
   a. Wire nuts and electrical tape
   b. Solder and adhesive-lined heat shrink or crimp-and-seal connectors
   c. Butt connectors
   d. Rosin-core solder and electrical tape

9. A module is also known as a _____.
   a. BUS
   b. Node
   c. Terminator
   d. Resistor pack

10. A high-speed CAN BUS communicates with a scan tool through which terminal(s)?
    a. 6 and 14
    b. 2
    c. 7 and 15
    d. 4 and 16

chapter 9

ELECTRONIC TRANSMISSION CONTROLS

LEARNING OBJECTIVES

After studying this chapter, the reader will be able to:

1. Prepare for ASE Automatic Transmissions (A2) certification test content area "A" (General Transmission and Transaxle Diagnosis).

2. Explain the procedure for monitoring engine load and vehicle speed for the proper functioning of hydraulically controlled transmission/transaxles.

3. Explain how the automatic transmissions/transaxles are controlled electronically.

4. Explain the function of sensors and switches for electronic control of transmission.

5. Identify the types of transmission solenoids.

6. Discuss adaptive strategies and controls for electronically controlled automatic transmissions/transaxles.

KEY TERMS

Adaptive control 172
Adaptive learning 172
Brake on/off (BOO) 169
Clutch volume index (CVI) 174
Default (Limp in) 174
Electronic pressure control (EPC) 171
Input speed sensor (ISS) 166
Output speed sensor (OSS) 167
Pressure control solenoid (PCS) 172
Scan tool 174
Torque management 172
Transmission adapt pressure (TAP) 174
Transmission control module (TCM) 164
Transmission fluid temperature (TFT) 168
Transmission range (TR) switch 165
Turbine speed sensor (TSS) 166
Vehicle speed (VS) sensor 167

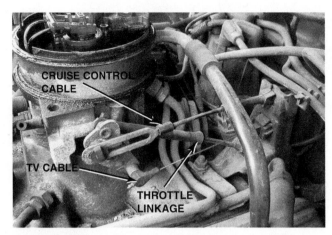

FIGURE 9–1 The throttle valve (TV) cable on a 4L-60 transmission.

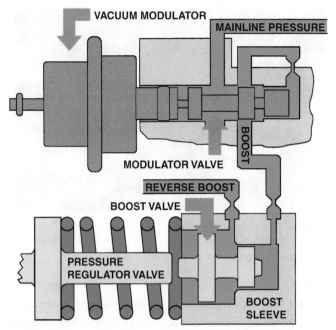

FIGURE 9–2 A vacuum modulator moves the modulator valve depending on the vacuum of the engine. A heavy load on the engine causes the vacuum to be lower than when the engine is operating under a light load. The spool valve applies mainline pressure to the boost sleeve of the pressure regulator valve, which causes the mainline pressure to increase.

HYDRAULICALLY CONTROLLED TRANSMISSIONS

BACKGROUND From the 1940s until the early 1990s, most automatic transmissions were hydraulically controlled. Hydraulically controlled automatic transmissions/transaxles use valves to control when to shift instead of sensors that are used in electronically controlled transmissions/ transaxles. These valves use mainline pressure to develop other hydraulic circuit pressures within the transmission. Pressure valves are normally spool valves that link to external components.

In order for hydraulically controlled transmission/transaxles to operate correctly, they must be able to monitor engine load and vehicle speed.

ENGINE LOAD Engine load can be detected using either a throttle valve (TV) or a vacuum moderator valve.

- **Throttle Valve**—The hydraulically controlled transmission throttle valve senses engine load and uses that information to delay the upshift on hydraulically controlled automatic transmissions. Throttle valves have linkages or cables that connect them mechanically to the throttle plates, and they respond directly to engine load. ● **SEE FIGURE 9–1**.

A low engine load develops low throttle pressure while a higher load develops higher throttle pressure. The throttle position (TP) sensor has replaced the need for throttle valves in electronically controlled automatic transmissions/transaxles.

- **Vacuum Modulator Valve**—A vacuum modulator is used to convert engine manifold vacuum into a signal pressure

that increases as engine vacuum decreases. The modulator is connected to the intake manifold vacuum with a rubber hose or steel line. A vacuum modulator can be used on hydraulically controlled transmissions/transaxles to help determine the shift point based on engine load. The purpose of the vacuum modulator is to delay the upshifting of the transmission based on the engine load. ● **SEE FIGURE 9–2**.

engine load examples:

- **Light engine load.** Manifold vacuum is high, shifts occur at lower speeds.

- **Heavy engine load.** Manifold vacuum is low, shifts occur at higher speeds.

The manifold absolute pressure (MAP) sensor or mass airflow (MAF) sensor and throttle position (TP) sensor serve in place of the vacuum modulator valve in measuring engine load on electronically controlled automatic transmissions/transaxles.

VEHICLE SPEED The governor valve monitors vehicle road speed and uses that operating signal to develop governor pressure. The governor valve normally follows transmission output shaft rotation speed, which increases with vehicle speed. Mechanical governors contain "flyweights" that move in relation to centrifugal forces caused by the speed of the output

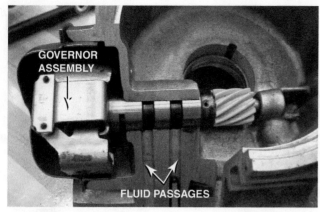

FIGURE 9–3 A governor assembly is used on older hydraulically controlled automatic transmissions/transaxles to control shift points based on vehicle speed.

shaft. As the output shaft speed increases flyweights move outward, this in turn moves an internal valve which controls the output pressure. As the speed increases, governor pressure also increases. Governor pressure opposes throttle pressure at the shift valves to control upshifts and downshifts in relation to vehicle speed. ● **SEE FIGURE 9–3.**

TRANSMISSION CONTROL MODULE

TCM All recent automatic transmissions are controlled by electronic components and circuits. Typical transmission control systems contain many components. An automatic transmission can be controlled by its own computer, called a **transmission control module (TCM)**, or a *transmission control unit (TCU)*. The transmission can also be controlled through either the body control module (BCM) or the powertrain control module (PCM). Each manufacturer has its own design criteria and terminology. The TCM is normally located outside the transmission in a protected, relatively cool and clean location. Some newer transmissions have the TCM mounted on the valve body inside the transmission. The primary advantage is the reduction of wiring and the elimination of electrical connectors, both sources of potential problems.

TERMINOLOGY When the TCM is located inside the transmission, this design is often called a *control solenoid valve assembly*, *mechatronic*, and *solenoid body* and reduces the number of wires entering the transmission because of the following:

- Input and output shaft speed sensors
- Transmission range sensor
- Fluid pressure sensors
- Fluid temperature sensor
- Shift and pressure control solenoids are connected directly to the TCM

The wire connections to the rest of the vehicle include:

- Hi and Lo CAN transmits data to and from the ECM, BCM, and PCM
- Ignition on
- Diagnostic connection
- Ground

The TCM in some transmissions is about the same size as a common credit card. A concern with an internal TCM is the possibility of overheating the electronic components. One design has a thermocouple temperature sensor(s) mounted in the TCM circuit board, and if the temperature rises above 288°F (142°C), it will go into failure mode/default. The TCM normally keeps relatively cool by contact with the transmission case, and a spring bracket is used to ensure tight contact. ● **SEE FIGURE 9–4.**

PURPOSE AND FUNCTION Many features of an electronic transmission, such as shift timing and quality, torque converter clutch apply timing, and quality, are software driven. A vehicle manufacturer can use the same transmission and adjust the operating characteristics with software for variations of particular vehicles. Some transmission control modules allow calibration values to be reprogrammed by technicians in the field.

The TCM receives data from the sensors and other control modules, and when these signals match the program stored in the TCM's memory, the TCM sends a signal to one or more electrical actuators to control the shifting operation of the transmission.

OPERATION The TCM can be programmed to incorporate several different operating strategies that are stored in the memory. The types of memory include:

- *Random access memory (RAM).* This is temporary memory that is cleared every time the vehicle is turned off.
- *Read-only memory (ROM).* The TCM/processor can read from ROM but cannot save any information to ROM.
- *Programmable read-only memory (PROM).* This is similar to a ROM but is programmed for a specific vehicle.
- *Electronically erasable programmable read-only memory (EEPROM).* This is similar to PROM but can be erased and reprogrammed. This is often called *reflashing*.
- *Keep alive memory (KAM).* ROM that is always connected to power so it retains memory. This can store

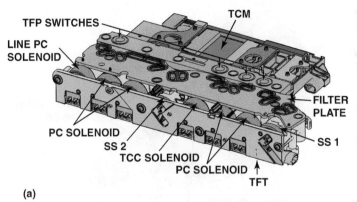

TFP SWITCHES

LINE PC SOLENOID

TCM

FILTER PLATE

PC SOLENOID

SS 2

TCC SOLENOID

PC SOLENOID

TFT

SS 1

(a)

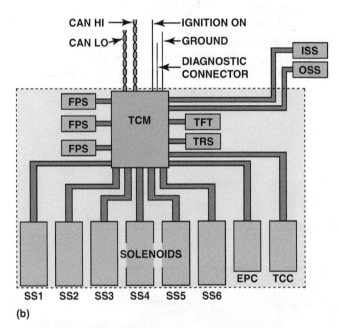

(b)

FIGURE 9–4 (a) This control solenoid assembly contains four transmission fluid pressure (TFP) switches, a line pressure control (PC) solenoid, four pressure control (PC) solenoids, two shift solenoids (SS), a torque converter clutch (TCC) solenoid, a transmission fluid temperature (TFT) sensor, and the transmission control module (TCM). It also has a vehicle harness connector and connectors to the shift position switch and the input and output speed sensors. (b) A simplified view is also shown.

information such as transmission adaptive strategies and the data will be lost if a battery becomes discharged or is disconnected.

SENSORS

PURPOSE AND FUNCTION Sensors are the TCM inputs. They monitor the things that can affect transmission operation: vehicle speed, input shaft speed, transmission fluid temperature, the selected gear range, and engine coolant temperature, RPM, and load. A typical transmission sensor can be a switch that is made to open or close at certain pressures or temperatures, a transducer that senses pressure, a thermistor that senses temperature, or a speed sensor that measures vehicle speed or shaft RPM. The various sensor types (organized by the type of electrical signal) include the following:

- Frequency generators (creates an AC signal with a frequency relative to speed and the TCM monitors the signal frequency)
- Voltage generator (creates a voltage signal that is relative to speed and the TCM monitors the voltage)
- Potentiometer or variable resistor (alters resistance)
- Switches (an on–off signal)
- Thermistor (changes resistance relative to temperature)
- Transducer (changes resistance relative to pressure)
- Serial data (an on–off signal coming from another control module)

TRANSMISSION RANGE SWITCH The **transmission range (TR) switch**, also called the *manual lever position (MLP)* sensor, is used as an input to the PCM/TCM, which indicates the drive range requested by the driver. The transmission range switch is usually located on the outside of the case on the transmission/transaxle housing and attached to the shifter. As the gear range selector is moved, the TR switch can make a variety of switch connections for each gear range. These inputs allow the TCM to determine which gear range has been selected. The TR switch is used by the TCM to

- Keep the engine from starting in any gear position except park or neutral
- Allow a progressive 1–2–3–4 shift sequence in drive
- Limit upshifts in manual ranges
- Operate the backup lights in reverse. ● **SEE FIGURE 9–5.**

Some vehicles are equipped with a manual position where the driver can request one gear position by moving the shift lever to the manual position. ● **SEE FIGURE 9–6.**

SPEED SENSOR DESIGNS Speed sensors measure the speeds of the input and output shafts or sometimes of other shaft speeds in the automatic transmission or transaxle. The output shaft speed sensor is often used to provide vehicle speed information to the PCM and for adaptive learning. ● **SEE FIGURE 9–7.**

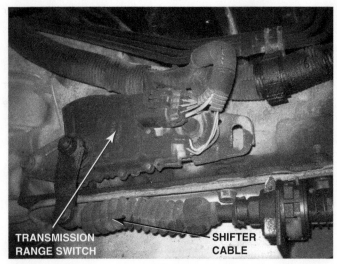

TRANSMISSION RANGE SWITCH

SHIFTER CABLE

FIGURE 9–5 The transmission range switch is usually located on the case where the shifter cable attaches to the manual valve lever. The switch also includes the switch for the backup lights and the park/neutral switch which is used to prevent the start being engaged unless the shifter is in park or neutral.

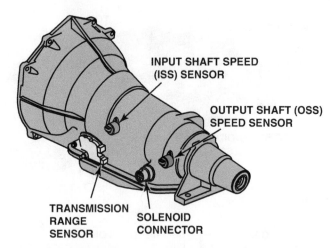

INPUT SHAFT SPEED (ISS) SENSOR

OUTPUT SHAFT (OSS) SPEED SENSOR

TRANSMISSION RANGE SENSOR

SOLENOID CONNECTOR

FIGURE 9–7 Speed sensors are used by the powertrain control module (PCM) or the transmission control module (TCM) to control shifts and detect faults such as slippage when the two speeds do not match the predetermined ratio for each gear commanded.

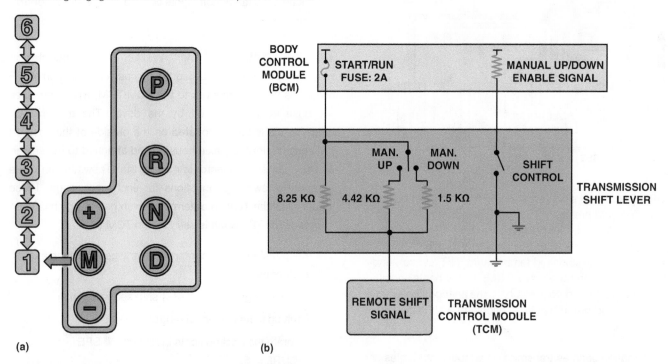

(a)

(b)

FIGURE 9–6 Moving the shift lever to the M (manual) position (a) activates the up/down, $+/-$ switches that will cause an upshift or downshift.

Speed sensor design includes:

- **Magnetic**—Most speed sensors use a coil of wire that is wrapped around a magnetic core. This sensor is mounted next to a toothed ring or wheel. As the toothed ring revolves, an alternating voltage is produced in the sensor. ● **SEE FIGURE 9–8.**

- **Hall-Effect**—Some speed sensors are Hall-Effect and create an on–off square wave signal that is used directly by the PCM/TCM for speed detection.

SPEED SENSOR LOCATIONS

- Speed sensors are used to detect the speeds of the input and output shafts on automatic transmissions/transaxles. **Input speed sensor (ISS)** measures the speed of the input shaft, which is the same or almost the same as the engine speed. This is also called **turbine speed sensor (TSS)** because it is used to determine the speed of the turbine shaft.

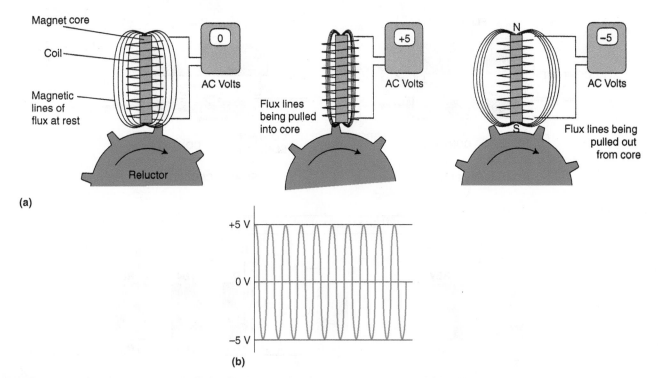

(a)

(b)

FIGURE 9–8 (a) The speed sensor switch will close as the magnet moves past it. (b) It will generate a sine wave signal, which is converted inside the PCM/TCM to a digital signal. The frequency of the signal is used to measure the speed.

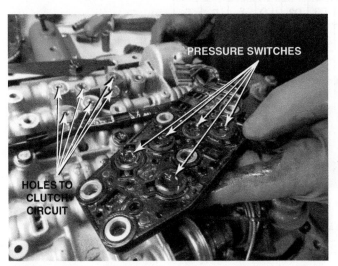

FIGURE 9–9 The pressure switch manifold (PSM) used in a GM 4L60-E consists of diaphragm switches with seals around each one that are bolted to the valve body over holes for each clutch circuit.

- The **output speed sensor (OSS)** is also called the **vehicle speed (VS) sensor** and is used by the PCM for speedometer and cruise control operation as well as for transmission/transaxle operation and shift-related fault detection.

PRESSURE SENSORS/SWITCHES Most pressure sensors use a transducer, which is a variable resistance that produces a signal that is relative to pressure. The *line pressure sensor (LPS)* is a transducer that converts line pressure to a variable resistance.

? FREQUENTLY ASKED QUESTION

What Is Pressure Logic?

Pressure switches are used to monitor which clutch has pressure but the PCM/TCM can use the information from the switches to verify which gear the transmission/transaxle is operating. Some pressure switches are normally open (N.O.) and others are normally closed (N.C.) and the gear that the unit is operating in can be determined by the switch positions. An open circuit is represented by a binary code "1" and measures 12 volts while a grounded circuit binary code is "0" and measures 0 volts. Depending on the position of the manual valve, fluid is routed to the pressure switch manifold (PSM). The PCM/TCM uses information from the on/off positioning of the switches to adjust line pressure, torque converter clutch (TCM) apply, and to control shift solenoid operation. ● **SEE FIGURE 9–10.**

Many transmissions include *pressure switches* at the valve body. The signal from the pressure sensor tells the TCM that the circuit has pressure. The TCM uses these signals along with other information to determine TCC lockup and shift timing. ● **SEE FIGURE 9–9.**

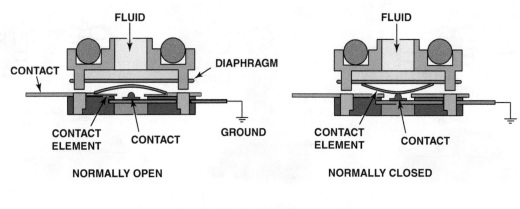

NORMALLY OPEN   NORMALLY CLOSED

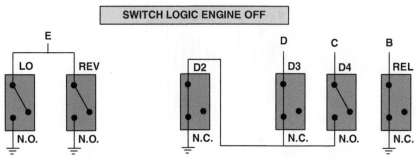

RANGE INDICATOR	FLUID					CIRCUIT		
	REV	D4	D3	D2	LO	E	D	C
PARK / NEUTRAL	0	0	0	0	0	0	1	0
REVERSE	1	0	0	0	0	1	1	0
OVERDRIVE	0	1	0	0	0	0	1	1
MANUAL THIRD	0	1	1	0	0	0	0	1
MANUAL SECOND	0	1	1	1	0	0	0	0
MANUAL FIRST	0	1	1	1	1	1	0	0

1 = PRESURIZED   0 = EXHAUSTED

1 = GROUNDED (RESISTANCE < 50 OHMS, 0 OHMS)

0 = OPEN (RESISTANCE > 50 K OHMS, 12 VOLTS)

FIGURE 9–10 Some switches are electrically normally open (N.O.) and others are normally closed (N.C.) and are used to provide gear selection information to the PCM/TCM.

TEMPERATURE SENSORS The **transmission fluid temperature (TFT)** sensor can also be called a *transmission oil temperature (TOT) sensor.* Most temperature sensors are thermistors, a type of variable resistor that changes electrical resistance relative to temperature. These are called negative temperature coefficient (NTC) thermistors. The signal from a thermistor is the inverse of the temperature because it has high resistance at low temperatures and a low resistance at high temperatures. For example, a particular transmission fluid temperature sensor has a resistance of 37 to 100 ohms (Ω) at 32°F to 58°F (0°C to 20°C) and 1,500 to 2,700 ohms (Ω) at 195°F to 230°F (91°C to 110°C). ● **SEE FIGURE 9–11.**

This sensor is used by the PCM or TCM to detect the temperature of the automatic transmission fluid. This signal is used to determine the best shift points and to regulate line pressure. It will cause the PCM or the TCM to engage the torque converter clutch (TCC) sooner and disable overdrive, to help reduce the fluid temperature if it reaches higher than normal.

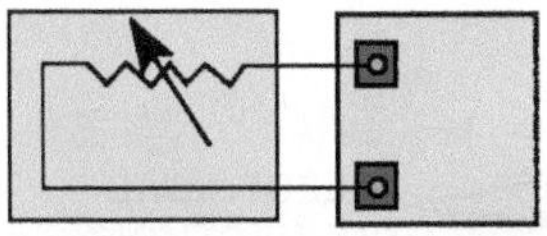

Temperature		Resistance (Ohms)
°C	°F	
140	284	0.6 K
120	248	1.1 K
100	212	2.1 K
80	176	3.8 K
50	122	10 K
30	86	27 K
10	50	69 K
−10	14	193 K
−30	−22	600 K

(a)   (b)

FIGURE 9–11 (a) A transmission fluid temperature sensor can be checked by connecting an ohmmeter to the harness connector terminals. (b) The resistance should change as the temperature changes.

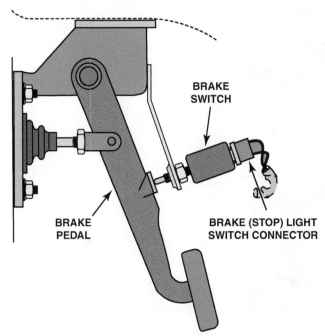

FIGURE 9–12 The brake (stop light) switch is mounted at the brake pedal. It provides a brake-apply signal to the TCM.

BRAKE SWITCH A brake switch mounted at the brake pedal provides a signal when the brake is depressed. It signals the TCM that the brake is applied, and the TCC should be released. The brake switch is also called a **brake on/off (BOO)** switch. ● **SEE FIGURE 9–12**.

INPUTS SHARED WITH THE PCM Many factors are used by the TCM to determine when to shift. Many sensors are used by the PCM for engine operation and are also used to help the engine and transmission/transaxle work together to provide smooth efficient operation and produce the best performance with the lowest possible exhaust emission and

the best possible fuel economy. The sensors that are used for both the engine and the transmission include the following:

- *Throttle position (TP) sensor.* This variable resistor (potentiometer) provides a voltage signal that is relative to throttle opening. It provides a throttle position signal to the TCM.

- *Engine coolant temperature (ECT).* This variable resistor (thermistor) monitors engine temperature. It signals the TCM that the engine is at operating temperature or approaching an overheat temperature.

- *Manifold absolute pressure (MAP)* and *mass airflow sensor (MAF).* These sensors provide engine load signal to the PCM.

TRANSMISSION SOLENOIDS

TYPES OF SOLENOIDS An electronic transmission controls the shift points by turning a solenoid(s) on and off. The solenoids in turn control the hydraulic pressure that moves the shift valves or operates the torque converter clutch. Solenoids used in electronically controlled automatic transmissions/transaxles are as follows:

- **On–off solenoids.** These can be normally open to fluid flow or normally closed to block fluid flow. Shift solenoids control the pressure force which in turn controls the position of the shift valve. They are commanded on or off by the PCM or TCM. The resistance of most on–off shift solenoids is 10 to 15 ohms. ● **SEE FIGURE 9–13**.

- **Linear solenoids.** This type of solenoid can be varied by changing the amount of on time to precisely control the

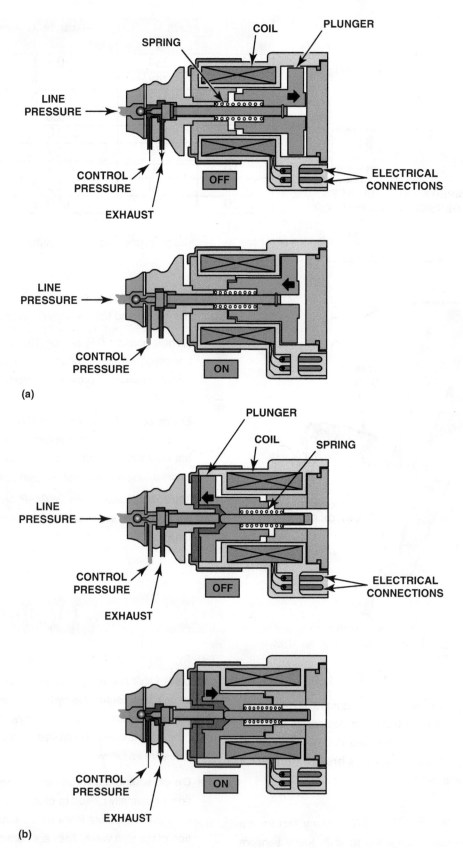

FIGURE 9–13 (a) The normally closed solenoid blocks fluid flow when it is off while opening the exhaust; and when it is on, it opens the valve. (b) The normally open solenoid allows fluid flow when it is off; and when it is on, it closes the valve while opening the exhaust.

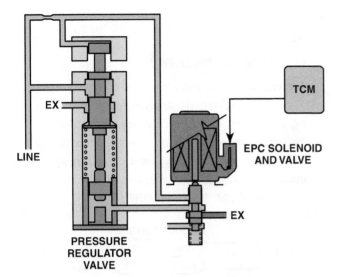

FIGURE 9–14 The signal from the TCM can cause the EPC solenoid to change the pressure regulator valve to adjust line pressure.

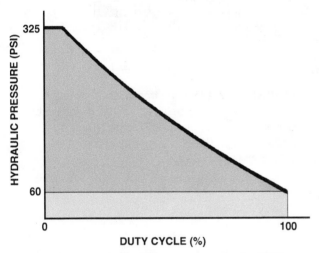

FIGURE 9–15 Line pressure increases as the duty cycle of the EPC solenoid decreases.

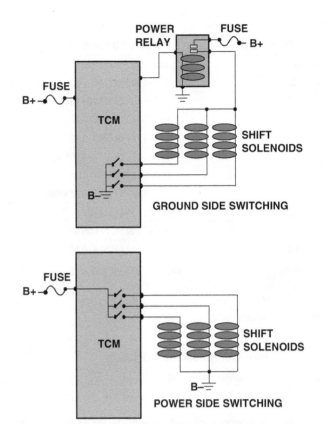

FIGURE 9–16 Solenoid control occurs when the PCM/TCM completes the circuit to ground (top) or switches on B+ (bottom). The ground connection is also B−.

fluid flow through the solenoid valve. The variable power or ground applied to the linear solenoids is pulse-width modulated (PWM) and allows the PCM precise control over the shifting and the fluid pressure. The resistance of most linear (PWM) shift solenoids is about half of the on–off type and range from 4 to 6 ohms. ● **SEE FIGURE 9–14**.

A PWM signal is a digital signal, usually 0 volts and 12 volts, which is cycling at a fixed frequency. Varying the length of time that the signal is on provides a signal that can vary the on and off time of an output. The ratio of on time relative to the period of the cycle is referred to as duty cycle. The torque converter clutch (TCC), pressure control solenoids (PCS), and some shift solenoids are pulse-width modulated-type solenoids. ● **SEE FIGURE 9–15**.

LOW-SIDE AND HIGH-SIDE DRIVERS Low-side drivers (LSD) are transistors that complete the ground path in the circuit. Ignition voltage is supplied to the solenoid and the computer output is connected to the ground side of the shift solenoid. The computer energizes the solenoid by completing the ground path. Low-side drivers can often perform a diagnostic circuit check by monitoring the voltage from the solenoid to check that the control circuit is complete. A low-side driver, however, cannot detect a short-to-ground.

High-side drivers (HSD) control the power side of the solenoid from the PCM/TCM. A ground is provided to the solenoid, so when the high-side driver switches, the solenoid will be energized. High-side drivers inside modules can detect electrical faults such as a break in continuity when the circuit is not energized. ● **SEE FIGURE 9–16**.

ELECTRONIC PRESSURE CONTROL

- The transmission's hydraulic pump pressure regulator valve is controlled by the pressure regulator valve that is controlled by a pulse-width-modulated solenoid called **Electronic pressure control (EPC)** or

EPC Amperes	Pressure PSI (kPa)
0.0	169–195 PSI (1165–1345kPa)
0.1	167–194 PSI (1151–1338 kPa)
0.2	161–190 PSI (1110–1310 kPa)
0.3	155–186 PSI (1069–1282 kPa)
0.4	144–177 PSI (993–1220 kPa)
0.5	133–167 PSI (917–1151 kPa)
0.6	120–153 PSI (827–1055 kPa)
0.7	102–138 PSI (703–952 kPa)
0.8	83–119 PSI (572–821 kPa)
0.9	62–97 PSI (427–669 kPa)
1.0	53–69 PSI (365–476 kPa)

CHART 9–1

Typical electronic pressure control (EPC) current and line pressure comparison.

- **Pressure control solenoid (PCS)** or
- *Variable force solenoid (VFS)* or
- *Force motor*

The EPC is normally closed, which results in high regulated pressure.

- Current (a maximum of about 1 ampere) allows the solenoid to open, which reduces the regulated pressure. The EPC PWM by the PCM/TCM operates at a fixed frequency, usually at 300 to 600 Hz depending on the unit.

- The higher the duty cycle, the more current and the lower the pressure.

- The lower the duty cycle, the less the current and the higher the pressure. ● **CHART 9–1**.

HOW IT ALL WORKS

ELECTRONIC The transmission control module (TCM) uses information from the various engine and transmission/transaxle sensors and then commands the shift solenoids to operate, which controls the timing of the shifts. ● **SEE FIGURE 9–18**.

HYDRAULIC A solenoid can be cycled (pulsed on and off) or line pressure can be increased or decreased by adjusting the electrical signal to the electronic pressure control (EPC) or shift solenoid. The solenoids in turn control the hydraulic pressure that moves the shift valves or operates the torque converter clutch. ● **SEE FIGURE 9–19**.

? FREQUENTLY ASKED QUESTION

What Is Torque Control?

Accurate control of shift timing and quality provides a smoother driving experience. In addition to improving shift quality, altering the ignition timing during the shift decreases the load on the transmission and increases transmission life. This is called **torque management** or *torque reduction* and is controlled by the PCM/TCM. ● **SEE FIGURE 9–17**.

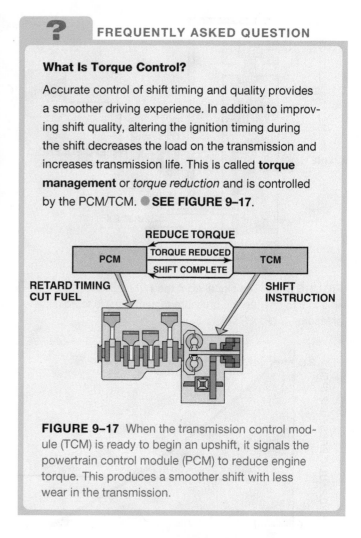

FIGURE 9–17 When the transmission control module (TCM) is ready to begin an upshift, it signals the powertrain control module (PCM) to reduce engine torque. This produces a smoother shift with less wear in the transmission.

ADAPTIVE STRATEGIES

DEFINITION Most late model electronically controlled automatic transmissions/transaxles use the PCM or TCM to monitor the time it takes to complete a shift. The PCM can determine this from the comparison between the engine speed and the output speed sensor data. When a shift is commanded, there should be a change in the speed of the output shaft. If the change in speed is more than normal, which could indicate normal wear in the clutch pack, the PCM can learn from this and start the shift sooner to allow time for the clutch to be fully engaged. The adjustment is called **adaptive control**, or **adaptive learning**, which keeps shift duration within a certain time period as determined by the driver's habits.

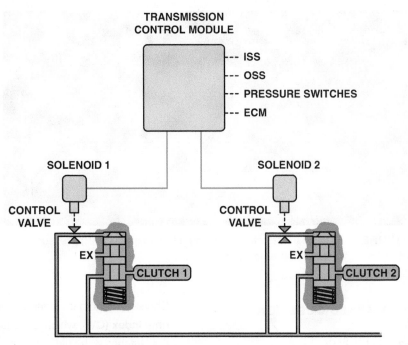

FIGURE 9–18 Using data from the various sensors, the TCM can apply or release the clutches. During an upshift, solenoid 1 can control how fast clutch 1 releases as solenoid 2 controls how fast clutch 2 applies to keep the shift time at the proper speed.

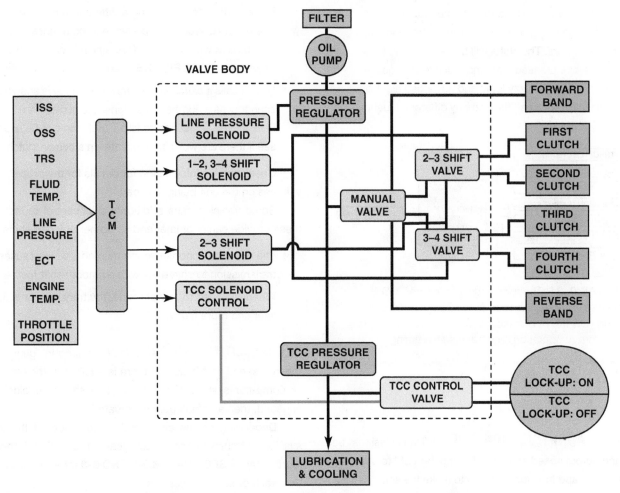

FIGURE 9–19 A diagram showing the relationship between the electronic and hydraulic controls.

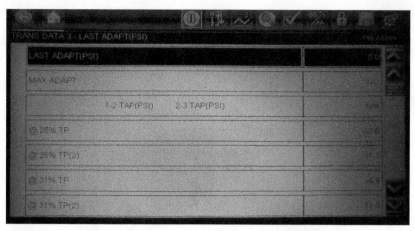

FIGURE 9–20 A scan tool display showing the adaptive (TAP) pressure changes at various throttle positions.

? **FREQUENTLY ASKED QUESTION**

What Is Fuzzy Logic?

A method used to improve shift timing is through a process called *fuzzy logic*. In most situations, shifts simply match vehicle speed and throttle position. Fuzzy logic adapts shifts to driving conditions such as mountains, upgrades and downgrades, and while turning corners. The shifts will be delayed and firmer because of increased load and multiple changes in throttle position. Fuzzy logic and advanced electronics allow improved shifts for many different situations. **SEE FIGURE 9–21.**

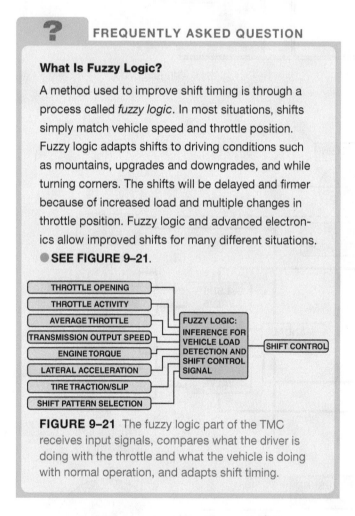

FIGURE 9–21 The fuzzy logic part of the TMC receives input signals, compares what the driver is doing with the throttle and what the vehicle is doing with normal operation, and adapts shift timing.

TYPICAL ADAPTIVE CONTROLS Transmissions use input and output speed sensors, allowing the TCM to determine the gear ratio and how long it takes to make the shift.

- Chrysler refers to the adaptive control as the **clutch volume index (CVI)**, which is the length of time it takes to fill the clutches with fluid.

- General Motors call their adaptive control **Transmission Adapt Pressure (TAP)** system, which manages oil pressure to control clutch fill rates. The TAP values are sorted by cell, with each cell being a different throttle opening. The PCM/TCM can add pressure to compensate for clutch pack wear up to 30 PSI, which is displayed on a **scan tool. SEE FIGURE 9–20.**

- Honda calls it *clutch fill volume index* which is shown on a scan tool as a number. The higher the number, the more fluid volume is required to fill a clutch and can be used to see if there are worn friction plates in a certain clutch pack.

Check service information for details for the proper clutch volumes on the unit being serviced.

Some vehicles have additional shift control modes, and these provide earlier or later and smoother or faster shifts.

- The driver can choose economy mode, which causes the transmission to shift early with a smooth shift feel.

- When switched to power mode, the transmission shifts later and more firmly.

DEFAULT (LIMP-IN) A default (or limp-in) gear is the forward speed that is used if there is a failure in the electronic or computer system. If neither of two shift solenoids were engaged, then a default gear is actuated.

Depending on the exact make and model of the transmission or transaxle, the default gear can be second, third, or fourth gear. **SEE CHARTS 9–2 AND 9–3** for examples of two General Motors transmissions.

GENERAL MOTORS 4T60-E (FRONT-WHEEL-DRIVE TRANSAXLE)		
Gear Range	Solenoid A	Solenoid B
First gear	ON	ON
Second gear	OFF	ON
Third gear	OFF	OFF
Fourth gear	ON	OFF

CHART 9–2

In this example, the vehicle would start out and remain in third gear if there was a fault with the computer or wiring.

GENERAL MOTORS 4L80-E (REAR-WHEEL-DRIVE TRANSMISSION)		
Gear Range	Solenoid A	Solenoid B
First gear	ON	OFF
Second gear	OFF	OFF
Third gear	OFF	ON
Fourth gear	ON	ON

CHART 9–3

In this example, the vehicle would start out and remain in second gear if there was a fault with the computer or wiring.

SUMMARY

1. Electronic controls are used for accurate automatic operation of the transmission/transaxle.
2. Electronic controls use sensors to monitor various operational inputs that will be used to control the operation of the transmission.
3. The hydraulic operation of the transmission is controlled by solenoids that are switched to redirect pressurized fluid to move shift valves or change the operational pressures.
4. The PCM/TCM receives the signals from the sensors and operates the solenoids to produce upshifts and downshifts at the proper speed.

REVIEW QUESTIONS

1. What are the four sensors that are used by the automatic transmission/transaxle controller to determine when to shift?
2. What are the types of computer memory used in the PCM/TCM?
3. What is the purpose and function of the input and output speed sensors?
4. What is the purpose and function of the pressure sensors inside the automatic transmission/transaxle?
5. What is meant by adaptive controls?

CHAPTER QUIZ

1. What electronic control module is used to control the shifting of an electronically controlled automatic transmission/transaxle?
   a. PCM
   b. TCM
   c. TCU
   d. Any of the above depending on application
2. What type of sensor measures temperature?
   a. Potentiometer
   b. Thermistor
   c. Transducer
   d. Frequency generator
3. What type of sensor measures speed?
   a. Potentiometer
   b. Thermistor.
   c. Transducer
   d. Frequency generator
4. The transmission range (TR) switch is used to _____.
   a. Keep the engine from starting in any gear position except park or neutral
   b. Limit upshifts in manual ranges
   c. Operate the backup lights in reverse
   d. All of the above

5. The input speed sensor is also called a _____.
   a. Output speed sensor (OSS)
   b. Vehicle speed (VS) sensor
   c. Turbine speed sensor (TSS)
   d. Any of the above depending on make and model

6. The output speed sensor is also called a_____.
   a. Input speed sensor (ISS)
   b. Vehicle speed (VS) sensor
   c. Turbine speed sensor (TSS)
   d. Any of the above depending on make and model

7. What type of sensor is the transmission fluid temperature (TFT) sensor?
   a. Negative temperature coefficient (NTC) thermistor
   b. Potentiometer
   c. Rheostat
   d. Transducer

8. Linear solenoids are used for _____.
   a. TCC
   b. Pressure control
   c. Transducer
   d. All of the above depending on application

9. What does electronic pressure control (EPC) solenoid use to control mainline pressure?
   a. Resistance
   b. Torque
   c. Current
   d. Voltage

10. Adaptive control means _____.
    a. The time it takes to make a shift
    b. The delay between the command and when the shift occurs
    c. The change in the pressure or timing to keep the shift occurring at the same time to make up for wear
    d. The default position which may be second, third, or fourth gear depending on application

chapter 10

HYBRID ELECTRIC VEHICLE TRANSMISSIONS AND TRANSAXLES

LEARNING OBJECTIVES

After studying this chapter, the reader will be able to:

1. Prepare for ASE Automatic Transmissions (A2) certification test content area "A" (General Transmission and Transaxle Diagnosis).

2. Identify the types of hybrid vehicles.

3. Identify the levels of hybrids.

4. Explain how an automatic transmission can be converted for use in hybrid electric vehicles.

5. Identify the components of a two-mode hybrid transmission system and explain its operation.

6. Discuss the operation of different hybrid vehicle transmissions.

KEY TERMS

Electronically variable transmission (EVT) 182

Internal combustion engine (ICE) 178

Traction battery 193

Traction motor 193

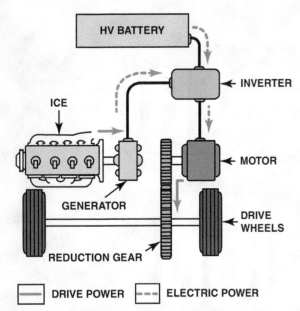

FIGURE 10–1 The power flow in a typical series-hybrid vehicle.

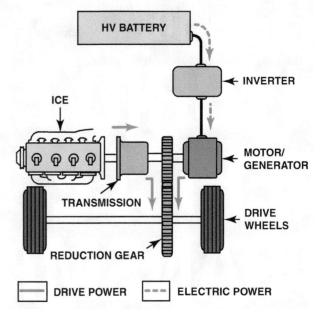

FIGURE 10–2 The power flow in a typical parallel-hybrid vehicle.

TYPES OF HYBRID VEHICLES

SERIES HYBRID The types of hybrid electric vehicles include series, parallel, and series–parallel designs. In a series hybrid design, sole propulsion is by a battery-powered electric motor, but the electric energy for the batteries comes from another on-board energy source, such as an **internal combustion engine (ICE)**. In this design, the engine turns a generator and the generator can either charge the batteries or power an electric motor that drives the transmission. The internal combustion engine never powers the vehicle directly. ● **SEE FIGURE 10–1.**

The engine is only operated to keep the batteries charged. Therefore, the vehicle could be moving with or without the internal combustion engine running. Series-hybrid vehicles also use regeneration braking to help keep the batteries charged. The engine is designed to just keep the batteries charged, and therefore, is designed to operate at its most efficient speed and load.

ADVANTAGES An advantage of a series-hybrid design is that no transmission, clutch, or torque converter is needed. A series hybrid does not give the owner "range anxiety" that often affects owners of electric vehicles who are concerned that they may not have enough electric power to make it home or to a charging station.

DISADVANTAGES A disadvantage of a series-hybrid design is the added weight of the internal combustion engine as compared to an electric vehicle. The engine is actually a heavy on-board battery charger. Also, the electric motor and battery capacity have to be large enough to power the vehicle under all operating conditions, including climbing hills. All power needed for heating and cooling must also come from the batteries so, using the air conditioning in hot weather and the heater in cold weather reduces the range that the vehicle can travel on battery power alone.

PARALLEL HYBRID In a parallel-hybrid design, multiple propulsion sources can be combined, or one of the energy sources alone can drive the vehicle. In this design, the battery and engine are both connected to the transmission. The vehicle using a parallel-hybrid design can be powered by the internal combustion engine alone, by the electric motor alone (full hybrids only), or by a combination of engine and electric motor propulsion. In most cases, the electric motor is used to assist the internal combustion engine.

ADVANTAGES One of the advantages of using a parallel-hybrid design is that by using an electric motor or motors to assist the internal combustion engine, the engine itself can be smaller than would normally be needed. ● **SEE FIGURE 10–2.**

NOTE: A parallel-hybrid design could include additional batteries to allow for plug-in capability, which could extend the distance the vehicle can travel using battery power alone.

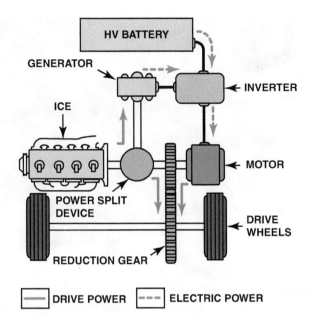

FIGURE 10–3 A series–parallel hybrid design allows the vehicle to operate in electric motor mode only or in combination with the internal combustion engine.

DISADVANTAGES One disadvantage of a parallel-hybrid design is that complex software is needed to seamlessly blend electric and ICE power. Another concern about the parallel-hybrid design is that it has to be engineered to provide proper heating and air-conditioning system operation when the ICE stops at idle.

SERIES–PARALLEL HYBRID The Toyota and Ford hybrids are classified as series–parallel hybrids because they can operate using electric motor power alone or with the assistance of the ICE. Series–parallel hybrids combine the functions of both a series and a parallel design. The internal combustion engine may be operating even though the vehicle is stopped if the electronic controller has detected that the batteries need to be charged. ● **SEE FIGURE 10–3.**

NOTE: The internal combustion engine may or may not start when the driver starts the vehicle depending on the temperature of the engine and other conditions. This can be confusing to some who are driving a hybrid electric vehicle for the first time and sense that the engine did not start when they tried to start the engine.

LEVELS OF HYBRIDS

MILD HYBRID A mild hybrid will incorporate idle stop and regenerative braking but is not capable of using the electric motor to propel the vehicle on its own without help from the internal combustion engine. A mild hybrid system has the advantage of costing less, but saves less fuel compared to a full hybrid vehicle and usually uses a 42-volt electrical motor and battery package (36-volt batteries, 42-volt charging). An example of this type of hybrid is the General Motors parallel-hybrid truck (PHT) pickup truck and the Saturn VUE. The fuel savings for a mild type of hybrid design is about 8% to 15%.

MEDIUM HYBRID A medium hybrid uses 144- to 158-volt batteries that provide for engine stop/start, regenerative braking, and power assist. Like a mild hybrid, a typical medium hybrid is not capable of propelling the vehicle from a stop using battery power alone. Examples of a medium-hybrid vehicle include the Honda Insight, Civic, and Accord. The fuel economy savings are about 20% to 25% for medium-hybrid systems.

FULL HYBRID A full hybrid, also called a strong hybrid, uses a 201-300 volt battery, and provides for idle stop, regenerative braking, and is able to propel the vehicle using the electric motor(s) alone. Each vehicle manufacturer has made its decision on which hybrid type to implement based on its assessment of the market niche for a particular model. Examples of a full or strong hybrid include the Ford Escape SUV, Toyota Highlander, Lexus RX400h, Lexus GS450h, Toyota Prius, and Toyota Camry. The fuel savings are about 30% to 50% for full-hybrid systems.

ONE-MOTOR/TWO-MOTOR/THREE-MOTOR SYSTEMS

ONE-MOTOR HYBRIDS Hybrid electric vehicles that use one electric motor include VW, Nissan, Honda, and General Motors. In these units, an electric motor is attached to the engine crankshaft and is used to perform two functions:

1. Start the gasoline engine (ICE)
2. Act as a generator to charge the high-voltage batteries.

General Motors also uses a belt alternator starter (BAS) system, which uses a belt-driven motor/generator attached to the front of the engine. Hybrids that use one motor are often mild hybrids and usually are not able to power the vehicle using electric power alone.

TWO-MOTOR HYBRIDS Hybrid electric vehicles that use two motors are the most commonly used hybrids and are used

FIGURE 10–4 The rear electric motor on a Lexus RX 400h SUV.

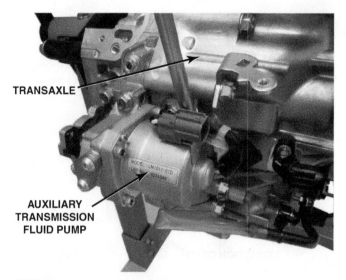

FIGURE 10–5 Honda Accord Hybrid auxiliary transmission fluid pump. This pump operates only when the ICE enters idle stop (stop–start) mode.

by Toyota, Ford, and General Motors in their full-size two-mode trucks. Each electric motor serves two purposes:

- The motor/generator attached to the engine, usually labeled M/G1, is used to start the gasoline engine and to charge the high-voltage batteries.
- The motor/generator that is connected to the drive wheels, usually labeled M/G2, is used to propel the vehicle and to recharge the high-voltage battery during deceleration (regenerative braking).

Two-motor hybrid electric vehicles are full (strong) hybrids and are capable of propelling the vehicle using electric motor power alone for short distances.

THREE-MOTOR HYBRIDS Three-motor hybrid electric vehicles are usually two-motor hybrids that use an additional electric motor to propel the rear wheels for all-wheel-drive capability. Hybrid electric vehicles that use three electric motors include the Toyota Highlander and Lexus Rx400/450h SUVs. ● **SEE FIGURE 10–4.**

HYBRID ELECTRIC VEHICLE (HEV) TRANSMISSIONS

AUTOMATIC TRANSMISSIONS CONVERTED FOR USE IN HYBRID VEHICLES In order to adapt a conventional automatic transmission to a hybrid power train, an electric auxiliary pump is used to maintain fluid pressure in the transmission during internal combustion engine (ICE) idle stop.

This pump is powered by a DC brushless (AC synchronous) motor, which requires a special controller to provide the correct operating frequency and pulse width. When the auxiliary pump is operating, it sends hydraulic pressure to the transmission regulator valve, and then on to the manual valve where it is directed to the appropriate clutches. This prevents the transmission from shifting into "neutral" when the ICE is in idle stop. Once the ICE restarts, the auxiliary pump is turned off and hydraulic pressure is again supplied by the mechanically driven transmission fluid pump. ● **SEE FIGURE 10–5.**

GM PARALLEL HYBRID TRUCK

DESCRIPTION AND OPERATION The transmission in the 2004–2008 Chevrolet Silverado/GMC Sierra parallel-hybrid pickup is based on the 4L60E electronically controlled automatic transmission design with minor modifications to adjust for its role in a hybrid power train. It has four forward speeds and one reverse, with the fourth speed being an overdrive. It is designed primarily for medium- and large-displacement engines and is used extensively in GM pickups and SUVs. The specific model used in the hybrid pickup is known as the M33. The transmission is controlled by the PCM, which receives signals from other vehicle sensors to determine load and speed and command appropriate transmission operation.

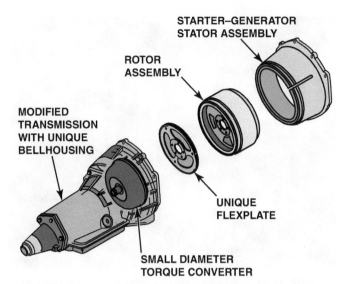

FIGURE 10–6 Integrated starter–generator (ISG) assembly adapted to a production 4L60E transmission. Note that the torque converter diameter is smaller to fit inside the rotor assembly.

The transmission gear selector lever can be placed in seven positions, as follows:

- P—Park
- R—Reverse
- N—Neutral
- D—Drive
- 3—Manual third
- 2—Manual second
- 1—Manual first

The gear shift linkage attaches to the manual valve lever on the transmission case. This lever incorporates a transmission range switch, which signals the PCM of the selected gear.

CONSTRUCTION The transmission case and the bell housing are made from die-cast aluminum, the same as the conventional model. However, changes were made to accommodate the addition of the *integrated starter–generator* (*ISG*) inside the bell housing assembly. The transmission was modified where it was absolutely necessary, but otherwise used as much of the original design as possible. The primary change was a decrease in the diameter of the torque converter in order for it to fit inside the rotor assembly of the ISG. ● **SEE FIGURE 10–6.**

The original torque converter is 300 mm in diameter, whereas the hybrid torque converter is 258 mm. The rotor assembly is bolted directly to the engine crankshaft and wraps around the torque converter. A separate flex plate inside the rotor is used to drive the torque converter. The bell housing is

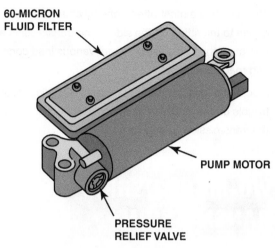

FIGURE 10–7 Electric secondary fluid pump from a 4L60E transmission in a GM hybrid pickup.

a separate part of the most recent 4L60E transmission case design, and this was replaced with a special unit that was large enough to enclose the ISG stator assembly.

To limit heat buildup in the smaller torque converter, a different TCC control strategy was used so that lockup would be commanded earlier. This also required the use of a torque converter with a multi-plate clutch (TCC) in order to handle the torque generated by the V-8 engine.

OPERATION In start/stop (idle stop) mode the engine stops, which will in turn stop the transmission oil pump and cause the transmission to go into "neutral." To prevent this, an electric secondary fluid pump is installed on the valve body inside the transmission oil pan. Whenever the engine goes into idle stop, the electric fluid pump is turned on to maintain oil pressure on the transmission forward clutch and keep the drivetrain connected to the engine. This results in a smoother transition between idle stop and engine restarting as the vehicle resumes operation. ● **SEE FIGURE 10–7.**

To enable regenerative braking, the hybrid version of the 4L60E transmission is made to apply the overrun clutch during coasting or braking in the D4 range and either third or second gear. This allows power to be transmitted back through the torque converter, which can then be used to generate electric current for recharging the 42-volt battery pack.

SERVICE Service and diagnostic procedures include:

- Transmission service for the 4L60E model M33 is limited to fluid and filter changes. This transmission requires Dexron VI fluid. The filter on the electric secondary fluid pump is replaceable but is not a regular maintenance item.

- Transmission pressure testing can be performed using the line pressure tap located on the transmission case.

These tests are most often done by attaching a pressure gauge to the fitting on the side of the transmission and operating the transmission under various load conditions and road speeds.

- A scan tool can be used to access DTCs (diagnostic trouble codes) and also to perform bidirectional testing of the transmission solenoids.

TWO-MODE HYBRID TRANSMISSION

POWER FLOW The transmission used in the GM two-mode hybrid (2008–2014) is designed specifically for use in hybrid vehicles. The two-mode hybrid transmission used in General Motors hybrid trucks is labeled 2ML70 and is also used by Dodge and Chrysler. This unit features two 60-kW motors inside the transmission, a 300-volt battery pack, and a V-8 engine.

A two-mode hybrid electric vehicle is capable of increasing fuel economy by about 25%, depending on the type of driving conditions. Like all hybrids, the two-mode combines the power of a gasoline engine with that of electric motors and includes:

- Regenerative braking that captures kinetic energy that would otherwise be lost

- Idle stop (start/stop)

COMPONENTS This two-mode unit is called an **electronically variable transmission (EVT)**. It includes three simple planetary gear sets with four multi-plate clutches. It has four fixed gear ratios with two EV ratios for smooth, more efficient operation. The components of the two-mode transmission include the following:

- Two 60-kW electric motor/generators assemblies called motor/generator A and B, usually abbreviated MG A and MG B.

- Three planetary gear sets (one is located in front of motor/generator A , called M/G A; another is located between the two motor/generators, and the last planetary gear set is located behind motor/generator B, called M/G B).

- Four wet plate clutches (two friction [rotating] and two [reaction/stationary] clutch assemblies). ● SEE FIGURE 10–8.

FIGURE 10–8 The two-mode transmission has orange high-voltage cable entering the unit to carry electric energy from the high-voltage battery pack to propel the vehicle and also to charge the battery during deceleration.

The vehicle starts moving in EV 1 with a variable ratio from infinite low to 1.7:1. If the vehicle is launched with the engine off, M/G A will spin the engine crankshaft so it can start running.

EV 2 has a ratio between 1.7:1 and 0.5:1.

FIRST MODE OF OPERATION The first mode is for accelerating from standstill to second gear. At low speed and light load, the vehicle can be propelled by:

- Either electric motor alone

- The internal combustion engine (ICE) alone

- Or a combination of the two (electric motor and/or ICE)

In this mode, the engine (if running) can be shut off under certain conditions and everything will continue to operate on electric power alone. The hybrid system can restart the ICE at any time as needed. One of the motor/generators operates as a generator to charge the high-voltage battery, and the other works as a motor to assist in propelling the vehicle.

SECOND MODE OF OPERATION The second mode takes the vehicle from second gear through to overdrive. At higher loads and speeds, the ICE always runs. In the second mode, the motor/generators and planetary gear sets are used to keep torque and horsepower at a maximum. As the vehicle speed increases, various combinations of the four fixed ratio planetary gears engage and/or disengage to multiply engine torque, and allows one or the other of the motor/generators to perform as a generator to charge the high-voltage battery. ● SEE FIGURE 10–9.

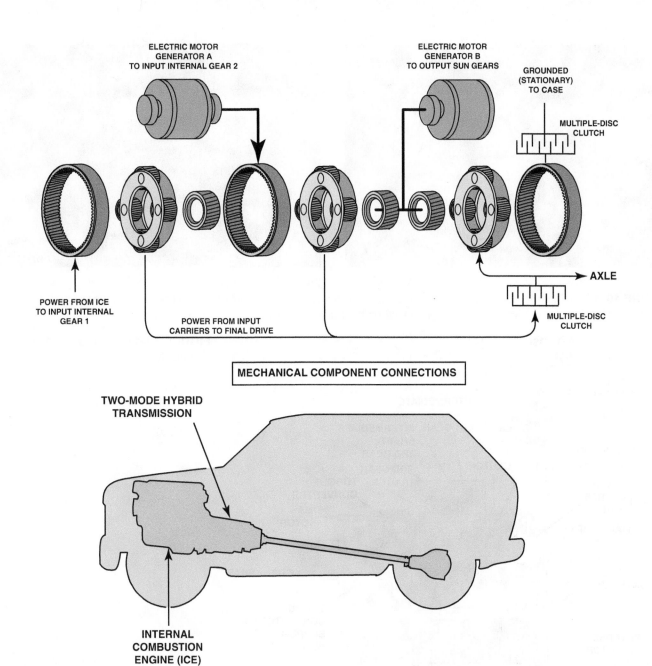

MECHANICAL COMPONENT CONNECTIONS

FIGURE 10–9 Using two planetary gear sets, the ICE can be maintained in the most efficient speed of about 2000 RPM under most operating conditions.

TWO-MODE SERVICE Routine service is all that is needed or required of the two-mode transmission. Fluid level check and visual inspection should be all that is required until the first scheduled fluid change. Always use Dexron VI. Faults in the system will often set a diagnostic trouble code (DTC). Unit repair requires an engine hoist or the lift arm of a vehicle lift to remove the motor assembly. ● **SEE FIGURE 10–10.**

HONDA ACCORD FIVE SPEED

DESCRIPTION AND OPERATION Honda uses an automatic transmission (transaxle) in the 2005–2007 Accord Hybrid that is similar to the units used in its vehicles with conventional nonhybrid power trains. This transmission has

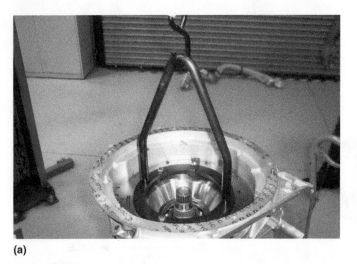

(a)

(b)

FIGURE 10–10 (a) Disassembly of the 2ML70 transmission requires the use of a lift or engine hoist to remove the motor assembly. (b) The motor assembly after being removed for the transmission.

FIGURE 10–11 Cutaway view of Honda Accord Hybrid automatic transmission.

REVERSE IDLER GEAR

REVERSE IDLER GEAR SHAFT

INTERMEDIATE SHAFT 4TH GEAR

INTERMEDIATE SHAFT 3RD GEAR

MAINSHAFT 5TH GEAR

4TH CLUTCH

5TH CLUTCH

3RD GEAR CLUTCH

TORQUE CONVERTER

MAINSHAFT REVERSE GEAR

IMA ROTOR

MAINSHAFT

CRANKSHAFT

COUNTERSHAFT

TORQUE CONVERTER SUPPORT HUB

REVERSE SELECTOR HUB

FINAL DRIVE GEAR

SECONDARY SHAFT

2ND CLUTCH

COUNTERSHAFT REVERSE GEAR

1ST-HOLD CLUTCH

DIFFERENTIAL ASSEMBLY

COUNTER SHAFT 5TH GEAR

1ST CLUTCH

ONE-WAY CLUTCH

FINAL DRIVEN GEAR

five forward speeds and one reverse, and uses a standard torque converter with lockup clutch. There are four parallel shafts, including the main shaft, countershaft, secondary shaft, and the intermediate shaft. This design is similar to the Honda manual transaxles, as constant-mesh helical gears and a reverse idler are used to create the gear ratios. Planetary gear sets are not utilized in this design. The various speeds are selected through the application of six multiple-disc clutches and a single one-way clutch. ● **SEE FIGURE 10–11.**

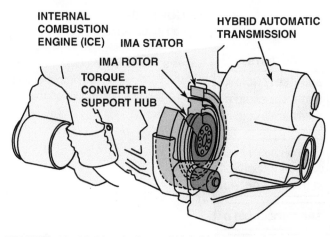

FIGURE 10–12 Honda Accord Hybrid power train, including 3.0-liter V6, IMA assembly, and 5-speed automatic transmission.

The integrated motor assist (IMA) assembly is located between the ICE and the transmission. The torque converter drive plate (flex plate) is attached to the IMA rotor, which in turn is driven by the ICE crankshaft. ● **SEE FIGURE 10–12.**

Most transmission control functions are performed electronically. Input signals from the sensors are processed by the PCM, which operates seven solenoid valves in the transmission to control shift points, shift quality, and torque converter lockup. In order to accommodate the hybrid power train, an electric auxiliary pump is used to maintain fluid pressure in the transmission during ICE idle stop. This pump is powered by an AC synchronous motor, which requires a special controller to provide the correct operating frequency and pulse width.

The vehicle gear selector has seven positions, including:

- P—Park
- R—Reverse
- N—Neutral
- D—Drive (first through fifth)
- D3—Drive (first through third)
- 2—Second
- 1—First

The gear shift linkage attaches to the manual valve lever on the transmission case. This lever incorporates a transmission range switch, which signals the PCM concerning the selected gear.

CONSTRUCTION The Honda Accord Hybrid automatic transaxle is housed in an aluminum case, which attaches in line with the ICE and the Integrated Motor Assist (IMA) assembly. The various gears are engaged and disengaged through the application and release of hydraulically operated multiple-disc clutches. Since there are no planetary gears used in this transmission, there is no need for holding devices (brakes). Power is directed through the transmission by applying a clutch and locking a gear to its associated shaft. The clutches are similar in function to the synchronizers in a manual transaxle.

As with any electronically controlled transmission, the mechanical workings are relatively simple but the control strategy is complex. The PCM is responsible for the automatic transmission functions, and it receives input data from many different sensors in order to make the transmission operate smoothly and efficiently. ● **SEE FIGURE 10–13.**

DIAGNOSIS AND SERVICE If a fault is detected with the hybrid transmission, the "D" indicator on the transmission range display is flashed on the instrument panel. ● **SEE FIGURE 10–14.**

The DTC related to the malfunction can be retrieved using a Honda or enhanced aftermarket scan tool. The scan tool is plugged into the data link connector (DLC) and the ignition switch is turned to the RUN position. The scan tool can then communicate with the PCM and identify any diagnostic trouble codes along with other sensor information that can help diagnose the problem at hand.

There is no specified service procedure required because the fluid is a "fill for life" system. Always check service information for the exact procedures to follow for the vehicle being serviced.

TOYOTA/LEXUS POWER-SPLIT SYSTEM

APPLICATIONS The Toyota/Lexus power-split device drive system is used in the following models:

- Toyota Prius
- Toyota Camry hybrid
- Lexus CT200h
- Toyota Highlander
- Lexus RX400h and RX450h

DESCRIPTION The power-split transaxle is a series–parallel hybrid technology. During most phases of vehicle operation, the system is operating as both series and parallel at the same time. While the control system is complex, the basic

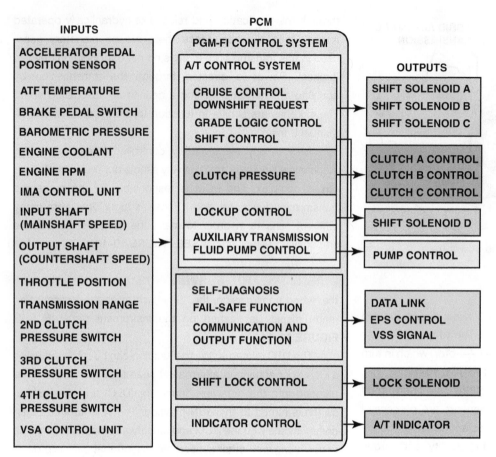

FIGURE 10–13 Control schematic for a Honda Accord Hybrid automatic transmission. Note that all sensor inputs are shown to the left of the PCM, while the output signals and actuators are shown on the right.

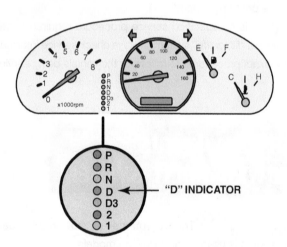

FIGURE 10–14 The Honda Accord Hybrid will alert the driver of a transmission malfunction by flashing the "D" indicator on the instrument panel.

transaxle is very simple in design as it is built around a single planetary gear set (power-split device) and two electric motor/generators, called MG1 and MG2. ● SEE FIGURE 10–15.

A planetary gear set is comprised of three main components:

1. Ring gear
2. Planet carrier
3. Sun gear

In the power-split transaxle, a large electric motor/generator (MG2) is directly attached to the transaxle final drive and to the planetary ring gear. The ICE is connected to the planet carrier, and the small electric motor/generator (MG1) is connected to the sun gear. ● SEE FIGURE 10–16.

The planetary ring gear always turns in the same direction as the drive wheels and its speed is directly proportional to vehicle speed. In other words, if the ring gear is not moving, the vehicle is not moving.

The power-split device is so named because the ICE (attached to the planet carrier) splits its torque output between the sun gear (MG1) and the ring gear (MG2 and drive wheels). The gear ratio of the planetary gear set causes the ICE to send 72% of its torque to the ring gear and the remaining 28% to the sun gear. The torque split percentages remain the same regardless of what mode the transaxle is operating in because they are determined by the number of teeth on the planetary ring gear and the sun gear. ● SEE FIGURE 10–17.

While torque split percentages are always the same, power split percentages will vary depending on the RPM of the various components. Horsepower is the rate at which work is performed and is a function of torque and RPM. If a shaft has torque applied to it but remains at zero RPM, no

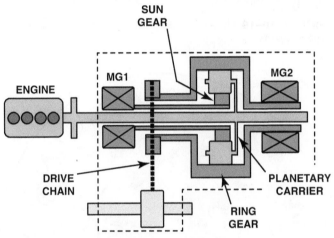

FIGURE 10–15 The Toyota Hybrid System uses two electric motor/generators (MG1 and MG2) and an ICE, all connected together by a power-split device, which is a simple planetary gear set.

FIGURE 10–16 The power-split device from the Toyota Hybrid System. Note that the vehicle will move only when MG2 (and the ring gear) is turning.

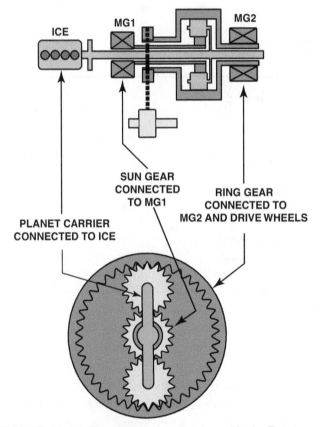

FIGURE 10–17 The planetary gear set used in the Toyota Hybrid System (THS) has 2.6 times the number of teeth in its ring gear as it has in its sun gear. This means that the ICE (attached to the planet carrier) will send 72% of its torque to the ring gear (drive wheels), and 28% of its torque to the sun gear (MG1).

work is being performed and no horsepower is transmitted through the shaft. The same principle applies to the torque split planetary gear set. If the sun gear is stationary, it will still receive 28% of the torque of the ICE, but all of the engine horsepower will be directed through the ring gear and on to the drive wheels.

OPERATION

▪ **Vehicle Stopped.** When the vehicle is stopped, nothing is happening within the vehicle drive system. The ICE is shut off, and both electric motor/generators are shut off as well. There are circuits within the vehicle that will use electrical energy from the auxiliary battery, but the drive system itself is effectively inert. The Toyota hybrid system does not use an auxiliary starter but instead uses the

motor/generator (MG1) for starting under all conditions. ● **SEE FIGURE 10–18.**

▪ **Light Acceleration.** When the vehicle is driven at low speeds and light acceleration, it is driven by MG2 alone. ● **SEE FIGURE 10–19.**

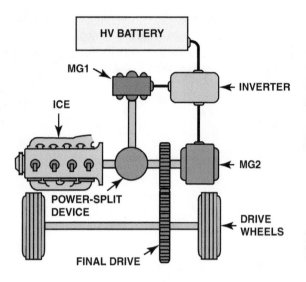

VEHICLE STOPPED

FIGURE 10–18 When the vehicle is stopped, the ICE is shut off along with both motor/generators.

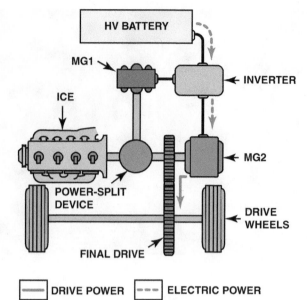

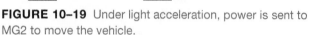 DRIVE POWER --- ELECTRIC POWER

FIGURE 10–19 Under light acceleration, power is sent to MG2 to move the vehicle.

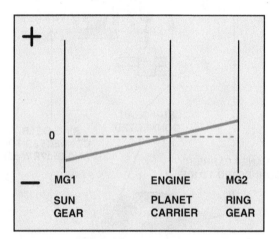

FIGURE 10–20 Light acceleration—the engine is stopped (0 RPM), MG2 is turning forward (+), and MG1 is turning backward (–).

- This is because the electric motor is more efficient than the ICE at low vehicle speeds. Current from the high-voltage (HV) battery is sent through the inverter and on to MG2 to move the vehicle. A special graph, known as a monograph, shows the speed relationship between the various elements. When the engine is stopped (0 RPM), MG2 is turning forward (+), and this causes MG1 to turn backward (–). ● **SEE FIGURE 10–20.**

- **Normal Driving.** When higher vehicle speeds are required, the ICE must be started so that its output can be combined with that of MG2. The ring gear is already turning clockwise as the vehicle travels in a forward direction. Since the planet carrier (attached to the ICE) is

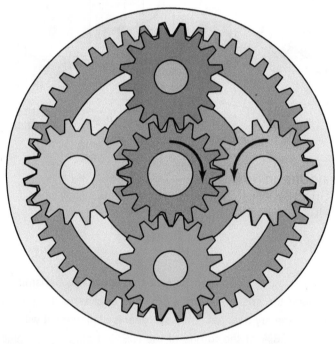

FIGURE 10–21 To start the ICE, MG1 (sun) acts as a motor and turns clockwise (CW), causing the planet carrier (attached to the ICE) to also turn CW.

stationary, the sun gear (driven by MG1) is used to drive the planet carrier clockwise and start the ICE. Current from the HV battery is directed through the inverter and operates MG1 as a motor, turning clockwise and spinning the ICE up to 1000 RPM for starting. ● **SEE FIGURE 10–21.**

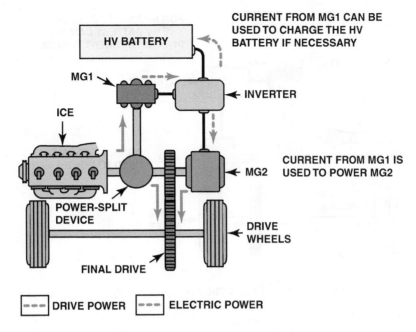

DRIVE POWER ⸺ ⸺ **ELECTRIC POWER**

NORMAL DRIVING

FIGURE 10–22 Normal driving—the ICE is now running and some of its torque is used to drive MG1. Electricity generated by MG1 is used to power MG2 or recharge the HV battery.

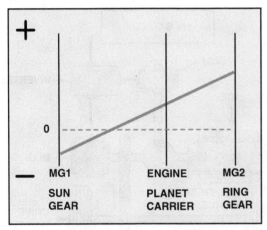

FIGURE 10–23 Normal driving—the engine is running, MG2 is turning forward (+), and MG1 is turning backward (–).

Once the ICE is started, MG1 operates as a generator, but turns in the counterclockwise direction. ICE output is now divided or "split" between the drive wheels (ring gear) and MG1 (sun gear). Power generated by MG1 is either directed to MG2 to help move the vehicle or is used to recharge the HV battery if necessary. ● **SEE FIGURES 10–22 AND 10–23.**

▪ **Full-Throttle Acceleration and High-Speed Cruise.** When greater acceleration is required, both MG2 and the ICE continue sending torque to the vehicle drive wheels,

but MG2 can also receive power from the HV battery to increase its output. As demand increases further, the ICE speed is increased for more output. To enable an increase in ICE speed, the sun gear (MG1) must rotate in a clockwise direction. It is during these times that MG1 can be configured as a motor and will draw power from MG2 during a phase known as energy recirculation. ● **SEE FIGURES 10–24 AND 10–25.**

▪ **Deceleration and Braking.** As the vehicle is decelerating, MG2 is configured as a generator. The kinetic energy (energy of movement) of the vehicle is then converted into electrical energy by MG2. The ICE and MG1 are shut off, and current from MG2 is sent through the inverter and is then used to recharge the HV battery. ● **SEE FIGURE 10–26.**

▪ **Reverse.** If reverse is selected, power is sent from the HV battery to the inverter and then on to MG2. MG2 operates in the reverse direction to back up the vehicle, but the other components in the drive system are turned off at this time. The ICE does not run when the vehicle is being driven in reverse. ● **SEE FIGURE 10–27.**

CONSTRUCTION   The Toyota power-split transaxle is built with an aluminum case composed of two major assemblies. These are known as the MG1 assembly and the MG2 assembly,

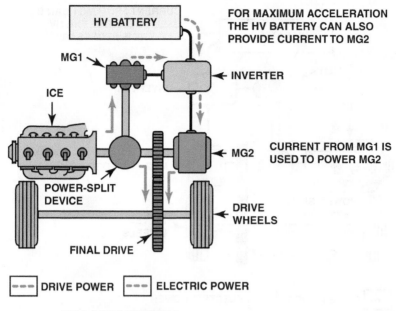

FOR MAXIMUM ACCELERATION
THE HV BATTERY CAN ALSO
PROVIDE CURRENT TO MG2

CURRENT FROM MG1 IS
USED TO POWER MG2

- - - DRIVE POWER   - - - ELECTRIC POWER

FULL ACCELERATION &
HIGH-SPEED CRUISE

FIGURE 10–24 Full-throttle acceleration and high-speed cruise—with greater demand for acceleration, power from MG1 is combined with power from the HV battery to generate higher output from MG2. It is also possible to configure MG2 as a generator and send its power to MG1 (which then acts as a motor).

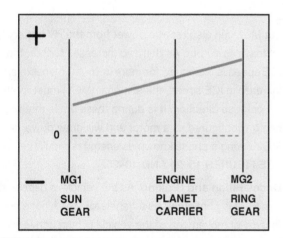

FIGURE 10–25 Full-throttle acceleration and high-speed cruise—this graph shows MG1 acting as a motor using power from MG2. This increases the speed of the ICE, allowing it to produce higher output.

and each houses its respective motor/generator. Each of these major assemblies has its own water jacket for cooling the motor/generator windings in the housing. There are two water jacket unions installed in each major assembly, and these send coolant to the motors from the separate inverter cooling system. ● **SEE FIGURE 10–28.**

The following components are assembled on a common axis:

- Internal combustion engine (ICE)
- MG1

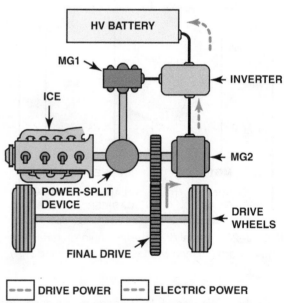

- - - DRIVE POWER   - - - ELECTRIC POWER

DECELERATION AND BRAKING

FIGURE 10–26 Deceleration and braking—MG2 is configured as a generator and recharges the HV battery.

- Power-split device
- MG2
- Oil pump

The final drive is housed between the two major assemblies and utilizes a conventional open differential for sending torque

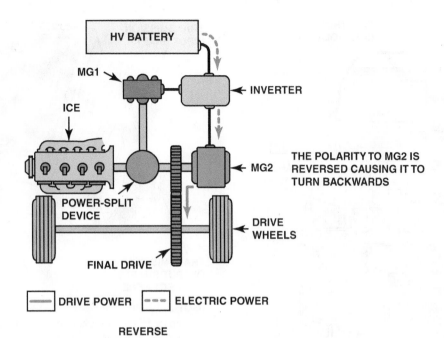

FIGURE 10–27 Reverse—MG2 alone is used to move the car in reverse. This is accomplished by reversing the direction of MG2.

FIGURE 10–28 Excessive heat created in the electric motors must be controlled and proper maintenance of the cooling system is important for long life to help avoid overheating motor winding as shown.

to the front drive wheels. A chain drive attaches the ring gear of the power-split device to the counter drive gear, which drives the counter driven gear that is meshed with the ring gear of the differential assembly. This system does not use a conventional clutch or torque converter. With this design, there is no need to disconnect the engine from the input shaft. This is because the engine can turn at any speed while the vehicle is stopped (ring gear is therefore stopped) by using MG1 (sun gear) as a generator. The ICE is connected directly to the transaxle input shaft using a damper disc mechanism. The transaxle oil pump

is housed in the rear of the MG2 assembly and is attached to the input shaft from the ICE. This means that oil is circulated by the pump only when the ICE is running. When the vehicle is driven by MG2 only, the transaxle is splash-lubricated by the movement of the final drive gears. The transaxle for the 2001–2003 Prius has a cable-operated parking lock mechanism. This was replaced with an electrically actuated mechanism starting with the 2004 model year.

SERVICE Service procedures to be performed at specified intervals include changing the transaxle oil and the coolant for the inverter (high voltage) system. There are drain plugs for both at the bottom of the transaxle assembly. The transaxle oil is refilled through a hole in the front of the case, with the level being brought up to a specified distance from the bottom of the hole. The coolant is refilled at the reservoir that is located on the inverter assembly, and must be bled properly before placing the vehicle back into service. Always use the recommended fluids and procedures when servicing any vehicle.

NOTE: The fastest and most reliable way to refill the inverter cooling system is to use an airlift fluid exchange machine. This pulls the cooling system into a vacuum and then injects the coolant into the evacuated system. This method fills the system quickly and eliminates air bubbles.

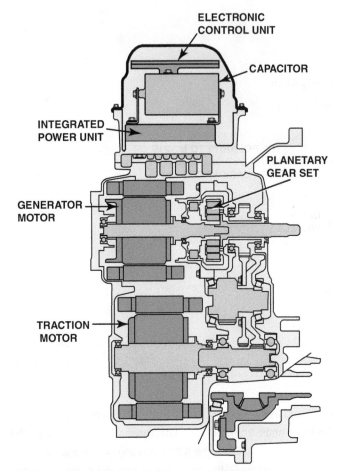

FIGURE 10–29 Cutaway view of the Ford Escape Hybrid transaxle.

Labels on Figure 10–29:
ELECTRONIC CONTROL UNIT
CAPACITOR
INTEGRATED POWER UNIT
PLANETARY GEAR SET
GENERATOR MOTOR
TRACTION MOTOR

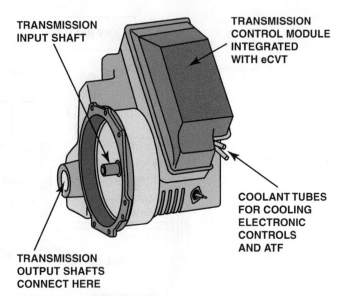

Labels on Figure 10–30:
TRANSMISSION INPUT SHAFT
TRANSMISSION CONTROL MODULE INTEGRATED WITH eCVT
COOLANT TUBES FOR COOLING ELECTRONIC CONTROLS AND ATF
TRANSMISSION OUTPUT SHAFTS CONNECT HERE

FIGURE 10–30 The Ford Escape Hybrid transaxle operates very similar to the one used in the Toyota Hybrid System, but is constructed very differently.

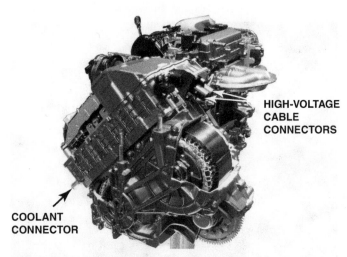

Labels on Figure 10–31:
HIGH-VOLTAGE CABLE CONNECTORS
COOLANT CONNECTOR

FIGURE 10–31 A Ford eCVT transaxle assembly showing the electrical connectors on the top of the assembly.

FORD ESCAPE HYBRID ECVT

PARTS AND OPERATION   The Ford Escape Hybrid uses an electronically controlled continuously variable transmission (eCVT) that is very similar in operation to the Toyota power-split transaxle. It is built differently, however, in that the traction motor is on a different axis and is placed above the generator motor. This was done to keep the length of the transaxle similar to that of a conventional automatic transaxle. ● SEE FIGURES 10–29 AND 10–30.

Another difference is that the transmission control module (TCM) is an integral part of the eCVT. This encloses the high-voltage cables and also makes it possible to cool the motors and the electronics with one heat exchanger. ● SEE FIGURE 10–31.

Coolant in the transaxle/electronic cooling system is sent through the water channel and absorbs heat from the ATF channel below and the heat sink for the electronic control unit above. A small oil pump inside the eCVT circulates ATF for lubricating the gear train and for cooling the two electric motors. This oil pump is driven directly by the ICE through the planet carrier of the planetary gear set. Like the Toyota system, the oil pump will not circulate ATF unless the ICE is running. This means that the gear train is splash-lubricated when the vehicle is in electric-only operation.

The traction motor in the eCVT can be used to accelerate the vehicle from a standstill. If more power is required, the ICE is started. The starting function is performed by the generator motor, which in most cases acts as a generator to provide current to the traction motor or to the high-voltage battery when

TECH TIP

Traction Motors Move the Vehicle

Traction motors are so named because anything that propels the vehicle is said to provide a *traction force*. Traction force is also known as *tractive force*. The high-voltage battery in a Ford Escape Hybrid is used to power the traction motor in the eCVT, so it is known as **a traction battery**.

FIGURE 10–32 The Honda CVT is connected directly to the ICE through a drive plate and flywheel mechanism.

required. Like the Toyota, the Escape hybrid does not use an auxiliary starter and relies on the generator motor for starting under all conditions. The generator motor is also responsible for supplying all the electrical current for vehicle operation. The high voltage from the generator is sent through a DC/DC converter to provide the 12 volts necessary for powering the vehicle accessories. During vehicle braking, the traction motor becomes a generator and provides electrical current to recharge the battery (regenerative braking).

SERVICE The eCVT is lubricated-for-life with a special Mercon fluid. There is a fill plug and a drain plug located on the left side of the case, but these are used only in special service situations.

HONDA HYBRID BELT AND PULLEY CVT

PURPOSE AND FUNCTION Internal combustion engines run most efficiently in a relatively narrow RPM range. In order to achieve the best efficiency, there must be a means of controlling the RPM of an ICE during the entire vehicle operating range. Both manual and automatic transmissions have increased the number of speed ratios used in order to keep the ICE as close as possible to the most efficient RPM at all times, and the best type of transmission to use is a continuously variable transmission (CVT).

DESCRIPTION AND OPERATION One CVT design being used in hybrid electric vehicles is the belt-and-pulley system as used by Honda in the Civic and Insight. Much of this system is similar to other automatic transmissions, in that

it uses a planetary gear set and multiple-disc clutches with electrohydraulic controls. However, there are no distinct speed ranges (or "shifts") in this design, as variable drive and driven pulleys are used with a special steel belt to provide nonstaged speeds forward.

There is no clutch or torque converter utilized in this design. Instead, the transmission input shaft is splined directly to the ICE through the drive plate and flywheel. This assembly is built similar to a dual-mass flywheel and is designed to dampen torsional vibrations from the engine. ● **SEE FIGURE 10–32.**

There are three multiple-disc clutches used in the internal gear train.

1. One for the forward clutch,
2. One for the reverse brake, and
3. The third for the start clutch.

In park (P) or neutral (N), none of the clutches have hydraulic pressure applied to them, which prevents engine torque from being applied to the drive pulley shaft.

The forward clutch and the start clutch are in operation whenever the transmission is placed in a forward gear position (D or L).

The start clutch has multiple responsibilities, including the following:

1. The start clutch is engaged whenever the vehicle is moving, in either forward or reverse.
2. It must help the vehicle accelerate from a standstill by slipping and then fully engaging once the vehicle is moving, similar to a manually operated clutch.

FIGURE 10–33 The Honda Accord V-6 hybrid electric vehicle use a Honda non-planetary gear type automatic transaxle equipped with a small electric pump motor to maintain hydraulic fluid pressure during idle stop operation.

IMA

ELECTRIC PUMP

How Does a Hybrid Work Without a Transmission?

The Honda Accord hybrid starting with the 2014 model year (MY) uses a two-motor hybrid drive system that is totally different from that used by Toyota and Ford. It does not use a transmission. Instead, the two motor/generators are separated by a clutch and each performs two functions:

- **Primary motor/generator.** It propels the vehicle and recharges the high-voltage battery during deceleration.
- **Secondary motor/generator.** It is used to start the gasoline engine and supply electrical energy to the primary motor/generator or charge the high-voltage battery. ● SEE FIGURE 10–34.

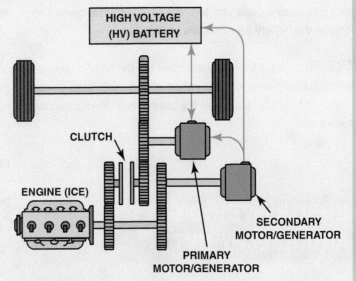

HIGH VOLTAGE (HV) BATTERY

CLUTCH

ENGINE (ICE)

SECONDARY MOTOR/GENERATOR

PRIMARY MOTOR/GENERATOR

FIGURE 10–34 The primary motor/generator is used to propel the vehicle and the secondary motor/generator is used to start the engine and charge the high-voltage battery.

HONDA HYBRID AUTOMATIC TRANSAXLE

SYSTEM OVERVIEW Honda Accord hybrids (2005–2007) used a conventional automatic Honda transaxle and added the integrated starter/generator between the engine and the transaxle. The unit used a torque converter and a small electric motor mounted on the side of the unit to provide hydraulic pressure during idle stop mode operation. ● SEE FIGURE 10–33.

CAUTION: When servicing a hybrid vehicle transmission, be careful of any orange-colored electrical wire. Orange indicates the presence of high-voltage current.

SUMMARY

1. Automatic transmissions used in HEVs incorporate an electric auxiliary pump to provide transmission fluid pressure at engine idle stop.

2. Continuously variable transmissions (CVTs) utilize an infinite number of speed ratios to allow the ICE to operate in its most efficient RPM range during all phases of vehicle operation.

3. The two major types of CVTs include the belt-and-pulley system and the power-split system.

4. The power-split transaxle utilizes two electric motor/generators and a planetary gear set to create infinite speed ratios.

5. The belt-and-pulley CVT uses a special steel belt and two variable-diameter pulleys to create infinite speed ratios and a planetary gear set for reverse.

REVIEW QUESTIONS

1. What are the differences in the operation of an automatic transmission that has been modified for use in a hybrid electric vehicle?

2. What is the difference between a mild and full hybrid?

3. How does a two-mode hybrid work?

4. How does a Honda two motor/generator system work?

CHAPTER QUIZ

1. In a GM two-mode hybrid electric vehicle, when can the vehicle be powered by electric power alone?
   a. During the first mode
   b. During the second mode
   c. During either the first or second mode
   d. During heavy load conditions regardless of mode

2. Modifications to automatic transmissions used in hybrid vehicles include _____.
   a. Electric auxiliary transmission fluid pump
   b. Larger torque converter
   c. Increased number of plates in multiple-disc clutches
   d. Both a and b are correct

3. Technician A says that power-split transaxle use a torque converter. Technician B says that power-split transaxle use an electric transmission fluid pump. Which technician is correct?
   a. Technician A only
   b. Technician B only
   c. Both technicians A and B
   d. Neither technician A nor B

4. All of the following statements concerning power-split transaxles are true, except _____.
   a. The ICE and motor/generators are all connected through a planetary gear set
   b. One of the planetary members must be held to make the power-split transaxle work
   c. The power-split transaxle can operate in electric mode only
   d. Power-split transaxle systems do not use a separate starter motor

5. The Honda CVT is connected to the ICE with a _____.
   a. Torque converter
   b. Manually operated clutch mechanism
   c. Drive plate and flywheel
   d. None of the above

6. In a Toyota/Lexus hybrid electric vehicle, how is reverse achieved?
   a. The ICE reverses direction and powers the drive wheels
   b. MG2 is used to power the vehicle in reverse
   c. MG1 is used to power the vehicle in reverse
   d. Either b or c depending on exact model and year

7. A Toyota hybrid is what type of hybrid?
   a. Series
   b. Series/parallel
   c. Parallel
   d. None of the above

8. Which type of hybrid vehicle cannot propel a vehicle from a stop using electric motor power alone?
   a. Mild hybrid
   b. Medium hybrid
   c. Strong hybrid
   d. Both a and b

9. What is meant by "range anxiety"?
   a. When the driver notices that the ICE has stopped during a stop
   b. When a driver is driving an electric only vehicle
   c. A passenger who notices that the engine starts and then stops when riding in a hybrid electric vehicle.
   d. Any of the above

10. In a Toyota power-split hybrid, what type of transmission is used?
    a. Single planetary gear set
    b. CVT
    c. A manual transmission transformed to function in a hybrid electric vehicle
    d. A conventional automatic transaxle converted for hybrid use

chapter 11

CONTINUOUSLY VARIABLE TRANSMISSIONS

After studying this chapter, the reader will be able to:

1. Prepare for ASE Automatic Transmissions (A2) certification test content area "A" (General Transmission and Transaxle Diagnosis).
2. Describe the construction of a continuously variable transmission and discuss its advantages and disadvantages.
3. Discuss the electronic controls and operation of a CVT.
4. Explain the diagnosis of a CVT, including pressure testing and CVT fluid and noise issues.

Continuously variable transmission (CVT) 197

Input speed sensor (ISS) 200

Line pressure solenoid (LPS) 201

Output speed sensor (OSS) 200

Primary oil pressure (POP) 200

Primary pressure sensor (PPS) 200

Pull chain 199

Push belt 199

Ratio control motor 201

Rubber band effect 198

Secondary oil pressure (SOP) 200

Secondary pressure sensor (SPS) 200

Transmission range sensor (TRS) 200

Transmission temperature sensor (TTS) 200

Variators 198

DRIVE PULLEY: WIDE/SMALL DIAMETER

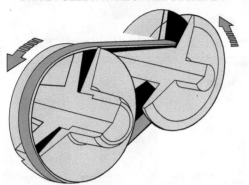

DRIVEN PULLEY: NARROW/LARGE DIAMETER
LOW RATIO, ABOUT 2.5:1

(a)

DRIVE PULLEY: NARROW/LARGE DIAMETER

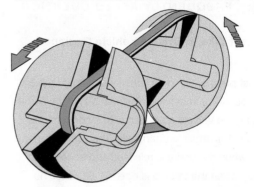

DRIVEN PULLEY: WIDE/SMALL DIAMETER
HIGH RATIO, ABOUT 0.5:1

(b)

FIGURE 11–1 A belt and pulley CVT uses variable-width pulleys to provide an infinite number of speed ratios.

CONTINUOUSLY VARIABLE TRANSMISSION (CVT)

PURPOSE AND FUNCTION A **continuously variable transmission (CVT)** is usually found on some front-wheel-drive vehicles that use a transaxle. A CVT varies the gear ratio in a continuous manner instead of in a series of steps or fixed gear ratios. The power flow is through a steel belt between two pulleys that change their width and effective diameter. When the vehicle accelerates from a standing start, the driving pulley is small and the driven pulley is large. This gives a gear reduction identical to a small gear driving a large gear, which provides an increase in torque and a decrease in speed. CVTs are more efficient than either manual or automatic transmissions while still providing the driving ease of an automatic transmission.

ADVANTAGES A CVT offers the following advantages over a planetary-gear automatic transmission.

- Compact, very short
- Lighter weight
- Constant, stepless acceleration with engine staying at the RPM for maximum power
- Efficient fuel use and emissions, cruise with engine staying at the RPM for maximum efficiency
- Lower internal power loss

One method used to compare transmissions is the engine revolutions for a specific driving cycle. A test vehicle using a 3.0-L engine and a CVT showed 3% fewer revolutions than the same vehicle with a five-speed transmission and 11% less than with a four-speed transmission. This should equal a gain of about

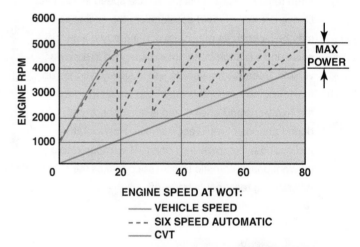

ENGINE SPEED AT WOT:
—— VEHICLE SPEED
--- SIX SPEED AUTOMATIC
—— CVT

FIGURE 11–2 Engine speed and vehicle speed of a CVT transaxle compared to a typical six-speed conventional automatic transaxle.

12% in fuel economy. These transmissions are used by Audi, Dodge, Ford, Honda, Subaru, Toyota, and Nissan.

CONTINUOUSLY VARIABLE GEAR RATIOS As the speed increases, the diameter of the driving pulley increases as the sides of the pulley move together. While this happens, the driven pulley is made wider and therefore smaller in diameter. At cruising speeds, the driving pulley is larger than the driven pulley, which produces an overdrive ratio.

The pulleys change size smoothly and evenly, which produces a somewhat odd sensation when the vehicle accelerates from a stop. When the throttle is depressed, the engine speed increases to the point of good torque output, the gear ratio selected by the CVT causes the engine to stay at this RPM while the vehicle accelerates. The pulleys move to higher ratios as vehicle speed increases. This is a different sensation than the familiar engine speed increase in each gear and the engine speed decrease after an upshift. ● **SEE FIGURES 11–1 AND 11–2.**

What Is It Like to Drive a Vehicle Equipped with CVT?

For most people, driving a vehicle equipped with a continuously variable transmission (CVT) is the same as driving the vehicle equipped with a conventional automatic transmission/transaxle. The vehicle creeps slightly when the brake is released and accelerates normally when the throttle is opened. Because no shifts occur, the first thing the driver and passenger notice is that it is very smooth. If the vehicle is equipped with a tachometer, the driver may notice that the engine speed increases when first accelerating and often remains higher until the vehicle speed increases. During periods of rapid acceleration, the engine speed may be close to its maximum and thereby create noise and vibration often not experienced in a similar vehicle. Because the vehicle speed slowly catches up to the engine speed, this effect is often referred to as the **"rubber band effect"** and is most noticeable only during periods of rapid acceleration. However, the fuel economy improvement of a CVT compared to a conventional automatic transmission makes the slight difference a reasonable trade-off.

CONSTRUCTION

TERMINOLOGY Instead of using three or more gears, a continuously variable transmission uses two variable-width pulleys, sometimes called **variators,** to change the gear ratio.

OPERATION The pulleys used in CVT design can vary their width by varying the hydraulic pressure applied to them. Each pulley has a movable face and a fixed face.

- The movable face for each pulley is attached to a piston that has hydraulic control pressure applied to it.

- Higher application pressure on the movable face causes the pulley to become narrow and this makes the steel belt ride closer to the outside diameter of the pulley. A lower application pressure will allow the pulley to become wider and the belt will ride closer to the pulley axis.

If a low hydraulic pressure is applied to the drive pulley and a high hydraulic pressure is applied to the driven pulley, a low speed ratio is achieved.

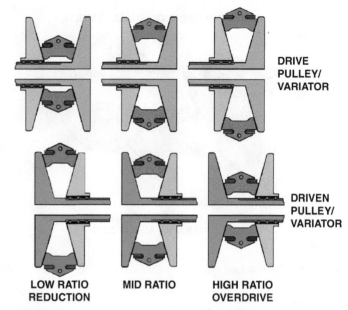

DRIVE PULLEY/ VARIATOR

DRIVEN PULLEY/ VARIATOR

LOW RATIO REDUCTION MID RATIO HIGH RATIO OVERDRIVE

FIGURE 11–3 The drive pulley is wide while the driven pulley is narrow for a low ratio vehicle start (left). The ratio changes by making the drive pulley narrow and the driven pulley wider.

A CVT (continuously variable transmission) has an infinite number of gear ratios between its lowest ratio (about 3.7:1) and highest ratio, which is a 0.27:1 overdrive.

A CVT improves efficiency by changing ratios from underdrive/reduction to overdrive in a gradual, continuous manner. The primary/drive pulley is attached to the input shaft. The secondary/driven pulley is on the output shaft and drives the final drive gears. Each pulley, also called a *sheave*, has two sides:

1. One is fixed so it cannot move

2. The other can float sideways to change pulley width.

When the vehicle is at rest, the primary pulley is wide so the belt sits low on the pulley, and the secondary pulley is narrow so the belt sits high. This produces the lowest underdrive ratio. ● SEE FIGURE 11–3.

The secondary pulley is spring loaded to force it to a narrow position. The primary pulley is adjusted to control the gear ratio, and the secondary pulley is adjusted to maintain tension on the belt. The belt must never be loose between the pulleys.

- At start, the pulley halves/discs on the input (primary) shaft are spread apart, and the pair of pulley halves on the output (secondary) shaft are pushed together. This produces a small pulley driving a large pulley, which produces the lowest drive ratio.

- As the vehicle moves, the floating side of the primary pulley moves inward, making the pulley narrower and forcing the belt to move out to a wider diameter. This produces a higher gear ratio.

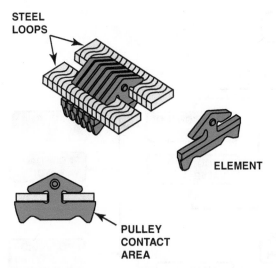

FIGURE 11–4 A Typical push-type CVT belt construction.

Vehicles That Use A Push-Type CVT (Belt-Type)	Vehicles That Use A Pull-Type CVT (Chain-Type)
Honda (Accord, Civic, Civic hybrid, Insight hybrid)	Audi (A4, S4, RS4)
Dodge Caliber	Ford (500, Freestar, Freestyle)
Jeep (Compass, Patriot)	Mercury (Montego, Monterey)
Mini Cooper	Subaru Lineartronic (Legacy, Forester, Impreza, Outback)
Mitsubishi (Lancer, Outlander)	
Nissan (Altima, Cube, Maxima, Murano, Rogue, Sentra, Versa)	
Saturn (Aura, Ion, Vue)	
Subaru Justy	
Suzuki SX4	
Toyota Corolla	

CHART 11–1

Vehicles that use a CVT transaxle, separated by type: either push-type (belt) or pull-type (chain). Check service information for the exact years and types of transmissions used for each model.

■ Both pulleys must maintain enough pressure on the drive belt to transfer the required torque. Fluid pressure is used to force the drive piston/pulley to a narrower position and the driven pulley to a wider position. The secondary pulley is spring loaded to force it to a narrow position. The primary pulley is adjusted to control the gear ratio,

FIGURE 11–5 The pull chain looks similar to a silent chain.

and the secondary pulley is adjusted to maintain tension on the belt. The belt must never be loose between the pulleys.

A reverse gear set, controlled by a multi-plate clutch pack, is used to produce reverse.

DRIVE BELT   Two different styles of fixed-length steel belts are used.

1. **Push belt** It is made up of about 400 wedge-shaped segments that are held together by two steel bands. Each band is made of multiple layers to allow flexibility. The segment sides contact the pulley sides. A push belt is often called the *Van Doorne design*. This style of belt is directional, and is usually marked with an arrow to show belt direction. ●**SEE FIGURE 11–4**.

2. **Pull chain** It is made up of links and link pins, much like a silent chain. The ends of the link pins contact the pulley sides. This style is also called a *Luk chain drive*. ●**SEE FIGURE 11–5**.

VEHICLES THAT USE A BELT OR A CHAIN   ●**SEE CHART 11–1** for list of vehicles that use each type of continuously variable automatic transaxles.

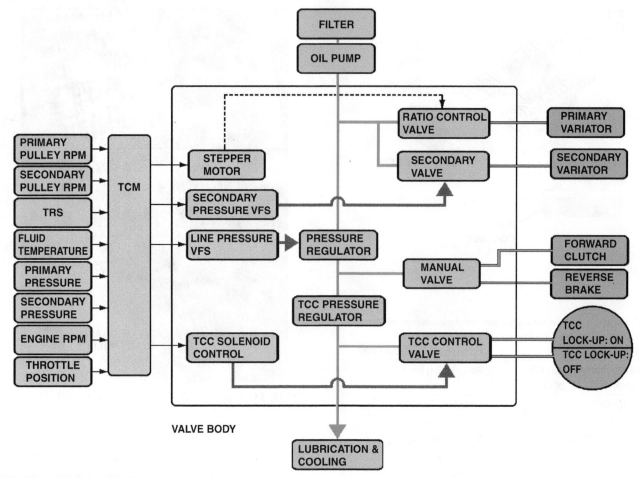

FIGURE 11–6 Block diagram showing the relationship between the TCM, electrical actuators, valve body, and hydraulic actuators for a CVT transmission.

CVT ELECTRONIC CONTROLS

The transmission control module (TCM) of a CVT uses direct and indirect inputs to monitor transmission and engine operation. ● **SEE FIGURE 11–6**.

INPUTS Direct inputs are as follows:

- **Transmission range sensor (TRS).** A multi-contact switch operated by the manual shift lever
- **Input speed sensor (ISS).** Can be a magnetic or a Hall-effect sensor
- **Output speed sensor (OSS).** Can be a magnetic or a Hall-effect sensor
- **Primary pressure sensor (PPS).** A pressure transducer to monitor primary pulley pressure. The pressure measured is called the **primary oil pressure (POP)**

- **Secondary pressure sensor (SPS).** A pressure transducer to monitor secondary pulley pressure. The pressure measured is called the **secondary oil pressure (SOP)**
- **Transmission temperature sensor (TTS).** A negative temperature coefficient (NTC) thermistor used to measure temperature of the transaxle

INPUTS FROM CAN BUS Indirect inputs from CAN bus include:

- PCM requests
- Engine output torque
- Brake switch
- ABS status signals
- Charging system voltage
- Engine RPM
- Engine coolant temperature

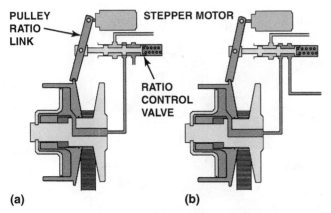

(a)　　　　**(b)**

FIGURE 11–7 (a) The stepper motor and pulley ratio link with the CVT in low ratio. (b) The stepper motor has extended, moving the ratio link and ratio control valve; this should cause the primary pulley to become narrower to produce a higher ratio.

- Accelerator pedal position
- Vehicle speed
- A/C system requests

OUTPUTS The TCM controls the drive ratio to match vehicle needs. It can adjust the ratio during vehicle cruise to produce the maximum fuel economy, best emissions, or maximum pulling power. It continuously monitors ISS and OSS signals to ensure that the speeds match the desired ratio.

- The stepper motor, also called a **ratio control motor,** is a linear position motor that changes the position of the upper end of the pulley ratio link. The stepper motor controls the hydraulic ratio valve through the link, which in turn controls fluid flow to the piston. The lower end of this link moves with the floating side of the primary/drive pulley and the *ratio control valve* is connected to the center of this link. Movement of the stepper motor or the floating sheave will move the ratio control valve to produce a ratio change. ● **SEE FIGURE 11–7.**
  TCM outputs include:

- Stepper motor that operates the ratio control valve which controls the ratio changes commanded by the TCM.
- **Line pressure solenoid (LPS) ,** which controls the line pressure to the transmission hydraulic system.
- *Secondary pressure solenoid (SPS),* which controls the pressure to the secondary pulley system.
- TCC lockup solenoid, which controls the torque converter clutch operation.

The TCM controls the drive ratio to match vehicle needs. It can adjust the ratio during vehicle cruise to produce the

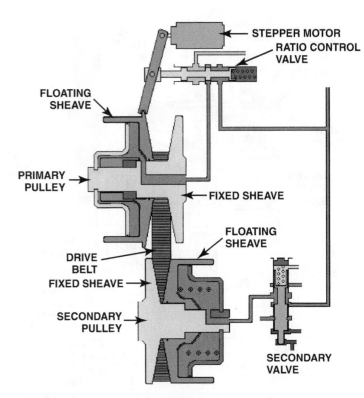

FIGURE 11–8 Movement of either the stepper motor or primary floating sheave will move the ratio control valve to add or remove fluid from the primary pulley. The secondary valve maintains the necessary pulley pressure on the drive belt.

maximum fuel economy, lowest emissions, or maximum pulling power. ● **SEE FIGURE 11–8.**

The TCM also controls fluid pressure to the secondary/driven pulley and torque converter as well as TCC lockup. Some vehicles use predetermined stepper motor position to mimic upshifts and downshifts.

CVT OPERATION

STARTING With no fluid pressure, the secondary pulley spring forces the floating side to a narrow, high-belt position, which in turn moves the primary pulley to a wide, low-belt position. This produces an underdrive that is always used as the vehicle starts moving. Continued fluid flow to the primary piston will change the ratio from an underdrive/reduction through 1:1 to an overdrive.

REVERSE A planetary gear set is needed for reverse-direction operation, and this is a simple planetary with a carrier that can be held by the reverse clutch. The input shaft drives the ring/internal gear, and the sun gear drives the shaft to the primary pulley.

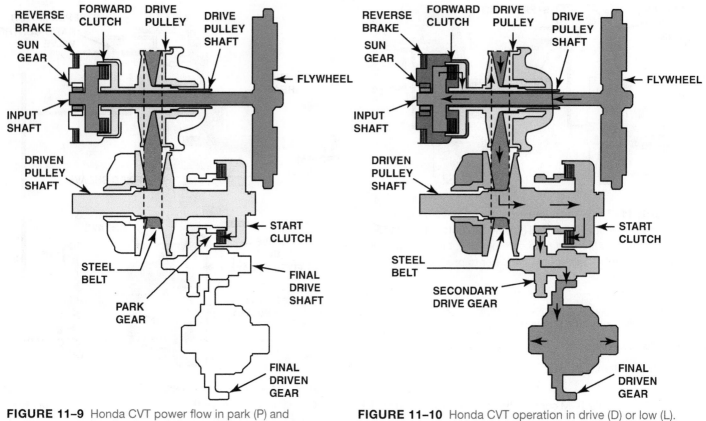

FIGURE 11–9 Honda CVT power flow in park (P) and neutral (N).

FIGURE 11–10 Honda CVT operation in drive (D) or low (L).

FORWARD OPERATION A forward clutch is mounted on the input shaft from the torque converter; it is mounted inside a clutch drum that also contains the planetary ring gear. When it applies, the forward clutch drives the planetary sun gear so both the sun and ring gears are driven. This locks the gear set to produce a 1:1 ratio.

CVT TORQUE CONVERTER

DESIGN Most CVT transmissions use a low-profile elliptical torque converter with a lockup clutch. Since CVTs are infinitely variable, the torque converter is not needed once the vehicle is moving. Therefore, the converter is used to multiply the torque to get the vehicle moving from a stop, and then becomes a mechanical connection between the engine and the CVT. The torque converter clutch apply will occur at about 12 MPH (20 km/h) and stay locked until the vehicle comes to a stop. Some small vehicles with CVTs do not use a torque converter. The forward and reverse clutches are released for stops and one will be applied to start the vehicle moving.

HONDA CVT

OPERATION The Honda CVT is also used as part of the hybrid system on some Honda vehicles. There are three multiple-disc clutches used in the internal gear train, one for each of the following:

- Forward clutch
- Reverse brake
- Start clutch

In the Honda Civic CVT, a start clutch, which slips when the vehicle is stopped with the engine running, is used instead of a torque converter. ● **SEE FIGURE 11–9**.

In park (P) or neutral (N), none of the clutches have hydraulic pressure applied to them, which prevents engine torque from being applied to the drive pulley shaft. The forward clutch and the start clutch are in operation whenever the transmission is placed in a forward gear position (D or L). ● **SEE FIGURE 11–10**.

For the reverse function, a planetary gear set is used in conjunction with the reverse brake. When the reverse brake is applied, the planet carrier is held and the sun gear (splined to

FIGURE 11–11 Location of the Honda CVT start clutch.

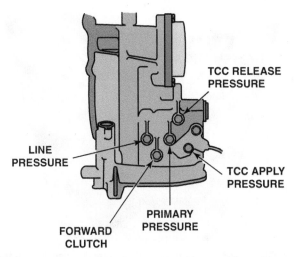

FIGURE 11–12 The pressure tap locations as found on a Dodge Caliber CVT transaxle.

the input shaft) causes the ring gear to turn backward. The ring gear is attached to the drive pulley through the forward clutch drum, so the drive pulley also turns backward. This torque is sent through the start clutch and the vehicle moves in reverse.

START CLUTCH The start clutch has multiple responsibilities, including:

1. The start clutch is engaged whenever the vehicle is moving, in either forward or reverse.

2. It helps the vehicle accelerate from a standstill by slipping and then fully engaging once the vehicle is moving, similar to a manually operated clutch. ● **SEE FIGURE 11–11.**

The Honda CVT, like any other automatic transmission, uses hydraulic pressure to perform its various functions. The belt drive, the multiple-disc clutches, and the control system will all stop functioning without hydraulic pressure. This pressure is supplied by a chain-driven pump that is driven by the transmission input shaft.

NOTE: Some vehicles equipped with a continuously variable transmission (CVT) have shifter paddles on the steering wheel or a manual shift mode on the gear selector. When using these paddles to upshift or downshift, the transmission control module selects preprogrammed ratios, which give the driver a sense that it is actively shifting gears.

SERVICING A HONDA CVT The Honda CVT can be pressure tested and stall tested just like any other automatic transaxle when diagnosing transmission malfunctions. These tests must be performed according to manufacturer-approved procedures, and test results compared to charts published by the manufacturer.

One service item that is unique and very important is the *start clutch calibration.* This procedure must be performed whenever any of the following vehicle components is replaced or removed.

1. Battery
2. Backup fuse
3. Transmission control module (TCM)
4. Transmission assembly
5. Lower valve body assembly
6. Engine assembly replacement or overhaul

Details for performing these procedures can be found in Honda service information. The purpose of the procedure is to allow the TCM to memorize the feedback signal for the start clutch control. Malfunctions in the start clutch control system can occur if this procedure is not performed at the appropriate time.

PRESSURE TESTING A CVT

TYPICAL PRESSURES Measuring the CVT oil pressures is similar to performing pressure testing on conventional automatic transmissions/transaxles. Always check service information for the exact procedures to follow and the location of the pressure tap. ● **SEE FIGURE 11–12.**

Typical pressures include:

▪ Mainline pressure 70 to 900 PSI (485 to 6,200 kPa))

▪ Primary pressure 15 to 900 PSI (100 to 6,200 kPa))

▪ Secondary pressure 15 to 900 PSI (100 to 6,200 kPa)

FIGURE 11–13 Using the exact fluid recommended by the vehicle manufacturer is the preferred choice when servicing a CVT transaxles.

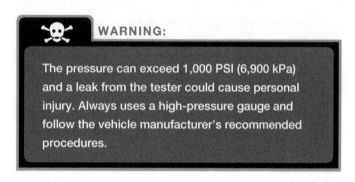

☠ **WARNING:**

The pressure can exceed 1,000 PSI (6,900 kPa) and a leak from the tester could cause personal injury. Always uses a high-pressure gauge and follow the vehicle manufacturer's recommended procedures.

CVT FLUID

CHECKING CVT FLUID LEVEL A dipstick is used to check the level in some units, and fluid may be poured into the dipstick pipe to bring the level up if it is low. CVT fluid is usually green to help distinguish it from conventional ATF.

CAUTION: Wipe off the dipstick before removing it to prevent any dirt from falling into the fill tube when checking the level of the fluid. Any dirt in the fluid can cause severe damage to the CVT transaxles.

REPLACING CVT FLUID When replacing the CVT fluid, make sure that the specified CVT fluid is used. There is often a drain plug on the transmission pan, and a filler hole located on the transmission case. When refilling the CVT, be sure to check the level regularly to make sure it is not being overfilled. Both the drain and filler plugs should have their gaskets replaced before installing them in their respective holes. Be certain to observe

Diagnostic Trouble Code (DTC)	Description
P0219	Engine speed excessive—check for speed sensor or transmission slip codes
P0571	Brake switch fault detected
P0707; P0708	TCM detects improper signal from transmission range switch (P0707—signal low; P0708—signal high)
P0711; P0712; P0713	Transmission temperature sensor (TSS) fault detected (P0711—circuit performance; P0711—signal low; P0713—signal high)
P0716; P0717	Transmission input speed sensor (ISS) fault detected (P0716—circuit performance; P0717—no signal).
P0721; P0722	Transmission output speed sensor (OSS) fault detected (P0721—circuit performance; P0722—no signal).
P0730	Incorrect gear ratio detected (transmission slip)
P0746	Line pressure sensor performance issue detected
P0776; P0777	Secondary pressure sensor (SPS) fault detected (P0776—performance fault; P0777—stuck on).
P0842; P0843	Primary oil pressure (POP) sensor fault detected (P0842—sensor circuit low; P0843—sensor circuit high).
P0847; P0848	Secondary oil pressure (SOP) sensor fault detected (P0847—sensor circuit low; P0848—sensor circuit high).

CHART 11–2

Typical continuously variable transmission (CVT) diagnostic trouble codes (DTCs) and code description. Transmission-related DTCs are usually P07XX or P08XX, where XX represents the specific fault code.

torque specifications when tightening these plugs to prevent damage to the threads in the transmission case and oil pan.

CVT FLUID OPTIONS The shop has two options when filling or replacing CVT automatic transmission fluid:

Option 1. The use of the exact specified fluid as recommended by the vehicle manufacturer is preferred in all cases. A minor disadvantage is that some fluids may be hard to find from local parts suppliers and may have to be purchased from a dealer. ●**SEE FIGURE 11–13**.

Option 2. Use a multi-vehicle fluid, also called *universal CVT fluid,* that is designed to meet the specifications of several different makes and both belts and chains used in CVTs. This is commonly used by many shops and can be successfully used if the fluid is within the specified viscosity and the fluid manufacturer states that it meets the O.E. requirement for friction coefficient.

3. A "ticking" heard in park and neutral caused by a faulty input bearing. Replacement of the bearing requires transmission disassembly or replacement of the entire assembly based on the vehicle manufacturer's recommendations.

Always follow the specified vehicle manufacturer's recommended diagnosis and repair procedures.

CVT NOISE ISSUES

Some CVTs tend to have three types of noise issues.

1. A "growl" caused by a faulty gear bearing, which can be repaired in-vehicle in most cases.
2. A "whine" that is usually caused by a damaged gear. This gear plus the intermediate shaft output gear and differential ring gear must be replaced, requiring transmission disassembly.

CVT-RELATED DIAGNOSTIC TROUBLE CODES

For some of the diagnostic trouble codes (DTCs) associated with a CVT transmission and the description, see ● CHART 11–2.

SUMMARY

1. A continuously variable transmission (CVT) varies the gear ratio in a continuous manner instead of in a series of steps or fixed gear ratios.
2. A pair of hydraulically controlled variable-size pulleys is used with a steel-link drive belt or chain.
3. Two different styles of fixed-length steel belts are used. A push belt or a pull chain is used.
4. The transmission control module (TCM) of a CVT uses direct and indirect inputs to monitor transmission and engine operation.
5. The stepper motor, also called a ratio control motor, is a linear position motor that changes the position of the upper end of the pulley ratio link.
6. Measuring the oil pressure is similar to performing pressure testing on conventional automatic transmissions/transaxles.

REVIEW QUESTIONS

1. What is the advantage of a CVT compared to a regular six-speed transmission?
2. What are the types of belts used in a CVT?
3. What controls the movement of the variator?
4. What is the purpose and function of the ratio control motor?

1. How is a variable ratio achieved in a CVT?
   a. By using multiple gears
   b. By using a steel belt with two variable-width pulleys
   c. By using a start clutch assembly
   d. By using a variable-torque converter

2. What is meant by "rubber band effect"?
   a. A CVT uses a large rubber band
   b. A rubber band is used to apply the clutches inside a CVT
   c. The vehicle speed slowly catches up to the engine speed
   d. Just a slang term for the variator pulleys

3. What is the difference between a push belt and a pull chain?
   a. A push belt is made up of about 400 wedge-shaped segments
   b. A pull chain is made up of links and link pins
   c. A pull chain looks similar to a silent chain
   d. All of the above

4. Which is NOT an advantage of a CVT?
   a. Larger in size
   b. Lighter weight
   c. Lower internal power loss
   d. Efficient fuel use

5. Which statement is *false*?
   a. The primary/drive pulley is attached to the input shaft
   b. Both sheaves are fixed so they cannot move
   c. The movable face for each pulley is attached to a piston that has hydraulic control pressure applied to it
   d. The primary pulley is adjusted to control the gear ratio, and the secondary pulley is adjusted to maintain tension on the belt

6. Which of these is a *direct input* to the TCM?
   a. Accelerator pedal position
   b. Primary pressure sensor (PPS)
   c. Vehicle speed
   d. Brake switch

7. TCM outputs include_____.
   a. Stepper motor that operates the ratio control valve
   b. Line pressure solenoid (LPS)
   c. Secondary pressure solenoid (SPS)
   d. All of the above

8. Mainline pressure on a CVT can exceed_____.
   a. 500 PSI (3,450 kPa)
   b. 750 PSI (5,200 kPa)
   c. 900 PSI (6,200 kPa)
   d. 2,000 PSI (13,800 kPa)

9. The recommended fluid to use in a CVT is usually _____.
   a. Dexron VI ATF
   b. Specific CVT fluid
   c. Mercon V or Dexron VI
   d. Any of the above depending on the specific unit

10. Which diagnostic trouble code is associated with secondary pressure sensor (SPS)?
    a. P0776   c. P0440
    b. P0300   d. P0172

chapter 12
DUAL CLUTCH AUTOMATIC TRANSMISSIONS/ TRANSAXLES

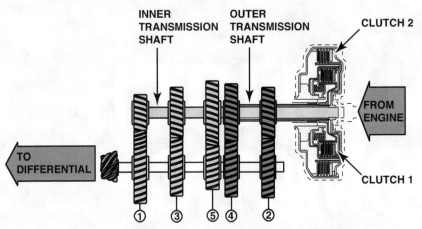

FIGURE 12–1 A dual clutch automatic uses the best features of an automatic transmission without the power loss of a torque converter.

PURPOSE AND FUNCTION

A dual clutch automatic transmission or transaxle uses a manual-type transmission and two clutches that engage either the inner or outer transmission shaft. This type of transmission is designed to achieve the following goals, compared to a conventional automatic transmission or transaxle equipped with a torque converter and planetary gear sets.

1. Improve fuel economy.
2. Reduce the cost of assembly by using manual transmission components.
3. Improve the speed of gear changes.
4. Provide smoother operation.

TERMINOLOGY A dual clutch automatic transmission/transaxle can also be referred to as

- **Direct shift gearbox (DSG).** Most commonly used by the VW/Audi Group (VAG) of vehicles.
- **Porsche Doppelkupplung (PDK).** The Porsche term used to describe their dual clutch automatic.
- **Automated manual transmission (AMT).** Original term no longer commonly used.
- **Twin clutch transmission.** Another variation of the term used for a dual clutch automatic transmission.

PARTS AND OPERATION

A dual clutch automatic transmission/transaxle uses two clutches that are mounted together. One clutch drives the odd number gears (first, third, fifth, and seventh). The other clutch

FIGURE 12–2 Dual clutch automatic transaxles that use two dry clutches. The larger clutch drives the odd number gear ratios (first, third, and fifth) and the smaller clutch drives the even numbered gear ratios (second, fourth, and sixth).

drives the even number gears (second, fourth, and sixth).
● **SEE FIGURE 12–1**.

The shifts occur without interrupting the torque from the engine by applying torque to the clutch while at the same time disconnecting the other clutch. These actions result in a rapid shift without the slight delay usually associated with an automatic transmission.

There are two types of clutches used depending on application.

1. Dual dry clutches are used in low powered vehicles such as small front-wheel-drive vehicles. ● **SEE FIGURE 12–2**.
2. Dual wet clutches are often used in higher powered vehicles.

Vehicles that use a dual clutch automatic-type transmission/transaxle include certain models of Audi, Nissan, Mercedes, BMW, Porsche, Ford, Ferrari, VW, and Mitsubishi.

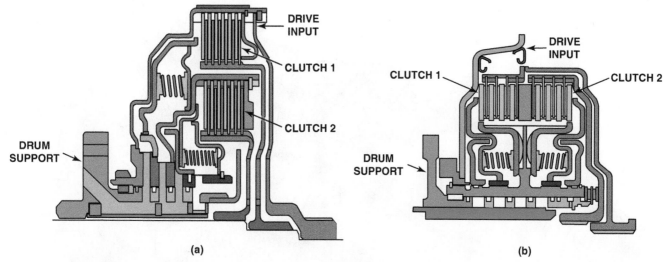

FIGURE 12–3 (a) A concentric (nested) clutch design, the assembly is shorter in length but taller in height. (b) A parallel clutch design is longer but has a smaller diameter drum assembly.

ADVANTAGES The advantages of a dual clutch automatic transmission/transaxle compared to a conventional automatic transmission include:

1. Quicker throttle response
2. No drop in engine speed when the driver releases the throttle
3. Instant gear changes
4. Improved fuel economy

DISADVANTAGES The disadvantages of a dual clutch automatic transmission/transaxle compared to conventional or continuously variable automatic transmissions include:

1. No torque multiplication advantage of a torque converter
2. Not as fuel efficient as a continuously variable transmission (CVT) or transaxle

DUAL CLUTCH TRANSAXLE

TERMINOLOGY A dual clutch transaxle is essentially two transmissions built into one case. Each portion is driven by one of the clutches, and these clutches are applied, one at a time, to transfer power. A dual clutch transmission is essentially an automatic transmission that uses manual transmission-style gear layout and synchronizers with two countershafts. The shifts can occur vary rapidly, being controlled by how fast each clutch can be applied and with partially engaging one clutch while slipping the other during shifts.

CONCENTRIC AND PARALLEL CLUTCH DESIGNS There are two basic wet clutch designs used in dual clutch automatic transmissions.

1. A **concentric clutch** (also called a *nested-type clutch*) is a design where both plates share the same vertical plane and provides a shorter assembly.
2. A **parallel clutch** design is used in a side-by-side arrangement. ● **SEE FIGURE 12–3.**

GEAR ARRANGEMENTS The 1–3 and 5 synchronizer assemblies are driven by clutch #1 and the 2–4 and 6-reverse synchronizers are driven by clutch #2. Vehicle movement begins with the 1–3 synchronizer shifted to first gear and clutch #1 applied. The 2–4 synchronizer is then shifted into second gear by a hydraulic servo, and the 1–2 upshift will occur when clutch #1 is released and clutch #2 is applied. The remaining upshifts occur in the same manner, with the synchronizer preshifted or shifted early, and the actual shift occurring when the clutches are cycled. ● **SEE FIGURE 12–4.**

The driver can control the transmission/transaxle using a floor-mounted shift lever or one of a pair of paddles mounted on the steering wheel.

- Clutches #1 and #2 are applied by hydraulic pressure, similar to automatic transmission clutches.
- The hydraulic flow to the clutches and servos is controlled electronically by a control module.

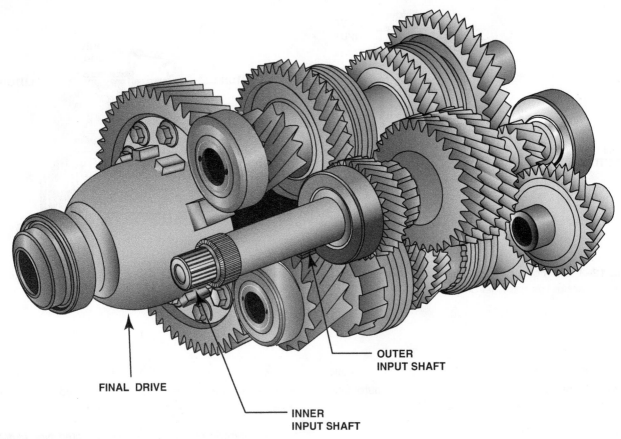

FINAL DRIVE

INNER
INPUT SHAFT

OUTER
INPUT SHAFT

FIGURE 12–4 Notice the two concentric input shafts. Each shaft is splined to a clutch.

GETRAG DCT 450

A Getrag DCT 450 transaxle is a dual clutch automatic trans-axle commonly used in a number of Ford and Volvo vehicles starting in 2008. This is a six-speed unit and uses clutch 1 for the odd-numbered gears (1, 3, 5) and clutch 2 for the even-numbered gears (2, 4, 6).

GEAR CHANGE EXAMPLE Using the DCT 450 as the example, the shift from first to second includes the following actions:

STEP 1 Clutch 1 is on and drives the inner shaft. ● **SEE FIGURE 12–5**.

STEP 2 Second gear control device is pressurized to get ready to shift to second gear.

STEP 3 Clutch 2 is starting to be filled with hydraulic pressure (both clutches work at the same time during shifting).

STEP 4 First gear torque delivery through clutch 1 is being reduced as clutch 2 in being applied and starting to transmit engine torque.

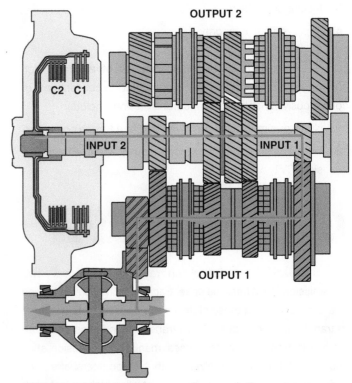

OUTPUT 2

C2 C1

INPUT 2

INPUT 1

OUTPUT 1

FIGURE 12–5 First gear engaged using clutch 1 (C1) to transmit engine torque.

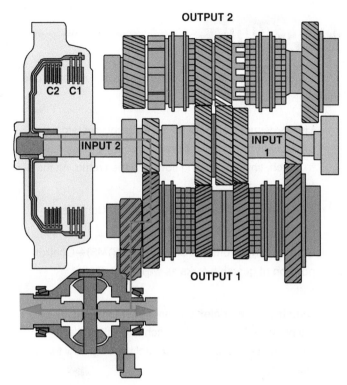

FIGURE 12–6 Second gear engaged using clutch 2 (C2) to transmit engine torque.

STEP 5 Engine torque through clutch 1 is zero and full engine torque is being transmitted through clutch 2. ● **SEE FIGURE 12–6**.

SHIFT FORKS
There are four gearshift forks in this Getrag DCT 450 transaxle. The gear positions per gearshift fork include:

- Gearshift fork 1 (odd): R-N-5
- Gearshift fork 2 (odd): 3-N-1
- Gearshift fork 3 (even): 2-N-4
- Gearshift fork 4 (even): P-N-6

The gearshift forks mechanically engage the gears. The forks are moved by hydraulic pistons, which are controlled by shift solenoids. The transmission control module (TCM) operates shift solenoids. The solenoids move pistons, which in turn apply force to the shift forks through lever points to help increase the force applied. Both an even and an odd gear can be commanded at the same time in parallel.

- Fifth gear and neutral are blocked if the reverse gear is engaged
- Neutral and first gear are blocked if third gear is engaged. ● **SEE FIGURE 12–7**.

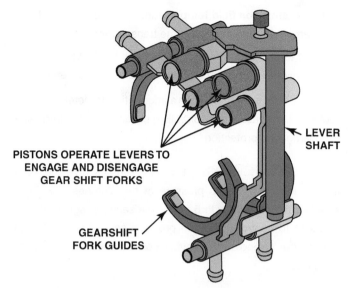

FIGURE 12–7 The shift forks are similar to those used in a manual transmission but are moved using hydraulic pistons.

SPEED SENSORS
Speed sensors include:

- **Engine RPM sensor.** Inputs the engine RPM to the TCM from the sensor located on the clutch drum housing.
- **Speed sensor input shaft odd gears.** Gives the TCM information on input shaft RPM (after the C1 clutch) for odd gears, 1, 3, 5, and R.
- **Speed sensor input shaft even gears.** Gives the TCM information on input shaft RPM (after the C2 clutch) for even gears, 2, 4, and 6.

TEMPERATURE SENSORS
Temperature sensors include:

- **Clutch fluid temperature.** Used to measure the temperature of the fluid leaving the clutches.

- **Transmission fluid temperature.** Used to measure the temperature of the fluid in the transmission.
- **Oil temperature sensor.** Located on the TCM, which provides information on transmission oil temperature.

The TCM uses temperature information to determine correct system pressure, for controlling clutch, for cold starts, and for overheating protection.

PRESSURE SENSORS Pressure sensors give the TCM information on hydraulic pressure of the clutches. The TCM supplies the sensors with 5 volts. The sensors register the oil pressure to control the clutch pressure so that the TCM can control the solenoids to provide correct clutch pressure for each clutch.

POSITION SENSORS Position sensors include:

- *Fork position sensors*—These sensors give the TCM information on the position of the four gear shift forks that handle shifting in the transmission. Includes 1-R; 3-5; 2-4; and 6-N.
- *Transmissions Range Sensor (TRS)*—This sensor provides the actual P R N D gear selection.

The transmission electronic control module uses information from the sensors to determine the proper clutch and shift servo operation. Once the TCM determines the required gear range and driving conditions, actuators are turned on or off to control hydraulic pressure, gear selection, clutch control, and shift lock.

FREQUENTLY ASKED QUESTION

Why Is the TCM Using the Position of the Steering Wheel?

The steering wheel position (SWP) sensor information is sent to the transmission control module (TCM) over the network to prevent the transmission from upshifting when cornering. This helps the driver by allowing the vehicle to be accelerated when exiting a corner. If the steering wheel position was not part of the shift program, the transmission might likely upshift to a higher gear as the vehicle slows then the transmission may have to downshift again when the vehicle exits the corner.

SOLENOIDS

A typical dual clutch automatic transmission/transaxle includes the following solenoids:

- **Line pressure solenoid (LPS)**—Controls system pressure in the transmission by directing the hydraulic oil to clutch, shifting, cooling flow, and then returning the oil to the oil sump.
- **Clutch cooling flow solenoid (CCFS)**—Controls hydraulic oil for cooling of clutches.
- **Shift cooling multiplex solenoid (SHCMS)**—Controls position of gearshift forks as well as cooling of clutch.
- **Clutch shift multiplex solenoid (CSMS1)**—Leads the pressure between odd clutch and shifting, activates odd gears, as well as controls cooling flow for clutches.
- **Clutch shift multiplex solenoid (CSMS2)**—Leads the pressure between even clutch and shifting, controls cooling flow for clutches, and can turn off the valve for dumping clutch pressure.
- **Clutch shift pressure solenoid (CSPS1)**—Controls hydraulic pressure for odd clutch or shifting.
- **Clutch shift pressure solenoid (CSPS2)**—Controls hydraulic pressure for even clutch or shifting.
- **Clutch pressure cut (CPCUT)**—Safety valve that controls pressure dumping in the hydraulic system.
- **Shift select solenoid (SHSS1)**—Controls shifting for gearshift fork 1 and 3.
- **Shift select solenoid (SHSS2)**—Controls shifting for gearshift fork 2 and 4.

SHIFT FORK POSITION The transmission control module (TCM) operates shift solenoids. These pistons apply force to the shift forks through lever points to help increase the force applied. Both an even and an odd gear can be commanded at the same time in parallel. Position sensors are located inside the case and this information is used by the TCM to determine the actual position of each shift fork. ● **SEE FIGURE 12–8.**

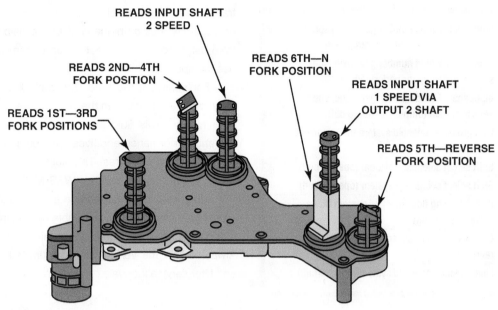

READS INPUT SHAFT
2 SPEED

READS 2ND—4TH
FORK POSITION

READS 6TH—N
FORK POSITION

READS INPUT SHAFT
1 SPEED VIA
OUTPUT 2 SHAFT

READS 1ST—3RD
FORK POSITIONS

READS 5TH—REVERSE
FORK POSITION

FIGURE 12–8 Fork position and shaft speed sensors are used as inputs to the TCM.

DIAGNOSIS AND SERVICE

DIAGNOSTIC PROCEDURES To diagnose faults with dual clutch automatic transmission/transaxle system, follow the recommended procedures found in service information. The usual procedure involves the following steps:

STEP 1 Verify the customer concern (complaint). This step includes trying to duplicate what the customer or driver is concerned about.

STEP 2 Perform a thorough visual inspection, including:

- Checking the level and condition of the fluid
- Checking the drivetrain mounts for damage or faults

STEP 3 Check service information for the specified procedure to follow. Most vehicles require the use of a factory-brand scan tool. ● **SEE FIGURE 12–9.**

STEP 4 Follow the troubleshooting procedure as specified to fix the root cause of the problem. This means following the instructions displayed on the scan tool or service information.

STEP 5 Repair the fault.

STEP 6 Road test the vehicle under the same conditions that were performed to verify the fault to ensure that the repair is completed.

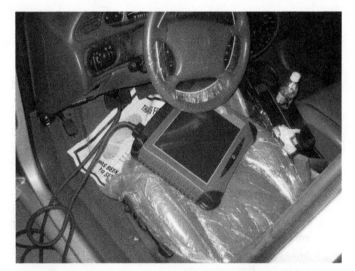

FIGURE 12–9 The use of a factory or a factory-level after-market scan tool is often needed to diagnose the dual clutch transmission system.

TYPICAL DIAGNOSTIC TROUBLE CODES As part of any diagnostics, checking for diagnostic trouble codes is one of the first steps. ● **SEE CHART 12–1** for some examples of dual clutch automatic transmission related DTCs.

FLUID AND FILTER SERVICE The transmission fluid is usually high-quality synthetic oil which is unique for this type of

P0715	Input shaft 1 (odd number gear axle) speed sensor system (output high range out)
P0716	Input shaft 1 (odd number gear axle) speed sensor system (poor performance)
P0717	Input shaft 1 (odd number gear axle) speed sensor system (output low range out)
P0746	Line pressure solenoid system (drive current range out)
P0753	Shift select solenoid 1 system (open circuit)
P0758	Shift select solenoid 2 system (open circuit)
P0776	Clutch cooling flow solenoid system (drive current range out)
P0842	Clutch 1 pressure sensor system (output low range out)
P0960	Line pressure solenoid system (open circuit)

CHART 12-1

Selected dual clutch transmission-related diagnostic trouble codes.

transmission. Dual clutch transmission fluid is usually green to help identify it as a unique fluid and to help prevent someone from using conventional automatic transmission fluid. Always use the specified fluid.

For example, the Ford Dry Dual Clutch Fluid is specifically formulated for use in the DPS6 power shift twin dry clutch transmission. This fluid is manufactured with synthetic base oils and performance additives, providing improved shifting at all ambient temperatures. This fluid is used only in transmissions requiring a fluid meeting WSS-M2C200-D2.

Most dual clutch automatic transmissions/transaxles use an external filter that is serviceable and an internal filter that is a nonserviceable part unless the unit is totally disassembled. Always follow the vehicle manufacturer's recommended fluid and filter service intervals.

SUMMARY

1. A dual clutch automatic transmission or transaxle uses a manual-type transmission and two clutches that engage either the inner or outer transmission shaft.

2. A dual clutch automatic transmission can also be referred to as direct shift gearbox (DSG), Porsche Doppelkupplung (PDK), automated manual transmission (AMT), or a twin clutch transmission.

3. A dual dry clutch system is mostly used for lower-powered front wheel drive vehicles, whereas dual wet clutches are used for most high-powered front and rear wheel drive vehicles.

4. There are two basic wet clutch designs used in dual clutch automatic transmissions.

- A concentric clutch (also called a nested-type clutch) is a design where both plates share the same vertical plane and provides a shorter assembly.
- A parallel clutch design is used in a side-by-side arrangement.

5. Speed sensors are used to measure the speed of the odd gear shaft and the even gear shaft.

6. Position sensors are used to detect the positions of the shift forks.

7. Solenoids are used to make the actual shifts by moving the shift forks.

8. Dual clutch automatic transmissions use a unique fluid.

REVIEW QUESTIONS

1. What are the benefits of using a dual clutch automatic transmission compared to a conventional automatic transmission?

2. What are the disadvantages of a dual clutch automatic transmission?

3. What type of vehicles use two dry clutches?

4. What are the two designs of wet clutches?

5. How is a shift made from first to second on a dual clutch automatic transmission?

6. What sensors are used in a typical dual clutch automatic transaxle?

1. All of the following are advantages of a dual clutch automatic transmission/transaxle *except*.
   a. Instant gear changes
   b. No torque multiplication advantage of a torque converter
   c. Quicker throttle response
   d. Improved fuel economy

2. A dual clutch automatic transmission/transaxle may be called _____.
   a. Direct shift gearbox (DSG)
   b. Porsche Doppelkupplung (PDK)
   c. Automated manual transmission (AMT)
   d. Any of the above

3. A dual dry clutch system is used in what type of vehicle?
   a. Small front-wheel drive
   b. Heavy rear-wheel drive
   c. All-wheel drive trucks and SUVs
   d. High power front-wheel drive

4. A concentric clutch is _____.
   a. A type of wet clutch
   b. A type of dry clutch
   c. Also called a nested-type clutch
   d. Both a and c

5. How does a dual clutch transmission/transaxle achieve better fuel economy compared to a conventional automatic transmission?
   a. By using a high capacity torque converter
   b. By engaging neutral when the vehicle is stopped
   c. By skipping gears
   d. By slipping the clutches to achieve smoother operation

6. In a Getrag DCT 450 transaxle what does gear shift fork 2 control?
   a. R-N-5   c. 2-N-4
   b. 3-N-1   d. P-N-6

7. Why is the steering wheel position sensor used as an input to the TCM?
   a. Used to help determine when to shift when driving straight
   b. Used to help control line pressure based on steering wheel angle
   c. Used to prevent an upshift if the vehicle is turning
   d. Used as a diagnostic input to help retrieve DTCs.

8. The fluid used in dual clutch automatic transmissions and transaxles is usually _____.
   a. Dexron VI
   b. Special synthetic fluid often green in color
   c. Mercon V
   d. Any of the above depending on make, model, and year

9. What is the purpose of the clutch shift multiplex solenoid (CSMS2)?
   a. Leads the pressure between even clutch and shifting, controls cooling flow for clutches, and can turn off the valve for dumping clutch pressure
   b. Controls hydraulic pressure for odd clutch or shifting
   c. Safety valve that controls pressure dumping in the hydraulic system
   d. Controls shifting for gearshift fork 2 and 4

10. A P0753 diagnostic trouble code (DTC) means that the TCM has detected a fault with _____.
    a. Input shaft 1 (odd number gear axle) speed sensor system
    b. Line pressure solenoid system (open circuit)
    c. Shift select solenoid 1 system (open circuit)
    d. Input shaft 1 (odd number gear axle) speed sensor system (output high range out)

chapter 13
TRANSMISSION CONDITION DIAGNOSIS

LEARNING OBJECTIVES

After studying this chapter, the reader will be able to:

1. Prepare for ASE Automatic Transmissions (A2) certification test content area "A" (General Transmission and Transaxle Diagnosis).

2. Outline the procedures involved in the first step of the automatic transmission diagnostic process—verifying customer concern.

3. Outline the procedures involved in the second step of the automatic transmission diagnostic process—fluid level and condition.

4. Outline the procedures involved in the third and fourth steps of the automatic transmission diagnostic process—retrieving diagnostic trouble codes and checking for technical service bulletins.

5. Outline the procedures involved in the fifth step of the automatic transmission diagnostic process—scan tool testing.

6. Outline the procedures involved in the sixth step of the automatic transmission diagnostic process—visual inspections.

7. Outline the procedures involved in the seventh step of the automatic transmission diagnostic process—finding the root cause.

KEY TERMS

Clutch volume index (CVI) 226

Powertrain control module (PCM) 222

Recalibration 224

Transmission control module (TCM) 222

THE DIAGNOSTIC PROCESS

STEPS INVOLVED When diagnosing automatic transmission concerns, perform the following steps:

STEP 1 The first step is to verify the customer complaint. This step usually includes performing a road test to see if the complaint can be duplicated. If the problem cannot be duplicated, then the repair cannot be verified.

STEP 2 Check the fluid level and condition.

STEP 3 Check for stored diagnostic trouble codes (DTCs).

STEP 4 Check for any related technical service bulletins (TSBs).

STEP 5 Check scan tool data including checking the adaptive values.

STEP 6 Visual inspections, including the following:

- Check for obvious faults such as damaged or worn driveshafts or U-joints
- Check for evidence of recent transmission or drivetrain service work
- Check the body and frame for evidence of a collision or recent collision repairs
- Check for leaks

STEP 7 Locate the root cause of the problem. This step involves performing more detailed tests such as pressure testing.

STEP 8 Replace all components that do not meet factory specifications.

STEP 9 Perform an adaptive relearn and drive the vehicle to verify that the repairs corrected the customer concern.

NOTE: Steps 8 and 9 are discussed in Chapter 17 after the transmission/transaxle has been repaired or rebuilt and reinstalled in the vehicle.

STEP 1—VERFIY THE CUSTOMER CONCERN

ROAD TEST A road test is used to verify the customer's concern and check the general overall condition of the transmission. The vehicle should be road tested at the start of the diagnosis and after the repair. The first road test helps the technician understand the customer's concern as well as

FIGURE 13–1 Selecting all of the shift modes of an automatic transmission/transaxle helps pinpoint the area where the fault is located.

the nature of the problem. The road test after repairs have been completed confirms that the repairs were successful. A road test may involve simply driving the vehicle and mentally reviewing the transmission operation.

ITEMS TO CHECK The following points are normally checked during a road test:

- Quality of the garage shifts (neutral–drive and neutral–reverse) ● **SEE FIGURE 13–1**.
- Engagement time for the garage shifts
- Quality of each upshift and downshift at various loads
- Timing of each upshift and downshift at various loads
- Any hunting between gear ranges
- Operation of the torque converter and torque converter clutch (TCC)
- Slipping in any gear range
- Binding or tie-up in any gear range
- Noise or vibration in any gear range
- Engine (compression) braking during deceleration in drive and manual gear ranges
- Speedometer operation (shows output from the vehicle speed (VS) sensor)
- Proper engine operation

There are many shift quality and timing problems that can occur. The common terms used to describe abnormal shifts are described in ● **CHART 13–1**.

TERM	MEANING
Binding	A very noticeable drag that causes the engine to slow down and labor.
Bump	A sudden, harsh application of a clutch or band.
Chuggle	A bucking or jerking condition, similar to the sensation of clutch chatter or acceleration in too high of a gear with a standard transmission (could be engine related).
Delayed or late shift	The shift occurs some time after normally expected.
Double bump	Two sudden, harsh applications of a clutch or band, also called "double feel."
Dropout	An unexpected shift to neutral or a lower gear, also called "fallout."
Early	The operation occurs before normally expected. An early shift results in a laboring engine, poor acceleration, and sometimes a chuggle.
End bump	A shift feel that becomes noticeably firmer as it is completed, also called "end feel" or "slip bump."
Firm shift	A quick, easily felt shift that is not harsh or rough.
Flare	A rapid increase in engine speed, usually caused by slippage.
Harsh or rough shift	An unpleasantly firm band or clutch application.
Hunting	A repeated up-and-then-down shifting sequence that produces noticeable repeated engine RPM changes.
Shudder	A more severe form of chuggle.
Slipping	A noticeable loss of power transfer that results in an increase in engine RPM.
Soft shift	A very slow shift that is barely noticeable.
Stacked shifts	An upshift that occurs immediately after a prior upshift.

CHART 13–1

Typical automatic transmission/transaxle fault descriptions and their meaning.

THROTTLE POSITION VERSUS SHIFT POINTS The technician operates the vehicle at various throttle positions during the road test. Light-, medium-, full-throttle, and through detent or wide-open throttle (WOT) upshifts are made to check shift quality and timing under each of these conditions. The vehicle is also operated under different closed-throttle conditions. The various throttle positions used are defined as follows:

- Minimum—the least throttle opening that produces acceleration
- Light—when the throttle is about one-fourth open
- Medium—when the throttle is about one-half open
- Heavy—when the throttle is about three-fourths open
- Wide-open throttle (WOT)—fully opened throttle without forcing a downshift
- Closed—a complete release of the throttle, which results in coasting
- Engine braking—a closed-throttle manual downshift to produce a condition where engine compression slows the vehicle

Manufacturers publish shift points. These are the vehicle speeds at which upshifts and downshifts should occur relative to the different throttle openings. To check the shift points, accelerate the vehicle using different throttle openings, and watch the tachometer or listen for the engine speed change that indicates a shift. Have an assistant record the speed for comparison with the specifications. If no specifications are available, the approximate shift points are shown in ● **CHART 13–2**.

STEP 2—FLUID LEVEL AND CONDITION

The driver of a vehicle should periodically check the fluid level in an automatic transmission. A good time to check this is at every engine oil change. If the level is low, fluid of the correct type should be added. It usually takes 1 pint (0.5L) to move the fluid level from low to the full mark on the dipstick.

Most transmission dipsticks are marked for both cold and *hot fluid* temperatures. ● **SEE FIGURE 13–2**.

The most obvious markings are for the hot level, which is the normal operating temperature, about 150°F to 170°F (66°C to 77°C). Room temperature of about 65°F to 85°F (18°C to 29°C)

MINIMUM THROTTLE	SPEED MPH (km/h)	PART THROTTLE	SPEED MPH (km/h)	WOT	SPEED MPH (km/h)
1–2	5–10 (8–16)	1–2	15–30 (24–48)	1–2	35–45 (56–72)
2–3	15–25 (24–40)	2–3	25–45 (40–72)	2–3	55–65 (89–105)
3–4	30–45 (48–72)	3–4	40–55 (64–90)	3–4	Above 60/100
4–3	30–40 (48–64)	4–3	35–45 (56–72)	4–3	Above 60/100
3–2	10–15 (16–24)	3–2	30–40 (48–64)	3–2	55–65 (89–105)
3–1	5–10 (8–16)	2–1	10–20 (16–32)	2–1	25–40 (40–64)

CHART 13–2

Typical shift points for a four-speed automatic transmission/transaxle. Always observe all speed limits and traffic regulations during a road test.

FIGURE 13–2 A typical automatic transmission dipstick (fluid level indicator). Many use a clip to keep it from being forced upward due to pressure changes inside the automatic transmission. A firm seal also helps keep water from getting into the fluid, which can cause severe damage to the clutches and bands.

is considered cold for transmission fluid. If the fluid at the end of the dipstick is too hot to hold, then the fluid is hot. When the fluid is cold, use the cold markings on the dipstick. Some transaxles use a thermostatic valve to raise the fluid level in the upper valve body pan as the transaxle warms up. These units have a lower hot level and a higher cold level. The exact procedure for checking the fluid level can be found in the vehicle owner's manual, or occasionally it is printed on the dipstick.

OVERFILLED OR UNDERFILLED It is never a good idea to operate a transmission with the fluid level too high (an *overfill* condition) or too low (an *underfill* condition).

- An underfill is below the low, cold level on the dipstick and it is sometimes marked "Do not drive." An underfill condition can allow air to enter the filter and pump intake, which can cause mushy operation. It may go into neutral,

 REAL WORLD FIX

The Slipping Dodge Truck

A 2002 Dodge Durango (89,000 mi) transmission slips when taking off and during the 1–2 shift when cold. The fluid level was okay when it was checked with the transmission in park. However, the fluid level has to be checked in neutral, not park, and was found to be 1.5 quarts low. Adding the correct amount of fluid fixed this problem.

may slip, or the torque converter clutch (TCC) may fail to lock and unlock properly.

- Overfilling can cause slippage and mushy operation because of the air in the foamy fluid. An overfill condition can bring the fluid level up to the point where it contacts the spinning gear sets. This in turn causes foaming of the fluid and fluid may flow out through the vent or filler pipe. There have been cases of vehicle fires caused by the fluid spilling out of the filler pipe and onto a hot exhaust manifold.

CHECKING FLUID LEVEL WITH A DIPSTICK To check transmission fluid with a dipstick, check the procedure stamped on the dipstick. The usual procedure includes the following steps:

STEP 1 Park the vehicle on a level surface, apply the parking brake securely, and place the gear selector in park or neutral as recommended by the manufacturer. Start the engine, and let the temperature of the transmission come up to operating temperature.

STEP 2 Apply the service brakes firmly, and move the gear selector to each of the operating ranges. Leave the

FIGURE 13–3 The "add" mark on most automatic transmission dipsticks indicates the level is down 0.5 quart (0.5L). Always follow the instructions stamped or printed on the dipstick.

selector in each position long enough for each gear to become completely engaged.

STEP 3 Return the selector lever to park or neutral, depending on the transmission. Leave the engine running at idle speed.

STEP 4 Clean any dirt from the dipstick cap, and remove the dipstick.

STEP 5 Wipe the dipstick clean and return it to the filler pipe, making sure that it is fully seated.

STEP 6 Pull the dipstick out again and read the fluid level. ● **SEE FIGURE 13–3**.

Carefully grip the end of the dipstick between two fingers to get an indication of the fluid temperature.
  a. If it feels cold, use the COLD marks.
  b. If it feels warm, the correct fluid level will be between the HOT and COLD marks.
  c. If it is too hot to hold onto, use the HOT marks.

STEP 7 Replace the dipstick completely into the filler tube.

CHECKING FLUID LEVEL WITHOUT A DIPSTICK

Some units do not use dipsticks. Fluid level is checked by following the procedure stated in the service information. When checking sealed units, a general procedure is to bring the transmission to operating temperature, and then remove the fluid level plug. Fluid will trickle or weep out of the plug if the level is correct.

- If it runs out, the level is high.
- If there is no fluid, the level is low.

Some manufacturers require a special procedure or tool in order to check the fluid level of their sealed transmissions, so it is wise to review their fluid-checking procedures. A general procedure follows.

To check transmission fluid level on a vehicle without a dipstick, perform the following steps:

STEP 1 Check service information for the correct checking procedure.

STEP 2 Check the transmission temperature using a scan tool. This is very important and the vehicle will usually need

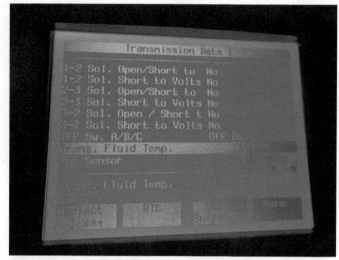

FIGURE 13–4 The temperature of the automatic transmission fluid is displayed on a factory or factory-level scan tool. It may require that the vehicle be driven under a load for the fluid to reach the specified temperature and can often be achieved by simply allowing the engine to idle.

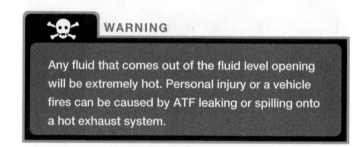

WARNING

Any fluid that comes out of the fluid level opening will be extremely hot. Personal injury or a vehicle fires can be caused by ATF leaking or spilling onto a hot exhaust system.

to be driven for several miles before the specified fluid temperature is achieved. ● **SEE FIGURE 13–4**.

STEP 3 Locate and carefully remove the fluid level plug. Note that the level plug can be small, like a pressure check plug, or large, like a conventional plug. The plug can be located in the transmission case or on the bottom or side of the pan. ● **SEE FIGURE 13–5**.

STEP 4 If fluid drips or seeps from the hole, the level is correct. If fluid runs out, the level is too high, allowing the excess fluid to drain out. Some transmissions use a stand pipe. ● **SEE FIGURE 13–6**.

If no fluid comes out, the level is low. Add additional fluid of the correct type until the level is correct. If necessary, add additional fluid by pumping it into the fill port located at the side of the case or up through the fluid level checking plug opening.

FLUID CONDITION Fluid condition should always be checked when checking fluid level. A transmission technician will normally smell the fluid and check the color for unusual

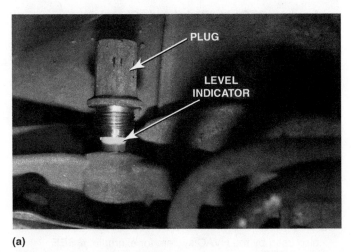

(a)

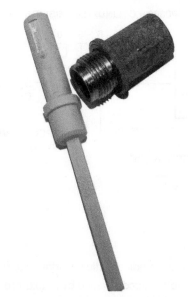

(b)

FIGURE 13–5 (a) The fluid level indicator is reached from under the vehicle on this Ford 6R80 rear-wheel-drive transmission. (b)The level indicator can be removed after removing the plug, and then the fluid level can be read on the stick.

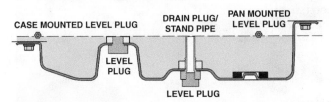

FIGURE 13–6 Fluid level on sealed units (without a dipstick) is checked by removing the level plug, which can be mounted in the bottom or side of the pan or in the case. It is normal for some fluid to drip from this type of level indicator because normal operation of the transmission causes fluid to fill the stand pipe.

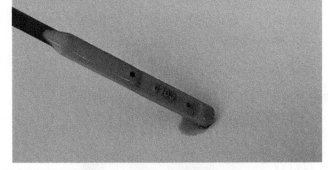

FIGURE 13–7 Fluid condition can be checked by placing a sample on clean, white, absorbent paper. Clean fluid will spread out and leave only a wet stain. Dirty fluid will leave deposits of foreign material.

 REAL WORLD FIX

The Automatic VW

A shop drained the dirty transmission fluid and replaced the filter in the VW Passat and then noticed that there was no dipstick to check the fluid level. The problem was how to properly adjust the fluid level.

On this vehicle, the recommended fluid level is to install 2 quarts of the proper fluid, start the engine, and monitor the transmission fluid temperature. At 96°F (35°C), fluid should flow from the fluid level port. If no fluid flows, the level is low and more should be added. The exact procedure published by the manufacturer for each transmission should be followed.

characteristics. The fluid should be a bright reddish color with a smell that is similar to new fluid. It should be noted that some fluids will normally darken and take on a definite odor after a few hundred miles. One manufacturer states that a smoky odor with light brown color is normal. ● **SEE FIGURE 13–7.** Following are indications of fluid breakdown:

- Dark brown or black color indicates dirt or burned friction material.

NOTE: Some highly friction-modified ATFs do tend to turn light brown after a short period of time and this should not be used as a sign of fluid breakdown.

- A definite burned odor indicates slippage or overheating.
- Pink fluid or a milky color indicates a coolant leak at the heat exchanger in the radiator.

EXAMPLE: P0302 = CYLINDER #2 MISFIRE DETECTED

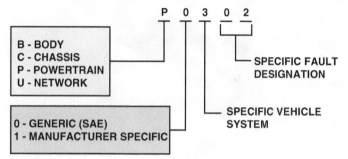

FIGURE 13–8 OBD-II DTC identification format.

- A varnish-like odor indicates fluid oxidation and break-down. This is often accompanied by a gold-brown varnish coating on the dipstick.

- Metallic appearance or very fine metal particles indicate wear.

- Foam might indicate a leak in the pump intake system or incorrect fluid level.

STEP 3—RETRIEVE DIAGNOSTIC TROUBLE CODES

HOW THE PCM/TCM SETS CODES One of the roles of the **powertrain control module (PCM)** and/or the **transmission control module (TCM)** is to monitor transmission operation and determine if malfunctions may be occurring. The PCM/TCM will run frequent self-tests of the electrical circuitry and will also analyze the sensor data to look for transmission slippage, overheating, or other problems. When a problem has been detected, the PCM will generate a diagnostic trouble code (DTC) and may also place the transmission in limp-home mode, depending on what sort of problem has been detected. Limp-home mode is when the transmission stays in one gear only (second gear is a common option) and gives the driver the ability to take the vehicle to the closest service center without having to call a tow truck.

If a diagnostic trouble code (DTC is present in the PCM/TCM memory, it may illuminate the malfunction indicator lamp (MIL), commonly labeled "check engine" or "service engine

TECH TIP

Look for DTCs in "Body" and "Chassis"

Whenever diagnosing a customer concern with a transmission, transfer case or other driveline components, check for diagnostic trouble codes (DTCs) under chassis and body systems and do not just look under engines. Engine or emission control type codes are "P" codes, whereas module communications are "U" codes. These are most often found when looking for DTCs under chassis or body systems. Chassis-related codes are labeled "C" and body system-related codes are labeled "B" codes and these can cause drivetrain issues if they affect a sensor that is also used by the HVAC system for example. ● SEE FIGURE 13–9.

FIGURE 13–9 A "C" diagnostic trouble code was stored along with a note "symptom 71" which gives additional information about the possible cause of this serial data fault code being set.

soon." Any code(s) that is displayed on a scan tool when the MIL is *not* on is called a pending code or a transmission code for a fault that would not result in an increase in exhaust emissions. Although this pending code is helpful to the technician to know that a fault has, in the past, been detected, further testing will be needed to find the root cause of the problem. ● SEE FIGURE 13–8. ● SEE CHART 13–3 for transmission-related diagnostic trouble codes.

TRANSMISSION-RELATED DTCs			
P0703	Brake switch input circuit	P0741	Torque converter clutch system performance or stuck off
P0705	Transmission range sensor circuit problem (PRNDL input)	P0742	Torque converter clutch system stuck on
P0706	Transmission range sensor circuit range or performance	P0743	Torque converter clutch system electrical
P0707	Transmission range sensor circuit low input	P0745	Pressure control solenoid problem
P0708	Transmission range sensor circuit high input	P0746	Pressure control solenoid performance or stuck off
P0710	Transmission fluid temperature sensor problem	P0747	Pressure control solenoid stuck on
P0711	Transmission fluid temperature sensor range or performance	P0748	Pressure control solenoid electrical
P0712	Transmission fluid temperature sensor low input	P0750	Shift solenoid A problem
P0713	Transmission fluid temperature sensor high input	P0751	Shift solenoid A performance or stuck off
P0715	Input or turbine speed sensor circuit problem	P0752	Shift solenoid A stuck on
P0716	Input or turbine speed sensor circuit range or performance	P0753	Shift solenoid A electrical
P0717	Input or turbine speed sensor circuit no signal	P0755	Shift solenoid B problem
P0720	Output speed sensor circuit problem	P0756	Shift solenoid B performance or stuck off
P0721	Output speed sensor circuit range or performance	P0757	Shift solenoid B stuck on
P0722	Output speed sensor circuit no signal	P0758	Shift solenoid B electrical
P0725	Engine speed input circuit problem	P0760	Shift solenoid C problem
P0726	Engine speed input circuit range or performance	P0761	Shift solenoid C performance or stuck off
P0727	Engine speed input circuit no signal	P0762	Shift solenoid C stuck on
P0728	Gear 6 incorrect ratio	P0763	Shift solenoid C electrical
P0730	Incorrect gear ratio	P0765	Shift solenoid D problem
P0731	Gear 1 incorrect ratio	P0766	Shift solenoid D performance or stuck off
P0732	Gear 2 incorrect ratio	P0767	Shift solenoid D stuck on
P0733	Gear 3 incorrect ratio	P0768	Shift solenoid D electrical
P0734	Gear 4 incorrect ratio	P0770	Shift solenoid E problem
P0735	Gear 5 incorrect ratio	P0771	Shift solenoid E performance or stuck off
P0736	Reverse incorrect ratio	P0772	Shift solenoid E stuck on
P0740	Torque converter clutch system problem	P0773	Shift solenoid E electrical

CHART 13–3

Transmission/transaxle-related diagnostic trouble codes (DTCs). For transmission-related diagnostic trouble codes for vehicles older than 1996, check service information on how to retrieve and read the codes.

STEP 4—CHECK FOR TECHNICAL SERVICE BULLETINS

Check for corrections or repair procedures in technical service bulletins (TSBs) that match the symptoms. According to studies performed by automobile manufacturers, as many as 30% of vehicles can be repaired following the information, suggestions, or replacement parts found in a technical service bulletin. DTCs must be known before searching for service bulletins, because bulletins often include information on solving problems that involve a stored diagnostic trouble code. ● SEE FIGURE 13–10

What Is Meant by Flashing a Module?

Flashing a module is the updating of the programming of an electronic control module such as the PCM or TCM to solve an issue or customer concern. Flashing a PCM/TCM, also called *programming, reprogramming,* and *calibrating,* can be done to correct possible software problems. Occasionally there is a concern that a transmission has improper shift points, delayed shifts, or just does not work right, and a thorough diagnosis fails to locate any problems. TCMs use an electronically erasable programmable read-only memory (EEPROM) that determines the operating parameters of the TCM. The TCM determines when the transmission upshifts or downshifts, when the TCC applies or releases, and the hydraulic system pressures in some transmissions. This memory function can be changed by connecting a computer interface to the TCM that will erase the old instructions and send new instructions to the vehicle TCM. Flashing will remove adaptive learned values.

A SAE J2534 compliant module is available that, with a computer (preferably a laptop) and the update program, can flash all vehicles. With some makes of vehicles, this will include all or most of the ECM/PCMs, while other makes limit flashing to the powertrain modules. A speedometer that is reading incorrectly can be recalibrated in some vehicles.

Recalibration is often necessary when a new TCM is installed. The process must be performed exactly as directed by the manufacturer. The TCM can be recalibrated outside of the vehicle in some cases. The TCM in some vehicles has a learn strategy that can compensate for some transmission faults such as low line pressure. These units should be recalibrated after a major repair or overhaul. ● **SEE FIGURE 13–11**.

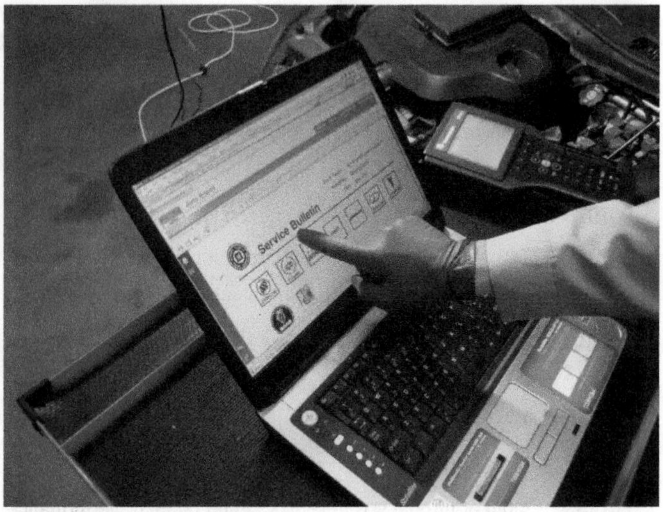

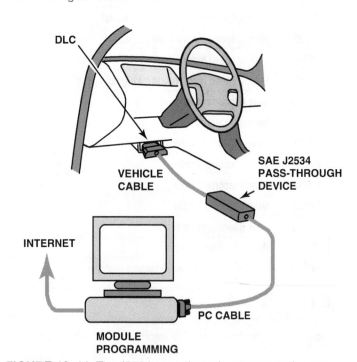

FIGURE 13–10 After checking for stored diagnostic trouble codes (DTCs), the wise technician checks service information for any technical service bulletins (TSBs) that may relate to the vehicle being serviced.

FIGURE 13–11 The J2534 pass-through reprogramming system does not need a scan tool to flash the PCM on most 2004 and newer vehicles.

STEP 5—SCAN TOOL TESTING

TYPES OF SCAN TOOLS Scan tools are the most important tools for any diagnostic work on all vehicles. Scan tools can be divided into the following three basic groups:

1. **Factory scan tools.** These are the scan tools required by all dealers that sell and service a specific brand of vehicle. Examples of factory scan tools include:
   - General Motors—TECH 2. ● **SEE FIGURE 13–12**.
   - Ford—WDS (Worldwide Diagnostic System) and IDS (Integrated Diagnostic Software)
   - Chrysler—DRB-III, Star Scan, or WiTECH

FIGURE 13–12 A TECH 2 scan tool is the factory scan tool used on General Motors vehicles.

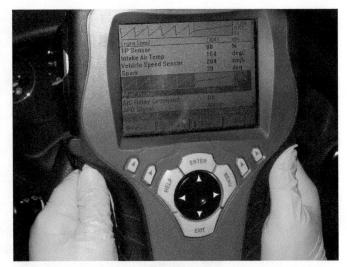

FIGURE 13–13 An OTC Genisys being used to trouble-shoot a vehicle. This scan tool can be used on most makes and models of vehicles and is capable of diagnosing other computer systems in the vehicles such as automatic transmissions.

- Honda—HDS or Master Tech
- Toyota—Master Tech and Tech Stream

All factory scan tools are designed to provide bidirectional capability, which allows the service technician the opportunity to operate components using the scan tool, thereby confirming that the component is able to work when commanded. Also, all factory scan tools are capable of displaying all factory parameters.

2. **Aftermarket scan tools.** These scan tools are designed to function on more than one brand of vehicle. Examples of aftermarket scan tools include the following:
   - Snap-on (various models, including the Ethos, Modis, Versus, and Solus).
   - OTC (various models, including Pegasus, Genisys, EVO, Nemisys, and Task Master). ● **SEE FIGURE 13–13**.
   - AutoEnginuity and other programs that use a laptop or handheld computer for display.

   While many aftermarket scan tools can display most if not all of the parameters of the factory scan tool, there can be a difference when trying to troubleshoot some faults.

3. **Global scan tools.** The vehicle diagnostic trouble codes (DTCs) and data can be acquired by looking at the global (generic) part of the PCM and does not need to have the vehicle information entered into the scan tool. All global scan tools display only emission-related data stream information and do *not* display faults or codes for any other system or transmission.

SENSOR VALUES A scan tool can display information about the various sensors and components that can assist the service technician in determining the cause of many automatic transmission/transaxle problems.

A properly operating engine should display the following readings with the engine at idle and operating in closed loop.

- **Engine coolant temperature (ECT)**—between 180°F and 215°F (82°C and 102°C)
- **Throttle position (TP) sensor**—usually between 0.5 and 4.5 volts and varying directly with throttle movement.
- **Accelerator pedal position sensor (APPS)**—usually two or more sensors on differing scales (0.4 to 4.6 volts) and varying with accelerator pedal movement
- **Fuel injector pulse width**—1.5 to 3.5 ms.
- **Upstream oxygen sensor (O2S)**—voltage varying between 200 and 800 mV
- **Air–fuel ratio sensor(s)** (if equipped)—scan tool to read fairly low and steady
- **Transmission fluid temperature (TFT)**—less than 275°F (135°C)
- **Brake switch**—scan data to show a change when brake pedal is pressed and released
- **Manifold absolute pressure (MAP) sensor**—with the engine idling in park or neutral, the voltage should be between 0.88 and 1.62 volts or between 102 and 109 Hz for a Ford MAP sensor.
- **Mass airflow sensor (MAF)**—warm engine in park with no load typically reads grams per second within 20% of

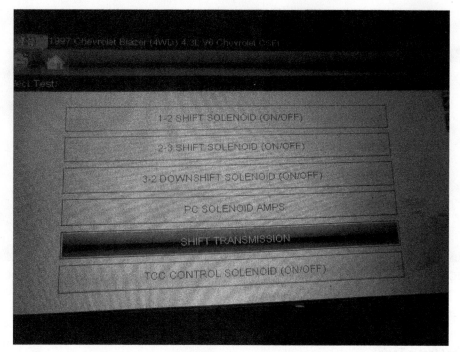

FIGURE 13–14 A Snap-on scan tool is able to shift the transmission and display pressure control (PC) solenoid current (amperes).

the engine's liters of displacement with a 3.5 L engine will show fairly close to 3.5 g/s of airflow at idle

- **Vehicle speed (VS) sensor**—source can vary: derived from ABS wheel speed sensors, output speed sensor of transmission, or a dedicated sensor on transmission or transfer case.

- **Idle speed**—check for normal idle speed. Vehicles with electronic throttle control will display 2% to 3% open at warm idle in park and vehicles with IAC (idle air control) valves will display 10 to 30 steps or counts on a scan tool.

- **Shift solenoids**—check for the proper voltage and current of the shift solenoids using a factory or factory-level scan tool.

Observe the operation of the command for the shift solenoids and the TCC solenoid while driving the vehicle. This information confirms that the PCM is commanding the operation and it does not mean that the solenoids are working correctly. Therefore, if the scan data indicate that a particular solenoid is being commanded on and nothing occurs, then the problem could be caused by a defect with the following:

1. Hydraulic component (clutch, band, etc.)

2. Solenoid

3. Fault in the wiring to the solenoid or from the solenoid to the PCM or TCM ● **SEE FIGURE 13–14.**

CLUTCH VOLUME INDEX Some vehicles include a code for **clutch volume index (CVI),** also called *transmission adapt pressure (TAP)* or clutch fill volume index. The index monitors the time needed to fill a clutch as it applies. Each clutch should fill and stroke the clutch in a specified time. This time period usually increases with normal wear.

The TCM determines CVI from the speed differential between the input and output speed sensors. The TCM can determine the actual ratio and how long it takes to complete a shift from the speed differential of the two speed sensors. A high CVI usually indicates a clutch with excessive slippage. ● **SEE FIGURE 13–15.**

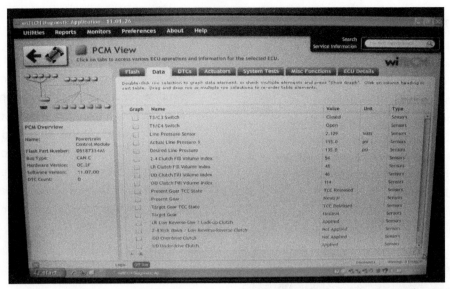

FIGURE 13–15 The clutch fill volume index as displayed on a Chrysler wiTECH scan tool.

STEP 6—VISUAL INSPECTIONS

ITEMS TO CHECK The diagnostic procedure should determine if the problem is *inside the transmission* (faulty hydraulic or mechanical operation) or *outside the transmission* (linkage or electrical problems).

Many technicians begin their diagnosis by making a visual check of the battery and wiring. Green, corroded battery terminals or loose terminals can easily cause improper electrical operation. Modified or altered wire connections also lead to unsuspected problems.

- The shifts can be forced electrically by providing the proper electrical signal to operate the solenoids using a special diagnostic tool or a factory level scan tool.

- Try removing the fuse that supplies power to the transmission control unit, and conduct a second road test. Without power, the TCM will shut down, causing the transmission operation to revert to a limp-in mode. In this mode, forward operation in the drive range is limited to a single gear, usually second or fourth. Gear operation is controlled by the manual valve, and there will be no automatic upshifts or downshifts. The transmission's operation will be purely hydraulic and mechanical, so it will start in a higher gear than first, and not upshift. If the second road test has the same problems as the first, then this confirms that the problem is not in the electronic controls.

 REAL WORLD FIX

The Starbucks Syndrome

A 1990 BMW 520i (122,000 miles) came in with only second gear, limp-in mode. The customer said the car would operate normally one day and have only second gear the next day. The fluid level is correct and appears in good condition.

The shop checked for fault codes and found two:

1. Gear position switch
2. Speed sensor

Testing revealed faults in the gear position switch and speed sensor circuits (called Starbucks syndrome). *Starbucks syndrome* is a name given to the results of coffee and food spills onto the center console control switches. Corrosion caused by the spills increases resistance at the wire connections. Replacement of these two components fixed the problem.

SOURCES OF NOISE The three most common sources of transmission noise are

1. Bearings
2. Gears
3. Hydraulic system.

Bearings, both ball and roller, consist of three parts: the bearing element (rollers or balls with cage), and the inner

Chassis Ears

A noise, vibration, and harshness (NVH) diagnostic tool, "Chassis Ears," consists of a headset and six sensors that can be attached to various locations under the vehicle. The vehicle can be driven on a road test while the technician listens to the six locations. This should help locate the exact source of the noise. ● **SEE FIGURE 13–16**.

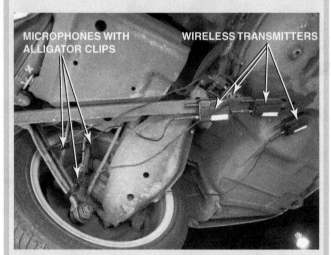

FIGURE 13–16 Chassis ear microphones attached to various under-vehicle components using the integral clamps. The sound is transmitted wirelessly to the receiver inside the vehicle where an assistant technician can listen for noises while the vehicle is being driven.

A Dodge 2005 Neon (87,000 mi) had a bad, tinny rattle noise coming from the torque converter area. The noise occurs whenever the engine is running. Visual inspection through the inspection cover area does not show a problem. A cracked flexplate is suspected. Removal of the transaxle allowed inspection of the torque converter and flexplate. Visual inspection showed that a balance weight had come loose. Replacement of the torque converter fixed this noise problem.

and outer races. The races can be separate parts or a hardened portion of a shaft, gear, or carrier. Bearing noise, often described as a *whine,* is caused by damage, pits, or scoring that makes the bearing surface rough.

Gear noise is usually the result of a rough gear surface or a worn bearing that allows the gear to change position. Gear noise usually shows up as a whine in a certain gear or multiple gears. Another type of gear noise is a *clack* or *clunk* that occurs when there is a change in power flow; it is the result of excessive clearance in the gear train. Worn differential gears and differential pinion shaft are a major cause of neutral-to-drive or neutral-to-reverse clunk.

Hydraulic noise, often described as a "buzz," is the result of rapid fluid pressure pulsations. With many transmissions, it will occur for a short time period while the fluid is cold and then go away.

When troubleshooting noise problems, it helps to determine how the noise fits into the following categories.

- **Speed relation**—related to engine or vehicle speed
- **Gear range**—related to gear range
- **Pitch/frequency**—low (rumble), medium (growl), or high (squeal)
- **Load sensitive**—heavy throttle, light throttle, or coast
- **Direction**—straight or right or left turn

LOCATING THE SOURCE OF THE NOISE To locate the cause of a transmission noise, perform the following steps:

STEP 1 Raise the vehicle so you have access to the transmission mounts. Visually check their condition, and if the mounts appear weak, pry upward on the transmission to check for possible separation of the mounts.

STEP 2 Start the engine and shift the transmission through its gear ranges while observing for any mount problems.

STEP 3 With the engine running and the gear selector in P or N, listen for the noise. Shift into D, and with the brake firmly applied, listen for the noise. A torque converter problem is indicated if the noise occurs with the transmission in gear but not in P or N. A pump problem is indicated if the noise occurs in both D and P or N. A faulty input drive chain and sprockets can also cause this problem.

STEP 4 With the engine running, shift from N to R while listening for the noise. A hydraulic problem is indicated if the noise increases when shifted into R. Shift into D and alter the signal to the EPC solenoid using a scan tool to boost line pressure. A hydraulic problem is indicated if the noise increases.

STEP 5 Perform a road test and listen for noise changes as the transmission shifts through the gear ranges. A transmission gear set problem is indicated if the noise

NOISE	PROBABLE CAUSE
Chain noise	A whine or growl that increases in frequency and amplitude with vehicle speed. Most noticeable under light acceleration. Input chain noise can be heard in park and neutral.
Final drive	A hum related to vehicle speed. Usually torque sensitive.
Gear noise	A whine or growl related to vehicle speed. Usually torque and gear-range sensitive.
Pump noise	A high-pitched whine that increases in amplitude with engine speed. Most noticeable in park or neutral with cold transmission fluid.

CHART 13–4

Typical noise problem descriptions.

FIGURE 13–17 A broken flexplate that made a lot of noise and then the engine would not crank when it finally broke.

changes depending on the gear range, especially if it is quiet during the range with a 1:1 ratio.

STEP 6 Repeat step 5 and listen for a noise that increases as the vehicle speed increases. A final drive problem is indicated if the noise intensity or frequency increases with vehicle speed. Note that the final drive can include transfer gears or chain drives depending on the transaxle.

Transmission noise problem areas usually fit into the categories shown in ● **CHART 13–4**.

VIBRATION CHECKS   Torque converter problems cause an engine-speed-related vibration problem. Output shaft vibration problems are vehicle-speed related. These are often accompanied by driveline clunk. FWD output shaft problems will usually be most noticeable on turns because of the increased differential and CV joint action.

- Engine-speed-related vibrations occur during particular engine speed ranges and these vibrations change when the transmission shifts gears. There are several causes leading to this, for example, belt-driven accessories such as the fan, alternator, air-conditioning compressor, or internal engine unbalance. Belt-driven problems can be identified by running the engine with the belt removed. If the vibration is gone, then the source of the vibration is one of the units being driven by the accessory drive belt.

- Identifying a torque converter problem begins with removing the converter cover and carefully inspecting the torque converter and flex plate. Look for a wobble

(runout) of the converter during engine rotation. Torque converter runout can be caused by the following:

- Improper tightening of the torque-converter-to-flex plate bolts

- A damaged flex plate. ● **SEE FIGURE 13–17**.

- Improper mounting of the torque converter into the crankshaft. If there is no runout, then replace the torque converter.

STEP 7—FIND THE ROOT CAUSE

OIL PAN DEBRIS CHECK   When it has been determined something is wrong with the transmission/transaxle, the next step is to drain the oil and remove the pan for inspection. The debris in the pan can give a good indication of what is occurring in the transmission.

- A small amount of debris with a blackish oil film is normal. A small amount of metal can be attributed to the wear that occurs during break-in and normal operation. ● **SEE FIGURE 13–18**.

- An excess of loose, black material is burned lining material from a slipping band or clutch. It usually has a burned smell.

- A heavy golden brown coating is from badly oxidized, old fluid. The lower part of the case and valve body will also

FIGURE 13–18 This is a normal amount of wear material in the bottom of an automatic transmission pan.

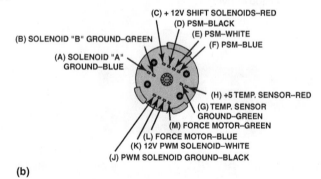

(a)

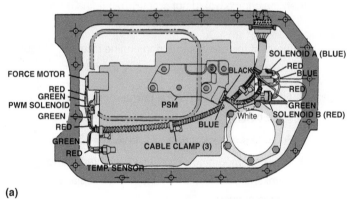

FORCE MOTOR
RED
GREEN
PWM SOLENOID
GREEN
RED
GREEN
RED
TEMP. SENSOR

SOLENOID A (BLUE)
RED
BLUE
BLACK
RED
GREEN
SOLENOID B (RED)
White
BLUE
PSM
CABLE CLAMP (3)

(C) + 12V SHIFT SOLENOIDS–RED
(D) PSM–BLACK
(E) PSM–WHITE
(F) PSM–BLUE
(B) SOLENOID "B" GROUND–GREEN
(A) SOLENOID "A" GROUND–BLUE
(H) +5 TEMP. SENSOR–RED
(G) TEMP. SENSOR GROUND–GREEN
(M) FORCE MOTOR–GREEN
(L) FORCE MOTOR–BLUE
(K) 12V PWM SOLENOID–WHITE
(J) PWM SOLENOID GROUND–BLACK

(b)

FIGURE 13–19 A visual inspection of the transmission electrical connector ensures that the terminals are clean and in good condition as well as being completely engaged.

have this varnish coating. It usually has a strong odor similar to varnish and indicates that the transmission ran hot.

- An excess of metal is from a gear set, thrust washers, bushings, or the transmission case. Steel and iron are usually from the gears, needle bearings, a spring, or a spring retainer. Aluminum is from the case, a carrier, or a clutch piston. Brass or bronze is from a bushing or thrust washer.

- Any plastic debris (broken or melted) is from a thrust washer, spacer, or clutch spring retainer.

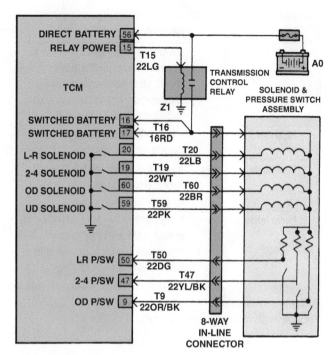

FIGURE 13–20 TCM terminals 16 and 17 receive B+ when the transmission relay is energized.

ELECTRICAL SYSTEM CHECKS An electronic system cannot function without adequate power or a good ground. The power and ground connections are often overlooked by the technician who is eager to solve a transmission problem. The case connector should be checked as it is exposed to road hazards as well as water, snow, and mud. ● **SEE FIGURE 13–19.**

After determining there is a problem in the electronic system, an experienced technician will check B+ voltage at the battery and then at the TCM and transmission power relay if there is one. There should be at least 12.6 volts with the engine off and 13.6 to 15 volts with the engine running. There should also be a minimum voltage drop between the TCM ground (B–) terminal and ground, 0.2 volt or less. ● **SEE FIGURE 13–20.**

- When checking a circuit, make sure that all connectors are properly latched. Disassemble the connector and check for loose, bent, or pushed-back pins, cracked connectors, and water intrusion that will cause corrosion.

- A signal generator can be used to input ISS and OSS signals, and if the TCM responds properly, the speed sensor in question must be faulty.

HYDRAULIC SYSTEM PRESSURE TESTS The operation of an automatic transmission is dependent on hydraulic pressure. A technician uses a pressure gauge to check the condition of the hydraulic system. Some hydraulic system

FIGURE 13-21 The locations (taps) for connecting a pressure gauge to measure the pressure of the various hydraulic circuits are usually found on the side of the automatic transmission/transaxle. Check service information for the exact locations for the vehicle being tested.

 REAL WORLD FIX

The Case of the Drips

The 1996 BMW 535i (86,000 mi) came in with a complaint of fourth-gear dropout. This occurs when it is hot with the A/C on. Normal operation returns after the car is shut off for a while. The technician checked the A/C evaporator drain and found that it was dripping water onto the transmission harness connector. Sealing/waterproofing this electrical connector fixed this problem.

problems can be cured with the transmission still in the vehicle. For example, it is not a good business practice to remove and replace (R&R) a transaxle if the problem was caused by a loose valve body, faulty governor, or electrical problems.

All transmissions have a pressure test port, and some have more than one. If there is only one port, it will usually be for line pressure. The additional ports provide the apply or release pressure of a particular clutch. Service information includes illustrations to identify these test ports. ● **SEE FIGURE 13-21.**

PRESSURE GAUGES A common analog hydraulic pressure gauge is normally dampened, so minor pressure fluctuations are lost. The electrical transducer of an electronic gauge can be connected to a scope, which can be used to watch small pressure changes and find an important clue to the cause of a problem. When using a hydraulic pressure gauge, it is recommended that the range of the gauge be 0 to 300 PSI (0–2 kPa) to prevent gauge damage while testing reverse gear pressure.

FIGURE 13-22 Six pressure gauges are installed on this vehicle to show students how the pressures vary and how the gauges can be used to find faults or possible problem areas before the unit is removed and disassembled.

To test transmission hydraulic pressures, perform the following steps:

STEP 1   Raise and securely support the vehicle on a hoist or jack stand.

STEP 2   Locate the pressure ports, remove the plugs, and connect the gauge(s) to the ports. Note that most domestic transmission ports use female, 1/8-inch National Pipe Threads (NPT). Always double-check that the fitting has the same threads as the transmission port by turning the adapter inward several turns using hand force only.

STEP 3   Connect a scan tool to the vehicle to monitor engine speed.

STEP 4   Route the various lines and wires so they can be read while the vehicle is operated. Be sure to keep them away from the hot exhaust system and rotating parts. Do not run the hydraulic lines or gauge inside the vehicle.

STEP 5   Place the gear selector in park, securely apply the brakes, start the engine, and note the readings on the various gauges.

STEP 6   Run the engine at idle speed, then shift the gear selector through each of the gear ranges and record the pressure readings. While testing pressure during a road test, watch the gauge pressure before, during, and after a shift. The pressure should drop and then come back. A lower pressure after a shift indicates a leaking fluid circuit.

STEP 7   Make sure the brakes are securely applied, then increase the engine speed to 1000 RPM and repeat step 6. ● **SEE FIGURE 13-22.**

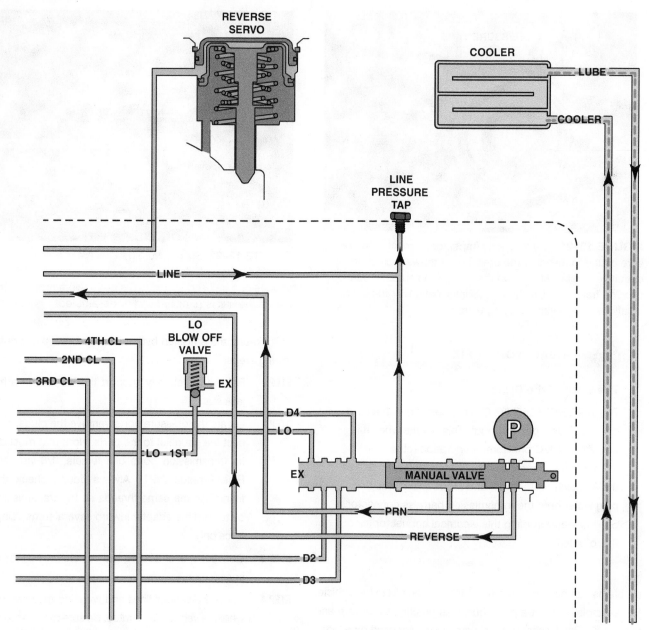

FIGURE 13-23 A portion of a typical hydraulic schematic showing part of the hydraulic system and pressure tap.

INTERPRETING PRESSURE READINGS A technician compares the pressure readings to specifications to determine if the system is operating correctly. The most likely causes for a pressure problem in park or neutral are the pump, intake filter, and pressure regulator because the fluid flow path is usually through the filter, valve body, transmission case, pump assembly, and back through the transmission case to the valve body. These are the circuits that are supplying fluid or are under pressure in that gear range. In park and neutral, the throttle valve, torque converter, and cooler are open to flow but the flow to the rest of the transmission is shut off at the manual valve. High or low pressures in neutral are usually caused by a problem in the throttle valve, torque converter, and cooler

circuits. If no specifications are available, the approximate pressures in most transmissions will be as follows:

- Neutral, park, and drive at idle: 50 to 60 PSI (350 to 400 kPa)
- M1 and M2: 50 to 60 PSI; in some transmissions: 100 to 125 PSI
- Reverse: 150 to 250 PSI

Increase the engine speed to 2000 RPM, observe the pressure gauge, and switch the ignition off. If the pressure increases to normal or above as the engine stops, there is a problem in the electronic pressure control (EPC) circuit. Any transmission that develops normal pressure in reverse is sure to have a good pump and pressure control circuit.

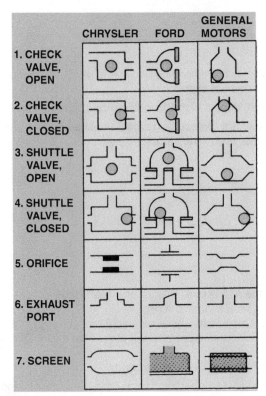

	CHRYSLER	FORD	GENERAL MOTORS
1. CHECK VALVE, OPEN			
2. CHECK VALVE, CLOSED			
3. SHUTTLE VALVE, OPEN			
4. SHUTTLE VALVE, CLOSED			
5. ORIFICE			
6. EXHAUST PORT			
7. SCREEN			

FIGURE 13–24 Hydraulic symbols used by domestic vehicle manufacturers.

Control pressure test results àre as follows:

- If normal in any range, the pump and pressure regulator pressure control solenoid and circuit are normal.

- If normal in reverse, the pump and pressure regulator valve or pressure control solenoid and circuit are normal.

- If low in all ranges, there is probably a clogged filter, defective pump, or defective pressure regulator valve, or faulty pressure control solenoid or circuit.

- If low in any gear range, there is a problem in that circuit, probably defective seals or sealing rings.

Clutch and band apply pressures are checked by moving the gear selector to the different gear ranges. For example, normal pressure in every range except drive-3 and reverse indicates leakage in the clutch that is applied for the drive-3 and reverse circuits. This pressure loss can cause slippage in high and reverse.

INDIVIDUAL CIRCUIT TEST PORTS When a transmission has test ports for individual apply circuits as well as line pressure, the condition of that circuit can be easily determined by comparing its pressure with line pressure. For example, if line pressure is 75 PSI (520 kPa) and third-gear pressure is also 75 PSI, then the third-gear circuit, and all of the piston seals, and sealing rings are in good condition. If any circuit is more than 10 PSI (70 kPa) lower than line pressure, there is a sealing problem in that gear circuit that must be corrected.

FLUID FLOW DIAGRAMS Manufacturers provide hydraulic schematics/fluid diagrams of the fluid passages and valves. ● **SEE FIGURE 13–23**.

They are used to locate the cause of a problem such as low fluid pressure or no upshift. The diagrams are used to trace the fluid flow through a circuit in the same way that you would use a street map to locate the roads between two points. The symbols (such as for check valves or exhaust ports) vary between manufacturers. ● **SEE FIGURE 13–24**.

SUMMARY

1. The diagnostic process includes the following steps:

   STEP 1 The first step is to verify the customer complaint. This step usually includes test driving the vehicle to see if the complaint can be duplicated. If the problem cannot be duplicated, then the repair cannot be verified.

   STEP 2 Check the fluid level and condition.

   STEP 3 Check for stored diagnostic trouble codes (DTCs).

   STEP 4 Check for any related technical service bulletins (TSBs).

   STEP 5 Check scan tool data including the adaptive values.

   STEP 6 Visual inspections.

   STEP 7 Locate the root cause of the problem.

   STEP 8 Replace all components that do not meet factory specifications and clear all codes and reset all adaptive factors.

   STEP 9 Test drive the vehicle to verify that the repairs corrected the customer concern.

2. A road test is used to verify the customer's concern and check the general overall condition of the transmission.

3. To check transmission fluid with a dipstick, check the procedure stamped on the dipstick.

1. What is the diagnostic procedure that most vehicle manufactures suggest be followed when diagnosing an automatic transmission/transaxle customer concern?

2. How is the automatic transmission fluid level checked on an automatic transmission/transaxle that does not have a dipstick?

3. What is the difference between a factory scan tool and an aftermarket scan tool?

4. What does a high CVI indicate on a scan tool display?

5. How are pressure gauges attached to an automatic transmission/transaxle?

CHAPTER QUIZ

1. Why should the transmission control system be checked for diagnostic trouble codes (DTCs) before checking for technical service bulletins (TSBs)?
   a. Some TSBs refer to stored DTCs
   b. If there are no DTCs then there will not be any TSBs
   c. The two are not related so it does not matter in which order they are checked
   d. TSBs refer to fluid level checking only

2. Why does the customer concern need to be verified?
   a. To make sure that there is a real concern
   b. To be able to verify the repair
   c. To determine under what conditions the fault is noticed or occurs
   d. All of the above

3. An "end bump" is best described as _____.
   a. The operation occurs before normally expected
   b. A shift feel that becomes noticeably firmer as it is completed
   c. A repeated up-and-then-down shifting sequence that produces noticeable repeated engine RPM changes
   d. The shift occurs sometime after normally expected

4. An automatic transmission or transaxle that is underfilled may experience which symptom?
   a. Mushy operation
   b. Goes into neutral
   c. Slipping
   d. Any or all of the above

5. What is needed to properly check the ATF level on an automatic transmission or transaxle NOT equipped with a dipstick?
   a. A special tool
   b. A scan tool to determine ATF temperature
   c. A scan tool to check the fluid level sensor reading
   d. A high-pressure gauge

6. If the ATF is pink, this usually means that _____.
   a. It is a synthetic ATF
   b. The fluid has been aerated (filled with air)
   c. Indicates a coolant leak at the heat exchanger in the radiator
   d. The fluid has been oxidized

7. A high CVI reading on a scan tool usually indicates _____.
   a. A worn clutch pack
   b. A defective one-way clutch
   c. Low ATF level
   d. Incorrect gear ratio detected

8. A factory or factory-level scan tool can _____.
   a. Read DTCs
   b. Read TSBs
   c. Command shifts
   d. Both a and c

9. During oil pan debris check, what is considered to be normal?
   a. Loose, black material
   b. Heavy golden brown coating
   c. A small amount of debris with a blackish oil film
   d. Plastic debris

10. If no specifications are available, the approximate pressures in most transmissions will be _____.
    a. Neutral, park, and, drive at idle: 50 to 60 PSI (350 to 400 kPa)
    b. Neutral, park, and, drive at idle: 100 to 120 PSI (690 to 827 kPa)
    c. Neutral, park, and, drive at idle: 120 to 160 PSI (827 to 1100kPa)
    d. Neutral, park, and, drive at idle: 160 to 200 PSI (1100 to 1380 kPa)

chapter 14

IN-VEHICLE TRANSMISSION/ TRANSAXLE SERVICE

LEARNING OBJECTIVES

After studying this chapter, the reader will be able to:

1. Prepare for ASE Automatic Transmissions (A2) certification test content area "B" (In-Vehicle Transmission and Transaxle Service).

2. Discuss fluid replacement.

3. Describe the procedure to follow when replacing seals.

4. Perform linkage adjustments in automatic transmissions.

5. Describe the correct procedure for replacing powertrain mounts and performing band adjustments.

KEY TERMS

Fluid flushing 238
Fluid change 236

Fluid exchange 238
Stop-off tool 240

Test Drive Before and After Every Service

The wise technician test drives any vehicle being serviced, especially one where a routine automatic transmission service is being requested. Sometimes, a vehicle owner will ask that a service be performed hoping that it will fix an issue that has been noticed. To help avoid misunderstandings and to insure good customer relations, test drive the vehicle and let the customer know if any transmission-related issues are discovered before performing a routine transmission service. Then, of course, test drive the vehicle after the service has been performed to verify that everything is normal and operating properly.

FLUID LIFE (miles/km)	TEMPERATURE (F/C)
100,000/160,000	175°/80°
50,000/80,000	195°/90°
25,000/40,000	215°/100°
12,550/20,000	235°/113°
6,250/10,000	255°/124°
3,125/5,000	275°/135°
1,560/2,500	295°/146°
780/1,250	315°/157°

CHART 14–1

The higher the ATF temperature, the shorter the life expectancy of the fluid.

IN-VEHICLE SERVICE ITEMS

OVERVIEW Automatic transmissions and transaxles can operate properly for many miles. Some that fail could have had a longer service life had they been properly maintained. Several surveys of transmission shops have shown that over 80% of transmission failures were the result of neglecting to change the fluid. Maintaining the correct fluid level and changing the fluid are primary maintenance tasks.

FLUID CHANGES

RECOMMENDED INTERVAL Most manufacturers recommend fluid changes every 100,000 miles (160,000 km) under normal driving conditions. Some recommend a **fluid change** at 50,000 miles (80,000 km). Fluid change recommendations are usually accompanied with a recommendation that the change interval be shortened to as low as 15,000 miles (24,000 km) when the vehicle is used under severe driving conditions. Such severe driving conditions include the following:

- Frequent trailer pulling
- Heavy city traffic, especially in areas where the temperature exceeds 90°F (32°C)
- Very hilly or mountainous conditions

- Commercial use such as taxi or delivery service
- Police or ambulance usage

The fluid should be changed when it starts to break down, which is best indicated by the fluid appearance and smell. It is wise to change the fluid early, before transmission damage occurs. Dirty fluid may cause the shift valves and solenoids to start sticking, which in turn can cause sluggish shifts and slippage and thus more fluid heat, breakdown, contamination, and damage.

ATF TEMPERATURE AND LIFE EXPECTANCY The main factor that determines transmission fluid life is heat or how hot the fluid is during vehicle operation. If the fluid temperature is kept below 175°F (79°C), the fluid should easily last 100,000 miles. At higher temperatures the fluid oxidizes, causing it to break down at a rate one-half its expected life for every increase of 20°F (11°C).

- Varnish begins forming at temperatures above 240°F (116°C)
- Rubber seals start hardening at temperatures above 260°F (127°C).

See transmission fluid life relative to temperature in ● **CHART 14–1**.

OLD FLUID CHANGE ISSUES If the old transmission fluid is extremely dirty, be aware that when the fluid is changed, the new ATF contains a fresh supply of detergents and dispersants that could result in the following:

- Loosen varnish and other deposits that have accumulated inside the transmission
- Carry this material throughout the transmission, including valves and solenoids

FIGURE 14–1 Draining the fluid from an automatic transaxle by allowing the fluid to flow into a container after most of the retaining bolts have been removed.

FIGURE 14–2 Always check that the filter is secured by a clip or other fastener to keep it from dropping out of its position.

- Possibly remove varnish that has formed over worn seals and open up a leak.
- The supply of new friction modifier will increase the "slippery" level of the fluid, which might increase slipping on upshifts.

SAFETY ISSUES The material safety data sheets (MSDS) (SDS) for most transmission fluids indicate that there are few safety hazards when working with new fluid. Some indicate a possible skin reaction. Used fluid, however, goes through an unknown change inside the transmission that might cause it to be more of a hazard. Experts usually recommend the following precautions:

- Wear goggles or a face shield.
- Wear gloves or barrier cream for skin protection.
- Clean any skin contact with ATF using soap and water.
- Change clothing that has contacted ATF.
- Wash any clothing that has contact with ATF.
- If ATF under pressure breaks the skin, medical attention should be sought.

FLUID CHANGING, DROPPING THE PAN

PROCEDURE The procedure for changing the fluid in a specific vehicle can be found in service information. To be specific, the procedure usually includes the following steps:

STEP 1 Safely hoist the vehicle.

STEP 2 Select the best direction for fluid to spill from the pan. Place a large drain pan in this area, and remove all but two of the pan bolts. The remaining two bolts should be at the end away from the drain pan and they serve as the "hinge" for lowering the pan. ● **SEE FIGURE 14–1**.

STEP 3 When the pan lowers to an angle of about 30° to 45°, support it by hand, then remove the remaining two bolts and finish draining the pan.

STEP 4 Remove the filter, which is usually attached to the valve body. Watch for any small parts that may come loose with the filter. Set aside the old filter for comparison with the new filter.

STEP 5 Inspect the pan, filter, and pan magnet for debris and varnish buildup. The magnet in most automatic transmission pans is used to collect steel particles to keep them from getting circulated throughout the transmission/transaxle. A few metal particles are considered normal. These result from wear and transmission break-ins. Inspect the inside of the transmission for any visible damage or varnish buildup.

STEP 6 Install a new filter using a new gasket or O-ring, and tighten the mounting bolts to the correct torque, if equipped. If an O-ring is used, it should be lubricated with transmission assembly lube, petroleum jelly, or automatic transmission fluid (ATF) before installation. ● **SEE FIGURE 14–2**.

STEP 7 Clean the oil pan and check and straighten if needed any bends at the pan bolt holes.

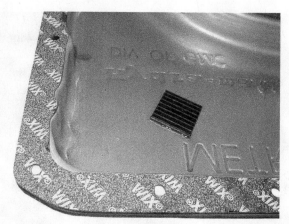

FIGURE 14–3 In this case, the cork-rubber gasket is glued to the pan and is ready to be installed. The retaining bolts need to be tightened in sequence, but be aware that over-tightening will cause a leak. Also, some manufacturers recommend using only an RTV sealer, but never use an RTV sealer and a gasket together.

STEP 8 Install a new gasket on the pan, and install the pan on the transmission. ● **SEE FIGURE 14–3.**

STEP 9 The bolts should be tightened in a back-and-forth, across-the-pan sequence to the specified torque.

STEP 10 Lower the vehicle, and add the proper amount of fluid. A rule of thumb is 4 quarts. Start the engine and check the fluid level. Add additional fluid to correct the level if necessary.

STEP 11 Dispose of the old transmission fluid according to Federal, State, and local laws and regulations.

NOTE: This procedure only changes the fluid in the pan, which is about one-quarter to one-third (1/4 to 1/3) of the total fluid capacity still in the transmission. The remaining fluid stays in the torque converter, clutches and band servos, accumulators, cooler, and fluid passages.

FLUID EXCHANGE AND FLUID UNITS

TERMINOLOGY **Fluid flushing** typically uses a chemical to dissolve varnish and other deposits. **Fluid exchange** usually means taking out the old fluid and replacing it with new fluid of the correct type. By using a fluid exchange machine, all of the fluid in the system is replaced.

If the flush is needed to remove solid debris, there must be enough flow velocity to break the material loose and carry it out of the component. More efficient flush machines will pulsate

FIGURE 14–4 The lines from the fluid exchange machine can often be connected to the cooling lines from underneath the vehicle as on this front-wheel-drive General Motors vehicle.

🚗 **REAL WORLD FIX**

TSB to the Rescue

A 2002 Dodge Durango came in to the shop with a customer complaint of delayed engagement into reverse after sitting for a while. A check in the pan showed metal, evidence of a converter failure, so the transmission was rebuilt. A new solenoid pack and pressure sensor were installed. A Quick Learn was done and the vehicle was driven 60 miles to relearn the harsh N–R and 2–3 shifts. The original problem of reverse shift delay is still there. A fellow technician told of a TSB (21-016-05) that describes filters with a faulty check valve. Replacement of the filter cured this problem.

the flow to increase the cleaning power. In severe cases, such as a plugged cooler, the flush can be set up to pump the solvent into the cooler outlet and remove it from the inlet.

TYPICAL PROCEDURE Fluid exchange machines are usually connected into the transmission cooler lines so that the machine can pump new fluid to the return line as it captures the fluid leaving the transmission. ● **SEE FIGURE 14–4.**

Running the engine will pump the old fluid out of the transmission, and a pump in the fluid exchange machine will pump new fluid into the return line. When new, clean fluid starts leaving the transmission, the fluid exchange is complete.

The Case of the Bent Pan

A 2002 Mercury Villager van (147,000 mi) would go into neutral under varying conditions. During a test drive it operated normally in all gears until accelerating from a stop but then it went to neutral and after a short period of time, back into gear. The fluid appeared and smelled normal. The transmission electrical connections were checked, and these were good. The pan was checked—it was bent upward, apparently blocking flow to the filter. The pan was removed, bent back to the proper shape, and replaced. This repair fixed the problem.

FIGURE 14–5 This seal is being removed using a seal puller.

Always follow the manufacturer's instructions when using a fluid exchanger, which usually includes the following steps:

STEP 1 Identify which cooler line is the return line.

STEP 2 Disconnect the return line from the cooler, and connect the line to the NEW FLUID connector of the machine. Connect the USED FLUID connector of the machine to the cooler.

STEP 3 Apply the parking brake and shift the transmission into park. Start the engine and observe the fluid flow in the machine. To prevent starving the transmission of fluid, new fluid should enter the machine at the same rate that used fluid leaves.

STEP 4 When the used fluid has the same appearance as new fluid, stop the engine.

STEP 5 Disconnect fluid connections to the machine, and reconnect the cooler return line.

STEP 6 Start the engine and check the line connection for leaks.

STEP 7 Check the transmission fluid level and adjust as necessary.

STEP 8 Dispose of the used transmission fluid in an approved manner.

SEAL REPLACEMENT

TWO SEALING SURFACES A standard metal-backed lip seal must seal against two different surfaces:

1. A dynamic seal with the movable shaft at the inner bore.

2. A static seal where it fits into its bore. The static seal is made when the slightly oversize seal backing is driven into the bore.

GENERAL REPLACEMENT PROCEDURE A chisel, slide hammer, or seal puller can be used to remove a seal after the shaft has been removed. ● **SEE FIGURE 14–5.**

Be careful when installing the seal over a shaft or a shaft into a seal. The sharp lip of the seal is easily cut or torn.

- When installing a seal over a shaft, it is good practice to protect the sealing lip with a seal protector, especially if there are any rough or sharp edges on the shaft. A piece of slick paper wrapped around the shaft will work as a seal protector in many cases.

- The lip of the seal should always be lubricated to prevent wear. Automatic transmission assembly lube, petroleum jelly, or automatic transmission fluid (ATF) can be used for a lubricant.

- Some seals include a garter spring to increase sealing lip pressure. This garter spring can be dislodged as the seal is driven into position. Filling the recess with assembly lube or petroleum jelly will keep the garter spring in place during installation. ● **SEE FIGURE 14–6.**

EXTENSION HOUSING SEAL To remove and replace a transmission extension housing seal, perform the following steps:

STEP 1 Raise and support the vehicle on a hoist that allows access to the transmission and driveshaft.

STEP 2 Place alignment marks on the rear universal joint and rear-axle pinion flange.

STEP 3 Disconnect the driveshaft from the rear axle. ATF will begin leaking out of the driveshaft opening. You

FIGURE 14–6 The lip of the seal around the garter spring is packed with assembly lube to help keep the spring from falling out when it is driven into the transmission housing.

FIGURE 14–7 Using a plug helps prevent fluid loss when the driveshaft is removed.

should either raise the rear of the vehicle enough to stop the flow or place a container to catch the flow. A **stop-off tool** or old U-joint slip yoke can be used to stop the fluid leak. ● **SEE FIGURE 14–7.**

STEP 4 Pull or pry out the rear seal using a suitable tool.

STEP 5 If necessary, remove the rear bushing using a suitable tool.

STEP 6 If the bushing is removed, use a suitable tool to drive the new bushing completely into place.

STEP 7 Use a correctly sized driver to drive the new seal into place. If the replacement seal does not have an outer sealant coating, a film of sealant should be spread around the outer surface of the seal case.

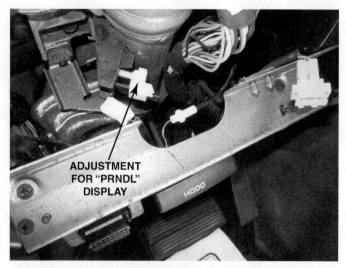

FIGURE 14–8 The position for the pointer ("PRNDL" display) on this Dodge truck is adjustable.

MANUAL LINKAGE CHECKS

NEED TO CHECK ADJUSTMENT The manual linkage is adjustable on most automatic transmissions. This ensures the manual valve is positioned correctly relative to the gear selector.

Detents are internal to the transmission and keep the manual valve aligned with the selected position. Because the detents act on the internal linkage, they normally stay correctly aligned with the valve position.

CHECKING MANUAL LINKAGE ADJUSTMENT To check manual linkage adjustment, the specified procedure usually includes the following steps:

STEP 1 Firmly set the parking brake and leave the engine off.

STEP 2 Move the selector level through the ranges, and observe the range pointer and the position of the internal detents. The detents engage as the pointer aligns with the gate for each gear position indicator.

STEP 3 Move the selector lever to park, and the parking pawl should freely engage to lock the transmission.

STEP 4 Check that the starter operates in park and neutral but not in other gear positions.

Always check service information for the proper procedure. ● **SEE FIGURE 14–8.**

MAKING A MANUAL LINKAGE ADJUSTMENT The manual linkage should be adjusted if the starter engagements

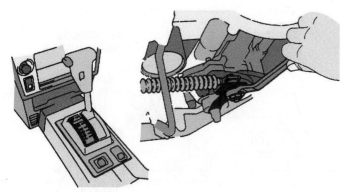

FIGURE 14–9 The manual shift lever is in park. The linkage is being tightened to lock the adjustment in after making sure that the transmission is in park.

occur in the wrong position or the transmission detents do not align correctly relative to the gear range pointer. The procedure will vary with vehicle makes and models. Check service information for the exact procedure for a particular vehicle. ● **SEE FIGURE 14–9.**

SHIFT INTERLOCK MECHANISM The shift interlock mechanism locks the shifter in park position when the ignition key is removed. On most vehicles, the brake pedal must be depressed before the shifter can be moved, and the ignition key cannot be removed unless the lever has been shifted into park. These systems operate either electrically or through a mechanical linkage. The mechanical systems usually have an adjustment to ensure proper positioning. These systems vary, so service information for that particular vehicle should be consulted when diagnosing problems or checking adjustments.

A shift interlock can get out of adjustment or fail to release. Vehicle manufacturers have incorporated a fail-safe mechanism so the vehicle can be operated. Located near the shift lever is a small lever or button that can be used to override the shift lock and release the lever. The release is often located under a cover that must be removed for access. This procedure is normally described in the vehicle owner's manual. ● **SEE FIGURE 14–10.**

POWERTRAIN MOUNTS

REPLACING MOUNTS Powertrain mounts often require replacement due to damage or wear. Defective powertrain (engine and transmission) mounts are replaced by lifting the engine and/or transmission slightly to remove the weight, and then removing the mounting bolts. The old mount is then removed and the new mount is installed.

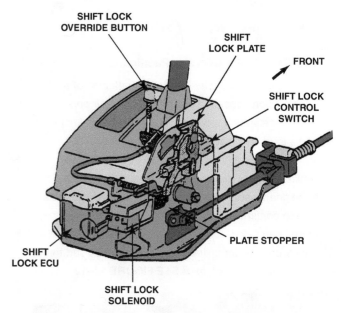

FIGURE 14–10 This shift lock mechanism includes a solenoid that can mechanically hold the shift lock plate. Note the shift lock override button that can be used to release the shift lock.

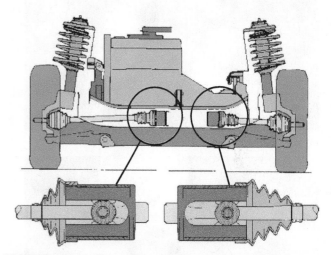

FIGURE 14–11 The enlarged views of the inner CV joints show that the engine and transaxle are misaligned; they should be moved toward the right.

The mount for a rear-wheel-drive (RWD) transmission is aligned by the bolts through slotted holes in the mount. Alignment is required so the engine, transmission, and exhaust system do not contact the frame or body. A front-wheel-drive (FWD) transaxle must be aligned to the two front driveshafts. The alignment check is accomplished by completely compressing both inboard CV joints, and measuring the distance between the joint and the transaxle. The position of the transaxle is then adjusted so that both distances are equal. Adjustment is accomplished by loosening the mounts and sliding the engine and transaxle sideways. ● **SEE FIGURE 14–11.**

The Case of the Chrysler Pacifica

The owner of a Chrysler Pacifica complained of a transmission concern that seemed to occur only when accelerating rapidly. The vehicle would shake and a loud knock sound was heard when decelerating, but everything seemed to be normal if the vehicle was accelerated slowly. Everything seemed to be fine when driven in reverse. The technician was able to confirm the situation and felt that an engine mount had failed. A visual inspection confirmed that the mount was torn. Replacing the mount solved the "transmission" problem. ● **SEE FIGURE 14–12.**

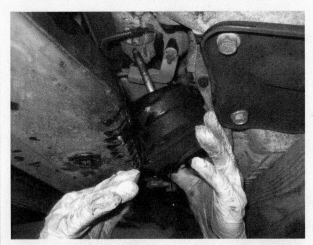

(a)

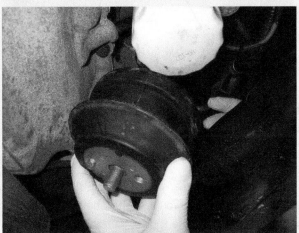

(b)

FIGURE 14–12 (a) The old front engine mount contained hydraulic fluid. The oil was leaking from the split in the mount. (b) The new original equipment (OE) mount ready to be installed.

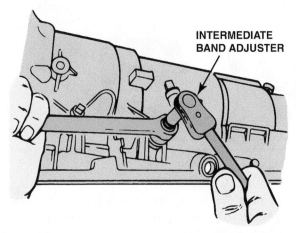

FIGURE 14–13 Adjusting the intermediate band on a Ford A4LD transmission.

BAND ADJUSTMENTS

The band in many transmissions is used only in manual ranges for engine compression braking and is expected to last the life of the transmission. Most recent transmissions have no provision for in-vehicle adjustments.

- Some older transmissions have threaded adjusters extending through the case to allow an easy readjustment of the band.
- Some band adjustments are made inside the transmission and it is necessary to drop the pan to gain access to the adjuster.

ADJUSTMENT PROCEDURE Service information should be checked to determine the exact adjustment procedure for each particular vehicle.

To readjust a band, the usual procedure includes the following steps:

STEP 1 Loosen the lock nut on the adjuster screw several turns. ● **SEE FIGURE 14–13.**

STEP 2 Tighten the adjuster screw to the specified torque. Special adjuster wrenches with preset torque settings are available for this operation.

STEP 3 Mark the adjusting screw position, and then back it off the specified number of turns. Hold the adjuster screw stationary and retighten the lock nut to the specified torque.

STEP 4 Road test the vehicle to check the adjustment.

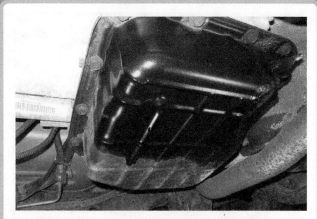

1 The owner of this Dodge pickup complained that automatic transmission fluid was leaking from the pan gasket.

2 The transmission fluid leak is found to be from small holes that had rusted through the steel pan.

3 The retaining bolts being removed from the pan.

4 The retaining bolts on one side are kept attached and then loosened to allow fluid to drain from one side of the pan.

5 The pan is then gently lowered and the ATF is caught dripping from the valve body.

6 The pan is then emptied into an oil drain unit.

CONTINUED ▶

7 The old filter is removed.

8 The shop purchased a new original equipment filter and a new, improved transmission pan gasket.

9 The new filter is installed.

10 The replacement pan is installed and the fasteners tightened to factory specifications. The new pan is galvanized steel compared to painted steel on the original.

11 The specified ATF is installed.

12 The level is checked with the engine running and the gear selector in neutral as per the instructions on the dipstick.

SUMMARY

1. Maintaining the correct fluid level and changing the fluid are primary maintenance tasks.

2. Most manufacturers recommend fluid changes every 100,000 miles (160,000 km) under normal driving conditions.

3. Fluid flushing typically uses a chemical to dissolve varnish and other deposits. Fluid exchange usually means taking out the old fluid and replacing it with new fluid of the correct type.

4. The material safety data sheets (MSDS) (SDS) for most transmission fluids indicate that there are few safety hazards when working with new fluid. Some indicate a possible skin reaction. Used fluid, however, goes through an unknown change inside the transmission that might cause more hazards.

5. A chisel, slide hammer, or seal puller can be used to remove a seal after the shaft has been removed.

6. The manual linkage should be adjusted if the starter engagement occurs in the wrong position or the transmission detents do not align correctly relative to the gear range pointer.

7. Defective powertrain (engine and transmission) mounts are replaced by lifting the engine and/or transmission slightly to remove the weight, and then removing the mounting bolts. The old mount is then removed and the new mount is installed.

REVIEW QUESTIONS

1. What are severe driving conditions that may require the automatic transmission fluid to be changed more often than when driven under normal conditions?

2. What issues may be the result of replacing fluid in a vehicle that has not had the specified fluid changes?

3. What is the difference between a fluid flush and a fluid exchange?

4. What is the general seal replacement procedure?

5. What are the typical steps involved with a band adjustment?

CHAPTER QUIZ

1. Most manufacturers recommend fluid changes every _____.
   a. 10,000 miles (16,000 km)
   b. 25,000 miles (40,000 km)
   c. 50,000 miles (80,000 km)
   d. 100,000 miles (160,000 km)

2. Severe service includes _____.
   a. Extensive highway driving
   b. Commercial use, such as police or taxi use
   c. A combination of city and highway driving
   d. Driving in temperatures below freezing

3. The life of ATF is reduced if the temperature of the fluid is above _____.
   a. 32°F (0°C)   c. 175°F (80°C)
   b. 100°F (38°C)   d. None of the above

4. The material safety data sheets (MSDS) (SDS) for most transmission fluids indicate which safety hazards when working with new fluid?
   a. Possible skin reaction
   b. Possible skin cancer
   c. Possible exposure to HIV
   d. Possible swelling of spots exposed to the fluid

5. When being exposed to ATF, what should a technician do?
   a. Wear goggles or a face shield
   b. Wear gloves or barrier cream for skin protection
   c. Clean any skin contact with ATF using soap and water
   d. All of the above

6. Fluid flushing typically _____.
   a. Uses a chemical to dissolve varnish and other deposits
   b. Another name for fluid exchange
   c. Pulsates the flow to increase the cleaning power
   d. Both a and c

7. Why is there a magnet in the bottom of many automatic transmission pans?
   a. To keep the pan in place as it is being installed
   b. To attract any steel particles and keep them from flowing through the transmission
   c. Used in assembly only
   d. Any of the above depending on make and model

8. A lip seal requires what type of tool to remove?
   a. A chisel or slide hammer and/or a seal puller
   b. A plastic trim removing tool
   c. A large ball peen hammer
   d. A clutch installation tool

9. What is the purpose of the shifter interlock system?
   a. Keep the transmission from being forced into reverse when the vehicle is moving forward
   b. Allows for the selection of all forward gears and reverse when the vehicle is stopped
   c. Prevents the shifter from being moved into drive or reverse unless the brake pedal has been depressed
   d. Prevents the vehicle from rolling backwards on a hill if in the drive position.

10. Which statement(s) is/are true about band adjustments?
    a. The band in many transmissions is used only in manual ranges for engine compression braking and is expected to last the life of the transmission
    b. Most recent transmissions have no provision for in-vehicle adjustments
    c. Some older transmissions have threaded adjusters extending through the case to allow an easy readjustment of the band
    d. All of the above are correct

chapter 15

TRANSMISSION/ TRANSAXLE REMOVAL AND DISASSEMBLY

LEARNING OBJECTIVES

After studying this chapter, the reader will be able to:

1. Prepare for ASE Automatic Transmissions (A2) certification test content area "C" (Off-Vehicle Transmission/Transaxle Repair).

2. Describe automatic transmission repair options.

3. Describe the automatic transmission/transaxle inspection process.

4. List the steps need to be followed to remove an automatic transmission/transaxle.

5. Explain the procedure for disassembling a transmission/transaxle.

KEY TERMS

Aftermarket 251
Hard parts 251
Overhaul 248
Rebuild 248
Remanufactured transmission/ transaxle 248
Retaining bracket 250
Selective 254
Soft parts 251

REPAIR OPTIONS

REPAIR A repair is an operation that replaces faulty parts and performs the needed labor to correct a transmission fault. Most transmission shops are equipped to perform all repairs needed to the vehicle's transmission. Repairing the original transmission ensures that the transmission will be the proper one for the vehicle.

REPLACEMENT A replacement is the removal and installation of the automatic transmission/transaxle. The replacement may be new, remanufactured, or wrecking (recycling) yard unit. For example, many shops install remanufactured transmissions because they are often less expensive than rebuilding or updating the original transmission. A **remanufactured transmission/transaxle** is a unit that has been disassembled, cleaned, inspected, and reassembled using new or like-new parts. It will have any necessary modifications and updates required for proper operation of the transmission. These units are commonly used by dealers to repair transmission problems that occur while a vehicle is still under its new-vehicle or extended warranty. Remanufacturing is done on a production line, with many transmissions of the same model being rebuilt at the same time. Many smaller shops will use remanufactured transmissions when the vehicle's unit is so badly damaged that the cost of the parts comes close to or exceeds the cost of a remanufactured unit.

COMPLETE OVERHAUL A complete overhaul includes disassembling the entire transmission/transaxle and replacing all needed parts, gaskets and seals to restore the transmission to perform like a new unit. A defective transmission with considerable mileage, damage, or wear is a candidate for overhaul or replacement. An **overhaul** implies a **rebuild**, which is generally considered to include the following steps:

- Transmission teardown or disassembly
- Replacement of all gaskets and seals
- Replacement of all friction materials
- Replacement of worn bushings
- Replacement of the filter and modulator, if equipped
- Cleaning and inspection of the planetary gears
- Cleaning and inspection of the valve body and all related components
- Cleaning and inspection of the torque converter
- Reassembling with a check of all necessary clearances

Some states have rules and regulations that define what an automatic transmission rebuild or overhaul must include. The California Bureau of Automotive Repair (BAR) states that a rebuilt, remanufactured, reconditioned, or overhauled transmission must include the following steps:

- Cleaning and inspection of all internal and external parts
- Valve body disassembly, cleaning, and inspection
- Front and intermediate bands replaced with new or relined units
- Replacement of the following parts: lined frictions, internal and external seals, rotating metal sealing rings, gaskets, and organic media filters
- All worn or defective parts repaired or replaced with new, rebuilt, or good parts
- Torque converter inspected or replaced with a new or rebuilt unit

NOTE: The California Bureau of Automotive Repair (BAR) regulations require that if a transmission is "exchanged," a descriptive term such as *new, used, rebuilt, remanufactured, reconditioned,* or *overhauled* shall accompany the exchange.

VERIFY THE NEED FOR UNIT REPAIR

VERIFY THE FAULT It is not unusual for a transmission or transaxle to be removed from the vehicle when the fault could have been repaired with the unit still in the vehicle. The fault could also be due to an electrical or engine-related fault outside the transmission/transaxle. Check with all of the following to be sure that the unit needs to be removed from the vehicle.

- A knowledgeable technician
- The archives at www.iatn.net
- A hotline service provider, such as Identifix (www.identifix.com)

Use these resources to verify that the fault is inside, not outside, the unit.

IN-VEHICLE REPAIRS Not all mechanical faults require that the automatic transmission/transaxle be removed from the vehicle. Faults that can usually be repaired with the unit still in the vehicle include any valve-body-related concerns. ● **SEE FIGURE 15–1.**

(a)

(b)

(c)

FIGURE 15–1 (a) This Saturn did not shift correctly and one technician was ready to replace the unit. However another technician thought that the problem could be due to a fault in the valve body. (b) Removing the valve body shows the non-planetary gears used in the Saturn automatic transaxle. (c) The valve body was disassembled and a broken pressure regulator spring was found to be the cause of the customer concern.

Depending on the transmission/transaxle, it may be possible to disassemble and repair many mechanical components of the unit while it remains in the vehicle. Parts and components that may be replaced with the transmission/transaxle still in the vehicle include the following:

- Pressure switches
- Transmission range switch
- Turbine and output speed sensors
- Extension housing gasket
- Drive axle seals
- Valve body replacement

Check service information for details on what can be replaced with the unit in the vehicle.

IDENTIFY THE UNIT Before removing the transmission/transaxle for replacement or repair, be sure that the unit is properly identified. This identification is critical because of the following:

1. The final drive ratio in transaxles can vary depending on the application; and using the wrong unit can cause shifting and other issues such as gear ratio–related diagnostic trouble codes.

2. The internal gear ratios can vary depending on exact application of the unit.

3. Sometimes the vehicle identification number (VIN) is needed to obtain the correct parts, but more often the transmission/transaxle identification number, also called the *tag number*, is the identification needed to be assured of ordering and receiving the proper parts. ●**SEE FIGURE 15–2**.

REMOVING THE AUTOMATIC TRANSMISSION/ TRANSAXLE

STEPS INVOLVED Removing an automatic transmission/transaxle from a vehicle includes many steps to avoid, which would otherwise cause damage to the vehicle or harm the personnel working on it. Always follow the vehicle manufacturer's recommended procedures. Most procedures include the following steps.

STEP 1 Disconnect the negative (–) battery cable from the battery. This prevents the possibility of an accidental

FIGURE 15–2 A transmission identification number on the side of the unit. The information on this tag is needed when ordering parts, as there are often several versions of the same transmission used in similar vehicles and the differences could affect the parts needed.

FIGURE 15–4 A transaxle being supported by a transmission jack prior to removal of the unit from underneath the vehicle.

FIGURE 15–3 A chain and holding fixture being used on this front-wheel-drive vehicle to support the engine when the transaxle is removed.

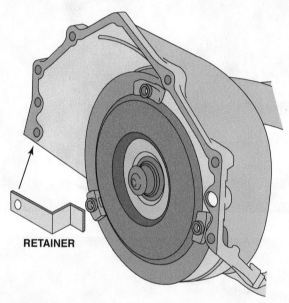

RETAINER

FIGURE 15–5 When the transmission/transaxle is being removed from the vehicle, either remove the torque converter or install a retaining bracket to keep it from falling off the splines.

short circuit that could damage the vehicle or cause a spark that could start a fire.

STEP 2 Hoist the vehicle safely and drain the fluid from the unit.

STEP 3 Disconnect the driveshaft or drive axle shafts.

STEP 4 Disconnect all cooler lines, linkage, and electrical connections. Be sure to label each to ensure proper reinstallation.

STEP 5 Disconnect the torque converter from the flex (drive) plate of the engine.

STEP 6 Support the engine before disconnecting the automatic transmission/transaxle. ● SEE FIGURE 15–3.

STEP 7 Remove the transmission/transaxle mounting fasteners.

STEP 8 Support the transmission/transaxle on a jack and remove the attaching bolts at the bell housing of the engine. ● SEE FIGURE 15–4.

STEP 9 Remove the transmission/transaxle from the vehicle.

CAUTION: There is a possibility that the converter can slide off its splines and fall as the transmission is being removed. It is heavy and can cause injury or damage if it falls. Some manufacturers recommend installing a converter retaining bracket. ● SEE FIGURE 15–5.

(a)

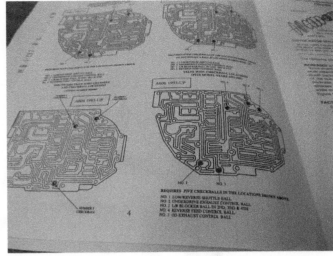

(b)

FIGURE 15–6 (a) A Typical automatic transaxle overhaul kit for a Chrysler 41TE. (b) The kit includes instructions and diagrams to help identify the unit being overhauled so that the correct parts are used from the kit.

AUTOMATIC TRANSMISSION PARTS

HARD PARTS Major transmission components such as pumps, clutch drums, or gear sets are called **hard parts**. New hard parts are generally available only from the manufacturer or an aftermarket supplier of automatic transmission parts. Some aftermarket companies specialize in used or rebuilt hard parts.

SOFT PARTS On the other hand, **soft parts** are those parts that are normally replaced during an overhaul. These include the gaskets, seals, and friction material.

The parts needed to overhaul a transmission are available from various sources. The vehicle manufacturer can supply all parts needed to repair or overhaul a transmission. Soft parts can be purchased from **aftermarket** sources (a supplier other than the vehicle manufacturer). These parts are usually available as individual components or as part of a kit. Kits are available in several forms, and the contents of a kit will vary between suppliers.

KITS A kit is more convenient and often less expensive than buying individual parts. A variety of kits is available to fit the needs of the particular job. Some of the kits available include the following:

- *Banner kit*—an overhaul kit plus the friction clutch plates
- *Bearing kit*—all bearings for the transmission
- *Compliance kit*—includes all parts that must be replaced as required for a rebuilt transmission in particular states

- *Deluxe or super kit*—a master kit plus filter, band(s), bushings, modulator (if used), and bonded pistons as required for the transmission
- *Filter kit*—the filter and pan gasket
- *Master kit*—an overhaul kit plus the friction and steel clutch plates
- *Overhaul kit*—all gaskets, O-rings, metal-clad seals, and lip seals
- *Sealing ring kit*—all seals made from Teflon, metal, or other materials
- *Solenoid kit*—shift, PWM, and force motor solenoids, which may include the wiring harness
- *Valve body kit*—additional parts needed for replacing worn valve body parts, including check balls, filters, springs, valves, and other needed parts. ●**SEE FIGURE 15–6.**

TRANSMISSION/ TRANSAXLE DISASSEMBLY

PREDISASSEMBLY CLEANUP Cleanliness is a must during a transmission overhaul. Many shops steam clean or pressure wash the outside of the transmission as soon as it is removed from the vehicle. Pre-cleaning removes all exterior dirt and other debris and helps keep the work area clean. An alternate cleanup method is to use solvent or an engine degreaser with a parts-cleaning brush and scraper. Always

FIGURE 15–7 A power washer being used to remove the road grime from the unit before it is disassembled.

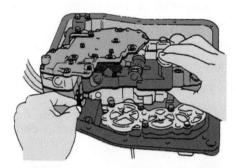

FIGURE 15–9 The valve body can be removed after the pan has been removed.

dispose of hazardous waste following the appropriate disposal procedures and requirements. ● **SEE FIGURE 15–7**.

TEARDOWN BENCH AND HOLDING FIXTURES Many shops use a teardown bench that has a steel top designed to catch the fluid and drain it into a catch pan. During disassembly, the transmission is placed on the bench and torn down. It is usually placed upside down and rolled over as needed. Some shops use transmission holding fixtures during overhaul. Holding fixtures allow the unit to be easily rotated to the best working position, which makes the work faster and easier. When using a holding fixture, a drain pan should be placed under the transmission to catch the dripping fluid. ● **SEE FIGURE 15–8**.

FIRST THINGS FIRST The first teardown step is to remove the oil pan, filter, and valve body. The procedure is to remove the pan, inspect the debris (if it has not been done already), wash the pan in solvent, and air dry it. Next, the filter

FIGURE 15–8 Using a holding fixture is the preferred method to use when disassembling and assembling an automatic transmission/transaxle. It allows the unit to be tilted and rotated as needed to get access to the internal and external components.

and gasket are removed and set aside for comparison with the new filter. The valve body is then removed and set aside for cleaning and inspection. ● **SEE FIGURE 15–9**.

CAUTION: Valve body bolts are often of different lengths. Either identify where they belong or leave them in the valve body holes after they are loosened.

Inspect for check balls as the valve body is removed, and note their location. Save the valve body gasket (if used) so it can be compared with the replacement gasket. Remove any check balls and screens under the valve body.

The valve body of some transmissions can serve as the cover for the accumulator or servo piston(s). Note the position of the piston(s) and spring (if used), and remove them. In other transmissions, a separate cover is used for the accumulator or servo. Each accumulator has its own spring and piston configuration. They may look alike, but there are slight differences. Improper assembly will cause shift timing and quality problems. ● **SEE FIGURE 15–10**.

RETAINING RINGS Retaining rings are used to hold many parts in the proper position. One example is like a standard snap ring and another looks like a round wire. The two types of retaining rings are external and internal. External rings fit over a shaft and need to be expanded for removal or installation. Internal rings fit into a bore and are contracted or compressed for removal or installation. ● **SEE FIGURE 15–11**.

Snap-ring pliers are often used to remove and install retaining rings and specially designed snap-ring pliers are

FIGURE 15–10 The accumulators used in a Chrysler 41TE look the same but use different springs.

FIGURE 15–11 A round retaining ring being removed after the accumulator piston plate/cover has been compressed using a compressing tool.

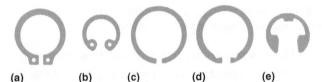

(a)   (b)   (c)   (d)   (e)

FIGURE 15–13 The most common types of retaining rings are (a) external pin type, (b) internal pin type, (c) plain external, (d) plain internal, and (e) E-clip.

⚠ **WARNING:**

Use caution during servo cover removal because some servos use a strong piston spring.
These require a special tool to hold the spring compressed during retainer ring removal and then allow the spring to be safely extended.

sometimes required for snap rings that are hard to remove. The correct type and size of snap-ring pliers must be used. Once removed, it is recommended that the retaining ring be replaced with a new one. ● **SEE FIGURE 15–13**.

END-PLAY CHECK   It is standard practice to measure the input shaft end play before removing the pump. End play is the in-and-out movement of the shaft.

- If there is no end play, there will be drag and a possible binding of the internal components.
- Too much end play allows misalignment of the internal parts which could cause damage from the excess movement.

FIGURE 15–14 Using a dial indicator to check the end play before the transmission is disassembled.

- If the end play is correct, the internal thrust washers are probably in good shape. If the end play is excessive, there is internal wear, which must be corrected during the rebuild. End play is normally measured using a dial indicator.

To measure input or output shaft end play, the usual method includes the following steps:

STEP 1 Place the transmission in a vertical position with the input shaft pointing up. Some transmissions require that a special fixture be used to hold the output shaft during end-play checks.

STEP 2 Attach a dial indicator onto the case or front pump, and position the measuring stylus against the end of the input shaft.

STEP 3 Pull the shaft slightly upward and then push it inward as far as it goes. Now adjust the indicator to read zero. ● **SEE FIGURE 15–14.**

NOTE: On some transmissions, the input shaft is not attached and can be easily pulled out of the transmission. On these units, end play is checked by measuring the distance from the end of the stator support to the end of the turbine shaft. End play on some of these units can be measured by prying upward on the gear train or specifying that the tailshaft (output) be lifted up and allowed to fall when checking total end play. This allows the entire stacked unit to be checked.

STEP 4 On most transmissions, pull up on the shaft and read the movement on the dial indicator. This is the amount of shaft end play.

STEP 5 Repeat steps 3 and 4 until you get consistent, reliable readings. Then make three more measurements and, if there is a slight difference, average them.

STEP 6 Record your reading and compare it to the specification.

Some manufacturers specify gear train end-play checks at the output shaft or other locations or require additional end-play checks. This helps locate excessive wear in specific areas or determine if the correct selective thrust washers or spacers are being used. For example, a transmission with a center support should have end play on each side of the center support. Manufacturers specify end-play checks between various components of the gear train. **Selective** washers or snap rings are produced in various sizes. This lets the technician select the proper size thrust washer for the best end play or clearance.

PUMP REMOVAL The pump assembly is the front cover that holds the gear train inside the case on RWD transmissions. Its removal allows the disassembly of the rest of the internal parts. The pump is held in place by a set of bolts. The close fit between the outer pump diameter and the case plus a rubber sealing ring and/or gasket makes pump removal a little difficult. Several methods can be used to remove the pump. These include:

- Slide hammers,
- Special screw-type pullers. ● **SEE FIGURE 15–15.**

TRANSAXLES USING INPUT CHAIN DRIVE Some transaxles use a chain and sprockets for gear train input. The main gear train is behind the valve body. Removal of these parts provides access to the driven sprocket support, which supports the input end of the gear train.

The drive chain and sprockets are exposed after the valve body and case cover/channel plate assembly have been removed. The chain should be checked for:

- Wear/link stretch—If the chain has stretched, it should be replaced.
- The master link—It may be a different color. Also note which side is up or down. ● **SEE FIGURE 15–16.**

NOTE: If the chain is replaced with the master link in the opposite position, it can be noisy. This noise will occur whenever the engine is running, even in park and neutral.

(a)

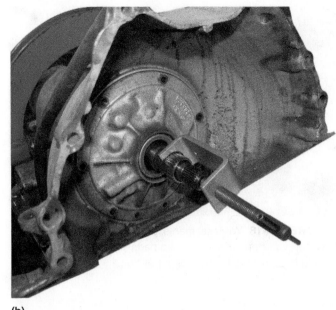

(b)

FIGURE 15-15 (a) Two slide hammers are used to removed the pump in some transmissions/transaxles. (b) A special puller being used to remove the pump.

FIGURE 15-16 The master link in this GM 4T65-E is facing upward and is colored black.

FIGURE 15-17 A snap ring being removed after the clutch piston has been compressed to allow access to the snap ring on this GM 4T65-E transaxle.

CASE DISASSEMBLY Service information should be followed for the disassembly procedure. To complete transmission disassembly, the usual procedure includes the following steps:

STEP 1 To remove a band, carefully note the position of the band struts, loosen the band adjusting screw, and remove the servo cover and piston. Remove the band struts and band. On transmissions using a clutch mounted next to the pump, remove the clutch friction, steel, and pressure plates. Be sure to note the position of the various clutch plates.

STEP 2 Remove the driving clutch assemblies. ● **SEE FIGURE 15-17.**

STEP 3 Remove the bolts retaining the extension housing, if equipped. It may be necessary to remove the snap ring and the extension housing.

STEP 4 The planetary gear train can be slid out of the case as one assembly on some transmissions. The condition of each part should be checked as it is removed.

STEP 5 If the transmission uses a center support, remove the retainer, usually a large snap ring, and lift the center support out of the case.

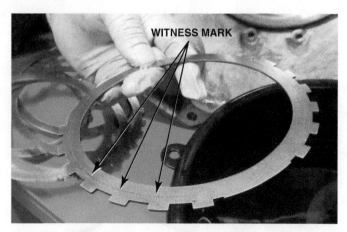

FIGURE 15–18 Witness marks are sometimes hard to see but there is often wear when two parts operate together, thus should be reinstalled in the same position.

FIGURE 15–19 The final drive assembly on a GM 4T65-E.

TECH TIP

Look for Witness Marks

Many transmissions use a drive shell that is connected to a clutch through a set of lugs, and a wear pattern will be established between them. These wear patterns are commonly referred to as *witness marks*. While reassembling, it is important to assemble them in the original position. While disassembling, it is a good practice to place index marks on both parts.
● **SEE FIGURE 15–18**.

STEP 6 As the park gear is removed, the gear and park pawl should be inspected for wear and damage. Also, the pawl return spring should be checked to ensure that the park pawl is moved completely away from the gear when released.

STEP 7 On rear-wheel-drive (RWD) transmissions, remove any remaining parts as required by the manufacturer's instructions. On transaxles, remove the final drive gears and differential plus any other remaining parts.
● **SEE FIGURE 15–19**.

1 For safety purposes, remove the negative battery cable before starting the transaxle removal procedure.

2 Remove engine bay cross members that may interfere with access to the transaxle fasteners.

3 Remove the air intake and air filter assembly, which is covering the transaxle in this vehicle.

4 Install a support for the engine.

5 Safely hoist the vehicle and remove the wheels.

6 Remove the retaining nut from the drive axle shaft.

CONTINUED ▶

7 Disconnect the lower ball joint on the front-wheel-drive vehicle to allow removal of the drive axle shaft.

8 Remove the drive axle shaft from the transaxle using a pry bar.

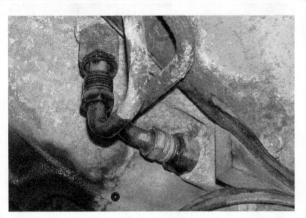

9 Disconnect the cooler lines from the transaxle using a line wrench.

10 Unbolt the torque converter from the flexplate, then remove the transaxle mounts.

11 With the transaxle supported on a transmission jack, remove the retaining bolts from the bell housing.

12 Carefully remove the transaxle from the vehicle.

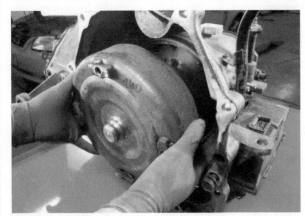

1 The torque converter is removed.

2 The input (left) and output (right) speed sensors are being removed. They are different sizes so they can't be mixed up.

3 A pressure sensor sealing ring being removed.

4 The cover for the TCM is made of rubber and is attached to the case using plastic "Christmas tree"-type clips.

5 After the pan has been removed, the filter can be accessed and then removed before removing the valve body assembly.

6 Removing the valve body.

CONTINUED ▶

7 The accumulator bores are checked for wear after removing the accumulator pistons.

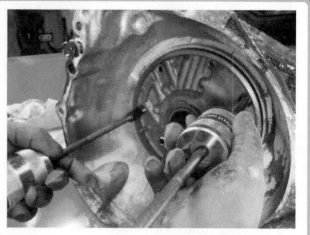

8 The pump is being removed using two slide hammers.

9 The input clutch assembly is being removed.

10 The 2/4 clutch return spring is being compressed so the retaining ring can be removed.

11 Removing the 2/4 clutch pack assembly.

12 The rear carrier assembly is removed after the retaining bolts are removed.

1 The first step before disassembling, it is preferred that the unit be mounted on a holding fixture.

2 The unit is tipped and fluid drained. The fluid looked burned and watery.

3 After removing the pan, the filter is removed.

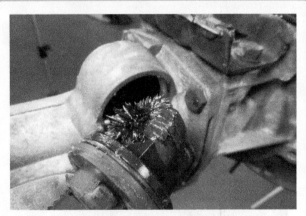

4 When the magnetic vehicle speed sensor was removed, it showed lots of metal fillings which indicates that something is worn or damaged inside the unit.

5 The pressure switch manifold being removed prior to removing the valve body.

6 The pump assembly is being removed from the unit.

CONTINUED ▶

7 Removing the input housing and shaft assembly.

8 The cause of the metal shavings was found to be an excessively worn planet carrier.

9 The reaction carrier and shaft with internal bushing being removed.

10 Removing a snap ring used to retain the low-reverse clutch assembly.

11 Removing the second gear apply piston assembly from the side of the case.

12 Visual inspection of the fluid in this unit shows that it has been overheated and, of course, there are hard parts needed to return this unit to useful service.

SUMMARY

1. Transmissions are removed to make repairs, for overhaul, or for replacement.
2. The removal procedures are similar for most transmissions and transaxles.
3. Always check the service information before removing an automatic transmission/transaxle as per the required tools and procedures that are specified.

REVIEW QUESTIONS

1. What is the difference between a transmission repair and an overhaul?
2. What parts and components may be replaced with the transmission/transaxle still in the vehicle?
3. Why is the proper identification of the automatic transmission/transaxle critical?
4. What are the steps involved in removing an automatic transmission/transaxle from a vehicle?
5. What is the difference between hard parts and soft parts?
6. How is end play measured?

CHAPTER QUIZ

1. What component or part cannot be replaced with the transmission/transaxle in the vehicle?
   - a. Torque converter
   - b. Shift solenoids
   - c. Valve body
   - d. Output speed sensor

2. What is the first step usually specified by vehicle manufacturers when removing an automatic transmission (rear-wheel drive) from the vehicle?
   - a. Remove the driveshaft
   - b. Remove the torque converter inspection cover
   - c. Disconnect the negative battery cable
   - d. Hoist the vehicle

3. What parts can usually be removed with the automatic transmission/transaxle still in the vehicle?
   - a. Pressure switches
   - b. Transmission range switch
   - c. Turbine and output speed sensors
   - d. Any of the above

4. What information is often needed when ordering parts for an automatic transmission/transaxle?
   - a. Number of bolts used on the pan
   - b. VIN/Tag number
   - c. The length of the extension housing
   - d. The diameter of the torque converter

5. Some states have rules and regulations that define what an automatic transmission rebuild or overhaul must include when performing which service or repair?
   - a. Fluid exchange service
   - b. Filter replacement
   - c. Overhaul
   - d. Extension housing seal replacement

6. What can be used to prevent the converter from sliding off its splines and falling as the transmission is being removed?
   - a. Keep the torque converter attached to the flexplate
   - b. Pack assembly lube into the splines
   - c. Use a retaining bracket
   - d. Tilt the transmission upward at the rear

7. An overhaul kit may be called _____ depending on the parts that are included.
   - a. Compliance kit
   - b. Master kit
   - c. Overhaul kit
   - d. Any of the above

8. After the automatic transmission/transaxle has been removed from the vehicle, many service technicians use _____ to clean the road grime and dirt from the unit before starting disassembly.
   - a. A power washer
   - b. Hot soapy water and a steel wire brush
   - c. An acid bath
   - d. A scraper and a used tooth brush

9. It is standard practice to _____ before removing the pump assembly.
   - a. Remove the extension housing
   - b. Remove the direct (forward) clutch assembly
   - c. Check end play
   - d. Loosen the band adjustment

10. What is the preferred tool to use when removing a pump?
    - a. A chain
    - b. Slide hammers
    - c. Special screw-type puller
    - d. Either b or c

chapter 16

VALVE BODIES AND VALVE BODY SERVICE

After studying this chapter, the reader will be able to:

1. Prepare for ASE Automatic Transmissions (A2) certification test content area "A" (General Transmission and Transaxle Diagnosis).
2. Describe the purpose and function of the valve body.
3. Describe the parts and operations of a valve body.
4. Discuss valve body service and replacement procedures.

Actuator 266
Accumulator 268
Check ball 266
Free fall test 272
Manual valve 266
Orifice 267

Rooster comb 266
Separator plate 265
Shift valve 268
Valve body 265
Worm tracks 265

FIGURE 16-1 A typical valve body as installed on a GM 4T65-E transaxle.

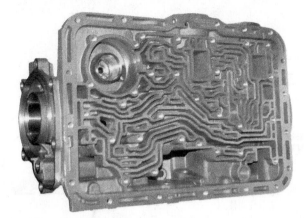

FIGURE 16-2 A typical upper valve body showing the fluid passages ("worm holes").

VALVE BODY

PURPOSE AND FUNCTION The **valve body** enables an automatic transmission/transaxle to operate automatically and is often referred to as the "brain" of the transmission. It supplies the force to apply the clutches, bands, and the valves that control pressure and direct the fluid for automatic shifts. A valve body is where most of the hydraulic valves in a transmission/transaxle are located, and is attached to the case with bolts. Valve bodies can be made of either cast aluminum or cast iron. The valve body in most rear-wheel-drive transmissions is located inside the transmission oil pan at the bottom of the case. A transaxle valve body may be at the bottom of the case, on the backside of the torque converter housing, or on the top or side of the transaxle housing depending on the specific application. ● SEE FIGURE 16-1.

FUNCTIONS OF A VALVE BODY The basic functions of the valve body assembly include:

- Schedule shifts to optimize engine performance
- Safely shift into reverse when requested
- Provide driver control of the operating ranges
- Provide for proper shift timing
- Provide engine braking to help control vehicle speed on downgrades
- Lock or unlock the torque converter clutch

PARTS Valve bodies have many fluid passages for the various transmission hydraulic circuits cast into them.

These are sometimes called **worm tracks** or *worm holes*.
● SEE FIGURE 16-2.

Some of these passages may be widened to form pockets that contain steel, nylon, or rubber check balls. Most valve bodies consist of two cast sections that bolt together with a flat metal separator plate between them.

- The upper section of the valve body is part of the transmission case and is often called the case side.

- The **separator plate**, also called a *transfer plate*, *restrictor plate*, or *spacer plate*, is located between the case side and the valve body side of the valve body assembly. It provides rigidity and contains calibrated drilled holes and openings that help manage fluid flow.

- The lower part of the valve body is located in the valve body itself and is often called the valve body side.

- Valve bodies contain specialized valves and circuits that are particular to a specific transmission.

Electronic solenoids are used in place of some valves on electronically controlled transmissions/transaxles. Some transmissions/transaxles incorporate the transmission control module (TCM) right on the valve body. This eliminates the wiring harness between the TCM and the solenoids, which in turn eliminates connector problems.

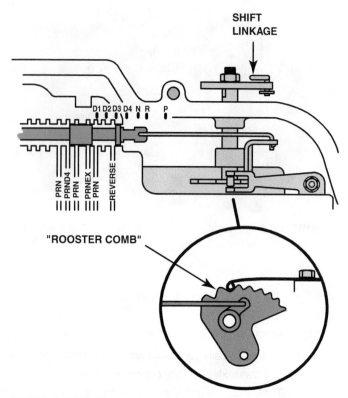

FIGURE 16–3 A rooster comb is the detent that helps retain the manual valve in the various positions in the valve body.

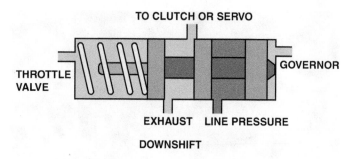

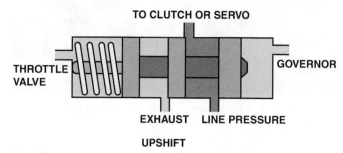

FIGURE 16–4 A typical shift valve has a spring to move the valve to a downshift position where the throttle pressure works with this spring. When governor pressure gets high enough, the valve will move to an upshift position.

MANUAL VALVE

PURPOSE AND FUNCTION The **manual valve** is the only hydraulic valve in the transmission that is "manually" controlled by the driver and therefore, it is called a "manual valve" or sometimes *selector valve*. It controls the fluid flow to the band servos and to clutch apply pistons for drive, low, and reverse gears plus to the shift valves. It receives the fluid from the pump at line pressure. This valve is connected to the shift lever in the driver's compartment.

OPERATION The manual valve is moved by mechanical linkage when the driver moves the shift lever. The valve is held in position by the detent cam at the valve body. This detent is a spring-loaded roller or ball that drops into notches in the cam to position the manual valve properly in its bore. The detent cam is commonly called a **rooster comb**. ● **SEE FIGURE 16–3**.

When the gear selector is in neutral or park, fluid flow through the manual valve is blocked by a land or trapped between two lands. In the other gear selector positions, the valve is moved to allow fluid flow through the valve to various valves and friction-apply circuits. Most three- and four-speed transmissions have six gear selector positions. Some four-speed transmissions have seven positions that allow

fourth-gear operation in overdrive and limit the transmission to first- through third-gear operation in drive.

Nearly all transmissions also have one *shift valve* for each automatic upshift. ● **SEE FIGURE 16–4**.

The largest volume of fluid flow is to the **actuator**, which is usually a hydraulic piston. The hydraulic actuators of an automatic transmission are the servos that apply and release the bands and the pistons that apply the clutches.

In automatic transmissions, the valves are positioned so that fluid pressure is exerted on the actuator piston all the time that the actuator is applied. When the actuator is released, fluid pressure is exhausted. ● **SEE FIGURE 16–5**.

CONTROL VALVES

CHECK BALLS A **check ball** is the simplest device for controlling fluid flow. A *one-way check valve* resembles a steel bearing or plastic ball located over a hole in the separator plate. ● **SEE FIGURE 16–6**.

An upward fluid flow moves the ball aside and fluid flows around it. A downward fluid flow forces the ball against the hole and stops the flow. The flow of fluid is possible in only one direction, upward. Often there are check balls in both the case side and valve body side of the valve body assembly. ● **SEE FIGURE 16–7**.

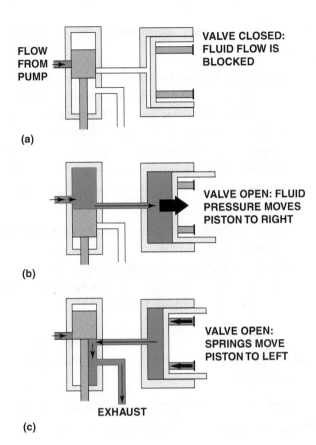

(a)

VALVE CLOSED:
FLUID FLOW IS
BLOCKED

FLOW
FROM
PUMP

(b)

VALVE OPEN: FLUID
PRESSURE MOVES
PISTON TO RIGHT

(c)

VALVE OPEN:
SPRINGS MOVE
PISTON TO LEFT

EXHAUST

FIGURE 16–5 Operation of the valve controls fluid flow to the actuator. It can (a) block operation, (b) cause apply, or (c) cause release.

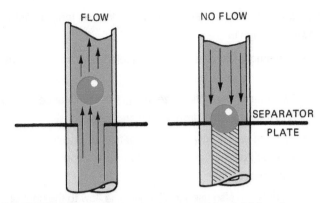

FLOW   NO FLOW

SEPARATOR
PLATE

FIGURE 16–6 A check valve is opened by fluid flow in one direction (left) and closes when the fluid tries to flow in the reverse direction.

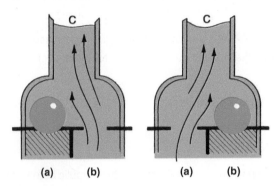

C   C

(a)   (b)   (a)   (b)

FIGURE 16–8 When fluid flows through this shuttle valve from port B to port C, the check ball moves over to close port A (left). Fluid flow from port A will close port B (right).

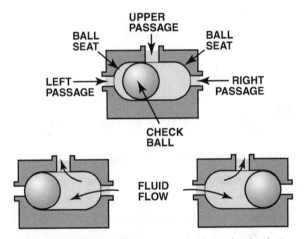

UPPER
PASSAGE

BALL
SEAT

BALL
SEAT

LEFT
PASSAGE

RIGHT
PASSAGE

CHECK
BALL

FLUID
FLOW

FIGURE 16–7 Check balls are used in the valve body to allow hydraulic circuits to share a common passage.

> ### TECH TIP
>
> **Do Not Use a Magnet on Check Balls**
>
> It is easy to use a magnet to retrieve the steel check balls out of the pockets in the valve body. However, using a magnet or placing the steel check balls in a magnetic tray may cause them to become magnetized. If the balls become magnetized, they may be attracted to the steel separator plate and not be free to move to block passages as designed.

Check balls are usually made from steel, but they can be made of nylon, rubber, or some composite material as well. The type of material used depends on the manufacturer and application. Steel balls generally hold up better, but cause greater seat wear because of their hardness. The softer composite balls are easier on seats and they cannot be magnetized.

Some transmissions use a *two-way check valve,* also called a *shuttle valve.* The ball is positioned above two side-by-side holes with another flow passage extending upward or to the side. Upward flow through one of the holes in the plate causes the ball to move over and seal the other hole. Fluid flow upward through the second hole causes the ball to move over and seal the first hole. ● **SEE FIGURE 16–8.**

ORIFICES   An **orifice** is simply a small hole, usually in the separator plate. An orifice produces a resistance to fluid flow and therefore causes a pressure drop as long as fluid is flowing through it.

- The amount of pressure drop is relative to the size of the orifice and the flow volume.
- The smaller the orifice size, the greater resistance to flow and the larger the drop in fluid pressure.
- As soon as the flow stops, the orifice no longer has an effect on the flow, and the pressure on both sides becomes equal.
- An orifice is also used to dampen fluid flow to the control valves. There is usually one in the passage between the pump and reaction land of the pressure regulator valve and this orifice helps soften pressure pulses from the pump that can cause the valve to overreact. ●**SEE FIGURE 16–9.**

SPOOL VALVES The fluid flow from the pressure regulator valve to the manual valve and into the control circuit can be called

- Mainline pressure
- Line pressure
- Control pressure.

Flow to and from a transmission hydraulic actuator is controlled by one or more valves. Spool valves sliding in a round bore are used for this purpose. A spool valve can be made from steel or aluminum. They usually have two or more lands that fit the valve bore tightly enough so that fluid cannot escape past the valve land but loosely enough so that the valve can slide freely in the bore.

- The valleys or grooves between the lands serve as fluid passages. Typically the valve-to-bore clearance is about 0.003 to 0.004 inch (80 to 100 μm). The close fit requires the valve to expand and contract at the same rate as the valve body. This prevents the valve from sticking or having excessive leakage. The outer edges of the lands have sharp corners to help prevent debris from wedging between the land and the valve bore.
- The faces serve as pressure surfaces, also called *reaction surfaces*, to produce valve movement. Some valves are relatively long with a series of lands and grooves so fluid flow through two or more passages are controlled at the same time. ●**SEE FIGURE 16–10.**

HYDRAULIC SHIFT VALVES A **shift valve** is a spring-loaded spool valve that controls the transmission upshift and downshift circuits.

- Throttle pressure works against one side of the valve.
- Governor pressure works against the other side.
- When one pressure is greater than the other, the valve moves to the upshift or downshift position and the valve lands uncover the ports to the relative circuits.

Transmission shift valves may be referred to as "snap valves" because they shift almost instantly in response to

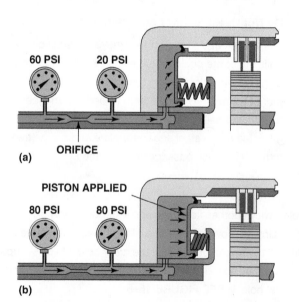

(a)

(b)

FIGURE 16–9 (a) An orifice will cause a pressure drop as fluid flows through; (b) when the flow stops, the pressure on both sides of the orifice will be the same.

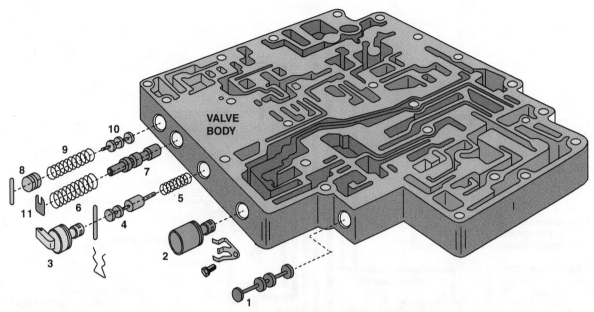

1 VALVE, MANUAL

2 VALVE ASSEMBLY,
  PRESSURE CONTROL SOLENOID

3 VALVE ASSEMBLY,
  TCC PWM SOLENOID

4 VALVE,
  TCC REGULATOR APPLY

5 SPRING, TCC REGULATOR APPLY VALVE

6 SPRING, ACTUATOR FEED LIMIT VALVE

7 VALVE, ACTUATOR FEED LIMIT

8 PLUG, ACCUMULATOR VALVE BORE

9 SPRING, ACCUMULATOR VALVE

10 VALVE, ACCUMULATOR

11 RETAINER, ACCUMULATOR FEED LIMIT VALVE SPRING

FIGURE 16–10 A typical valve body showing some of the valve and solenoids as well as the clips and pins used to retain the parts in the valve body.

pressure differential changes. Since these valves cause upshifts and downshifts, they are also known as "event-causing valves." There are only two positions for a shift valve:

- Fully to one end of the stroke or
- Fully to the other end of the stroke

Otherwise, hydraulic pressure could apply control devices for two gears at once and damage the transmission. ● **SEE FIGURES 16–12 AND 16–14** on page 272.

VALVE BODY SERVICE

PURPOSE   Despite its complexity, the valve body is one of the more reliable parts in a transmission, probably because the valves are so well lubricated. In a way, valves do little, as they move only slightly and only once in a while. The biggest "enemies" of a valve body include

1. Dirt (from dirty fluid or dirt getting into the fluid through the dipstick tube or opening).

2. Overheated fluid, which can cause varnish buildup on the valves and bores.

3. Solenoids can fail and, being magnetic, can attract iron and steel particles which can restrict their flow and prevent them from working properly in many cases.

4. All filter screens should be replaced and are usually included in most overhaul kits.

Most valve body service operations consist of the following:

- disassembly
- cleaning
- checking for free movement
- replacing defective solenoids
- replacing all filter screens
- reassembly. ● **SEE FIGURE 16–15** on page 273.

VALVE RETAINING METHODS   Several methods are used to retain the valve(s) in a bore.

- Many units use a cover plate that holds one or more valves. Removal of the retaining screws allows removal of the plate, valve(s), and spring(s).

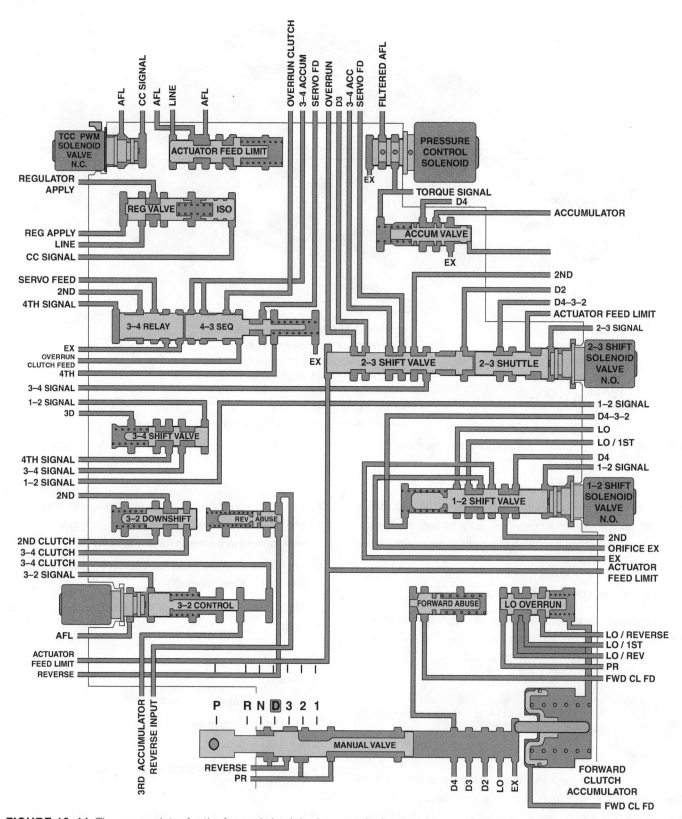

FIGURE 16–11 The accumulator for the forward clutch is shown at the lower right part of this valve body.

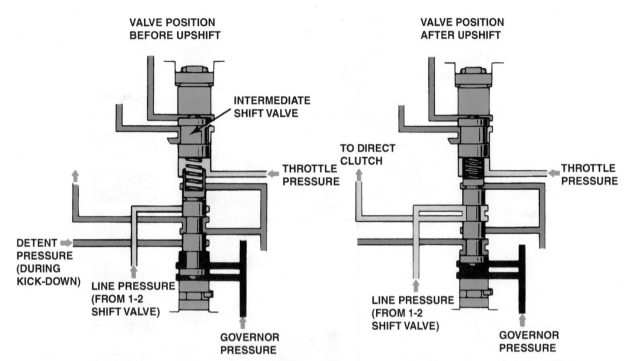

VALVE POSITION BEFORE UPSHIFT

VALVE POSITION AFTER UPSHIFT

INTERMEDIATE SHIFT VALVE

TO DIRECT CLUTCH

THROTTLE PRESSURE

THROTTLE PRESSURE

DETENT PRESSURE (DURING KICK-DOWN)

LINE PRESSURE (FROM 1-2 SHIFT VALVE)

LINE PRESSURE (FROM 1-2 SHIFT VALVE)

GOVERNOR PRESSURE

GOVERNOR PRESSURE

FIGURE 16–12 Shift valves move when there is a difference in pressure. In a hydraulically controlled automatic transmission/ transaxle, the shift valves compare governor pressure force against throttle valve (TV) pressure force to determine when to upshift or downshift.

 REAL WORLD FIX

The Case of the Stalling Ford

A 2000 Ford Mustang (61,000 mi) came in with a complaint of stalling when shifted to drive after the transmission warmed up. A scan-tool check showed no unusual activity of the shift or TCC solenoids. The TCC solenoid seemed sticky so it was replaced along with the Manual Lever Position Sensor (MLPS), which did not help. The valve body was checked, and several of the aluminum valves were severely scored and worn. Valve body replacement fixed this problem.

- Many valves use a plug or sleeve at the end of each bore. The plug/sleeve is retained with a keeper, which can be a pin, plate, or key. Some valve bodies use a coiled spring pin (roll pin) to hold the valve plug/sleeve in place. In some cases, this coiled pin can be pulled out by gripping it with a pair of pliers or using an extractor tool.

VALVE BODY CHECKS AND TIPS Most technicians place a lint-free shop cloth(s) or a carpet scrap under the valve body while disassembling it. The cloth helps keep the check balls, screws, and pins from rolling away and might prevent a nick or dent in a valve if one happens to drop.

 **TECH TIP**

Technician-Made Valve Body Organizer

Some technicians make a valve organizer by folding a piece of cardboard into an accordion shape. The biggest problem during valve body repair is getting it back together with everything in the right order and location and using something like this helps with the organization. ● **SEE FIGURE 16–13**.

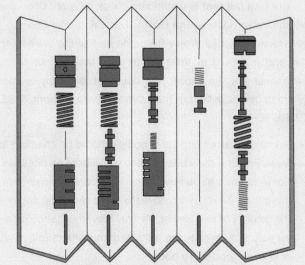

FOLDED CARDBOARD VALVE HOLDER

FIGURE 16–13 A sheet of stiff paper has been folded to create this simple valve holder. Note that a valve group can be placed in order and be labeled.

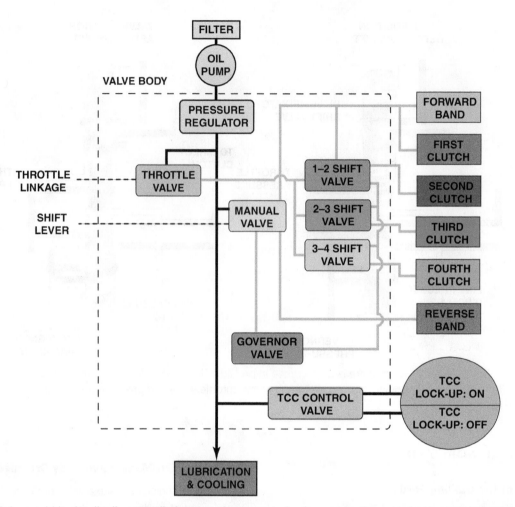

FIGURE 16–14 In an old hydraulically controlled automatic transmission/transaxle, the valve body contains valves that control fluid pressure and flow to various apply devices that, in turn, produce proper shifts at the proper time.

The **free fall test** is a standard check for a sticking valve. Hold the valve body so the bore is vertical. In this position, a steel valve should fall freely from one end of the bore to the other and it should at least fall through the area of normal valve movement. Any valve that does not fall freely is sticking, which can be a fault of the valve, the bore, or both. ● SEE **FIGURE 16–16.**

- Aluminum valves and valve bodies should be checked for wear. Position the valve as deep in the bore as possible. Some valves can be inserted into the bore backward for this check. Next, try to move the valve vertically, and note the amount of movement. Vertical movement should be very small. Compare the amount of movement to a new or known-good valve body.

- A wet air test can also be used to check for wear. Valve body wear can also be checked using a vacuum test;

more information for this test can be found at www.sonnax.com/

- Fluid can leak out of the end of the bore, past the plug. If a round, aluminum plug is used, it can be enlarged by using a tubing cutter to score a groove around the plug. This displaces and raises metal and should create a tighter fit.

- Short valves that are located between fluid pressure and a spring tend to tip in the valve bore. This can cause ridges in the bore, leading to jamming of the valve.

- Carefully inspect the valve and valve body for varnish, which can be a light brown or golden brown coating. It can be cleaned off with brake cleaner. ● SEE **FIGURE 16–17.**

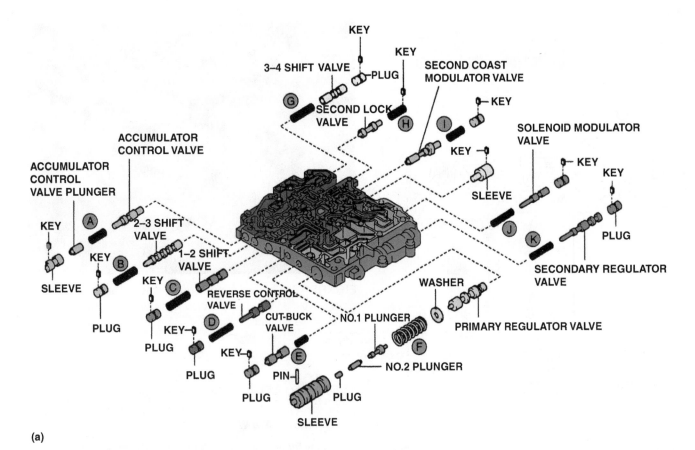

(a)

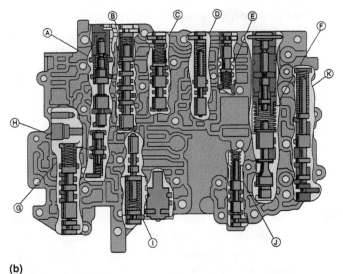

(b)

FIGURE 16–15 (a) An exploded and (b) cutaway view of the valve body from a four-speed transaxle. Note the various valve groups and how they are retained in their bore.

- If a valve is smooth but still sticks in the bore, carefully examine the bore for debris or nicks that might cause raised metal.

- A valve that has excessive movement, such as a pressure regulator valve, can wear into the bore and cause excess leakage.

? FREQUENTLY ASKED QUESTION

How Is a Solenoid Tested That Has a Diode Across the Leads?

Some solenoids include a diode to eliminate voltage spikes that might occur when the solenoid is de-energized. As the solenoid is tested, the diode is also checked to see if it allows a flow in one direction but not in the other.

Measure the solenoid coil resistance with the analog (needle-type) ohmmeter, the reading should be about 20 to 40 Ω depending on the coil temperature. If the reading is less than 20 Ω, the coil or diode is shorted. If the reading is greater than 40 Ω or infinite, there is an open or broken circuit. In either case, the solenoid is faulty.

To check the diode, reverse the meter leads. The meter reading should now be lower than it was before, usually about 2 to 15 Ω. If the reading does not change, the diode is open or shorted, and the solenoid is faulty.

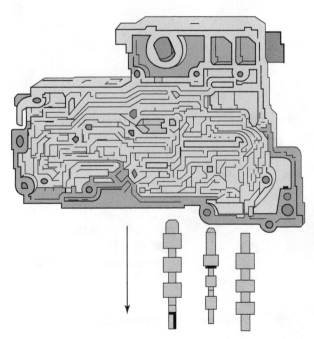

FIGURE 16–17 A valve body being washed and air dried in a parts washer. It will be cleaned again when the two major parts are separated.

FIGURE 16–16 If the valve body is moved to a vertical position, steel valves should slide freely from the bore. Be prepared to catch the valves when making this check.

TESTING SHIFT SOLENOIDS   Shift solenoids control the pressure force which in turn controls the position of the shift valve.

To test a solenoid, perform the following steps:

STEP 1   Disconnect the solenoid connector and connect one ohmmeter lead to each of the solenoid electrical terminals.

STEP 2   Read the resistance, and compare the reading to the specifications.

STEP 3   Move one of the leads to the solenoid body or base to check the ground circuit.

NOTE: A two-wire solenoid should not have continuity to ground. A single-wire solenoid will be grounded through the solenoid case, and it should have continuity when one of the ohmmeter leads is connected to the case and the other to the solenoid terminal.

STEP 4   A quick solenoid check is to apply power to the solenoid and listen for a click. This is done by connecting a jumper wire from the solenoid lead to the battery for a single-wire solenoid. A two-wire solenoid will also need to be grounded. The solenoid should click indicating the coil windings are complete and the plunger is moving. ● **SEE FIGURE 16–18.**

CAUTION: Do not perform this quick check on a PWM solenoid because the lower coil resistance will allow excessive current flow that can damage the solenoid.

STEP 5   The mechanical operation of a solenoid also should be checked. Because solenoids are basically electromagnets operating in an area that might have some metal debris, they tend to attract metal particles. These can cause sticking or binding of the solenoid plunger or blocking of the fluid passage. Test the solenoid by blowing air into the fluid passage while energizing and de-energizing the coil. ● **SEE FIGURE 16–19.**

VALVE BODY REPAIR KITS   A kit has been developed to repair some valve bores. This kit contains a drill jig (reamer

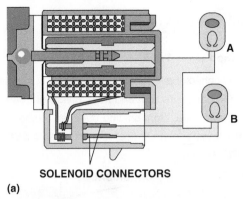

(a)

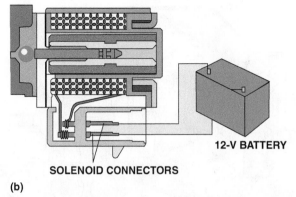

(b)

FIGURE 16–18 (a) Ohmmeter A is checking for a grounded solenoid coil; the reading should be infinite. Ohmmeter B is measuring the coil resistance; it should be within the specifications for this solenoid. (b) Connecting a solenoid to a 12-V battery should cause it to operate. Make sure the battery is connected using the correct polarity in case the solenoid has an internal diode.

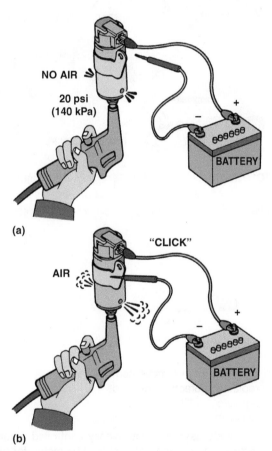

FIGURE 16–19 Air should not be able to flow through this solenoid if it is not activated. If it is connected to a 12-V battery, it should make a "click," and air should be able to flow through it.

guide), a replacement valve, and a spring. The reamer is used to restore the bore to be round, straight, and to the correct size for the new valve.

FIGURE 16–20 Using assembly lube is a great way to keep check balls in place during the reassembly of the valve body.

REASSEMBLY   After all the valves, springs, and valve body are cleaned and the valves move freely in their bores, the valve body can be reassembled.

- The springs should be checked to make sure they are not damaged and do not have distorted coils.

- Each valve should be dipped in ATF before installation. The reassembly procedure is generally the reverse of the disassembly procedure. As each valve is installed, make sure that it moves freely in its bore.

- Ensure that all check balls and filter screens are replaced in their proper locations. ● **SEE FIGURE 16–20.**

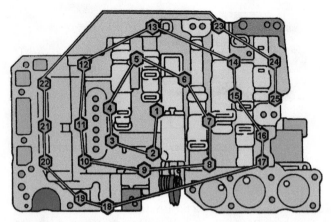

FIGURE 16–21 The valve body bolts should be tightened in order, starting from the center and working in an outward spiral.

- Be sure to tighten each fastener to the correct torque.
  ● SEE FIGURE 16–21.

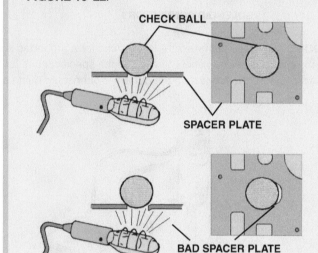
SUMMARY

1. The valve body is often referred to as the brain of the automatic transmission because the valves in the valve body are used to apply and release clutches and bands.

2. Various types of valves are used to direct the fluid flow and regulate the pressures used to operate the transmission, including spool valves and check balls.

3. Most valve body service operations consist of the following:

- disassembly
- cleaning
- checking for free movement
- replacing defective solenoids
- replacing all filter screens
- reassembly.

4. All solenoids used in electronically controlled automatic transmissions and transaxles should be tested for proper operation during valve body service.

REVIEW QUESTIONS

1. What is the purpose and function of a valve body?
2. Where is the separator plate located?
3. What does an accumulator do?
4. What is the purpose and function of orifices and check balls?
5. What is the free fall test?
6. What steps are needed to be performed to test solenoids?

1. The purpose and function of a valve body includes
   _____.
   a. Schedule shifts to optimize engine performance
   b. Provide for proper shift timing
   c. Safely shift into reverse when requested
   d. All of the above

2. Valve bodies have many fluid passages for the various transmission hydraulic circuits cast into them, and they are called _____.
   a. Manual valve passages
   b. Worm holes or worm tracks
   c. Control pressure lines
   d. Actuator channels

3. What part separates the lower valve body from the upper valve body?
   a. Separator plate
   b. Divider
   c. Valve body channel
   d. Valve springs

4. Where are most orifices located?
   a. In the valve body channel
   b. Under the valve springs
   c. In the separator plate
   d. Between the gaskets

5. An accumulator _____.
   a. Cushions a shift
   b. Applies fluid pressure to a clutch or band
   c. Releases fluid pressure from a clutch or band
   d. Increases fluid pressure

6. What valve body service operations are usually performed?
   a. Disassembly
   b. Cleaning
   c. Replacing all filter screens
   d. All of the above

7. The biggest "enemies" of a valve body include
   _____
   a. City and highway driving
   b. Cold ATF
   c. Dirt and overheated fluid
   d. Magnetism

8. The free fall test is a standard check for _____
   a. Check balls   c. Accumulators
   b. Shift valves   d. Shift solenoids

9. Technician A says that if a check ball is magnetized, it may not work as designed. Technician B says a solenoid is magnetic and can attract metal particles and affect its operation. Which technician is correct?
   a. Technician A only
   b. Technician B only
   c. Both technicians A and B
   d. Neither technician A nor B

10. What can be used to make sure that a check ball is properly seated to a spacer plate?
    a. A magnet
    b. A light
    c. Low pressure air from an air nozzle
    d. ATF from a squirt can

chapter 17

TRANSMISSION/ TRANSAXLE ASSEMBLY AND INSTALLATION

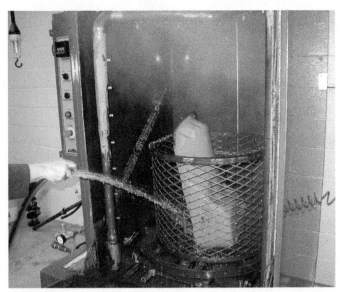

FIGURE 17–1 A pressure jet washer is similar to a large industrial-sized dishwasher. This type of cleaning unit can be used for most automotive components including engines and transmissions. Each part is then rinsed with water to remove chemicals or debris that may remain there while it is still in the tank.

COMPONENT CLEANING

CLEANING OPTIONS The internal parts, case, and extension housing are cleaned after disassembling. Some technicians set major components aside to be thoroughly cleaned as they are disassembled and serviced. Cleaning methods that are commonly used include:

- Hot spray wash
- Solvent wash
- Water (aqueous) solution wash
- Microbe cleaning

The parts should be dried using compressed air after washing. Each technician or shop has a preferred method of cleaning.

HOT SPRAY WASHING A hot spray wash cabinet resembles a large dishwasher. The parts are placed inside the cabinet, and the washer sprays the parts with a hot-water-based detergent solution as the parts are rotated. It is an effective and quick cleaner. Newer machines are designed to trap the sludge and dirt to make waste disposal easy and inexpensive. The used cleaning solution, sludge, and dirt waste is an identified hazardous waste that is carefully monitored in many areas. ● **SEE FIGURE 17–1**.

FIGURE 17–2 Transmission parts being cleaned in a water-based solvent cleaning tank.

 WARNING

The petroleum solvent–air mixture from drying the parts is highly flammable. Never use cleaning solvent around an open flame, spark, or source of ignition.

SOLVENT WASHING Solvent washing is usually done for small parts. Rubber seals, Teflon thrust washers, bands, and lined friction plates should not be cleaned in petroleum solvent because the solvent can destroy the seals and other friction materials. This method of cleaning parts is labor intensive. The parts are brushed as they are dipped or sprayed with a petroleum- or water-based solvent. Petroleum solvents are flammable and can cause redness and soreness of the skin. They are also considered pollutants because of the emissions released into the atmosphere and are treated as a hazardous waste when disposed.

WATER-BASED CHEMICAL CLEANING Because of environmental concerns, most chemical cleaning is now performed using water-based solutions (also called **aqueous-based solutions**). Most aqueous-type chemicals are silicate based and are mixed with water. Aqueous-based solutions can be used in one of two ways.

- Sprayed on
- Used in a tank for soaking parts. ● **SEE FIGURE 17–2**.

MICROBIAL CLEANING Microbial cleaning uses microbes that are living organisms (single-celled bacteria) that

FIGURE 17–3 A microbial cleaning tank uses microbes to clean grease and oil from parts.

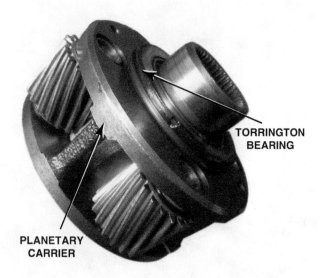

FIGURE 17–4 A Torrington bearing used to absorb thrust loads on a planetary gear set.

literally "eat" the hydrocarbons (grease and oils) off the parts being cleaned. The typical microbial cleaning system includes three steps.

1. A liquid assists the microbes by breaking the hydrocarbons to a smaller (molecular) size.

2. The microbes, stored in a dormant phase until ready for use, give an indefinite shelf life to the product. Once the microbes come into contact with the liquid, they wake up from the dormant state and begin to feed.

3. A third part is a blend of nutrients to ensure that the microbes start to multiply in the shortest possible time to help speed the cleaning time needed.

Microbial cleaning is environmentally friendly, but is slower to clean parts. ● **SEE FIGURE 17–3.**

BUSHING, BEARING, AND THRUST WASHER SERVICE

DESCRIPTION **Bushings** and **bearings** are used to support rotating shafts. **Thrust washers** are used to separate rotating parts from each other or from stationary parts. Bushings are plain metal bearings that require a flow of ATF lubricant to reduce friction. Bearings have much less friction because they have rolling members, either balls or rollers, as well as a lubricant to reduce friction. Bushing, bearing, or thrust washer failure causes wear as the hard parts turning at different speeds rub against each other.

Thrust washers can be made from plastic, fiber, or bronze- or tin-lined iron. When end-play positioning is critical or thrust loads are very high, a radial needle bearing commonly called a **Torrington** is used. This bearing type uses needle bearings to absorb the loads. These bearings must run against a very smooth, hard surface—either the face of a gear or a race. A bushing or thrust washer must have an operating clearance of about 0.003 to 0.005 inch (0.076 to 0.157 mm) to allow a good oil flow across the bearing surface. The condition of a Torrington is checked by feeling for rough operation under load. ● **SEE FIGURE 17–4.**

BUSHING REMOVAL A bushing is a metal sleeve that is lined with a soft bearing material, usually bronze, tin, or both. Any scoring, galling, flaking, excess wear, or rough operation is cause for replacement. A bushing is relatively inexpensive, but the damage caused by a worn bushing is very expensive to repair. The front (pump) and rear (extension housing) bushings are usually replaced during every transmission rebuild. If the bore is straight, the bushing is normally pressed or driven straight out the other end of the bore. The driving tool is usually a stepped disk that fits into the bushing bore and has a raised shoulder to press against the end of the bushing. Most manufacturers do not publish clearance or size specifications for bushings. Generally, anything over 0.006 inch (0.15 mm) clearance is excessive. ● **SEE FIGURE 17–5.**

BUSHING INSTALLATION Replacement bushings are available as individual items or as part of an overhaul kit.

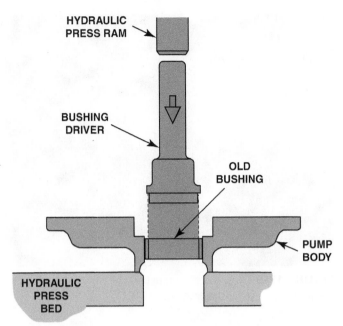

FIGURE 17–5 Worn pump bushings can be removed using a hydraulic press and a tool that applies force only to the bushing.

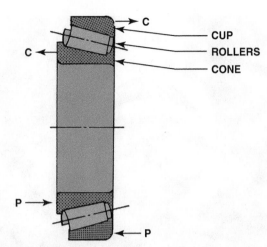

FIGURE 17–6 The cup, rollers, and cone of a tapered roller bearing are machined at an angle as shown. This allows them to resist a thrust in the direction indicated by the P arrows. The bearing is preloaded in this direction; any clearance at the sides of the bearing (C arrows) is called free play.

A bushing installer should be used to push the new bushing into its bore to prevent damaging it or the bore. This is often the same tool that was used to remove the bushing. In most cases, the bushing is placed on the tool and pressed or driven into the bore to the correct depth. Some bushing drivers have steps so they "bottom out" and stop at the correct depth. A bushing with a groove or oil passage should be aligned in the original position.

After staking a bushing (making a dent at the end using a blunt chisel), remove any raised metal with a scraping tool or sharp knife. Some bushings have a hole that must be aligned with an oil passage to permit lubrication of other parts. It is recommended to use a locking compound such as Loctite® to prevent the bushing from rotating in its bore and shutting off the lube flow.

TAPERED ROLLER BEARING SERVICE

Some transaxles use tapered roller bearings. The bearing consists of the *inner race*, *rollers*, *cage*, and *cup*. ● SEE FIGURE 17–6.

These bearings are checked by visual inspection and by rotating the cleaned and lubricated bearing with a pressure between the bearing and the cup. Any scoring or flaking of the cup or roller surfaces, or a rough feel is cause for replacement. These bearings are often press-fit onto the shaft, and the cup is press-fit into the bore. Special tools are usually required to

FIGURE 17–7 The selective spacer used at the final drive on a Chrysler 41TE. This unit uses two tapered roller bearings facing each other to support the final drive.

remove and replace the bearing and its cone. If a bearing or its cup is damaged, both should be replaced. If the bearings and cups are to be reused, they should be marked or tagged so a bearing will be installed with the original cup.

Tapered roller bearings must be adjusted to get the correct end play or preload. This adjustment is normally accomplished by changing **selective**-sized shims that can be positioned under the cup. A shim of the proper size is selected to provide the correct end play or preload. The procedure for this adjustment varies between manufacturers. ● SEE FIGURE 17–7.

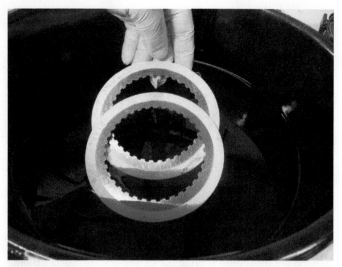

FIGURE 17–8 All lined friction material should be submerged in a shallow pan of ATF and allowed to soak before being installed in the automatic transmission/transaxle.

FIGURE 17–9 Steel plates can usually be reused if no faults are found during a visual inspection.

FRICTION MATERIAL SERVICE

LINED PLATE SERVICE   If lined plates are to be reused, they should be carefully inspected. The requirements for reuse of a lined plate include the following:

- The lining wear is minimal.
- There must be no breaking up or pock marks in the lining.
- There must be no metal particles embedded in the lining.
- The lining must not come apart when scraped with a coin, fingernail, or knife blade.
- The lining must not have a glazed, shiny appearance.
- The lining material must not be severely discolored.
- The plate must be flat.
- The splined area must be flat and even.

New lined material should be soaked in ATF for at least 20 minutes before installation and some shops soak the plates overnight. ● **SEE FIGURE 17–8.**

STEEL PLATE SERVICE   Unlined steel plates are often reused. They must be carefully inspected before reuse for the following:

- The plate must be flat (except for wave or Belleville plates).
- There must be no sign of surface irregularities.

- The notches must be flat and even.
- Slightly burned plates must be replaced or reconditioned.

A "good" steel plate is reusable. Other than cleaning, no further preparation is needed. The friction surface of the lined plate has to wear slightly until it matches the surface of the unlined plate. Too rough a steel plate surface produces severe operation and rapid friction material wear. The ideal surface finish for a used steel plate is a tumbled-finish, smooth, very flat surface like that of a new steel plate. ● **SEE FIGURE 17–9.**

BAND SERVICE   If a band is to be reused, it should be checked to ensure the following:

- The lining material is sound with no breaking up or pock marks. ● **SEE FIGURE 17–10.**
- The lining material does not come apart when scraped with a thumbnail or knife blade.

FIGURE 17–10 A badly chipped and pitted band. This band requires replacement.

- The lining thickness is almost the same as that of a new band.
- The lining material is not badly discolored or does not appear burned.
- There are no metal particles embedded in the friction material.
- The end lugs appear tight and unworn.

The drum surface for a band must also be in good condition. The drum surface should be very smooth and flat. A rough, badly scored drum should be replaced.

INTERNAL SEAL AND RING SERVICE

RUBBER SEALS An O-ring seal (round or square-cut) is first checked by placing it in the bore by itself. The seals can be checked for size by placing them one at a time in their operating position. A round O-ring should produce some drag and a square-cut seal is normal if it produces a barely noticeable drag. A lip seal is checked the same way. Just like an O-ring seal, it must produce a drag on the way into the drum, but it is okay if it falls outward when turned over. On a

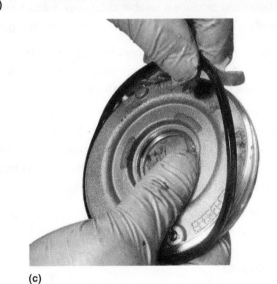

FIGURE 17–11 (a) Piston seals as supplied in an overhaul (OH) kit. (b) These seals are being lubricated in ATF before installation. (c) Installing a lip seal.

piston that uses three lip seals, each one should be checked, one at a time. A seal should never be installed dry. Both the bore and the seals should be lubricated with ATF, transmission assembly lubricant, or petroleum jelly. ● **SEE FIGURE 17–11.**

FIGURE 17–12 A round flat plastic ring is often included in overhaul kits and makes seal installation easier.

FIGURE 17–13 A dial indicator is set up to measure clutch pack clearance and then it is air checked to verify proper operation.

INSTALLING PISTONS WITH LIP SEALS

The clutch piston should be inspected before seal installation. A piston that is manufactured from sheet metal stampings should be checked for broken welds or cracks. Also make sure that the check ball moves freely in its cage and seals properly.

During installation, a lip seal often catches the edge of the bore and will roll outward. This will probably cut the seal lip and cause a fluid leak. Several procedures can be used to ease installation and produce a reliable clutch: use a wax lubricant, an installing tool, a seal guide, and compress the seal lip.

- Seal installation tools are commercially available. As the piston is being installed, use this tool to coax the seal lip into the bore. ● **SEE FIGURE 17–12.**

- Seal guides are available for some clutch units. These are smooth steel bands with a slight funnel or cone shape. They are placed in the drum and lubricated. As the piston is being installed, the guides prevent the seal lips from catching on the edge of the bore.

After the clutch is completely assembled, it should be air checked to ensure that the seals are good, the piston strokes properly, and the clutch applies and releases. ● **SEE FIGURE 17–13.**

FITTING SEALING RINGS

A sealing ring has to make a seal on one of its sides and at the outer diameter. Fluid pressure plus the elasticity of the ring pushes the ring outward, where it engages the bore. If the bore is rotating, the sealing ring rotates with the bore. Rubbing action should always take place between one side of the sealing ring and the groove. Some sliding action takes place between the ring and the bore.

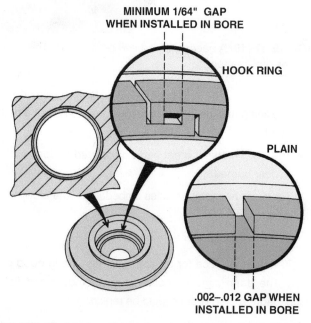

MINIMUM 1/64" GAP
WHEN INSTALLED IN BORE

HOOK RING

PLAIN

.002–.012 GAP WHEN
INSTALLED IN BORE

FIGURE 17–14 A metal sealing ring has been hooked and placed into its bore. It should enter with a slight pressure and make full contact with the bore. There should be a slight gap at the ends of the ring as shown.

End play allows the bore along with the drum to move forward and backward.

A metal sealing ring, either *open/plain end* or *hook ring*, should be checked by placing it in its bore. There should be a tight and close fit between the outer diameter of the ring and the bore. Open-end metal rings should have a slight gap, about 0.002 to 0.015 inch (0.05 to 0.3 mm), between the ends of the ring to allow for expansion of the ring metal. ● **SEE FIGURE 17–14.**

Next, check the ring in the groove. A hook- or interlock-type ring should be hooked after installation. There should be

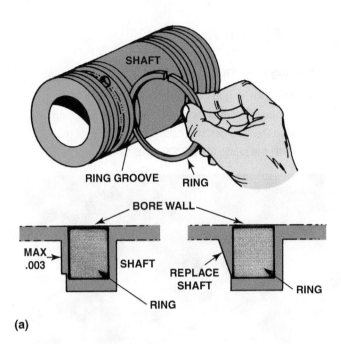

RING GROOVE RING

BORE WALL

MAX .003 SHAFT

REPLACE SHAFT

RING RING

(a)

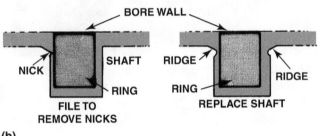

BORE WALL

NICK SHAFT RIDGE

RIDGE

RING RING

FILE TO REMOVE NICKS REPLACE SHAFT

(b)

FIGURE 17–15 (a) Side clearance of a metal sealing ring is checked by placing the ring into the groove and measuring the clearance using a feeler gauge. (b) While making this check, look for damage to the seal groove.

a maximum of about 0.003 inch (0.07 mm) of groove wear, and the sides of the groove should be smooth and straight. Small imperfections can be smoothed using a small file. Excessive or tapered wear requires shaft or clutch support replacement. ● **SEE FIGURE 17–15**.

INSTALLING TEFLON SEALING RINGS **Scarf-cut**, Teflon sealing rings are installed by placing them in the groove with the ends lapped in the correct direction. ● **SEE FIGURE 17–16**.

Uncut Teflon rings require two special tools for installation:

1. An installing tool
2. Resizing tool.

To install a Teflon ring,

- place the installing tool over the shaft
- adjust it to the correct depth if necessary
- lubricate the ring and the tool
- slide the ring over the tool and into its groove

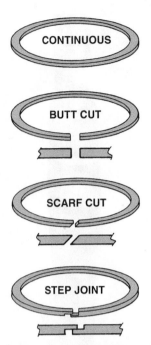

CONTINUOUS

BUTT CUT

SCARF CUT

STEP JOINT

FIGURE 17–16 Four styles of Teflon rings; the uncut, continuous ring requires special tools for installation. The other styles are placed into the groove with overlapping ends positioned properly.

The ring will stretch during installation. Next, lubricate the ring and the resizing tool, and work the resizing tool over the ring, being sure the ring enters its groove correctly. The resizing tool should compress the ring to the correct diameter. Once the transmission operates and the ring gets hot, it will take the shape of the bore. ● **SEE FIGURE 17–17**.

SUBASSEMBLIES

TYPICAL PROCEDURES Inspection, service, and repair operations are done to each of the transmission **subassemblies** as part of the transmission overhaul. Subassemblies include clutch packs, the pump, and the valve body. Most technicians disassemble the transmission and then service each of the subassemblies separately before starting to reassemble the transmission.

CASE SERVICE

FLUID PASSAGES Several areas of the case should be checked or serviced after it has been cleaned. These include the bushings, all fluid passages, the valve body worm tracks (grooves for the valve body fluid flow), all bolt threads, the clutch plate lugs, and the governor bore, if equipped.

(a)

(b)

(c)

FIGURE 17–17 (a) Using a seal installation tool allows the seal to slide down over the shaft without harming the seal. (b) After the seal has been placed in the groove, use a sizing tool to reduce the size of the seal. (c) The seal after it has been sized.

TECH TIP

Sealing Ring Tip

Warming the ring in hot water will soften the material and make installation and resizing easier. It is helpful to leave the seal-resizing tool on the seal until ready to install the shaft. ●**SEE FIGURE 17–18**.

FIGURE 17–18 Using water that has been heated in a microwave to help soften a Teflon sealing ring before installing it on the shaft.

Some cases have an output shaft bushing, and it should be checked and replaced if it is worn or scored. Occasionally a bushing will seize and spin with the shaft, which can ruin the case. The repair procedure is to ream the bore oversize and install an oversized bushing.

Every fluid passage in the case must be clean and open. It is a good practice to

- Blow air into each passage and make sure that it comes out through the other end.

- Next, plug off one end of the passage while air pressure is applied and if air is escaping, there is a leak.

WARPAGE Check for **warpage** in the worm track area. Warpage can produce a **cross leak**, which is a leak from one passage to another. A cross leak can cause an unwanted, partial application of a clutch or band that can lead to an early failure. Case warpage is checked by placing a precision straightedge over the area to be checked and trying to slide a feeler gauge between the case and straightedge. Check service information for the specified maximum warpage, which is usually less than 0.002 inch (0.05 mm).

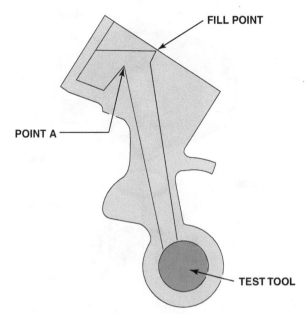

FIGURE 17–19 Filling the passage with ATF and then seeing how long it takes for the fluid to leak down to point A. A test tool instead of the component can be used to check for leakage around a bore if available.

FIGURE 17–20 A pump assembly after the cover has been removed.

FIGURE 17–21 The pump housing should be inspected for wear and replaced if grooved or damaged.

CHECK BORES   Check all bores in the case.

1. Accumulator bore size can be checked by placing the accumulator into its bore and filling the passages with ATF. The bore should be repaired if the fluid leaks out too quickly (to point A in less than 30 sec.). ● SEE FIGURE 17–19.

2. Some accumulator bores tend to wear because of repeated accumulator piston oscillation. This produces leakage at the accumulator piston and will ruin the case. A repair sleeve can be installed into the accumulator bore, and this sleeve along with a matching piston will allow the case to be reused.

BOLTS   Most faulty bolt threads are found during disassembly. It is good practice to check all bolt threads visually to make sure they are in good shape. Always replace questionable bolts. The telltale sign of failure is when the bolts come out with aluminum on the threads. If aluminum is found to be on the treads of a bolt, the threaded hole has to be repaired using a Heli-coil® or other type of thread insert.

PUMP SERVICE

STEPS INVOLVED   Servicing most pumps involves the following operations:

- Disassembly
- Inspection of the pumping members, stator support shaft, front bushing, clutch support surface, and sealing ring grooves
- Checking of all valves
- Cleaning of all fluid passages, including the drain back hole
- Replacement of the front seal and bushing
- Reassembly

To disassemble a pump, simply remove the bolts that secure the cover onto the body. ● SEE FIGURE 17–20.

VISUAL INSPECTION   Experienced technicians check a pump by visual inspection—carefully checking the areas where wear normally occurs. The pump has a high-pressure area, and this high pressure tries to force the gears outward. Inspect the following areas for wear.

- Sides of the gears or rotors
- Body and cover where the gears move. ● SEE FIGURE 17–21.

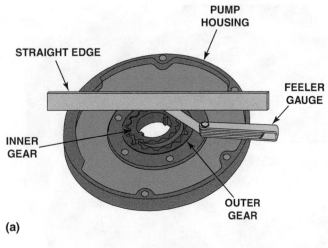

(a)

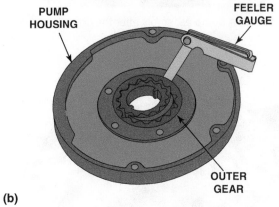

(b)

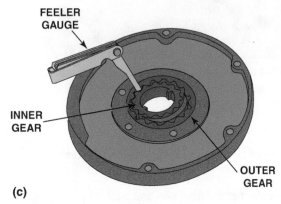

(c)

FIGURE 17–22 Clearance checks of the pump gears include (a) end clearance, (b) gear-to-housing clearance, and (c) gear-tooth clearance.

- Flanks of the gear teeth/rotor lobes for score marks
- Pump bushing

Manufacturers sometimes publish clearance specifications for the pump wear locations. These clearances can be checked using a feeler gauge. A worn pump requires replacement with a new or rebuilt unit. ● **SEE FIGURE 17–22.**

Vane-type pumps are also checked by visual inspection by checking the following:

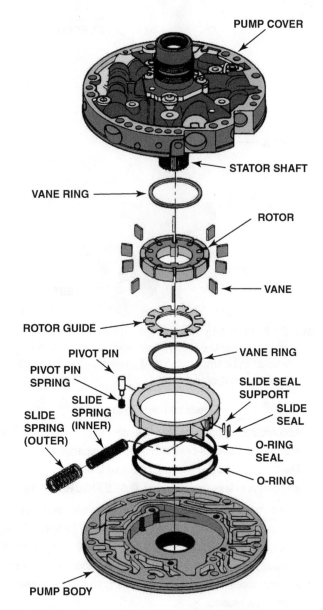

FIGURE 17–23 An exploded view of a vane-type pump. Wear checks include the rotor, vanes, slide, pump body, and pump cover.

- pump guide rings
- vanes
- rotor
- pump guide
- slide
- slide seals
- seal support
- slide pivot pin
- spring
- slide sealing ring
- backup seal. ● **SEE FIGURE 17–23.**

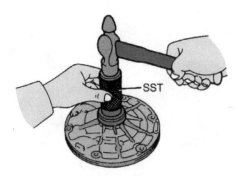

FIGURE 17–24 A new front seal is being installed using a seal driver which is a special service tool (SST).

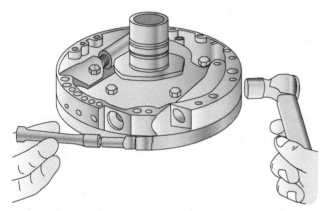

FIGURE 17–25 Using an alignment band to assemble both pump halves to ensure proper alignment. Many experts recommend lightly tapping the outer edges of the pump while tightening the clamp.

FRONT SEAL INSTALLATION The pump is disassembled usually when the front seal and bushing are to be replaced. It should be noted that some manufacturers recommend replacing the pump assembly if the front bushing is damaged. A seal driver should be used when installing the new front seal. ● **SEE FIGURE 17–24.**

ASSEMBLING THE PUMP After the pump has been cleaned, thoroughly checked, and the bushings and seal replaced, it can be reassembled. The gears or rotor and slide assembly should be well lubricated and placed in the pump body.

On some pumps, the cover has a much smaller diameter than the body. In this case, the cover is placed in position and the bolts are installed and tightened to the correct torque. Other pump covers and bodies have the same outer diameter. These diameters are only slightly smaller than the bore in the transmission case. The two outer diameters have to be exactly aligned before tightening the bolts. Pump cover alignment can be accomplished by using various commercially available band-type aligning tools or a large screw-type hose clamp. ● **SEE FIGURE 17–25.**

FIGURE 17–26 A compressor tool is usually necessary to compress the springs of the clutch piston to remove the snap ring.

CLUTCH ASSEMBLY

TYPICAL PROCEDURE The service procedure for most clutch assemblies is as follows:

- Remove the clutch plates and disassemble the return spring(s) and piston using the specified clutch compressor. ● **SEE FIGURE 17–26.**
- Thoroughly clean the parts
- Inspect the drum, piston, and check ball as well as the bushing and seal ring area
- Install new seals on the piston
- Install the piston and return spring(s)
- Soak all new friction plates in ATF
- Install the clutch plates
- Check the clutch clearance

CLUTCH PACK DISASSEMBLY Clutch plate removal first requires taking the snap ring out of its groove using a screwdriver or a seal pick. The pressure plate and clutch plates are removed next. ● **SEE FIGURE 17–27.**

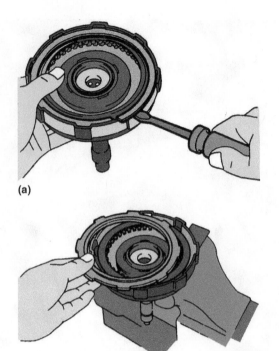

(a)

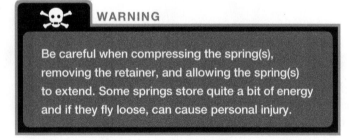

(b)

FIGURE 17–27 (a) The large snap ring can usually be removed using a screwdriver or a seal pick, and then (b) the pressure plate and clutch plates can be removed.

☠ **WARNING**

Be careful when compressing the spring(s), removing the retainer, and allowing the spring(s) to extend. Some springs store quite a bit of energy and if they fly loose, can cause personal injury.

A spring compressor is usually required to remove the piston return spring(s) and retainer. There is a large variety of spring compressors, and no one unit will work best for all clutches, because some have a bore in the center, a shaft in the center, or are in the case. Many shops use bench- or floor-mounted spring compressors because these are usually faster.

Some clutch pistons almost fall out of the bore when the springs and retainer are removed. Other pistons have to be coaxed with air pressure in the clutch apply oil hole or by tapping the clutch drum piston side down onto a block of wood. With the piston out, remove the old seals, wash the parts in solvent, and dry them using compressed air.

The clutch check ball should be captured in its cage but still be free to rattle when shaken. It should move with either an air blast or with the use of a seal pick. Fill the drum with

FIGURE 17–28 The check ball should be free to move inside its cage. It should also seal low-pressure airflow in one direction (left) and leak in the other (right).

🚗 **REAL WORLD FIX**

The Case of the Abused Minivan

A 2004 Dodge Caravan (143,000 mi) was working fine when the fluid was replaced a few weeks ago. Since the fluid change, it got stuck in snow, and had to be rocked out. Now it moves forward in all shift lever positions, even neutral. The shift linkage was checked and found to be working normally. When the transmission was disassembled, the front clutch plates were found to have gotten so hot that they welded together. Rebuilding the transmission fixed this problem.

ATF and check that it does not leak. The check ball assembly can be removed and replaced in stamped steel drums. ● **SEE FIGURE 17–28.**

ASSEMBLING A CLUTCH PACK When the clutch parts check out and are thoroughly clean, perform the following operations:

- Soak all frictions plates in ATF. ● **SEE FIGURE 17–29.**
- Install the new seals.
- Thoroughly lubricate the seals and bore.
- Carefully install the piston completely into the bore.
- Replace the return springs and retainer.

If three piston seals are used, be sure they all face in the proper direction.

A clutch is assembled by stacking the parts in the correct order. Some units use a thick apply plate next to the piston to distribute the apply force onto the plates. The stack is an alternating series of lined and unlined plates followed by a backing/pressure plate. Some units use a wave, Belleville, or selective plate under the backing plate.

FIGURE 17–29 All new friction plates should be soaked in ATF for at least 20 minutes or until bubbles no longer rise to the surface of the shallow pan of ATF.

When a clutch pack is assembled, the clearance should always be checked and adjusted if necessary. The clearance check ensures that the clutch is assembled correctly and will produce a smooth shift. Depending on the transmission and the particular clutch, different selective parts may be used to adjust clutch clearance. The parts that can be of variable (selective) thickness are the piston, pressure plate, snap ring, apply ring, steel plate, and lined plate. Typically, a selective snap ring is used. Most manufacturers publish clearance specifications for some, if not all, of the clutches used in their transmissions. If clearance specifications are not available, use the rule of thumb that the clearance should be 0.010 inch (0.5 mm) for each lined plate.

Clutch pack clearance, also called *piston travel*, is normally measured using a feeler gauge placed between the pressure plate and the snap ring. If a waved snap ring is used, position the feeler gauge in the widest area under a wave portion. ● **SEE FIGURE 17–30**.

Clearance can also be measured using a dial indicator. Position the dial indicator and raise and lower the backing plate to measure its vertical travel, which is the clutch clearance. If a wave or Belleville plate is used, the pressure plate should be pushed downward with a light, even pressure so the cushion plate(s) is not distorted.

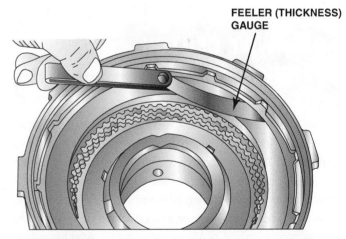

FEELER (THICKNESS) GAUGE

FIGURE 17–30 All clutch packs should be checked for proper clearance. Here, a feeler (thickness) gauge is used to check the clearance to make sure it is within factory specifications.

The clutch is ready for installation at this point. If the selective parts do not correct the clearance or are not available, clutch clearance can be reduced by using extra-thick steel plates or by adding an extra unlined steel or lined friction plate. ● **SEE FIGURE 17–31**.

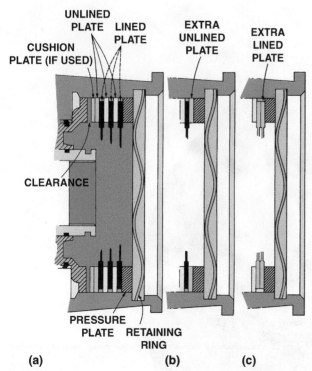

UNLINED
PLATE   LINED
PLATE
CUSHION
PLATE (IF USED)

EXTRA
UNLINED
PLATE

EXTRA
LINED
PLATE

CLEARANCE

PRESSURE
PLATE   RETAINING
RING

(a)   (b)   (c)

FIGURE 17–31 (a) and (b) Clutch clearance can be reduced by adding an extra unlined plate, or (c) lined plate. If two lined plates are next to each other as in (c), clearance can be increased by shaving the lining off one or both adjacent sides of the two lined plates.

ONE-WAY CLUTCH SERVICE

TYPICAL PROCEDURES One-way clutches (OWCs) are visually inspected during transmission disassembly and reassembly. The commonly encountered problems are severe wear from poor lubrication or metal fragments peeling from a failed part or wear or scoring of the race(s), rollers, or sprags. One-way clutches should always be lubricated using assembly grease, petroleum jelly, or ATF during assembly. After assembly, they should be tested to ensure that they rotate freely in the proper direction and lock up in the opposite direction. ● **SEE FIGURE 17–32.**

GEAR SET SERVICE

VISUAL INSPECTION Servicing gear sets is primarily a visual inspection of the various gears and a side play and rotation check of the planet gears. In some cases there

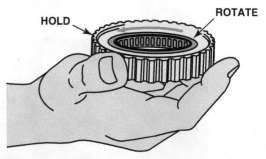

HOLD   ROTATE

FIGURE 17–32 Service information states that this one-way roller clutch shouldsbe installed as shown. Check by holding the outer race so that the inner race is free to rotate counter-clockwise as shown.

WORN
PLANET
CARRIER

FIGURE 17–33 This planetary gear set is excessively worn and wear metal form this failure has likely contaminated many other parts in the transmission.

is also an end-play check of the assembled gear train to ensure the thrust washers are not worn excessively. ● **SEE FIGURE 17–33.**

In many transmissions, the gear set comes out one part at a time. After cleanup, the parts are carefully inspected again. Parts to rebuild a planetary are available from aftermarket sources. All ring and sun gears should be checked for chipped or broken teeth and worn or stripped drive splines. The thrust surfaces at the sides of the gears and any support bushings or bushing surfaces should be checked for scores, wear, or other damage. Drive shells should be checked for stripped splines, damaged lugs, or cracks.

When checking a carrier, the pinion gears must be undamaged and turn freely. Check for worn or missing pinion thrust bushings and measure the pinion gear end play and/or side clearance. ● **SEE FIGURE 17–34.**

Some manufacturers provide pinion gear side clearance specifications, but if no specifications are available, use the rule

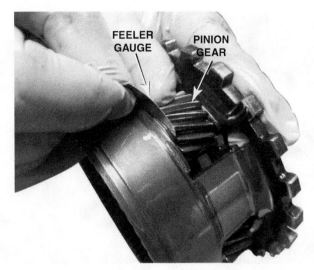

FIGURE 17–34 Using a feeler gauge to measure the pinion gear side clearance.

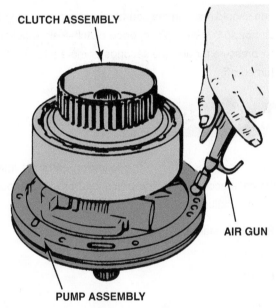

FIGURE 17–35 Air testing a clutch pack before installing it into an automatic transmission or transaxle.

of thumb of 0.005 to 0.025 inch (0.167 to 0.635 mm). In some cases, the pinion gear assembly can be removed from the carrier to replace the bearings, gear, or thrust washers. Shims are available to tighten the side clearance on some carriers.

AIR TESTING

PURPOSE OF THE TEST Air testing is a valuable diagnostic tool, which is also used as a final quality-control check during transmission assembly. Air tests are used to tell if a clutch or band servo operates, and if the passages are properly sealed. ● **SEE FIGURE 17–35.**

FIGURE 17–36 Using a rubber-tipped air nozzle in a passage to check the operation of a clutch or band.

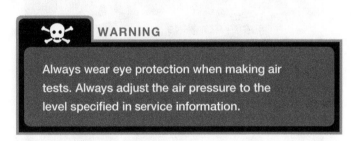

☠ **WARNING**

Always wear eye protection when making air tests. Always adjust the air pressure to the level specified in service information.

Many manufacturers provide illustrations in their service information that identifies these passages. A rubber-tipped air gun pushed against the end of the passage to make a seal is normally used when making air tests. ● **SEE FIGURE 17–36.**

It is possible to air check the whole transmission or an individual circuit by blowing air into the pressure test ports. If checking the whole transmission, insert the rubber tip of the air gun into the "line" test port, set the air pressure to about 90 PSI (620 kPa), and apply air pressure. Depending on the location of the test port in the hydraulic circuit, the airflow can be controlled using the manual valve. In some cases with the transmission on the bench, the pump will rotate, but it can be held stationary by installing the torque converter. If the transmission has pressure test ports for the different circuits, each of these circuits can be checked by pressurizing each port. While performing these checks, be sure to listen for escaping air, which indicates leaks.

As different components are air tested, the results can vary.

- **Band servos**—When air is applied, the band should apply with a very small amount of air leakage. Removal of the air gun from the passage should result in band release. Some bands require that air be used to apply the

Air Testing Tricks

Some technicians use an air gun that is modified with a piece of rubber tubing for hard-to-reach locations. An eraser with a hole drilled through the center can be used to seal passages. This makes air testing at the valve body easy. ● SEE FIGURE 17-37.

(a)

(b)

FIGURE 17-37 (a) An eraser with a hole drilled through it used to seal passages during an air test. (b) Using an air nozzle and the eraser to test hydraulic circuits at the valve body.

band and a second air nozzle position be used to release the band. When the second air nozzle is removed, the band will reapply, and when the first air nozzle is removed, spring pressure will release the band.

- **Clutches**—When air is applied to a clutch, a "kachunk" noise indicates the clutch applied. Removal of the air

FIGURE 17-38 Using an electronic torque wrench to tighten the pump retaining bolts to factory specifications.

gun should result in the sound of a clutch release. If the air nozzle is kept in place, good clutch seals should hold air pressure for about 5 seconds or more after the air is turned off.

FINAL ASSEMBLY

ASSEMBLE THE UNIT   The following parts are installed into the case according to the prescribed procedure found in service information:

- Planetary gear sets
- Clutch packs
- Bands

PUMP INSTALLATION   After the planetary gear sets, clutches, and bands are assembled, the pump is installed and the retaining bolts torqued to factory specifications. Always follow the vehicle manufacturer's specified assembly procedures and final checks. ● SEE FIGURE 17-38.

END PLAY CHECK   Perform all end play checks during assembly to ensure that the unit was properly assembled and that the proper internal clearances are achieved. ● SEE FIGURE 17-39.

TRANSAXLE DIFFERENTIALS/CHAINS   Transaxle differentials should be checked to make sure that the differential gears, thrust washers, and the differential pinion shaft are in good condition. A differential can usually be disassembled by removing the lock pin and driving the differential pinion shaft

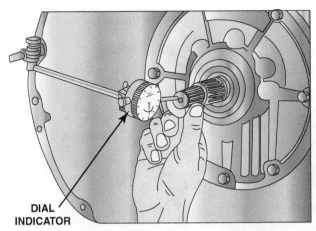

DIAL INDICATOR

FIGURE 17–39 A dial indicator being used to measure the end play of an input shaft. If the end play is not within factory specifications, the unit may not have been assembled correctly.

FIGURE 17–40 Checking gear clearance using a dial indicator on a final drive assembly on a Chrysler 41TE transaxle.

out. This allows removal of the gears and thrust washers. The gears should be inspected for chipped or broken teeth and scoring on the bearing surfaces. The thrust washers and differential pinion shaft should be checked for wear and scoring.

Some differentials are combined with a planet carrier that includes a set of planet pinions along with the differential. Like those inside the transmission, these pinion gears must turn freely on their shafts and not have excessive end play. The thrust washers and needle bearings can be replaced. If differential clearance is excessive, replace the thrust washers. In many cases, the new thrust washers will correct the clearance. ● **SEE FIGURE 17–40.**

Some transaxles use a chain/sprockets and need to be installed with the black link of the chain in the same direction (usually up) as when it was disassembled. Check service information for the specified procedure to follow.

 **TECH TIP**

TECH TIP

Avoid Using Red Assembly Lube

Assembly lube is used during the reassembly of automatic transmissions. If red assembly lube is used on seals, it may look like an automatic transmission fluid leak when the transmission gets hot and the lube melts. If you use blue, green, brown, or clear assembly lube, then the color will immediately identify it as assembly lube. ● **SEE FIGURE 17–41.**

Many transmissions have been disassembled because the service technician thought that the red liquid dripping from parts of the transmission was automatic transmission fluid when, in fact, it was only assembly lube that melted and ran when the transmission reached normal operating temperature.

FIGURE 17–41 Blue assembly lube.

VALVE BODY, FILTER, AND PAN INSTALLATION After completing all of the end play checks and air tests, the valve body can be installed. ● **SEE FIGURE 17–42.**

FINAL COMPONENTS INSTALLATION After the valve body and filter have been installed, the final components need to be installed:

- Turbine shaft seal
- Accumulators and transmission range switch
- Solenoid blocks
- Internal wiring harness
- Speed sensors. ● **SEE FIGURE 17–43.**

(a)

INTERIOR WIRING HARNESS

CASE CONNECTOR

(b)

FIGURE 17–42 (a) The valve body retaining bolts being torqued to factory specifications. (b) After the valve body has been installed, the interior wiring harness and case connector are installed. This unit is ready for the filter and pan to be installed.

 REAL WORLD FIX

The Case of the Broken Flex Plate

The 5.7-L engine in a 2005 Suburban was replaced at 185,000 miles with a reputable remanufactured engine. After 7,000 miles, it came back with a knock. Inspection revealed a broken flex plate, which was replaced. It returned again after another 7,000 miles with a knock, and another broken flex plate. A new GM flex plate was installed. It returned a third time with the same problem.

After the transmission was removed, it was discovered that the replacement engine did not come with the alignment dowels, and this omission was overlooked three times. Installation of the alignment dowels and a new flex plate solved this problem.

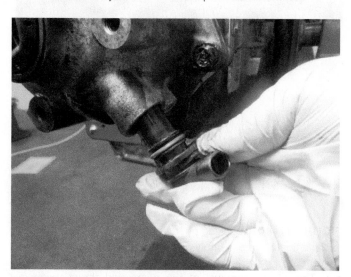

FIGURE 17–43 Installing an output speed sensor that has been equipped with a new O-ring seal.

DYNAMOMETER TESTING

- Carefully install the torque converter onto the input shaft, being sure to fully engage the following:

  1. Pump gear
  2. Stator splines
  3. Turbine splines

- Finally, conduct a visual check to make sure that all fasteners are properly tightened.

A rebuilt automatic transmission/transaxle can be tested for proper operation on a dynamometer powered by:

- An electric motor. ●**SEE FIGURE 17–44.**
- A gasoline engine. ●**SEE FIGURE 17–45.**

Most dynamometers are equipped with a load applying unit and pressure gauges so that their proper operation can be checked before installation.

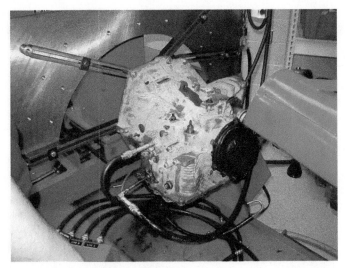

FIGURE 17–44 An electric motor-driven dynamometer being used to check the operation of a 41TE transaxle.

FIGURE 17–45 A gasoline-powered dynamometer being used to test a rear-wheel-drive automatic transmission.

TRANSMISSION INSTALLATION

STEPS INVOLVED   Installing a transmission is the reverse of the removal procedure. The last operation in the removal is usually the first step in the installation.

Installation of an automatic transmission or transaxle usually involves the following steps:

STEP 1   Before installing the transmission, make sure that the transmission alignment dowels and the wiring harness are in place and all of the connectors are properly connected.

STEP 2   Raise the transmission into position and slide it to place it against the engine.

CAUTION: Do not use the bolts to pull the transmission/ transaxle to the engine block.

STEP 3   Install the transmission-to-engine bolts and tighten them to the correct torque.

STEP 4   Place the transmission supports into position, lower the transmission onto the mounts, and tighten the mounting bolts to the correct torque.

STEP 5   Slide the converter forward to align with the flex plate. Install the bolts and tighten them to the correct torque.

STEP 6   Connect the cooler lines and tighten them to the correct torque.

STEP 7   Replace the driveshaft(s) and tighten any retaining bolts to the correct torque.

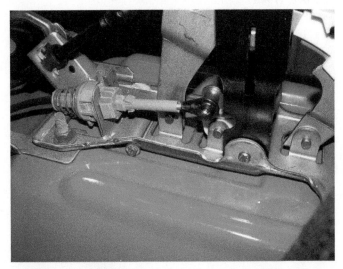

FIGURE 17–46 Check the linkage for proper adjustment so that the shift interlock works correctly and the PRNDL is aligned with the transmission range switch.

STEP 8   Reconnect all linkage and wire connections that were disconnected, making sure they are routed properly.
● **SEE FIGURE 17–46.**

After installation, the transmission should be filled with the correct amount of ATF and the engine started. Adjust the fluid level after starting the engine and operating the transmission in the different gear ranges.

FAST LEARN THE PCM/TCM   For an electronic transmission/transaxle to operate correctly, a "fast learn" or a "quick learn" should be performed with a scan tool before the vehicle is driven. This action will get the adaptive settings close to what they should be and will help prevent damage to the unit if this procedure is not done. In addition, Chrysler has a torque converter burnishing mode that can be activated on the scan tool for some models.

Adapts and fast-learn procedures should be performed if any of the following occur:

- Internal transmission repairs have been performed
- The valve body was replaced
- The control solenoid valve assembly was replaced
- The TCM was recalibrated or replaced
- Internal repairs such as replacing worn clutch friction plates were performed that could affect shift quality.

To perform a fast learn

- Use a scan tool capable of performing the fast-learn procedure. ● **SEE FIGURE 17–47**.
- Transmission fluid temperature (TFT) should be 158°F to 230°F (70° to 110°C). Move the selector in/out of gear three times.
- Select the fast learn process from the scan tool menu.
- Place the transmission in "drive" with the vehicle stationary. The TCM will individually apply the clutches and calculate the clutch volume.

FIGURE 17–47 A screen shot on a Snap-on Solus scan tool showing where to clear the adaptives prior to test driving the vehicle after an overhaul.

- Place the transmission in "reverse" with the vehicle stationary. The TCM will individually apply the clutches and calculate the clutch volume.
- Shut off the engine for at least 30 seconds.

ROAD TEST PROCEDURE Carefully drive the vehicle checking for proper operation and shift points. Hoist the vehicle and check for any possible ATF leaks before returning vehicle to the customer.

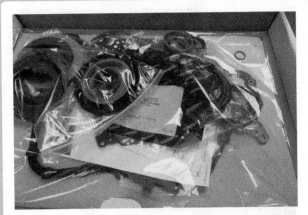

1 After cleaning all of the parts, read, understand and follow the instructions that come with the overhaul kit.

2 A new seal is installed.

3 All bearings and thrust washers should be lubricated with assembly lube during assembly.

4 The band is installed after soaking in ATF.

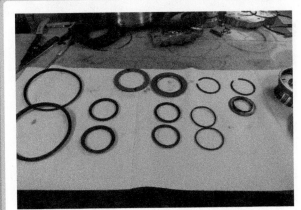

5 All of the seals being laid out and compared before being installed. They too should be covered with ATF or assembly lube before being installed.

6 All friction discs should be soaked in ATF for at least 20 minutes or until the bubbles stop.

CONTINUED ▶

7 All piston seals are replaced as part of the overhaul procedure. The piston is then installed using a lip seal plastic disc to help prevent the seal lip from curling over during installation.

8 Assembling a clutch pack with soaked frictions and then steel plates.

9 The return springs have to be compressed before installing the retaining ring.

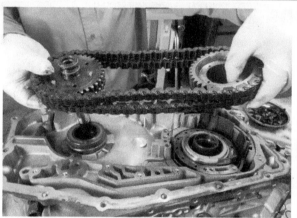

10 The drive chain being installed after checking that the black link is up the same way it was when it was disassembled.

11 Before assembling the valve body always check the valve body gasket labeled "V" and the gasket that goes against the case, label "C" to make sure that they match the ones that were removed when the unit was disassembled.

12 All fasteners should be tightened to factory specifications using a torque wrench.

SUMMARY

1. A transmission overhaul includes disassembling, cleaning, replacing worn parts, and reassembling to its original clearances.

2. Transmission parts cleaning methods that are commonly used include:
   - Hot spray wash
   - Solvent wash
   - Water (aqueous) solution wash
   - Microbe cleaning

3. Bushings and bearings are carefully checked and replaced as necessary. A bushing or thrust washer must have an operating clearance of about 0.003 to 0.005 inch (0.076 to 0.157 mm) to allow a good oil flow across the bearing surface.

4. Clutches are serviced by inspecting and replacing the friction material and seals.

5. Sealing rings must be replaced and the surfaces they seal against must be carefully inspected and serviced as needed. An O-ring should produce some drag and a square-cut seal is normal if it produces a barely noticeable drag.

6. Uncut Teflon rings require two special tools for installation:
   a. An installing tool.
   b. A resizing tool.

7. Warpage can produce a cross leak, which is a leak from one passage to another. A cross leak can cause an unwanted, partial application of a clutch or band that can lead to an early failure.

8. The pump is disassembled and inspected. The bushings and seals are replaced before reassembly.

9. When rebuilding a clutch, the friction plates, piston seals, and bushings are replaced.

10. Air testing is a valuable diagnostic tool and is also used as a final quality-control check during transmission assembly. Air tests are used to tell if a clutch or band servo operates, and if the passages are properly sealed.

11. For an electronic transmission/transaxle to operate correctly, a "fast learn" or a "quick learn" should be performed with a scan tool before the vehicle is driven.

REVIEW QUESTIONS

1. What cleaning methods can be used to clean automatic transmission/transaxle parts?

2. What is a Torrington bearing?

3. Uncut Teflon rings require what two special tools for installation?

4. What are the two ways to check clutch pack clearance?

5. Why should clutches and bands be air checked?

6. Why does the adaptive learning need to be reset after an overhaul?

CHAPTER QUIZ

1. Cleaning methods that are commonly used include _____.
   a. Hot spray wash
   b. Water (aqueous) solution wash
   c. Microbe cleaning
   d. All of the above

2. A radial needle bearing is commonly called a _____
   a. Bushing
   b. Torrington
   c. Bearing
   d. Cup

3. Tapered roller bearings must be adjusted to get the correct end play or preload. This is usually achieved by using _____.
   a. Selective thickness shims
   b. Various sizes of races
   c. Different size rollers
   d. Different tapers used for the bearings

4. New lined material should be soaked in ATF for at least _____ before installation.
   a. 5 minutes
   b. 10 minutes
   c. 20 minutes
   d. 60 minutes (an hour)

5. What is needed to properly fit a Teflon seal?
   a. An installation tool
   b. A sizing tool
   c. Hot water to soften the ring
   d. All of the above

6. Clutch pack clearance can be checked using _____.
   a. A feeler gauge
   b. A dial indicator
   c. Either a or b depending on the clutch and access to measure the clearance
   d. Both methods should be used to insure accuracy

7. Air testing is used to _____.
   a. Check the operation of the pump
   b. Test the valve body valve operation
   c. Test the clutches and bands for proper operation and to detect possible leaks
   d. Operate the speed sensors

8. Technician A says that an end play check should be performed to make sure that the unit has been correctly assembled. Technician B says that the end play check can be used to check for proper internal clearances. Which technician is correct?
   a. Technician A only
   b. Technician B only
   c. Both Technicians A and B
   d. Neither Technician A nor B

9. What should be done when installing a transmission/transaxle into a vehicle?
   a. Make sure that the transmission alignment dowels are installed.
   b. Connect the cooler lines and tighten them to the correct torque.
   c. Check the linkage for proper adjustment so that the shift interlock works correctly and the PRNDL is aligned with the transmission range switch.
   d. All of the above

10. "Fast learn" or a "quick learn" should be performed using _____ before the vehicle is driven.
    a. Pressure gauges
    b. Dial indicator
    c. Scan tool
    d. Valve body tester

SAMPLE A2 ASE CERTIFICATION-TYPE TEST

A GENERAL TRANSMISSION/TRANSAXLE DIAGNOSIS 25 QUESTIONS

1. Two technicians are discussing an electronically controlled automatic transmission that will not go into forward or reverse gears. Technician A says that a defective computer could be the cause. Technician B says that an excessively worn torque converter clutch could be the cause. Which technician is correct?
   a. Technician A only
   b. Technician B only
   c. Both Technicians A and B
   d. Neither Technician A nor B

2. A vehicle equipped with an electronically controlled transaxle stalls whenever slowing to a stop after being driven over 20 miles (32 km). Technician A says that one of the shift solenoids could be defective. Technician B says that a torque converter clutch solenoid is likely to be defective. Which technician is correct?
   a. Technician A only
   b. Technician B only
   c. Both Technicians A and B
   d. Neither Technician A nor B

3. An electronically controlled automatic transmission operates normally in reverse but the vehicle does not shift at all when moving forward. Technician A says that a defective torque converter is the likely cause. Technician B says that a defective computer could be the cause. Which technician is correct?
   a. Technician A only
   b. Technician B only
   c. Both Technicians A and B
   d. Neither Technician A nor B

4. An electronically controlled overdrive automatic transmission is equipped with a transmission fluid temperature sensor. Technician A says that the shift points may be changed if the fluid temperature is too low. Technician B says that overdrive may be disabled if the transmission fluid temperature is too high. Which technician is correct?
   a. Technician A only
   b. Technician B only
   c. Both Technicians A and B
   d. Neither Technician A nor B

5. An automatic overdrive transmission does not shift into overdrive. It functions normally in all other gear ranges. Technician A says that the gear selector display (PRNDL) or manual linkage may not be properly adjusted. Technician B says the governor may be defective. Which technician is correct?
   a. Technician A only
   b. Technician B only
   c. Both Technicians A and B
   d. Neither Technician A nor B

6. An automatic transmission in a rear-wheel-drive vehicle does not go into either drive or reverse. Which is the most likely cause?
   a. A defective vacuum modulator
   b. A defective governor
   c. An incorrectly adjusted TV cable
   d. A defective pump

7. An automatic transmission is not shifting correctly. A check of the fluid level indicates that the fluid is full of air bubbles. Technician A says that the fluid level may be too high (overfilled). Technician B says that the fluid level may be too low. Which technician is correct?
   a. Technician A only
   b. Technician B only
   c. Both Technicians A and B
   d. Neither Technician A nor B

8. A rear-wheel-drive vehicle equipped with an automatic transmission shudders during hard acceleration from a stop. Technician A says that the transmission mounts may be collapsed causing a change in the driveshaft angle. Technician B says that a slipping direct (forward) clutch is a possible cause. Which technician is correct?
   a. Technician A only
   b. Technician B only
   c. Both Technicians A and B
   d. Neither Technician A nor B

9. Two technicians are discussing the diagnosis of an automatic transmission that is not shifting correctly. Technician A says that the mainline pressure should be checked. Technician B says that the cooler pressure should be checked if a pressure tap is available. Which technician is correct?
   a. Technician A only
   b. Technician B only
   c. Both Technicians A and B
   d. Neither Technician A nor B

10. All of the following service operations should be performed during a routine troubleshooting procedure of an automatic transmission/transaxle fault except
   a. Checking the fluid level
   b. Adjusting the TP sensor
   c. Checking the line pressure
   d. A thorough test drive

11. The line to the vacuum modulator was removed and automatic transmission fluid ran out of the hose. Technician A says that this is normal and that the line should be reinstalled as quickly as possible to avoid spilling any additional fluid. Technician B says the line should only be removed when the engine is running. Which technician is correct?
   a. Technician A only
   b. Technician B only
   c. Both Technicians A and B
   d. Neither Technician A nor B

12. ATF is observed leaking out of the bell housing area of an automatic transmission. Technician A says that the fluid may have been overfilled and it is leaking out of the vent pipe. Technician B says that the front seal may require replacement. Which technician is correct?
   a. Technician A only
   b. Technician B only
   c. Both Technicians A and B
   d. Neither Technician A nor B

13. A vehicle equipped with an electronically controlled automatic transmission has a defective throttle position (TP) sensor. Technician A says that the transmission will default to second or third gear and will not upshift regardless of how fast the vehicle is driven. Technician B says that the transmission may or may not shift differently depending on the vehicle. Which technician is correct?
   a. Technician A only
   b. Technician B only
   c. Both Technicians A and B
   d. Neither Technician A nor B

14. Two technicians are discussing an electronically controlled automatic transmission that does not shift correctly. Technician A says that a shift valve may be stuck. Technician B says that the transmission range switch may be out of adjustment. Which technician is correct?
   a. Technician A only
   b. Technician B only
   c. Both Technicians A and B
   d. Neither Technician A nor B

15. An electronically controlled automatic transmission shifts harshly. Technician A says that the electronic pressure control (EPC) solenoid may be defective. Technician B says that the torque converter clutch solenoid may be defective. Which technician is correct?
   a. Technician A only
   b. Technician B only
   c. Both Technicians A and B
   d. Neither Technician A nor B

16. During a stall test, the engine speed is lower than specifications. Technician A says that the clutch inside the torque converter may be defective. Technician B says that the engine may have a drivability problem, which would cause it to produce less than normal power. Which technician is correct?
   a. Technician A only
   b. Technician B only
   c. Both Technicians A and B
   d. Neither Technician A nor B

17. A vehicle is slow in accelerating at low vehicle speed only yet shifts at the proper speeds. Technician A says that the torque converter may be defective. Technician B says that the torque converter clutch may be slipping. Which technician is correct?
   a. Technician A only
   b. Technician B only
   c. Both Technicians A and B
   d. Neither Technician A nor B

18. A customer complained of poor fuel economy. Technician A says that the torque converter clutch may be defective. Technician B says that the automatic transmission/transaxle may not be shifting into overdrive. Which technician is correct?
   a. Technician A only
   b. Technician B only
   c. Both Technicians A and B
   d. Neither Technician A nor B

19. Technician A says that a defective brake switch can prevent the operation of the torque converter clutch. Technician B says that a fault in the engine operation can be felt as a transmission fault by many drivers. Which technician is correct?
   a. Technician A only
   b. Technician B only
   c. Both Technicians A and B
   d. Neither Technician A nor B

20. Two technicians are discussing pressure gauge readings. Technician A says that if the pressure is too low, a clogged filter or an internal leak could be the cause. Technician B says if the pressure is too high at the wrong time, such as at gear changes, an internal leakage at a servo or clutch seal is likely. Which technician is correct?
   a. Technician A only
   b. Technician B only
   c. Both Technicians A and B
   d. Neither Technician A nor B

21. After an overhaul, an electronically controlled transaxle shifts too harshly. Technician A says that the electrical connector(s) at the transaxle may not be properly attached. Technician B says that the wrong type of ATF may be the cause. Which technician is correct?
   a. Technician A only
   b. Technician B only
   c. Both Technicians A and B
   d. Neither Technician A nor B

22. A pressure test is being performed with the engine running and the gear selector in park except where stated. All of the following test results are within standard parameters except
   a. Mainline pressure is 50 PSI
   b. Governor pressure is 50 PSI
   c. Cooler line pressure is 50 PSI
   d. Low/reverse is 150 PSI (in reverse)

23. A stall test is being performed with the results shown. The specification for this vehicle is 1850 to 1950 RPM. What is the most likely cause?
    a. A weak or excessively worn engine
    b. A slipping forward clutch
    c. A defective torque converter clutch
    d. A defective or out-of-adjustment manual valve

24. Pressure gauges are attached to the transmission and the vehicle is being test driven. The pressures are all within specifications until the vehicle is accelerated rapidly and the mainline pressure decreases. Which is the most likely cause?
    a. A slipping forward clutch
    b. A defective (slipping) torque converter clutch
    c. A stuck shift valve
    d. A clogged filter

25. A vibration is being diagnosed on a rear-wheel-drive vehicle. The torque converter was separated from the flexplate and the vibration was eliminated. Which is the *most likely* cause?
    a. A worn or damaged pump assembly
    b. A defective torque converter
    c. A defective U-joint(s)
    d. A worn extension housing bushing

B IN-VEHICLE TRANSMISSION/TRANSAXLE MAINTENANCE AND REPAIR 12 QUESTIONS

26. A technician performed an automatic transmission fluid service and refilled the unit with the incorrect automatic transmission fluid (friction modified instead of highly friction modified). Technician A says that the transmission will slip. Technician B says that shudder or harsher than normal shifts are likely to occur. Which technician is correct?
    a. Technician A only
    b. Technician B only
    c. Both Technicians A and B
    d. Neither Technician A nor B

27. The pan has been removed from an automatic transmission and nonmetallic material is found at the bottom. Technician A says that it is normal to have some friction material at the bottom of the pan. Technician B says that the transmission should be disassembled to find the exact location where the wear has occurred. Which technician is correct?
    a. Technician A only
    b. Technician B only
    c. Both Technicians A and B
    d. Neither Technician A nor B

28. Two technicians are discussing the adjustment of the band shown. Technician A says that the locknut should be loosened and the adjustment screw torqued to factory specifications, and then the locknut tightened. Technician B says the adjustment screw is used to adjust the clearance between the drum and the band. Which technician is correct?
    a. Technician A only
    b. Technician B only
    c. Both Technicians A and B
    d. Neither Technician A nor B

29. When checking for excessive voltage drop of the battery ground connection, what meter selection should be used?
    a. DCV
    b. ACV
    c. Hz
    d. A

30. Technician A says that the manual linkage may get out of adjustment if an engine or transmission mount were to fail. Technician B says that the shift selector (PRNDL) should be adjusted so it matches the manual valve detents. Which technician is correct?
    a. Technician A only
    b. Technician B only
    c. Both Technicians A and B
    d. Neither Technician A nor B

31. What is the usual method to tighten the retaining bolts for the pan on automatic transmission/transaxles?
    a. Start by hand to avoid cross threading
    b. Tighten gradually
    c. A torque wrench should be used to achieve the final torque
    d. All of the above

32. A hydraulically controlled automatic transmission is not shifting correctly. Which service operation should the technician perform first?
    a. Perform a pressure test
    b. Adjust the bands
    c. Check the transmission fluid
    d. Check for proper engine vacuum

33. An electronically controlled automatic transmission is not shifting correctly. All of the following should be performed to locate the cause except
    a. Checking the transmission fluid
    b. Checking scan tool data (PID)
    c. Retrieving stored diagnostic trouble codes (DTCs)
    d. Reflashing the computer

34. Proper operation of electronically controlled automatic transmission/transaxles depends on proper charging voltage. The proper charging voltage should be _____.
    a. 5 volts
    b. 10 to 12 volts
    c. 13 to 15 volts
    d. 16 volts or higher

35. Technician A says that the cooler should always be flushed whenever replacing an automatic transmission/transaxle. Technician B says that aqueous (water-based) solvent should be used to flush a cooler. Which technician is correct?
    a. Technician A only
    b. Technician B only
    c. Both Technicians A and B
    d. Neither Technician A nor B

36. An automatic transmission/transaxle pump volume test is being performed. Technician A says that a good pump should be able to pump about 2 quarts (2 liters) in 30 seconds through the cooler. Technician B says that the engine should be operated at about 1000 RPM during the cooler flow test. Which technician is correct?
    a. Technician A only
    b. Technician B only
    c. Both Technicians A and B
    d. Neither Technician A nor B

37. Two technicians are discussing an automatic transmission fluid leak from the rear seal of the extension housing on a rear-wheel-drive automatic transmission. Technician A says that the driveshaft has to be removed to replace the seal. Technician B says that the bushing in the extension housing may also need to be replaced. Which technician is correct?
    a. Technician A only
    b. Technician B only
    c. Both Technicians A and B
    d. Neither Technician A nor B

C OFF-VEHICLE TRANSMISSION/TRANSAXLES REPAIR 13 QUESTIONS

38. Regulated air pressure is often used to test _____.
    a. Clutch packs
    b. TV adjustment
    c. Vacuum modulators
    d. Governors

39. Technician A says that all friction and steel plates in a clutch pack should be replaced during an overhaul. Technician B says that the automatic transmission fluid cooler should always be flushed when a unit is rebuilt or replaced. Which technician is correct?
    a. Technician A only
    b. Technician B only
    c. Both Technicians A and B
    d. Neither Technician A nor B

40. What part(s) should be marked before removal?
    a. Pump gears
    b. The direction the steels are installed in the clutch packs
    c. The snap rings
    d. The planetary gears

41. Two technicians are discussing removal of an automatic transmission from a rear-wheel-drive vehicle. Technician A says that the cooler lines have to be removed before the driveshaft is removed. Technician B says that the engine should be supported before removing the transmission. Which technician is correct?
    a. Technician A only
    b. Technician B only
    c. Both Technicians A and B
    d. Neither Technician A nor B

42. Two technicians are discussing overhauling an automatic transmission/transaxle. Technician A says that all rubber seals and the friction discs should be replaced. Technician B says that all the steel discs should also be replaced as part of an overhaul. Which technician is correct?
    a. Technician A only
    b. Technician B only
    c. Both Technicians A and B
    d. Neither Technician A nor B

43. Technician A says that all clutch packs should be air checked before being installed into the automatic transmission/transaxle. Technician B says that the clutch pack clearance can be checked with a dial indicator. Which technician is correct?
    a. Technician A only
    b. Technician B only
    c. Both Technicians A and B
    d. Neither Technician A nor B

44. Technician A says that selective thickness snap rings or pressure or retaining plates are used to obtain the proper clutch pack clearance. Technician B says that air checking a clutch pack will determine whether or not the clutch pack clearance is okay. Which technician is correct?
    a. Technician A only
    b. Technician B only
    c. Both Technicians A and B
    d. Neither Technician A nor B

45. Technician A says that friction discs should be soaked in ATF before being assembled in a clutch pack. Technician B says that the seals and O-rings should be soaked for several hours before being installed in a clutch pack. Which technician is correct?
    a. Technician A only
    b. Technician B only
    c. Both Technicians A and B
    d. Neither Technician A nor B

46. Proper assembly of an automatic transmission/transaxle can be verified by performing the following tests except:
    a. End play measurements
    b. Clutch pack measurements
    c. Vacuum testing the regulator valve
    d. Air pressure checks

47. Technician A says that assembly lube can be used on all seals and O-rings during assembly of an automatic transmission/transaxle. Technician B says that automatic transmission fluid can be used to lubricate seals and O-rings during the assembly of an automatic transmission/transaxle. Which technician is correct?
    a. Technician A only
    b. Technician B only
    c. Both Technicians A and B
    d. Neither Technician A nor B

48. Technician A says that pulse-width-modulated solenoids have higher resistance than shift solenoids that are simply pulsed on and off. Technician B says that all solenoids should be checked for proper resistance before the automatic transmission/transaxle is installed in the vehicle. Which technician is correct?
    a. Technician A only
    b. Technician B only
    c. Both Technicians A and B
    d. Neither Technician A nor B

49. The clutch pack clearance is less than that specified. Technician A says that too many friction discs may have been installed. Technician B says that too thin a clutch pack pressure plate may have been installed. Which technician is correct?
    a. Technician A only
    b. Technician B only
    c. Both Technicians A and B
    d. Neither Technician A nor B

50. A technician left out the wavy spring from a clutch pack. Technician A says that the shift may be too soft. Technician B says that the shift may be too harsh. Which technician is correct?
    a. Technician A only
    b. Technician B only
    c. Both Technicians A and B
    d. Neither Technician A nor B

ANSWERS

1.	d	14.	c	27.	a	40.	a
2.	b	15.	a	27.	b	41.	b
3.	b	16.	b	29.	a	42.	a
4.	c	17.	a	30.	c	43.	c
5.	a	18.	c	31.	d	44.	a
6.	d	19.	c	32.	c	45.	a
7.	c	20.	a	33.	d	46.	c
8.	c	21.	b	34.	c	47.	c
9.	c	22.	b	35.	a	48.	b
10.	b	23.	b	36.	c	49.	a
11.	d	24.	d	37.	c	50.	b
12.	b	25.	b	38.	a		
13.	b	26.	b	39.	b		

2013 NATEF CORRELATION CHART

MLR—Maintenance & Light Repair
AST—Auto Service Technology (Includes MLR)
MAST—Master Auto Service Technology (Includes MLR and AST)

AUTOMATIC TRANSMISSION AND TRANSAXLE (A2)

TASK	PRIORITY	MLR	AST	MAST	TEXT PAGE #	TASK PAGE #
A. GENERAL: TRANSMISSION AND TRANSAXLE DIAGNOSIS						
1. Identify and interpret transmission/transaxle concern, differentiate between engine performance and transmission/transaxle concerns; determine necessary action.	P-1		✔	✔	217–233	34
2. Research applicable vehicle and service information fluid type, vehicle service history, service precautions, and technical service bulletins.	P-1	✔	✔	✔	2–4; 71–73	3, 4, 5, 17
3. Diagnose fluid loss and condition concerns; determine necessary action.	P-1	✔ Fluid condition and check for leaks only	✔	✔	218–219	35
4. Check fluid level in a transmission or a transaxle equipped with a dipstick.	P-1	✔	✔	✔	219	36
5. Check fluid level in a transmission or a transaxle not equipped with a dipstick.	P-1	✔	✔	✔	220	36
6. Perform pressure tests (including transmissions/transaxles equipped with electronic pressure control); determine necessary action.	P-1			✔	230–233	37
7. Diagnose noise and vibration concerns; determine necessary action.	P-2			✔	227–229	38
8. Perform stall test; determine necessary action.	P-3		✔	✔	91–92	12
9. Perform lock-up converter system tests; determine necessary action.	P-3		✔	✔	222–223	13
10. Diagnose transmission/transaxle gear reduction/multiplication concerns using driving, driven, and held member (power flow) principles.	P-1		✔	✔	102–120	39
11. Diagnose electronic transmission/transaxle control systems using appropriate test equipment and service information.	P-1			✔	144–157	30
12. Diagnose pressure concerns in a transmission using hydraulic principles (Pascal's Law).	P-2		✔	✔	73–76	10

TASK	PRIORITY	MLR	AST	MAST	TEXT PAGE #	TASK PAGE #
B. IN-VEHICLE TRANSMISSION/TRANSAXLE MAINTENANCE AND REPAIR						
1. Inspect, adjust, and replace external manual valve shift linkage, transmission range sensor/switch, and park/neutral position switch.	P-2	✔	✔	✔	240–241	42
2. Inspect for leakage; replace external seals, gaskets, and bushings.	P-2	✔	✔	✔	239–240; 243–244	44; 56
3. Inspect, test, adjust, repair, or replace electrical/ electronic components and circuits including computers, solenoids, sensors, relays, terminals, connectors, switches, and harnesses.	P-1		✔	✔	150–157; 272–275	42
4. Drain and replace fluid and filter(s).	P-1	✔	✔	✔	236–239	41
5. Inspect, replace, and align powertrain mounts.	P-2	✔	✔	✔	241–242	40
C. OFF-VEHICLE TRANSMISSION AND TRANSAXLE REPAIR						
1. Remove and reinstall transmission/transaxle and torque converter; inspect engine core plugs, rear crankshaft seal, dowel pins, dowel pin holes, and mating surfaces.	P-1		✔	✔	249–250; 257–258; 297–298	45
2. Inspect, leak test, and flush or replace transmission/transaxle oil cooler, lines, and fittings.	P-1		✔	✔	236–239	43
3. Inspect converter flex (drive) plate, converter attaching bolts, converter pilot, converter pump drive surfaces, converter end play, and crankshaft pilot bore.	P-2		✔	✔	93–95	14
4. Describe the operational characteristics of a continuously variable transmission (CVT).	P-3	✔	✔	✔	197–198	32
5. Describe the operational characteristics of a hybrid vehicle drivetrain.	P-3	✔	✔	✔	179–194	31
6. Disassemble, clean, and inspect transmission/ transaxle.	P-2			✔	251–262	46
7. Inspect, measure, clean, and replace valve body (includes surfaces, bores, springs, valves, sleeves, retainers, brackets, check valves/balls, screens, spacers, and gaskets).	P-2			✔	266–276	55
8. Inspect servo and accumulator bores, pistons, seals, pins, springs, and retainers; determine necessary action.	P-2			✔	134; 271–272	57
9. Assemble transmission/transaxle.	P-2			✔	279–300	58
10. Inspect, measure, and reseal oil pump assembly and components.	P-2			✔	79–80; 287–289	11
11. Measure transmission/transaxle end play or preload; determine necessary action.	P-1			✔	294–295	59
12. Inspect, measure, and replace thrust washers and bearings.	P-2			✔	280	47
13. Inspect oil delivery circuits, including seal rings, ring grooves, and sealing surface areas, feed pipes, orifices, and check valves/balls.	P-2			✔	266–272; 293–294	48
14. Inspect bushings; determine necessary action.	P-2			✔	280–281	49

TASK		PRIORITY	MLR	AST	MAST	TEXT PAGE #	TASK PAGE #
15.	Inspect and measure planetary gear assembly components; determine necessary action.	P-2			✔	292–293	50
16.	Inspect case bores, passages, bushings, vents, and mating surfaces; determine necessary action.	P-2			✔	260–268	51
17.	Diagnose and inspect transaxle drive, link chains, sprockets, gears, bearings, and bushings; perform necessary action.	P-2			✔	254–255	52
18.	Inspect measure, repair, adjust, or replace transaxle final drive components.	P-2			✔	295	53
19.	Inspect clutch drum, piston, check balls, springs, retainers, seals, and friction and pressure plates, bands, and drums; determine necessary action.	P-2			✔	282–285	54
20.	Measure clutch pack clearance; determine necessary action.	P-1			✔	284; 291	54
21.	Air test operation of clutch and servo assemblies.	P-1			✔	293–294	54
22.	Inspect roller and sprag clutch, races, rollers, sprags, springs, cages, and retainers; determine necessary action.	P-2			✔	292	16

GLOSSARY

Aboveground storage tank (AGST) A storage tank that stores used oil and is located above ground.

Accumulator A device used to dampen fluid apply pressure so as to cushion or soften a shift.

Actuator An electromechanical device that performs mechanical movement as commanded by a controller.

Adaptive control The PCM can learn how long a shift takes to complete and will command that the start the shift occurs sooner to allow time for the clutch to be fully engaged. The adjustment is called *adaptive learning*.

Adaptive learning See Adaptive control.

Additives Chemicals added to automatic transmission fluid (ATF) to improve the operating characteristics.

Aftermarket Referring to repair parts produced by companies other than OEM.

All-wheel drive (AWD) Vehicles are four-wheel-drive vehicles equipped with a center (inner-axle) differential so they can be operated on pavement in four-wheel drive.

Ammeter An electrical test instrument used to measure amperes (unit of the amount of current flow).

Ampere The unit of the amount of current flow. Named for André Ampère (1775–1836).

Aqueous-based solutions Water-type chemicals that are silicate based and mixed with water. Aqueous-based solutions can sprayed on or used in a tank for soaking parts.

Asbestosis A health condition where asbestos causes scar tissue to form in the lungs, causing shortness of breath.

Automated manual transmission (AMT) Another term used to describe a dual-clutch automatic transmission/transaxle.

Automatic transmission A transmission that changes forward-gear ratios automatically.

Automatic transmission fluid (ATF) The oil used in automatic transmissions.

Balance valve A valve that is in a balanced position between two opposing forces.

Battery Council International (BCI) A trade organization of battery manufacturers.

Bearings Nonfriction bearings that use balls or rollers as rolling elements to reduce friction.

Belleville plate A Belleville plate, like a Belleville spring, is not flat and are often called *cushion plates*.

Bench grinder A type of electric motor driven grinder that mounts to a bench.

Bevel gear A gear with teeth that are cut at an angle so it can transmit power between shafts that are not parallel.

Bolt The major type of threaded fastener used with a nut to secure parts together.

Breaker bar A long-handled socket drive tool.

Brake on/off (BOO) Another name for the brake switch.

Bushing A simple soft metal bearing surface that must use lubricants to reduce friction.

Bump cap A hard plastic hat to protect the head from bumps.

Calibration codes Codes used on many powertrain control modules.

Campaign A recall where vehicle owners are contacted to return a vehicle to a dealer for corrective action.

Casting number An identification code cast into an engine block or other large cast part of a vehicle.

Cheater bar A bar used on a wrench to increase the amount of torque that can be applied to a fastener. Not recommended.

Check ball A check ball is the simplest method of controlling fluid flow. A one-way check valve resembles a steel bearing or plastic ball located over a hole in the separator plate.

Chisels A type of hand tool used with a hammer to cut or mark metal and other materials.

Clean Air Act (CAA) Federal legislation passed in 1970 and updated in 1990 that established national air quality standards.

Clutch A device that controls the power transfer between two points. It can allow or stop the transfer.

Clutch cooling flow solenoid (CCFS) The solenoid that controls hydraulic oil for cooling of clutches of a dual clutch automatic transmission.

Clutch pack clearance The clearance in between the plates in a clutch pack and is normally measured using a feeler gauge placed between the pressure plate and the snap ring.

Clutch pressure cut (CPCUT) The safety valve that controls pressure-dumping in the hydraulic system in a dual clutch automatic transmission.

Clutch shift pressure solenoid Controls hydraulic pressure for odd clutch or shifting in a dual clutch automatic transmission.

Clutch volume index (CVI) Transmissions use an input and an output speed sensors allowing the TCM to determine the gear ratio and how long it takes to make the shift. Chrysler refers to the adaptive control as the clutch volume index (CVI), which is the length of time it takes to fill the clutches with fluid.

Clutch-to-clutch A transmission that shifts by releasing one clutch as it applies another clutch to change the power flow.

Code of Federal Regulations (CFR) A compilation of the general and permanent rules published in the federal register by the executive departments and agencies of the federal government.

Concentric clutch A clutch design where both plates share the same vertical plane provides a shorter assembly.

Conductors A material that conducts electricity and heat. A metal that contains fewer than four electrons in its atom's outer shell.

Connector The plastic part of an electrical connection that includes a locking tab to keep two parts together.

Constant-velocity (CV) joint A type of driveline joint that are designed to rotate without changing speed.

Continuously variable transmission (CVT) A transmission that uses two variable-width pulleys and a belt to change ratios from the lowest to the highest in a continuous, stepless manner instead of a group of fixed ratios.

Conventional theory The theory that electricity flows from positive (+) to negative (−).

Coupling phase A condition where the torque converter turbine speed is almost equal to that of the impeller.

Creep Creep is the slight movement of the vehicle when the engine is at idle speed and the brakes are released and is normal for a vehicle equipped with an automatic transmission.

Crimp-and-seal connectors A type of electrical connector that has glue inside which provides a weather-proof seal after it is heated.

Cross leak A cross leak can cause an unwanted, partial application of a clutch or band that can lead to an early failure.

Cushion plate See Bellville plate.

Damper assembly An assembly that uses springs to dampen engine power pulses from being transferred to the rest of the drivetrain.

Default (Limp in)   A default (or limp-in) gear is the forward speed that is used if there is a failure in the electronic or computer system. If neither of two shift solenoids were engaged, then a default gear is actuated.

Depth filter   A depth filter traps particles as they try to pass through the filter material. Depth filters use felt or a synthetic material of various thickness. The depth of the material allows room to trap particles as well as room for fluid flow.

Differential   A gear arrangement that allows the drive wheels to be driven at different speeds.

Digital multimeter (DMM)   A digital multimeter is capable of measuring electrical current, resistance, and voltage.

Digital volt-ohm-meter (DVOM)   A digital multimeter is capable of measuring electrical current, resistance, and voltage.

Direct clutch   The clutch in front of a Simpson gear train transmission. Also called a *front clutch* or a *high-reverse clutch.*

Directional grooving   Slanted grooves in the friction plates that must face the proper direction.

Direct shift gearbox (DSG)   Another term used to describe a dual-clutch automatic transmission/transaxle.

Double-wrap band   A type of transmission band gives more holding power, and are often used for reverse or manual first gears.

Drive axle   An assembly containing the differential assembly and the drive axles.

Driveshaft   A shaft that transfers engine torque from the output of the transmission to the rear axle (differential) assembly.

Drive sizes   The size in fractions of an inch of the square drive for sockets.

Driving devices   Driving devices connect the turbine shaft from the torque converter to the elements of the planetary gear train.

Drum   The drum, also called the *housing*, has internal splines that mate with external splines on the steel plates for the externally lugged discs, usually the unlined discs (steels). The inner diameter of the drum is machined for the apply piston and its inner and outer seals.

Dynamic friction   The relative amount of friction between two surfaces that are at different speeds. *See Static friction.*

Dynamometer   A machine used to measure engine torque.

Electricity   The movement of free electrons from one atom to another.

Electron theory   The theory that electricity flows from negative (−) to positive (+).

Electronically variable transmission (EVT)   The term used to describe the transmission used a General Motor's two-mode unit. It includes three simple planetary gear sets with four multi-plate clutches. It has four fixed gear ratios with two EV ratios for smooth, more efficient operation.

Electronic pressure control (EPC)   A pulse-width-modulated solenoid used to control the transmission's hydraulic pump pressure regulator valve.

Environmental Protection Agency (EPA)   A governmental agency that is charged with protecting human health and with safeguarding the natural environment: air, water, and land.

Extensions   A socket wrench tool used between a ratchet or breaker bar and a socket.

Eye wash station   A water fountain designed to rinse the eyes with a large volume of water.

Files   A type of hand tool used to smooth metal and other materials.

Final drive   The last set of reduction gears before the power flows to the differential and drive axles.

Fire blanket   A fire-proof wool blanket used to cover a person who is on fire to smother the fire.

Fire extinguisher classes   The classification of fire extinguishers by the type of fires they are designed to handle.

Flex band   A type of transmission band that is less expensive and, because of its flexibility, can easily conform to the shape of the drum.

Flexplate   The thin drive plate that connects the torque converter to the crankshaft of the engine.

Fluid change   The replacement of the automatic transmission fluid. Most manufacturers recommend fluid changes every 100,000 miles (160,000 km) under normal driving conditions. Some recommend a fluid change at 50,000 miles (80,000 km).

Fluid exchange   Fluid exchange usually means taking out the old fluid and replacing it with new fluid of the correct type. By using a fluid exchange machine, all of the fluid in the system is replaced.

Fluid flushing   Fluid flushing typically uses a chemical to dissolve varnish and other deposits.

Fluid Power   A method of transmitting motion and/or force using a fluid.

Force motor   *See* Pressure control solenoid.

Four-wheel drive (4WD)   Four-wheel drive (4WD) is often designated as "4 × 4" and refers to a vehicle that has four driven wheels.

Free fall test   The free fall test is a standard check for a sticking valve. Hold the valve body so the bore is vertical. In this position, a steel valve should fall freely from one end of the bore to the other and it should at least fall through the area of normal valve movement.

Freewheel shift   Freewheel shifts, also called nonsynchronous *shifts* use one or more one-way clutches as driving or reaction devices. A one-way clutch will self-release during a shift as soon as the next clutch applies, eliminating the need to synchronize the shifts.

Friction modifier   An additive that changes the lubricity of a fluid.

Friction plates   Plates lined with friction material, also called friction *discs* or simply *frictions*. These plates are also made from stamped steel with lining material bonded to each side.

Front clutch   The clutch in front of a Simpson gear train transmission and is also called a *direct clutch* or a *high-reverse clutch*.

Front-wheel drive (FWD)   A vehicle that uses the engine to drive the front wheels.

Garage shift   A shift from neutral to drive or reverse.

GAWR   Abbreviation for gross axle weight rating.

Gear ratio   The relationship between two gears determined by dividing the number of teeth on the driving gear by the number of teeth on the driven gear and expressed as a ratio to 1.

Gerotor   A design of oil pump

Grade   The strength rating of a bolt.

GVWR   Abbreviation for gross vehicle weight rating.

Hacksaws   A type of hand tool that is used to cut metal and other materials.

Half shaft   Drive axles on a front-wheel drive vehicle or from a stationary differential to the drive wheels.

Hall effect   A semiconductor moving relative to a magnetic field, creating a variable voltage output. Used to determine position and named for Edwin H. Hall, who discovered the Hall Effect in 1879.

Hammers   A type of hand tool used to force objects into position using a swinging motion.

Hard parts   Major transmission components such as the pump, a clutch drum, or a gear set.

Hazardous waste materials   Chemicals or components that are no longer needed and pose a danger to the environment or people.

Helical gear   A gear that has the teeth cut at an angle.

HEPA vacuum   High efficiency particulate air filter vacuum used to clean brake dust.

HEV   Hybrid electric vehicle.

High resistance   A type of electrical circuit fault that causes a reductions in current flow.

High-reverse clutch   The clutch in front of a Simpson gear train transmission and also called a *front clutch* or a *direct clutch*.

Horsepower   A measure of engine power derived from the torque and engine speed on revolutions per minute measurements.

Hydraulics   The transfer of power through fluids under pressure.

Hypoid gear   A special form of a bevel gear that has the teeth cut in a curvature and that positions the gear on nonintersecting planes; commonly used in rear-wheel-drive (RWD) final drives.

Impeller   The input member of the torque converter; also called *converter pump*.

Input speed sensor (ISS)   The sensor that measures the speed of the input shaft which is the same or almost the same as the engine speed. This is also called *turbine speed sensor (TSS)* because it is used to determine the speed of the turbine shaft.

Insulators   A material that does not readily conduct electricity and heat. A nonmetal material that contains more than four electrons in its atom's outer shell.

Internal combustion engine (ICE)   The term used to describe a gasoline or diesel fuel powered engine.

Internal–external gear   When an external gear drives an internal gear, the two gears will rotate in the same direction.

Land   The large-diameter portion of a spool valve.

LED   Light emitting diode.

LePelletier gear train   An automatic transmission gear train that combines a simple planetary gear set with a Ravigneaux gear set to produce six or more gear ratios.

Line pressure solenoid (LPS)   The solenoid that controls the line pressure to the transmission hydraulic system.

Mainline pressure   Regulated fluid pressure, also called, line, or control pressure is the working pressure for the entire hydraulic system.

Manual transmission   A transmission that is shifted by the driver.

Manual valve   The valve operated by the gear selector that directs pressure to the apply devices needed to put a transmission in gear.

Material safety data sheets (MSDSs)   Forms containing data regarding the properties of a particular substance.

Mechanical diode   A one-way clutch that uses a set of spring-loaded struts for a lighter but stronger clutch action.

Mercury   A heavy metal that is liquid at room temperature.

Metric bolts   Bolts manufactured and sized in the metric system of measurement.

Micron   A unit of measurement equal to one millionth of a meter.

MSDS   Abbreviation for *material safety data sheets,* now called *safety data sheets (SDS).*

Node   Another name for a control module used in a network.

Nonsynchronous   A design of an automatic transmissions where one clutch does not need to be released before the next clutch is applied. A nonsynchronous transmission is a unit that uses a one-way clutch to allow an upshift that requires only the application of the next driving or reaction member.

Nut   A threaded fastener that is used with a bolt.

Occupational Safety and Health Administration (OSHA)   A governmental agency that regulates workplace safety.

Ohmmeter   An electrical tester deigned to measure electrical resistance in ohms.

Ohms   The unit of electrical resistance. Named for George Simon Ohm.

Open circuit   Any circuit that is not complete and in which no current flows.

Open/plain end ring   A seal ring with the ends cut at a right angle.

Orifice   A restricted opening in a fluid passage designed to reduce fluid pressure while fluid is flowing.

Output speed sensor (OSS)   This speed sensor, also called the vehicle speed (VS) sensor, is used by the PCM for speedometer and cruise control operation as well as for transmission/transaxle operation and shift-related fault detection.

Overdrive   A gear arrangement that causes the output shaft to turn faster than the input shaft.

Overhaul   A complete overhaul includes disassembly of the entire assembly and replacing all needed parts and gaskets and seals to restore the transmission to like new performance.

Paper filter   A filter made of a woven screen of metal or synthetic material such as dacron or polyester.

Parallel clutch   A clutch design used in a dual clutch automatic where the clutches rearranged side-by-side.

Pinch weld seam   A strong section under a vehicle where two body panels are welded together.

Pinion gear   A small gear that meshes with a larger gear.

Pitch   The distance between threads of a bolt and nut; the relative number of teeth or spacing of the teeth on a gear.

Pitch diameter   The pitch diameter is the effective diameter of the gear. Note how the contact points slide on the gear teeth as they move in and out of contact.

Planetary gear set   A gear set that contains a sun gear, ring gear, and a carrier with planet pinion gear to produce one or more gear ratios.

Planet carrier   The part of a planetary gear set that contains the planetary pinion gears.

Pliers   A type of hand tool that has two moveable parts and are used to hold or rotate an object or fastener.

Porsche Doppelkupplung (PDK)   Another term used to describe a dual-clutch automatic transmission/transaxle used in Porsche vehicles.

Positive displacement pump   A type of pump where each rotation of the pump delivers the same volume of oil and everything that enters must exit.

Potentiometer   A 3-terminal variable resistor that varies the voltage drop in a circuit.

Powertrain control module (PCM)   The electronic control module that it is used to control both the engine and transmission systems.

Power transfer unit   The term used to describe the transfer case function used with a transaxle.

PPE   Personal protective equipment

Pressure balanced release   A clutch design that uses fluid pressure to help release the clutch.

Pressure control solenoid (PCS)   A computer-controlled solenoid that maintains the proper pressure in the hydraulic system of an electronically controlled automatic transmission. Also called a *variable force solenoid* or *force motor.*

Pressure regulator valve   The valve that maintains the proper pressure in the hydraulic system.

Primary oil pressure (POP)   The fluid pressure applied to the primary pulley in a CVT transmission/transaxle.

Primary pressure sensor (PPS)   The sensor used to measure the fluid pressure applied to the primary pulley in a CVT transmission/transaxle.

Pull chain   A type of chain used in a CVT transmission/transaxle that is made up of links and link pins, much like a silent chain. The ends of the link pins contact the pulley sides. This style is also called a Luk chain drive.

Pump   A device that transfers fluid from one point to another.

Punches   A type of hand tool used with a hammer to drive pins or other similar uses.

Push belt   A type of belt used in a CVT transmission/transaxle that is made of about 400 wedge-shaped segments that are held together by two steel bands. Each band is made from multiple layers to allow flexibility. The segment sides contact the pulley sides. A push-belt is often called the Van Doorne design.

Ratchet   A hand tool used to drive a socket wrench that is capable of being changed to tighten or loosen a fastener.

Ratio   The relative value between two things.

Ratio control motor   A stepper motor that changes the position of the upper end of the pulley ratio link in a CVT transmission/transaxle. The stepper motor controls the hydraulic ratio valve through the link, which in turn, controls fluid flow to the piston.

Ravigneaux gear set   Ravigneaux gear set combines one carrier that has two sets of planet gears with two sun gears, and one ring gear.

Reaction devices   The reaction devices connect (lock) a member of the gear train to the transmission case.

Rear-wheel drive (RWD)   A vehicle uses the engine to drive the rear wheels.

Rebuild   See Remanufactured.

Rebuilt   *See* Remanufactured.

Recall   A notification to the owner of a vehicle that a safety issue needs to be corrected.

Recalibration   Flashing a PCM/TCM, also called programming, reprogramming, and calibrating, is done to correct possible software problems.

Relay   An electromagnetic switch that uses a movable arm.

Remanufactured transmission/transaxle   See remanufactured.

Remanufactured   A term used to describe a component that is disassembled, cleaned, inspected, and reassembled using new or reconditioned parts.

Resource Conservation and Recovery Act (RCRA)   This law states that hazardous material users are responsible for hazardous materials from the time they become a waste until the proper waste disposal is completed.

Retaining bracket   A bracket that is used to hold a part(s) in place.

Right-to-know laws   Laws that state that employees have a right to know when the materials they use at work are hazardous.

Rigid band   A type of transmission band that a single thick, heavy band.

Ring gear   The outer gear of a planetary gear set; also called an *internal gear.*

Roller clutch   A one-way clutch that uses a series of rollers positioned in a special cam for the locking elements.

Rooster comb   A detent that is a spring-loaded roller or ball that drops into notches in the cam to position the manual valve properly in its bore.

Rotary flow   The fluid motion inside a torque converter in the same direction as the impeller and turbine.

Rubber band effect   A condition that affect some CVT units where the vehicle speed slowly catches up to the engine speed, and is most noticeable only during periods of rapid acceleration.

Scan tool   An electronic test device that can communicate with the vehicle's control module and determine operational data.

Scarf cut   A seal ring with the ends cut at an angle.

Schematic   a wiring diagram showing components and connecting wires.

Screwdrivers   A type of hand tool designed to remove screws.

Secondary oil pressure (SOP)   The fluid pressure applied to the secondary pulley of a CVT transmission/transaxle. The pressure measured is called the secondary oil pressure (SOP).

Secondary pressure sensor (SPS)   a pressure transducer used to monitor secondary pulley pressure. The pressure measured is called the secondary oil pressure (SOP).

Selective   Washers or snap rings are produced in various size which lets the technician select the proper size thrust washer for the best end play or clearance.

Semiconductor   A material that is neither a conductor nor an insulator; has exactly four electrons in the atom's outer shell.

Separator plate   The flat steel plate that separates the case part of the valve body from the valve body part. Also another name for an unlined steel plate used in a clutch pack.

Servo   A hydraulic device that changes fluid pressure into mechanical motion or force.

Shift cooling multiplex solenoid (SHCMS)   Controls position of gearshift forks as well as cooling of clutch in a dual clutch automatic transmission/transaxle.

Shift feel   A clutch or band application or release that is usually described, for example, as firm or soft.

Shift valve   Valves that controls the fluid flow to the band servos and to clutch apply pistons for drive, low, and reverse gears.

Short-to-ground   A short circuit in which the current bypasses some or all the resistance of the circuit and flows to ground. Because ground is usually steel in automotive electricity, a short-to-ground (grounded) is a "copper-to-steel" connection.

Short-to-voltage   A circuit in which current flows, but bypasses some or all the resistance in the circuit. A connection that results in a "copper-to-copper" connection.

Simpson gear train   The Simpson gear set consists of a double sun gear that is meshed with the planet gears of the two carriers and is a compound gear set.

Single-sided plate   Single-sided plates have friction material on one side only, and half of the plates have lugs on the inner diameter while the other half have lugs on the outer diameter.

Snips   A type of hand tool used to cut sheet metal and other thin materials.

Socket   A type of tool that fits over the top and used to remove a threaded fastener.

Socket adapter   An adapter that allows the use of one size of driver (ratchet or breaker bar) to rotate another drive size of socket.

Spiral bevel gear   Spiral bevel gears, like helical gears, have curved teeth for quieter operation.

Soft parts   Parts that are normally replaced during an overhaul. These include the gaskets, seals, and friction material.

Solvent   Usually colorless liquids that are used to remove grease and oil.

Special service tools (SSTs)   Tools that are developed by OEM so service or repair procedures can be done.

Spontaneous combustion   Self-ignition of oily rags without the use of an ignition source.

Solenoid   An electromagnet actuator that uses a movable core.

Spool valve   Spool valves sliding in a round bore are used to control fluid flow. A spool valve gets its name because it looks similar to the spool that holds thread.

Sprag   The locking element in a one-way sprag clutch.

Spur gear   A gear with straight-cut teeth.

Stall speed   The maximum engine RPM that can be achieved with an automatic transmission in gear, with the brakes applied and the accelerator wide open.

Static friction   The relative amount of friction between two stationary surfaces or two surfaces that are turning at the same speed. *See* Dynamic friction.

Static seal   A static seal is used to seal the space between two parts that are stationary relative to each other. Static seals include gaskets and O-rings that are placed between the two parts and squeezed tightly as the parts are fastened together.

Stator   A component in the torque converter that is used to change the direction of fluid motion.

Steels   Another name for the unlined clutch discs.

Stop-off tool   A stop-off tool or old U-joint slip yoke can be used to stop the fluid leak.

Stud   A short rod with threads on both ends.

Subassemblies   The major transmission components.

Sun gear   The gear in the center of a planetary gear set.

Supply pressure   The pressure-regulated fluid. Also called supply mainline pressure.

Surface filter   A surface filter traps the foreign particles at the outer surface.

Synchronous   A type of shift that requires that one apply device be timed or synchronized with the application of the apply device for the next gear range.

Technical service bulletin (TSB)   A form that describes a particular vehicle concern and the recommended correction procedure.

Tensile strength   The maximum stress used under tension (lengthwise force) without causing failure.

Terminal   The metal end of a wire which fits into a plastic connector and is the electrical connection part of a junction.

Thrust washers   Bearings that separate rotating parts that turn against each other.

Torque   Turning or twisting effort; usually measured in foot-pounds or Newton-meters.

Torque converter   A fluid coupling that transfers power from the engine to the transmission and can produce a torque increase.

Torque converter clutch (TCC)   The clutch inside the torque converter that locks the turbine to the impeller to prevent any slippage; also called a *lockup torque converter.*

Torque management   The program inside the powertrain control module that controls shift timing and quality to provide a smoother driving experience.

Torrington   Bearings that operate against a very smooth, hard surface— either the face of a gear or a race.

Torsional vibrations   Torsional vibrations are small speed increases and slowdowns as the crankshaft revolves between engine cylinder firing pulses. These vibrations can produce gear noise in the transmission and drivetrain as well as a noticeable vibration and harshness in the vehicle.

Traction battery   The high-voltage battery used to power the traction motor which can propel the vehicle.

Traction motor   The electric motor used propel the vehicle in an electric and hybrid electric vehicles.

Transaxle   A transmission that is combined with the final drive assembly; normally used in front-wheel-drive (FWD) vehicles.

Transfer case   A transfer case is normally attached to the rear of the transmission. It has a single input shaft from the transmission and two output shafts, one to the front drive axle and one to the rear drive axle. Some transfer cases are two-speed and include a set of reduction gears for lower-speed, higher-torque operation.

Transmission   A device in the powertrain that provides different forward-gear ratios as well as neutral and reverse.

Transmission adapt pressure (TAP)   The General Motor's term for which manages oil pressure to control clutch fill rates to allow for adaptive control and which compensates for clutch pack wear.

Transmission control module (TCM)   The term given to the computer that controls An automatic transmission and called a *transmission control unit (TCU).*

Transmission fluid temperature (TFT)   A temperature sensor that measures the automatic transmission fluid temperature.

Transmission range (TR) switch   The transmission switch, also called the manual lever position (MLP) sensor, is used as an input to the PCM/TCM which indicates the driver request for which drive range is being requested.

Transmission range sensor (TRS)   a multi-contact switch operated by the manual shift lever.

Transmission temperature sensor (TTS)   a Negative Temperature Coefficient (NTC) thermistor used to measure temperature of the transaxle.

Trouble light   A light used to help a service technician see while performing service work on a vehicle.

Turbine   The output member of a torque converter.

Turbine speed sensor (TSS)   The sensor that measures the speed of the input shaft which is the same or almost the same as the engine speed. This is also called input speed sensor (ISS).

Turbulator   A turbulator built into the inside of a cooler line causes turbulence in the fluid flow to ensure constant mixing and thorough cooling of all the fluid.

Twin clutch transmission   Another term used to describe a dual-clutch automatic transmission/transaxle.

UNC   Unified national coarse.

Underground storage tank (UST)   Underground storage tank used to store used oil.

UNF   Unified national fine.

Universal joint (U-joint)   A joint in a steering or drive shaft that allows torque to be transmitted at an angle.

Used oil   Any petroleum-based or synthetic oil that has been used.

Valve body   The valve body enables an automatic transmission to operate automatically and is often referred to as the "brains" of the transmission. It supplies the force to apply the clutches, bands and the valves that control pressure and direct the fluid for automatic shifts.

Vane pump   Vane pumps are also positive displacement in that they will pump a certain volume on each revolution, but the displacement, and therefore the fluid volume, can be changed.

Variable displacement pumps   allow a large output to produce the fluid volume needed for shifts and lubrication and a reduced output when it is not needed.

Variable force solenoid   *See* Pressure control solenoid.

Variators   Two variable width pulleys to change the gear ratio in a continuously variable transmission.

Vehicle emission control information (VECI)   An underhood label with emission control information.

Vehicle speed (VS) sensor   A sensor that measures the speed of vehicle. It can use the output speed sensor or the wheel speed sensor depending on the vehicle.

VIN   Vehicle identification number.

Voltmeter   An electrical test instrument used to measure volts (unit of electrical pressure). A voltmeter is connected in parallel with the unit or circuit being tested.

Volts   unit of electrical pressure.

Vortex flow   A recirculating fluid flow in the converter that is outward in the impeller and inward in the turbine.

Warpage   A fault that occurs when mating surfaces become less flat.

Washer   A thin metal disk with a hole used to support the load of a threaded fastener.

Wave plate   An unlined clutch plate that is wavy, not flat.

Worm gear   A type of gear used in an older type of steering gear, which is attached to the steering shaft.

WHMIS   Workplace Hazardous Materials Information Systems.

Worm tracks   The fluid passages in a value body for the various transmission hydraulic circuits cast into them. These are sometimes called *worm holes.*

Wrench   Any of various hand or power tools, often having fixed or adjustable jaws, used for gripping, turning, or twisting objects such as nuts, bolts, or pipes.

INDEX